NOW THAT WE HAVE MET

NOW THAT WE HAVE MET

IN THE GUISE *of a* STRANGER

WILLIAM MACCREA

Mill City Press

Minneapolis, MN

It has been my very great fortune to have known and shared my life with many strong women while on this earthly journey. Three such women have been my own angels: My Great Grandmother, whom I truly believe was the wisest human being whom I have ever known; my very dear partner in life, Dolores, who nourished my body with her home-made bread and my soul with her music (and ran the sort of "tight ship" mentioned in my book), and my very dear daughter in law, Debra, who has made the best kilts and who has the finest gardens in the county. Such women bring out the best traits in their husbands, sons and grandsons: men who are not afraid to follow their dreams and develop their talents. A bit intimidating perhaps to daughters and granddaughters, these younger ones learn to use wings they never knew they had. Thanks to all of them, the brave and loving sons and daughters move on with honor, dignity, faith and compassion. The "Old Way" remains very much alive.

William MacCrea, Locustbrae Farm, 2014

FOREWORD

Many years ago in a university classroom, not far from where I now sit, we were discussing the great cities of civilization and how the city serves as a catalyst for Empire and the hub of its balance. One lady in the class, a very cultured individual from Vienna, addressed a rather interesting question to the professor. If, she asked, the great cities were the hubs of civilization around which all else rotated, what purpose is served by places like Allegany County, New York? Everyone laughed, for there is no great bread-basket here, the land being hilly and the soil full of clay and poorly drained. It is not like Bucks County, Pennsylvania or Marin County, California. Allegany County is poor even when the nation has peak prosperity, sitting always at the fringe of Empire; contributing to its greatness only in the export of its very talented young people.

The professor stared out of the window as if he hadn't heard the question and after at least a full minute he gave his answer. He explained it something like this: No noticeable purpose is served by such a poor county, not one that can be seen immediately. Yet, when there is grass growing in the ruined shells of the skyscrapers, historians will come here and say to a farmer; "Tell me about the American Empire", and the farmer will put on his boots, take up a bucket and say with a smile that he really doesn't know much about it, at all. If the historian is wise he will follow the farmer, listen to all that he says and watch all that he does, for through listening to this farmer and watching him at work, the American Empire will be slowly revealed. Cities like London and New York do indeed act as the catalyst for history, but counties like Devon in England and Allegany in upstate New York are that history.

About the year 1818, Alexander Dewar left Scotland for Canada. The "Clearances" had begun; that blot on British history that saw Highland Scots burned out and loaded onto ships. Un-milked cows bawled in the Byres, men were sometimes bound hand and foot, sometimes separated from their families forever. Alexander Dewar was just another exile, sent out with his family to North America. He had little baggage and a very curious cane in his possession, but that 'cane' was the staff of authority of one of Scotland's earliest saints. The Dewars were its hereditary protectors, its keepers.

There were others who brought certain symbolic articles or relics with them. The landowners who had taken over the estates in the Highlands, the new "ruling class" had thought to rid itself of the Highland clan system once and for all. Instead, they had taken seeds from crowded, tired plants and sown them in a new and fertile soil. The clan system which was supposed to have died on the field of Culloden in 1746 is alive and well in tiny pockets all over the world. More interesting is the fact that a wild, half pagan, but terribly beautiful branch of primitive Christianity has blossomed into something which might actually save mankind. This novel is in three parts, but there is a continuum; a fiber made of two plies which runs through them all. What is here is not really fantasy. Much of it has actually taken place. Some of it is bound to come to pass.

PART ONE

CHAPTER 1

They had been telling the old stories since the evening light had faded away: the ones about gray seals and seal maidens, glastaigs and the" little people". Murdoch MacIan was the greatest story teller of them all. He would jut out his great jaw, point his bony nose straight ahead and save for the nodding of his head from time to time and the rolling of his eyes, he would always be facing in the same direction, as if his craggy face was required to look to the same point somewhere, beyond the stone walls, out over the many patches of close-cropped grass, scattered carpets of yellow green between mossy stones and lichen-covered rocks, and even further, into the horizon, the sea itself. His big hands, as work-worn and rough as they were, could form ideas and define sizes and shapes with a grace and versatility almost unbelievable for such a big, raw-boned man. He was telling about the man who had wounded the Seal King:

"He was moving along up one road and down another, and so fast was the horse galloping that he could catch the wind before him and not be caught by the wind at his back, and if he went those roads before he never traveled them again, for the roads themselves would be gone at the first breaking of the sun's light on the shoreline. And that would be the end of the story and it is true. All of the other ones are lies."

A bowl was passed around, he dipped into it with a drinking shell, being careful not to spill a single drop. Everyone waited while he brought the dram of whisky to his lips, holding the shell most carefully with two fingers to the edge and his third finger beneath it for balance. He tilted his head and took the dram, neatly and with appreciation, for the way that he gave an oblique shake to his head said, "That will be a good dram!"

"There was a woman near Kyle not long ago," someone was saying," who was one of the girls from a very old family there. The MacMath used to say that she was a gray seal. Isabel MacMath said that when the woman's husband was away at the fishing that you'd never find her at home after dark. Isabel said that she had taken her some bannochs that she'd made extra one night. The kettle was on the peat fire and a lamp stood by the window, but not a soul was in sight."

"What about the bairns?", An old lady asked. "Weren't they there, at all either? She wouldn't be leaving them alone, surely?"

"Och, well, I don't know about that, although they could have been asleep in the loft." (A pause) "Of course, she could have put a sea sleep on them before she went out. The seals have their own way of things, of course."

"Aye, well…", the old lady said, "maybe she wasn't a seal so much as she was a fairy."

"Na, I don't think so, for Isabel said that it happened every time the man was at the fishing. She said that she had seen a gray seal skin on the chair by the fire more than once."

"Aye, well, my grandmother told me that there are seals and there are seals that are something special," the old lady persisted. As far as the difference between that kind of a seal and one of the 'shee', well, 'Mu Tha Bran, tha e a bhrathair!'("If it is not Bran, it is his brother,!", as they say.)

There was a giggle in the corner by the door and away from the fire. The old lady swung her head to see who it was and other heads turned also. It was Morag and Alan. They had had their private jokes all night. They were at the Ceilidh only as bodies; minds and hearts on each other. MacIan the story-teller had uncrossed his legs and turned almost around toward them, for they had been off to his side. Turning and opening his eyes to their widest, to where the whites showed all around the iris, he clamped down on his pipe then eased it before taking it out of his mouth completely. He pointed toward the young couple with the pipe-stem, his eyes now narrowing to a squint. They'd heard the warning which was to follow many times in their lives. "There are people much smarter than you who have laughed at the faeries and lived to regret it, and that goes for the seals as well!"

"Alan isn't laughing at anyone, MacIan. He just doesn't

have any belief in the old stories," Morag told him.

"I thought you were a fisherman, Alan Lonn!", MacIan said to him.

"And so I am, MacIan." Alan's voice was soft, apologetic.

"No, No. You're a poor kind of fisherman if you have nothing at you about the ways of seals!"

"I leave the seals alone, and they do not bother me", Alan explained," "I can't abide the old stories, MacIan. They're all a lot of old lies and no one knows the truth of it. What people do not know they make up. There's no sense to the stories at all!"

The exchange went on for a while, as much a part of the Ceilidh as anything else could be. The old lady reminded Alan that his grandfather had been drowned at sea within a week of harming a gray seal. MacIan reminded them all that Morag's Aunt Eilidh had once been put under a spell by the faeries, but then they all wondered whether the girl had been stolen by the faeries, or had merely met a geancannach, one of those fallen angels who take on the form of a handsome young man: the 'love talkers'. In any case, the matter of belief vs. disbelief was soon dropped. Rory Mac Kinnon played some tunes on the pipes. Rory was Alan's older brother. Morag left Alan's side long enough to join her sister, Sine (Sheena) in some very old songs; appropriately enough; about the faeries. After the Macrae sisters had finished their songs refreshments were served: oat cakes, bannocks, barley scones, honey cakes, tarts and tea. A wedding loaf was broken above Morag's head and the women stepped back with chuckles and squeals of delight. The children present scrambled to find as many pieces as had fallen to the floor. The men were laughing too. When the pieces were gathered up it was discovered that the loaf had broken into eleven pieces. This, according to custom, was the number of children that the forthcoming marriage of Morag and Alan would produce.

"Who'll work your land or do your fishing, Alan?" one man called out. Another said that Alan would need to build a larger house. The comments and jokes went on and on. Morag glanced toward Alan who was surrounded by men who hadn't taken the least notice of the tea (Alisdair Ruadh, the host, had filled the bowl again), and Alan looked toward Morag in her new world, a woman's world of decisions, advice and accounts of other weddings;of fabric, lace and infants; of wedding plans and things to be done.

The men grew more solemn around the bowl. Their voices lowered until their conversation was inaudible a few feet away. One would say something and the others would laugh. Someone else would speak, everyone would laugh. Occasionally a loud "Slainte!" (Slahnjj) would rise up out of all of them as they raised their drinking shells. Every once in awhile a feminine voice would come over to them. "Rory! I hope that you won't be sick!" or "Alisdair! What are you men plotting over there?" It was an old, old state of affairs and one that may never change for all that we try: men huddled together in what looks like secrecy, women trying to be as open and sharing as possible.

"No wonder, at all, Duncan, but I haven't the heart to tell them that it's all a great game we play", Alan was saying to an older man

"Aye, well, as long as it's a game there's no harm done, I suppose. I'm certain that the women have their games too."

"I'm sure they have,, Duncan!"

"Not as sure as you'll be when you're married as long as I am, Alan! Ah, but it's games that make light work of things, whether cutting turf or living a life."

"Duncan, you're an old fox! I know what you're telling me, 'that the stories are part of the game too!"

"Is that what I'm telling you? Aye well, you do sometimes get worked up about the old things, Alan. They're not so bad, really. Let people have their stories, son! What does it matter really?"

"But they're not true and you know it!"

Duncan looked at Alan for a long time. There was something of himself in the young man. Alan must have sensed it early on in his own life, for even as a child he used often to go over to Duncan and Sara's to play. Duncan held to the land most of the time and was usually around his croft. He was a good builder and could fashion some really lovely things of wood or horn. When he cut his peat he did not object to the pieces of fir or bog oak which so often appear. He would very carefully pick them up and take them home with him. Sara had many fine kitchen utensils which Duncan had made from the bogwood and their children always had toys enough which had also come from the bog and from the same love and care of the material. Alan had learned a lot from Duncan and he knew that he could continue to learn for years to come.

"Morag told me this morning that you are going to go across to America, Duncan. I'm really sorry to hear that!", Alan told him.

"I have no choice, love-son. I do not want to go and it will be the breaking of Sara's heart. But, there is no way to stay. We've thought of everything! Do you know that my family has lived in the same place for over two hundred years? And, when they came to that place it was from only a mile away and they'd lived there longer than that! Did you know that, Alan?"

"That is all the more reason to stay!", Alan told him.

"Come outside, Alan," Duncan said to him, taking his arm.

"I have something to tell you."

The two men moved across the room and toward the door. Alan winked at Morag on the way. Poor Morag! She was cornered by the old lady, Mrs. MacPhee and her spinster sister. From the way that she looked, the expression on her face, Alan thought that he'd better rescue her soon, for she'd be talked out of marriage and motherhood altogether if she listened much longer to the old wives' tales that those two would be loading her down with.

"Marked for a chicken! I told her not to go near the hen house not the byres with her being eight months along! Anyway, she would never listen to anyone! Once that great mean rooster jumped up at her like that and pecked her I said that the child would be marked for a chicken, Didn't I, Una?"

Reaching the open doorway with its door post leaners telling about the battle of Waterloo, Duncan and Alan stepped to the night outside. Seeing them going through the door, one of the men inside the doorway said, "Ol suas ach minn sios, Alan!" (Drink up but piss down, Alan!) "Wonderful!", Alan thought with a shake of his head, "not very original, either! The oldest toast known to man and it has to be both in the Gaelic and stupid!"

Passing across the front of the house, the two men stopped by the light of the window. Duncan looked about at the landscape, the sea and into the house. The voices of many conversations taking place simultaneously came out to them and it occurred to Alan that it did have something like a sound of the sea in it. Alan thought that perhaps there could be some explanation for the Highland folk developing the legends as they did. "After all," he thought, "who can say for certain that the sound of the wave hitting the rocks or the beach isn't the rising battle cry of millions of sea things as row after row of them make one assault after another on the land. Then, each one is thrown back and the sizzling sound, the whisper of the defeated column can be heard. Once in a while it happens that the water is not thrown back, that the assault ends in a victory rather than a defeat. Waterloo with its columns of horse, its columns of 'foot', was not unlike those evenly spaced white rows of water soldiers that I saw yesterday."

Duncan could see the face of this young man clearly in the light given from the window. Alan was not like Neil and Angus in many ways, although they had grown up as brothers. Alan with his very dark hair and eyes contrasted sharply with Duncan's memory of his own two sons. When they were children playing at the croft or by the water's edge there was always that difference. Of course, it hadn't been as noticeable when they were very young, because Alan's hair was almost as light as the other boys' when he was yet a small, wee lad. His hair was like straw in its fairness. That is often the case with the children of the Gael. Yet by the time that Alan had become about ten or twelve years old, he could have passed for a Cornishman, or even a Spaniard, save for that very, very fair skin. "Now," thought Duncan, "he's all that is left. The only one of "my boys" to come back from fighting Napoleon, and I've had to borrow another man's son even to claim him! Well, there is Suibhan. At least I have one of my children yet alive! Thank God, they don't send women to war! I'd always hoped that..." His thought became his opening words.

"I'd always hoped that you and Siubhan would take an interest in each other, Alan. I would have liked that very much and I know that Sara would have given her all to have you two married."

"I think that I've known that for quite some time, Duncan. But, I hope that you know that I do love her and very much. Morag understands that too."

"Oh, aye, aye. I know that just as I know that Morag is a fine girl and will be a good wife to you. I like her fine enough. Still, I'd not be truthful if I said that there wasn't a small part of me that wishes that, even now and at this late date, something would drive you and Siubhan together."

"I know that, Duncan, and a part of me is very glad that you feel that way… but I do love Siubhan, as a brother loves a sister. We've grown up together and nothing can take away from that. I'm sure that you know that too. She is a beautiful woman in every way possible!"

"Aye. Och, you've spent too much time together to have it any other way. Mind, that's only part of what I wanted to say."

Duncan looked around him again and squinted at the window with the light coming out of the crowded house. He cleared his throat, turned away and spat before going on.

"Alan, I told you that we are forced to leave and…we are. For hundreds of years my family has kept the staff of St. Comgall, as you know. You also know that it is one of the most ancient and one of the holiest relics of the old church."

"Oh, we all know that, Duncan. Even though I am quick to make light of things, I would never be able to bring myself to laugh at the staff, nor those who believe in its power. I must confess that I've often wondered whether it worked its cures and won ancient battles because of its holiness or because people believed in its ability to help them."

Duncan looked away for a time and he seemed to have

another thought on his mind; something pulling him deeper into himself, yet at the same time further away; quite outside of the present space in which he found himself to be. Quite suddenly he came back to the moment and answered.

"We are back to 'Bran or his brother' when we try to decide about such things. As men we try to see everything as if all things were here at all because we want them to be. There is another world too, after all, and for all we know many other worlds and worlds within worlds! Maybe that's why we shouldn't scoff too much at the tales of the seals and the fairies, or the Glastaigs or the Blue men!" At this point, Duncan laughed and put his hand on Alan's shoulder. Alan smiled quite self-consciously in the semi-darkness.

"Who will go with you, Duncan?" Alan was quite serious now.

Duncan slid his hand from the young man's shoulder, straightened up, and with an air of pretended anticipation at a new adventure he spoke.

"Well, there is Sara and Siubhan, of course. Mairi and young Duncan and little Alisdair will come along too. I'll be glad to have them along, you may be sure! That will be the lot of us. Donald and Colin Macrae from Carr will go in the same party, also one of the MacKenzies from Gairloch, Angus MacDonald of the Sleat headland on Skye...oh, a lot of us who suddenly find ourselves pulled up by the roots. Like myself, there are so many folk who must leave".

"The new landlords!" Alan almost hissed.

"Oh, aye. The new landlords. We have a small holding, but on it we've had a good living; not that we've ever been able to be lavish, you understand! With the clan and the chief the fact that I guarded the staff paid my rent. In fact, that *was* the rent, the guarding of the staff and the lore that goes with it. The chiefs are, many of them, impoverished, and the land is now in the hands of proprietors, not patriarchs. Do you know what 'advice' I was given by the new factor? He said that if I was clever, I would "sell that piece of stick with its bits of silver and bronze to a museum of antiquities" in London or some such place! I could pay my rent then like a respectable and civilized man! Can you even imagine such a thing!? I told him that it will be a long day 'til we see that hour!"

Duncan and Alan stood in silence for a moment, their own silence, at least, although the voices from inside the house were a little less loud now. It was as if only one or two people in the house were talking and the rest were listening to them. Duncan suddenly took Alan by the arm and motioned with a movement of his head towards the house:

"Come! Morag will need to be rescued from Margaret MacPhee and her sister!" The two men moved back toward the doorway. Two young women came out of the door, giggling, and dashed around the corner. Duncan and Alan smiled. Duncan said,

"Aye, well, that's the way of it. What goes in must come out!" Just before reaching the doorway Duncan stopped short and said in a tone of urgency, "Alan! I am not sure that the staff is meant to leave Scotland! Should it not be left here? Think on it. I trust your judgment... and who else could I ask, my own two lads gone now? It's a strange thing how life can turn things around, isn't it? A few years ago who ever would have thought that I would someday be leaving my croft, that my two sons would not be on the land after me? But the staff is what I must concern myself with now. It is a great burden as well as a great honor to be responsible for it. I'm just not sure that it should leave Scotland."

Alan was a bit surprised by the suddenness of this request for advice on so weighty a matter, not to mention the fact that the advice had been requested of him by a man to whom he himself had long looked for guidance.

"I am not sure, Duncan, "he replied, a tone of wonder in his voice, almost as if he were thinking aloud "I would have to think about that before I could venture an opinion. I will put my wits to it and let you know what comes to me."

"Good lad! I could ask for no more than that. But, don't be too long at your thinking, for we will be leaving in two weeks' time."

Alan was happy enough that the darkness could hide his friend's expression, for he had heard the break in his voice. Duncan was, he thought to himself, about a finger's width in time from breaking down in tears at that moment......and perhaps only about two weeks from total heartbreak.

Alan followed Duncan into the house. Just as Duncan's

form filled the doorway he turned and said, "Isn't it grand that we'll not yet be gone when you're married? We'll still be here for the wedding! There's that to be thankful for!"

CHAPTER II

"What is redder than blood?" So goes an old Gaelic riddle, the answer being; "The face of an honest man who finds a stranger at his door and himself with no meat to give him." Alisdair Ruadh would have no red face on the wedding day of his niece, Morag NicLeannan. He was determined that, hard times or no, Morag and Alan would have a proper wedding worth remembering.

"Och," he would say, "It's little enough I can do for my own sister's lass!" Alisdair had five strong sons, but not one daughter of his own. His wife, Margaret, lamented the fact many times over, that Alisdair had so many hands to help him in the work with the herd and flock, and she with no one to lighten her load in the house. Everyone knew that she only half meant it, for her pride in her handsome young men was there for all to see,. Still, she would have liked to have had a girl; just someone to chat with about "women's things" during household chores. Morag and her mother would often fill part of that void, her coming every so often to assist with those chores that needed extra pairs of hands, but it was never a terribly close relationship. Margaret's sister-in-law, Catriona, was a quiet, dreamy sort of woman, moving about in a deliberate, quiet way. Oh, she got things done, and she did them well, but her heart or perhaps her mind seemed always to be far away. Margaret, on the other hand, was always bustling about, her little voice chiming away, delighted laughter as tinkling bells about this and that, talking to her hens at the door or the great cat by the fire. True enough! She laughed and one could almost hear bells and musical notes. Catriona, in contrast, would smile; a kind of tired, patient smile, but no one could remember her laughing very often. Some said that that was why her husband, Morag's father had died. "Mark what I say," Mrs. McPhee often said, "that young man died of a broken heart! A broken heart!...And why not, himself so bonnie and a strapping young man married to one who'd never give him so much as a bit of laughter! Men are like bairns! They never out-grow their need for affection and praise! Treat them with love and praise and they'll move heaven and earth for the one whom they love. Deprive them of it and they'll just waste away...or take to the drink!" At such a time, and only in this instance, Mrs McPhee's sister Una would say in a tiny protesting voice...,

"Well, Maggie, they do know that Donald had a terrible chill and a great fever come on him..." And Margaret McPhee (on cue) would counter, "Naaa! It was no fever, at all! Why would a fever take a strong young man like that?

He had a chill right enough! I'll agree he had a chill!"

In any case, Alisdair loved his niece dearly and his sister as well, and he was determined that Morag's wedding would be everything that a young bride could hope for.

The church, or what was left of it, was not visible from Alisdair and Margaret M'Cra's house. Between the two buildings was a rise of ground just sufficient in height to hide Killian Church yard. Still, Alisdair Ruadh would look out toward the rise every few minutes to see the first heads of the wedding party pop up over the hillock, listening closely also to hear the strains of the bagpipe which would be leading the company of friends and kindred from the church to his own holding. Alisdair hadn't gone to the wedding itself, nor had his youngest son, Dugall. Alisdair had set the lamb and bullock to roast at sun-up and had been fussing over the roasting ever since. He had been determined that no one would oversee the cooking of that meat but himself. As for Dugall, a lad of fourteen hasn't a great deal of respect for the institution of marriage and weddings are often regarded by the cynically young to be the worst part of that. Alan MacKinnon had been something akin to a folk-hero to him and now he, of all people, had fallen victim to the schemes of women and the preachments of priests and clan chieftains. So it was, that under the guise of giving help to his father, he had stayed home, to tend the fire. After all, it was an outside fire and would, he had said, require a great deal of fuel, for this was to be a wood fire! He knew that his father suspected his motives, but was saying nothing. This made him feel all the more guilty, but he had determined to live with what guilt there might be in it. Dugall threw another arm load of wood onto the ground near the roasting pit.

"Where did you learn to do a roasting with a pit like that, father? Was it from the red savages when you were in America?"

"No, Dugall, no. I never saw any red savages in America! Why would you think that? It was to Jamaica that they sent the regiment." A puff of smoke came forward, completely engulfing Alisdair, causing him to turn his head and hold his breath. His eyes stung with the smoke and tears ran onto his cheeks.

"Well," Dugall persisted, "Jamaica's part of the Americas, isn't it, father?" Alisdair moved to the other side of the fire. A gust of wind drove the smoke over and around him again and again he held his breath waiting for it to pass. The smoke remained and Alisdair backed up. "Aye," he puffed, answering his son, "but it's not the same as the main land."

"Well, aren't there red Indians in Jamaica, father?" Alisdair turned the meat, stirred the fire with a stick and retreated from the fire's heat. "Oh aye. There's some kind of people, part Indian, part African." The smoke again.

"Is Jamaica where they use such a pit, then?"

Coughing and wiping his eyes, Alisdair stood back, drew a breath, then answered with just the last bit of control of his vexation:

"Aye! They use pits in Jamaica!" Then louder; "and

there's all kinds of people there," (louder,) "and it's gentle winds, not Scottish gales they have to call their fires! Now! Will ye go and listen for the pipes before you drive me daft with your questions?"

Dugan smiled to himself. "Oh, he must have been a *braw* sodger, my father, when he got worked up!"

Dugall moved around to the side of the house that looked out toward the Loch. The morning sun was shining into his face, although it was fast climbing toward its' forenoon position, he still needed to shield his eyes with his hand. Looking down the slope toward the rise in the land, he could just see the torsos of some people coming up the far side and just appearing by the great outcropping of rocks which formed the knoll's crest. He listened but heard no pipes. He listened again but heard nothing. The figures, four of them were in plain view now. They were, all of them women, and they seemed to be hurrying as fast as they could over the rocky meadowland toward the house. At that moment, Alisdair came around the corner of the house and squinted toward the knoll next to his son. "It will be your mother and the others to get things ready." he said as if he were thinking it to himself. Dugall could see now that his father was quite right, and hear them too.

Margaret M'Cra's bell voice was chiming out suggestions to the others; orders really, which they had all agreed upon several times over in the preceding two weeks. Ella Frazier, Margaret McPhee and Una Matheson were bubbling away along with her, puffing between sentences as they half-trotted up the slope. Magaret M'Cra stopped a few paces in front of Alisdair and Dugall, looking at them as if she were trying to recall who they were. Mrs. McPhee wasn't ready for her sudden halt and almost ran her over, and Mrs. McPhee was a large woman! They stood motionless looking at Alisdair and Dugall.

"Well, what...are you two...standing there looking at?", asked Margaret M'Cra between pants and puffs. "We've only minutes until Donald Ban leads them thrice around the church yard and over the machair and up here, where we're all standing like cows! Oh, and haven't we a lot to be getting done!" And at that the women all flew into activity. The interior doors of a half dozen croft houses had been stacked at the side of the house and earlier that morning set up upon wooden horses to make two great, long tables. Once it had been decided that the day was to be a pleasant enough one after all, Margaret had had them set up outside of the house, leaving the dwelling itself for dancing and gathering as the day grew cooler, as it was bound to do in the afternoon. Over the tables the linens of several ladies' households were rolled out and then were set out the bowls, platters and trenchers filled with every kind of scone, oat-cake, bap and bannoch. There were cheeses and curds, fancy eggs, onions and leeks, salmon and trout, haggis, Col-cannon, clapshot and cream crowdie, tiers of currant-cakes, seed-cakes, honey-cakes, and a very large wedding cake as only were made years ago, with every kind of fruit and nut, reeking of spirit. Such a cake could have a dried part steamed into a very fine pudding to celebrate the 25th wedding anniversary, all that many years into the future, provided that the cake was kept dry and away from house mice. A place was left in the middle of one table for the punch bowl. Finally, over all of this, the ladies rolled out more linens.

Everyone crowded into this house for the witnessing of the wedding toast. Children were quick to station themselves on the steps to the loft of the house once the young couple had been led up the brae to the small farm. The piper, Donald Ban, had marched right through the door eyes straight ahead and, as is always the case with pipers, one had the feeling that were the door unopened, it would have been trodden underfoot with never a note nor doubling missed on the chanter. A piper leading people somewhere (in any direction) takes his duty very seriously. They all stood very quietly while Alisdair Ruadh embraced his new niece's new husband, whose tartan she now wore pinned over her right shoulder. He then handed a glass about two-thirds full of whisky to Morag. Morag took the glass in both hands and raised it to her lips, taking only a sip, then with both hands passed it to Alan. Alan ceremoniously drained the glass, blinked, strained for his voice and said, "And that shall be the last drink and the last pledge to be had with this glass!" At which point it was hurled into the fireplace. The glass almost exploded into fragments, which brought loud exclamations of wonder and happiness from all who were present. "And this."

cried Alisdair, "will be a grand marriage!" The pipes then started up, the couple then led to their wedding feast, with a beaming company of friends and kinsfolk behind them.

There was the usual dancing: reels and some jigs, and surely there was music enough. Alisdair Ruadh had managed to come up with no fewer than three fiddlers, the two pipers, a man from the Western Isles who played an Irish whistle, and a drummer. Surely there was enough food and more than enough drink (….and not a weak one), "Brose", that unbelievable Scottish mixture of oatmeal water, heavy cream whipped to peaks folded in along with whisky and spices, not to mention the fact that many extra bottles had been brought by the guests, as is always the case at Highland weddings. Yet, something was different at this wedding feast, for along with the great happiness of the day there was a strong undercurrent of uneasiness; of leave-taking or finality.

Morag and Siubhan had an opportunity to have a few words before the bride was called away to perform another small ritual or accept the best wishes of another person. Alan had engineered it in a way. He had whispered to Siubhan when she was near, "Take care of my bride for a few minutes for me, would you? Keep Mrs. McPhee and Una from settling her into a corner and frightening her to death! I have something to say to Duncan before you all leave." Siubhan had responded by wrinkling her nose at him and giving his head a little shove to one side in a very sister-like way.

"I really am happy for you, Morag!", proclaimed a soft voice beside her. Morag turned.

"Are you, Siubhan? I really hope that you mean that, for you mean so much to Alan!" Morag's eyes had a very anxious, sincerity about them as she searched Siubhan's face. "No wonder Alan chose her!", Siubhan thought. "She really is a lovely, very kind woman. I guess I never realized it before!" She answered Morag:

"Yes, I do mean it, Morag, Although I am not so certain that I am all that important to Alan."

"Oh, but you are! Alan speaks of you often...of your childhood together, your always taking his part, all of those things."

"I'm sure that Alan likes me. I am a 'sister' to him. I'm not in any way certain that he loves me."

"You're wrong, Siubhan. He does love you."

"It doesn't matter. He is your husband now. Anyway, I would think that it would bother you if you felt that he loved me!"

"Siubhan," (Morag's voice was very soft, almost comforting) "Alan married me, it's true, but he isn't the kind of man who can love just one person in his lifetime."

"Alan would never be unfaithful to you, Morag!"

Morag smiled before answering. Her soft, gray eyes turned to a great look of understanding, a patience, toward this other woman who had had so much of her husband's boyhood and youth, but who had not really met Alan, the man. Her dark hair tumbled out over her arm as she placed her hand upon Siubhan's.

"I know that, Siubhan. I know that he wouldn't...not in any physical sense of the word...but, Alan has too much love for others, so much to give! I couldn't expect him to give all that he has to one person and one person only in all his life!"

At this, Siubhan felt momentarily ugly, shrewish,... stupid. "How could I hope to compete in any way with this girl?" she asked herself. "She is so wise in her youth, so sure of herself...and I am shallow as she is wise, as much given to selfishness as she is given to trust and generosity!" Morag was speaking again.

"Siubhan, I am so glad that my husband grew up with someone like you! I am sure that so much of that trust and good feeling he has toward women is due to his having known a really fine girl in his childhood. You really are more than a sister to him. I had hoped that we could be such good friends. Now you will be going across to America.

"Canada." Siubhan corrected her. Seeing the look of bewilderment on Morag's face, she repeated, "Canada. Father and mother are going to upper Canada."

"Upper Canada! Oh, that must be a terribly cold place!"

"Well, I thought that it sounded to be a cold place too, but father has had letters, you know, and it seems that 'upper Canada' means 'western' or 'inland' rather than somewhere more northerly. We are going to a place by what they call the Great Lakes."

"Oh, I don't know where that would be or what the Great Lakes are.", Morag replied.

"Nor do I, Morag, but father says that it's not overly cold and that they do have very fine orchards there!", Siubhan replied, "Aye, well, it is said to be quite flat there." Suddenly she turned to look directly into Morag's face. Her grey-green eyes were wide and brimming with tears. "I'll die in a land that is flat and far from the sea, Morag! I really think that my heart is about to break, for I have never, never in my life looked upon a journey with such loathing and sadness." Siubhan looked down toward her lap, took a handkerchief from her sleeve and wiped her nose. Her face was invisible as her coppery hair fell down over her shoulders. Her head shook back and forth a few times, but before Morag could reach out to her, not knowing what else to do, Siubhan's head popped up, and with a red-nosed but smiling face she tossed her hair back. "Anyway, it will be an adventure! Maybe I'll be captured by a red Indian and be made to live on wild berries and nuts!"

"Or wear dresses made of animal skins!", laughed Morag. Out of the corner of her eye, Morag saw her mother across the room sitting next to Margaret M'Cra' and she saw too, her new husband stop by her mother's side. "Oh, thank you, Alan!", she thought toward him. "Thank you!", She saw Alan touch Catriona MacLeannan's shoulder and she saw her mother turn to look at him with the same tired, patient smile that she always wore.

The pipers had given the fiddlers another rest and it was almost impossible to hear anything. Alan bent down to hear what Catriona was saying, and as he did so, Catriona reached her hand up to his shoulder. Even across the room Morag could see something different about her mother's smile as she looked at her new son-in-law. "She really is smiling!" Morag thought. "She really looks happy!"

There were other conversations taking place. Mrs. McPhee looked well pleased with the whole thing. She was in fact telling Siubhan's mother that Morag was a fine girl.

"I've always said that Catriona MacLeannan would raise that girl up to be a fine and bonnie lass! And so she did! Mind you...it hasn't always been easy for Catriona, but you know that as I do..." on and on and on. Murdoch MacIan was still telling stories and the two M'Cra boys next to him were encouraging him.

"Well," Murdoch was saying, "after her long journey across from Scotland they finally landed in Carolina. Now, the ship was being tied up and all and some of the passengers came to the rail. She was just thinking her loneliest thoughts, and all around her they were speaking only English when suddenly the most lovely sound came to her ears! It was the sound of two men on the pier, and weren't they conversing in the Gaelic! Well, now, she brightened up at that, all right, and looked to see who it was. There on the pier they were: two Africans! Darkies,... raised, I suppose from childhood near Gaelic speaking folk. Well, it was a hot enough day, you know...and she saw these two with their dark skin and their short hair looking all the world as if it had been singed by a fire. She threw up her hands and said, "Gu Sealladh Dia! May God be looking! Is this what becomes of Gaels in this land of blistering sunlight?!" And, that's a true story sent over from America! And so it is, every word of it!" MacIan nodded solemnly and took his dram. The men around him smiled.

"Aye, Duncan," Ian Crubach MacKenzie was saying, "I wish I were going across with you! The rents we pay to men who couldn't care less about us and all! But I'm too old and broken up to start over again. But you, why you'll be picking your food from the very trees, or so I am told! Oh, aye. I'd go. I'd go alright if it wasn't to start all over again. It wouldn't do for me to try that now!"

Duncan looked over toward Sara and Mairi. Sara was holding up pretty well. Little Alisdair was curled up on her lap with his head against her bosom. Young Duncan had left Sara and his mother just an instant before to go running out the door with two of the other children. Someone had come up to Sara and Mairi and Mairi looked up to him. then to her dead husband's mother. Sara tossed her head and waved toward her. Mairi rose somewhat shyly to her feet and began to move away with the young man, who as he turned around, Duncan recognized as Seumais Donn M'Cra', Alisdair and Margaret's second son. As the young couple took to the jig, Duncan thought how fine they looked, happy too at the sight of Mairi enjoying herself for a change. Daughter-in-law or no, she was still a pretty thing, and "after all, Neill is gone now," he thought. Duncan couldn't resist glancing over toward Mrs McPhee. Sure enough, she stared, open mouthed. "Close your self-righteous mouth, Maggie McPhee" he was thinking with merriment, "or something will take it for a cave and fly inside." Sara sat with the child on her lap, tapping her foot to the music. There was a soft but beautiful smile on her face as she looked toward the dancing, and just the smallest hint of tears in her eyes. Her hand reached out and touched the arm of Dugall M'Cra' as he was passing and as he turned she measured a small space in the air between her thumb and index finger. Dugall went to fetch her the 'tiniest dram of brose.'

CHAPTER III

Morag had put just enough water in the pan to cover the salmon, added a spoon of vinegar, then pushed the iron fire arm back so that the fire would bring the water in the pan to an even boil. When the water would have boiled away the salmon would be cooked. Certainly a salmon wasn't needed for breakfast, what with all of the other things which had come down from Alisdair and Sara. There would still be a large group of people to feed; those who had come a great distance and who would be staying to rest before returning home, as well as the younger folk who could lengthen a marriage feast out for several days. Yet Alisdair had insisted that Ian and Dugall carry a tiny part of almost everything that was there to Catriona's house for the newlyweds' breakfast. A half hour ago, young Donald Macrae had stopped by with this wonderful salmon. As she poked at the peats in the fire place, the young bride thought of how these coals or a part of them would be carried to her own cottage, just as the fire which had been kindled in this house had been made of coal's carried from Catrionas's mother's house. Alan had hoped to have their cottage ready in time, but as the day of the wedding had come closer and closer it had looked to be impossible. As it had turned out, Catriona had announced her wish to visit a sister and her husband in Inverness for a few weeks. She would stay at Alisdair's for a day or two then go on to Inverness with Martha and Coll Frasier. Coll gathered local produce from the coast, from tweeds made by the island people to cheese or basketry made on the coast, and took them into Inverness for the market there. Catriona's sister, Helen, and her husband, Martin Chishom, had a small bakery where Catriona would busy herself and enjoy the sights and sounds of the Highlands' only real city. This would give Alan plenty of time to finish work on the cottage...and at that time, coals from Catrionas fire would be carried to kindle a new fire in Morag's house.

Alan had not had the opportunity to talk to Duncan on the previous night. He reckoned to day as he worked at securing his animals in a pen, which badly needed some repairs, that it had been foolish of him to have considered such a possibility on any wedding feast night, much less his own. There had been so many words of thanks to be expressed by him, so many people to be acknowledged and given some small part of his time! Here, in this temporary holding pen were some of the gifts: a six-month old heifer, a three month old bull calf and two ewes, a young ram and four lambs. He thought now of Duncan and Sara, of how they would need their friends around them at this time. He tugged at the knot in the rope a little angrily as he thought of these wonderful, gentle people leaving their home at a time in their lives when security, land and family are so important. "We fought their dammed war for them!," he was thinking, "and it's great the number of men who never came home! Well, at least they're not here to see the broken promises and lands of their fathers snatched from under their feet! My God! Here is poor Neil's mother and father, his sister, his wife and two lads put out of their homes and heading out for Canada! They can't move inland to a smaller holding because they are evicting people over there to make room for sheep! And Neil and Angus, both of them in heroes graves! Their medals wouldn't buy a boll of meal, not even a yard of cloth. Yes, we must go to Sara and Duncan today. In fact, we can do that after breakfast." As it turned out, neither Alan nor Morag had breakfast on that first morning of their married life.

Duncan and Siubhan were at the cottage when Alan came along the wall from the byre and pen. Siubhan was crying, Morag was crying and tears ran down Duncan's cheeks. Two young men came across the floor toward the doorway, one of them running the sleeve of his shirt across his eyes. Alan looked at each one of the people before him in wonder. "What's wrong?," he asked of no one in particular yet everyone in general. "Who are you lads? Where do you come from?" A muffled sound came from the direction of the fireplace. One of the young men stood silently looking at Alan and with a toss of his head he motioned toward the fireplace. Alan saw what appeared to be a bundle of rags. He looked closer.

On a pallet by the fire wrapped in what were once bed clothes, was a smallish human form. At one end was the head of a very old lady quietly shivering and sobbing. The bed clothes were scorched in several places and this bundle of fright and misery shook with the quickness of shivering and the violent depth of sobbing simultaneously. A patch of the woman's white hair had been burned and as she brought a hand up to her eyes, it was not difficult to see that her arm was thin, wasted; that she had been ill. A continuous sound, thin and tired, came from her; just a "'n'n, n'n'n "of pitiful crying. Alan looked and said, "Oh, my..., oh, my God!" He kept staring at her, reached out and patted her thin arm. "Who is she? What has happened to her?" One of the two young men spoke; the one who had motioned to her with his head a moment or two ago. "She is a MacDonnell woman. They evicted the people of the glen that she lived in. She's old and ill. We tried to tell those men that she couldn't be moved. The factor said "Well, you'll move her or she'll go up in flame with her cottage!" "And at that he set the cottage afire."

"These two young men carried her from that glen, Alan. All night they carried her!" Morag told her husband.

Alan knelt down by the old woman. He couldn't stop staring and he couldn't believe. Over and over he said "Oh... you poor thing! Oh, my God! How could anyone be so unfeeling?" Suddenly he looked around to the two young men. "Have you had anything to eat?", he asked them.

"Well, we have not," one of them said, "but there are others worse than ourselves. Some are old, some are children, there are nursing mothers, too."

"Yes, Alan," Duncan was saying. "There are others. Come!"

Alan followed Duncan out and around to the gable end of the house. Here one could see the other houses lining the small road. Along the path and sitting in small clusters were perhaps 20 or 30 people, people in various states of dress, or undress. (Two children were quite naked save for a plaid wrapped around one and the other clutching a sheet of bed linen about him." One man had a meal chest standing beside him. He had carried it roped to his back from his now burned cottage, about twelve miles away. Roped to his back, it had been about half full of meal and contained, as well, his three year old little girl. His wife and two other children had carried as much as each of them could manage.

"How long have they been here?" Alan asked Duncan.

"Oh, not more than the time it would take you to walk to Alisdair's house."

"Well, I heard the dog barking, but I paid no attention because he makes that much noise when he has a cat cornered!"

Alan shook his head and kept looking at the victims of a new order, a scheme of English and lowland Scots planners which would ultimately empty the Highlands of people and re-populate the north of Scotland with sheep. "What are we going to do with them?" his words came out.

"Well, we can find places for them for awhile and although it won't be all that easy I suppose that we can feed those who need help, for awhile, but laddie, it's not all that simple! I'm sure that there will be others, and then others! There's apt to be no end to it in our lifetime." Duncan looked at Alan for a long time, half turning himself to do so before going on. "That is really what made me decide that we had to leave, Alan! Sooner or later! Sooner or later! Ten years from now I wouldn't be able to swing an ax in Canada. Well, I could, of course, but not for a long enough day of it to get a proper start at a new life over there."

Both men stood looking in the direction of the people who had come over the heather tracks to take a brief rest before going on to whatever there was for them to go on to. Motioning to them with his walking stick, Duncan went on: "Those aren't just a lot of tinkers and vagrants you know, Alan!"

"What do you mean?"

"Well..." Duncan put his hand to his fore head sliding his 'bonnet' back bit, "they're reputable folk! These men and women aren't, or weren't, poor people, by any means! That auld woman in Catriona's house lying by the fire, for example. She's the widow of a very important man of that clan. Her husband's father raised one hundred and sixty-odd men for the Prince back in the '45. I know who she is. I recognized her despite all the terrible battering she's had!"

"I'd heard that people were being evicted here and there and that even old charters and documents were being called worthless...but seriously, Duncan, do you not think that this will pass?" Alan was almost asking Duncan to tell him what he instinctively felt to be bearing down on all of them was an illusion, something which would go away, yet he knew better. Alan had seen and heard things long before the news had reached this small hamlet of theirs.

"However will it pass away?" Duncan asked him. It was the same tone of voice that a father uses when he scolds a son. He could have easily been saying, "Who's to fix that broken window, or why are you talking nonsense?" "Na, Alan! It's not going to pass! The Scotland of the clan and the chief is gone. My grandfather stood with the prince at Culloden, as I'm sure you know. Anyway, he said that he knew on that day that, like it or not, what the Highlandman was facing was the world of the future: cold, heartless and very, very efficient...but...the future. Well, here we are, Alan. That 'future' is where we now stand."

Morag and Suibhan passed by the two men, Morag with a large wooden pail of milk and a metal dipper, Siubhan carrying a creel of scones, bannochs and whatever she'd been able to gather up in the way of 'loose' food. Over her shoulder, Morag told Alan that she'd set a great pot of oats to cook and asked him to have a look at it to see that it wouldn't boil over. As Duncan and Alan moved toward the door of the house, they saw Margaret M'Cra and Catriona coming down the path carrying baskets. Three of the lads,

Murdoch, Andrew and Dugall, were carrying some blankets and plaids. "The unbidden guests have come to what is left of the wedding feast." Alan mused.

"Aye." Duncan was saying aloud. "It's a good thing that Alisdair Ruadh thinks always to plenty!" The two men went in to look at the porridge.

There was a young man who refused to travel to the church five miles to the north. It had been arranged that the up-rooted and discarded people would gather by the church at Kil'urran and wait for three days. At that time a ship bound for Canada would come into the bay and they would embark, making that break with their past that would haunt them and even their children's children. In time the New World would give them more than they could ever have dreamed possible, but there would always be a certain restlessness, a longing for something left somewhere, someplace. The young man was, on this third day of the arrival to the coast, beginning to feel a deep and burning sense of bitterness, the like of which would carry him for the rest of his life. In the New World he would translate his anger and frustration into an energy which would enable him to clear a land of trees, dig wells for water, lay up stone for walls and end it all as a very venerable ancestor figure for future Canadians. He would be, after a half century of bouts with frost bite, near exhaustion and tasks normally beyond human endurance, a well-to-do old gentleman in a black suit with a gold watch chain, looking out of a photographic portrait with soft, down-turned eyes, a slight smile behind his patriarchal white beard. Despite the success of a long life of hard work and a home filled with love, his eyes would betray upon closer inspection, a look of hurt which would have begun upon this day on Scotland's rugged, rocky coast; here in this place where the rocks pierced the peaty grass roadway winding up among the small cottages.

Of course, he couldn't have known about his future at this time. This morning his head was reeling. Things were happening but he didn't know why. What he did know was that he wanted absolutely nothing to do with the established church of Scotland. Alisdair Ruadh had been trying to point out to him that the church up the coast was the best place to gather and that was where provision had been made for such a great number of people.

"Listen, a mhic", Alisdair was saying. "There are good ministers and bad ministers just as there are good and bad priests! Now, you cannot turn away from a church when it is all that has been set up to be of help to you! The ship will be here before long and that will be an end of your trouble. You'll find a new life and what is even more, you'll probably be better off than those of us who are to be staying here."

The young man squinted off toward the water of the loch where the sun danced and threw fairy darts of reflected light at his eyes. Those eyes were as cold as the sea beyond the loch itself. Impassive, giving no sign that he was hearing any of Alisdair Ruadh's, words he kept his head turned away, not with embarrassment, not in grief, but only in an empty sense of neither being nor caring. Alisdair Ruadh wanted to touch the young man's shoulder, to turn him 'round and tell him that all would be different someday soon. Yet, instinctively even Alisdair felt that any such statement would be little short of a lie. Somehow he knew that nothing would ever be as it had been.

Duncan and Sara moved up toward Alisdair but stopped a few yards away upon seeing the usually jovial redhead with such a look of concern on his face, not to mention the uncompromising back and shoulders to which he had been addressing his words.

Alisdair turned to look at them, a look of helplessness written on his ruddy face. He spread his hands, arched his brows and moved away from the silent figure, toward Duncan and Sara.

"I don't know what to tell him. He won't move on to Kil'urran." Alisdair explained. "That is where the emigrant ship will be coming in. He won't go near the church there. I don't know what is wrong with him."

"Perhaps he is Episcopalian or Catholic." Duncan said.

"Aye, well… what if he is?", Alisdair asked. "We've never cared one way or the other around here. Besides that, the church at Kil'urran is Episcopal, but more to the old religion than anything else."

"Yes." Sara put in. "In fact, Reverend MacLean is one even to go to the Belteine fires and take part in the procession. And didn't Flora MacLean tell Maggie McPhee that he wouldn't sleep in a house where the fire hasn't been smoored in the old way, with the prayers at the hearth!"

"Well, if Maggie McPhee said it it must be so," said Duncan. Alisdair and Duncan laughed at that; not in an unkind way, but in the way of people long accustomed to putting up with the well known eccentricities of a sometimes vexatious loved one. Sara made a little cuffing gesture toward Duncan's arm, at the same time trying to conceal her own smile and reluctant agreement with her husband's implication.

"Anyway," Duncan went on, "the lad has probably had his stomach full of the preachments of the ministers!"

"What do you mean?" Alisdair asked.

"Well apparently the ministers have been of little help whatever to the evicted folk of the glen yonder. A woman was telling me that the men made no attempt whatever to stop those hired drunkards from their burning and breaking up of the cottages...and do you know why?" Without waiting, but just after looking at the blank faces of Alisdair and Sara, he went on. "The ministers, many ministers...in more than one glen...have been telling their flocks that their loss of their homes is a part of God's judgment on them! In fact, the folk have been informed by these reverend gentlemen that if they so much as raise hand or voice to the factors or their men, that they will be going against some God-ordained plan to punish them for their having been a wild and savage people; that they'll lose not only their homes but their immortal souls, as well! Did you ever hear of such utter nonsense?"

"Wild and savage were they?", mused Sara. "How? Why,

they have been clansmen and they do not speak English, and they dance and sing. They've been known to make music with pipes, fiddles and harps! Aye! They'll take a dram now and then too!"

"Oh, well!", said Alisdair. "It is a wonder that they'd have a pipe or fiddle anyway. In the North and in Lewis the ministers of the Kirk broke up the fiddles and all! Burned them all too! Better to have a wee fire now of fiddles than a fire for all eternity and that one feasting on human souls, they'd told them!"

"How would anyone believe that?", Sara asked in astonishment. "They'd have to be simple to believe something like that!"

"Not really, Sara." Duncan turned to her. "You see, the ministers could point to their poverty or loss of property and say that it was because they spoke only the Gaelic and had no English and that their ignorance was holding them back...or that their sinful desire to wear bright colours or to be wild and free had made God angry. The God of John Knox is angry much of the time, I am thinking!"

"Oh, Aye," Sara and Alisdair answered in unison.

"It seems," Duncan went on, "that the minister of the glen told these people in no uncertain terms that they had to submit to the factor and the lawyer's writs which he carried in his hand." Duncan lowered his voice even more so than it had been. "These folk have had a terrible time. The men, those hired drunkards from the south were taking great delight in breaking up their cupboards...even their meal chests! Then, to have their own minister come out on the side of the factor, to see him practically defending the actions of some unfeeling, brutish men, well...it must have been enough to destroy much of what faith those poor folk had had in Southrons and ministers alike!"

The three of them stood silent for a time, looking about at various people who were, each of them, engaged in what was at that moment in time, a very important task. The lady who had come into the hamlet in a wagon with the fine horses was preparing to leave for the gathering place at the church up the coast. She was climbing up onto the seat next to a man not from the Highlands, a lowlander perhaps, or an Englishman. He was driving her team now, having bought them. Somewhere she had parted with the furniture and the bedding which had been in the back of the wagon when she first arrived. A wooden chest and a small clock roped to it were all that the wagon box held now. The lady carefully spread her skirts over her portion of the seat and a young man passed a small wooden box up to her which she placed squarely in her lap, before putting both hands on it, then folding her hands on its top, almost as if she were about to begin her prayers. She nodded to the driver and then lifted her chin and looked straight ahead. The driver pulled up the lines, gave them a shake, and the horses and wagon, the lady with her chest, clock and small box rolled northward. Her eyes never moved from some distant point far ahead of her. As the driver brought the team and wagon past Duncan, Sara and Alisdair, they could see the bodice of the lady's dress a blaze of reflected light, and glory, for there on prominent display were the service medals and battle decorations of three brave soldiers who had fallen in various engagements during the Napoleonic war: the honors of her husband and two sons. To the day of her death many years later she would never smile again.

Duncan looked over again toward the silent young man. It was as if he were becoming one with the stone that he sat upon; not a stir, not a sign of movement. He stared toward the water as one who wished to be carried off and into it, then to become a mist and be no more. Duncan moved up to the young man. Standing behind him for a moment he looked upon the slumped shoulders, the tweed coat and it's seam down the lad's back. "He'll need a better coat than this one in Canada." He caught himself thinking. Slowly and not knowing why, he raised his hand and placed it gently on the shoulder before him. The lad neither turned nor shrugged. He acted as if he didn't know that Duncan or anyone had touched him. Duncan heard himself say, "You'll come home with us. We all need our rest. Like yourself, my family and I will be boarding that ship tomorrow. I think, lad, there'll be many who will be needing the help of a strong young fellow." At that and without saying a word, the young man got to his feet. Duncan turned back toward Sara and a somewhat surprised looking Alisdair. As he walked back to his wife and friend he was aware that the young man had picked up a bundle from the ground and had started moving silently after him. Down they went to the center of the cluster of houses with the semblance of a road, a rocky ribbon of turfless earth which ran north to Camusclachan, the bay where the ship would be waiting the next morning.

Alisdair and Sara, Duncan and the young man came together without words, and as they turned to walk up the steep slope toward Duncan's cottage they were passed by a family moving slowly across their path: a man carrying a child of about three or four years of age, her little head of tangled red hair lying on his shoulder, a little boy, perhaps eight or ten, leading a Highland pony a pace or two behind them. There was an infant on the mothers back, held in place by the woman's plaid which had been fashioned into a kind of pouch or sling, passing over her shoulders then criss-crossed over her chest and secured by her belt. The pony had a woven creel fastened to it on each side and each creel contained the hastily gathered bits of bedding and clothing, the few keepsakes and cooking utensils of a life-time. The mother and father looked straight ahead, their sense of pride or self-esteem badly shaken. They were landless, homeless...without status; honest people who had kept the old ways and the old loyalties all of their lives, now reduced to the position of gypsies, tinkers...like the remnants of the "broken" clans...like MacGregors. "We are landless, landless, Grigalach, landless," the old song has it, and now there was a swelling legion of landless folk. Families and ancient proprietorships were being torn up by the roots as if by the torrent of a great flood, and like a flood, much of that which had been firmly rooted was now floating debris, carried along to some unknown destination.

The boy walking at his father's side did not look straight ahead. He looked from one side of him to the other, too young to have lost status never yet gained; too innocent of the game of life and the rules of conduct required of those who have entered into that game. His soft, grey-green eyes met those of Sara and she could feel the tears coming. She wanted to gather him up and pass her hand over his reddish hair, hug him to her and say, "Oh, let this moment pass away! Don't become bitter or angry in later years! Don't let it make a mean man of you." Women, who are mothers know of such things. Women who have brought forth life and cared for ailing children and their injured fathers know that the blank look on a child's face is no indication that all is well. There is no such thing as being too young to feel. They know that and they know that these glimpses of whatever is taking place today may well translate into some terrible resolve in future. And as Sara saw the child and felt what she did, she knew instinctively that what she was experiencing was a tremor of fear. That child and thousands of others just like him were, collectively, the future. Her fears were to be justified. The red-headed little boy with the soft grey eyes, the eyes of a poet who had just turned around to look at her another time, would be working for a printer in a few years. Before his death he would have owned a publishing house, a paper mill and thousands of Canadian acres. In his old age he would often tell of his leave-taking of Scotland. "I never knew my father to be as broken and ashamed as he was when we left the croft. I think that he seriously thought that he had lied to me...telling me about the land and the clan, how one could always be sure of those two things. "Well, it's money, laddie!," he would say to his young workers, sons, grandsons and business acquaintances, "Mind yer money, for it's all that stands between living and being out and on the road! I learned that lesson early enough!" Today, though, he was still a little boy walking up a stony road; kilted and barefoot, his brogues (for they weren't really shoes as we know them) hanging by their strings over his shoulder. What his Daddie did not know was that nothing he could ever have done could have shaken the love and trust that this child held for him.

The time of the short walk up the hillside to Duncan and Sara's was filled with the sights and sounds of the great upheaval. Small groups of two or three people seemed to be everywhere. Sometimes they would be speaking together in quiet voices while others spoke not at all. Close by them would be the few bundles which they were carrying with them, and the smaller children, now resting on the ground just as their parents, not too far away from them, in the unfamiliar setting, although a few of them made something of a holiday of the lack of organization. those were mainly the slightly older children, running and playing with the others whose homes these cottages were. Half way up the knoll, the four of them: Duncan, Sara, Alisdair and their still nameless new friend had turned around to look back toward the road. A lone rider had come into the hamlet at a gallop. He had called out that the expected ship had been sighted. "This means that it will be at Camusclachan by mid-afternoon", Duncan was thinking to himself. Duncan guessed that somewhere, in the back of his mind, he had been hoping that the ship might not come, or that maybe all ships large enough or having the ability to carry people across the sea might suddenly cease to exist. That would have been the end of this nightmare, he thought. But no, the nightmare was here, and it wasn't going away. In fact, perhaps the only end of the nightmare would be realized at the boarding of a ship.

Mairi was calling to young Duncan from the doorway of the cottage when the four got to the croft. "Where is Alisdair? I told you to watch your little brother!"

"He's in the byre!", came the answer of a yet unseen child

"Och hone!" came the exasperated reply. "A fine place for him! He'll be muck from end to end even if he hasn't eaten half of it by now! Tell him to come out of there, or rather, go fetch him and bring him to the house!" Young Duncan suddenly sprang from behind a low wall and ran off to the byre with a stick and a yelp, scattering hens and chicks in his path. His mother stood watching him. shaking her head in an absent sort of way. She looked up and saw the four, giving them an embarrassed smile and smoothing her apron. Seeing Alisdair Ruadh and the stranger with her parents-in-law had made her feel a bit foolish. "He is so forgetful! He really vexes me at times!", she said in the way of an apology.

"Oh, No, Mairi," Duncan smiled, "it is the wildness of the Macleannains he has on him!"

"From the Macleannains is it?" Mairi countered. "There'll be the dreamer of his daddie and grandad that is in him, if I am any judge!"

"I'll agree to that, Mairi." Sara put in. Turning to Duncan she said, "and its' only the better traits in a child that men will claim!"

"Only because that is the way of it, ladies."

"Well," Mairi persisted, "no Macleannain was ever late for a meal as you are now! Come now and I'll get you something."

"I'll see to that, Mairi." Sara said. "You've enough to do!"

"No, Mother. It is already well cooked and needs only to be dished up."

As they moved into the house they found themselves enveloped by the warm fragrance of baking. Siubhan was inside too, tending barley scones on a stone over the fire. On the table close by was a large wooden bowl covered with bits of dough and flour. There was something very special, very solemn, about this baking. It would be the last that any of Duncan's womenfolk would be doing in this house. In an attempt to use up as much of the flour on hand and to prepare some food for the journey, Siubhan and Mairi had been baking as if they expected to never bake again.

Siubhan turned away from the fire and back toward the table, bending her wrist and bringing the back of her small hand up to her up-turned forehead to push back a wisp of fine, auburn hair from her forehead. It is one of those very feminine gestures which men so often find to be absolutely fascinating, beautiful. The movement had not gone unappreciated, for as she looked up at that moment the first eyes to meet her own were those of the young man who had come into the house with her father and mother. She felt herself to be embarrassed, caught off guard, without knowing why.

"I'll move these things," she said. "None of you have had your meal yet."

"No, no.", Sara protested. "You go on with what you're doing. We'll just need the one end of the table." Sara started, almost jumped, and looked to the side of the fire place. Everyone: Duncan, Alisdair and the young man saw him at the same time. It was Seumais Donn, Alisdair's second son. He had been almost invisible by the side of the fireplace, but now he stepped forward, nodding to all of them.

"Why...a good day to you, Seumais." Sara Said.

"And a very good day to you, Sara,..Duncan."

Alisdair Ruadh looked surprised.

"I did not expect to find you here, a mhic," Alisdair said to him. "You've come to be of help, I see.

"I have", Seumais replied

"Well, I am sure that there is plenty to do," Alisdair said. "In fact, you can help me move the cows. I have bought

Duncan's two cows."

"They're good cows!" Seumais nodded.

"Aye, well...we won't have to move them just now, mind! They'll have the use of them before..." Alisdair's voice fell short.

"No, Alisdair,: Duncan argued. "take them along anytime. There is no place for any milk now. You take them along!"

Mairi had been ladling up a thick broth from an iron pot by the fire. She set four steaming bowls on the table. "Talk about that later," she said. "your broth will get cold!"

"Oh," said Alisdair on seeing the four bowls. "I am not staying to eat with you. I'll have something waiting for me at home...or is that for Seumais?"

"No, father, I've had something to eat with Mairi and Siubhan already."

"You'll eat that, Alisdair Ruadh or I'll never..." Mairi's voice trailed off. No, she would never be offering him a bowl of broth or a scone ever again in any case. The young man looked at Siubhan who glanced again, now for about the sixth time at him.

Duncan and Alisdair moved toward the table. Sara brought out some spoons and a plate for some scones. Duncan looked over at his young guest, glanced at Siubhan then back to the young man. He looked toward Sara too for any indication that she saw what he was seeing, but Sara's face had no expression other than squinting her eyes almost shut as she took some hot scones from the stone 'girdle'.

"Come on here!", Duncan called over to the dark young man. "I doesn't pay to be shy in this house!" Then, to everyone else he said, "I would tell you this young fellow's name, but I do not know what it is myself."

"Take my pardon!" The young man said. "My manners are bad ones today. My name is Ranald dubh MacAindreas, and I thank you for your offer of hospitality."

Seumais was looking in a hard way at Ranald and Alisdair was looking hard at his son, Seumais. The guest took a stool offered to him and sat down, at which point Seumais went over to Mairi who was folding some linens. A few words so low that no one could hear passed between them. They turned around to face the others.

Siubhan smiled to herself without raising her eyes.

"Duncan, Sara...and you, Father." Seumais stood next to Mairi as straight as a board, his face full of color.

"I...or...we have something to say. "He looked sideways at Mairi who was looking up at his face. He seemed to search the air for words, then went on. I wish that there was more time...to do things properly, with more dignity and all, but there is not." Duncan looked at Sara. Sara's expression was blank.

"Duncan," Seumais went on, "I cannot bear the thought of all of you going away, and especially of Mairi going away. I want you to know that I want her for my wife, and I can't think of anyone else being her husband." Sara started to cry into the crisp apron which she had just put on. Seumais went on.

"I like both of the lads and I think that they like me. They should have a father, and I will be good to them." He moved closer to the table, but his hand still held that of Mairi. There was a pause, a short pause, perhaps, but the room was absolutely still. Sara wiped her eyes, Duncan traced a scratch in the table's surface with his thumbnail, unable to look up. Siubhan was sitting by the fire staring at the glowing peats, and only the voices of the children at play outside invaded the silence, the surprise of the moment.

Alisdair spoke before Seumais could continue:

"This is a poor, a very poor time, to come up with such an idea! I am surprised at you, Seumais. Here are these people leaving everything to go to a new and strange place... everything in turmoil, and you come up with this!"

"Duncan, Sara," Seumais went on. "I want you to know that I would never let the boys lose thought or knowledge of their own daddie. I want them to know of Neill, what a fine man he was...and I am in a good position to do that for them, having known him so very well and all."

"But what of Duncan and Sara?" Alisdair put in. "What of them? It was all arranged that they were all going to Canada, all of them! Wee Duncan and Alisdair is all that they have of Neill now! Of Angus they have only their memories...Mairi is as their own daughter! It's bad enough they have to go, leaving their past behind! Now you'll take what future they have from them, as well! Seumais, you aren't thinking!"

"Stop, Alisdair!" Sara was speaking now. Her eyes were

red, her voice quavering but her expression was stern and her eyes level with his. "You or Duncan or I or anyone else hasn't the right to condemn Mairi, as young as she is, to endless widowhood...and those children need a father! It's true we love Mairi as our own daughter, although I admit that we first took her to us as Neill's wife. Well, we have been through a lot together and we do think of her as our daughter now. That is why her happiness is more important to us than her going along with whatever she thinks we expect her to do, or where we expect her to go."

"But you and Duncan and Siubhan will be in Canada and your Grandsons thousands of miles away! You can't be expected to..."

Alisdair was interrupted by his son. Seumais' voice took on a softness: a tone of affection which Alisdair had never heard from him.

"Dad, You're not understanding what is happening or what I am saying." Seumais turned his eyes toward Duncan, back to Mairi, then to Sara before returning his attention to Duncan. "Duncan, I know how you feel about Mairi as a daughter. I am, in a way, asking you to accept me as your adopted daughter's husband; a different sort of "son-in-law, because Duncan, you need another strong back and pair of arms to help you. I intend to go with you to Canada... or, no...I intend to take my wife and my adopted sons to Canada in the company of some people who mean a great deal to me!" Everyone in the room, save for Mairi and

Siubhan, the dark young Ranald with an expression of respect, stared at him.

"Oh, God of life!" Alisdair sprang to his feet and hugged his son. "This will kill your mother, a mhic!"

"She already knows, father. I wanted to speak with you alone, but this is the first chance that there has been to say much of anything to anyone."

Alisdair was crying, or trying hard not to; wiping his eyes and clearing his throat. He threw his arm up around his son's shoulders squeezing the far shoulder with his strong hand.

"You...you were always the lad for surprises, Seumais. This one, though! This one crowns all your past efforts."

Duncan had been studying Mairi. She looked toward him and he gave her a kind smile. "Well, Mairi, what do you think about all of this?"

"Seumais and I have cared for one another for a long time, Duncan. I've never been able to get past missing Neill. I know that I never will be able to. Seumais knows that and accepts it, and I love him all the more for his understanding."

Duncan rose from his chair, pulled Mairi and Seumais to him, one on each side. An arm around each of them he faced the others, smiling proudly he said, "Here we have it then! A small, last gathering of friends tonight will seal it for us all."

From his side of the fire, the darkly handsome young

stranger looked across at Siubhan, watching her as if he feared that she might vanish in the moment that he chanced to look away. At the same time, his face conveyed a certain determination, as if he had no intention of looking away....ever.

CHAPTER IV

Duncan couldn't make up his mind whether to believe that his neighbors were really as naive as they appeared to be or if they were just trying to cheer his family and himself on their way. Murdoch MacIan had just finished singing a song written several years before by Ian MacMhurchaidh, or "John MacRae" as he is called in the English world. The song, "Nise bho na Thrachair Sinn", ("Now That We Have Met") had been written by the Kintail bard in the late Eighteenth Century and depicts the leaving of a place of high rents and oppression for a new life in America. The lyrics of such songs often paint a very romantic picture of life in the New World. Duncan was thinking that perhaps it was the lilt, the cheerful melody which really had the great appeal to everyone. The singer would sing a verse, then everyone in the room would join in on the chorus:

"Tha tighinn fodham, fodham, fodham,
Tha tighinn fodham, fodham, fodham,
Tha lihinn fodham agus fodham,
Tha tighinn fodham eiridh."

Duncan smiled a quiet, soft smile throughout the evening as he and Sara sat with their friends who had come to be with them on this their last night under this roof. He was glad that everyone was keeping a happy face on things and not giving in to the gloomy side of the situation. It was, he was thinking, almost the extreme opposite of what he had feared; so much so that it became a reverse sadness. There was an excess of optimism; an attempt to cover the sadness of the moment with lavish hopes for the future. Duncan accepted it all, 'though by no means a believer.

Sara had almost enjoyed giving her things away; so many things which couldn't be taken along. The evening's refreshments were set out on her finest china. At the end of the evening Maggie McPhee was to take her grandmother's cake plate, Margaret M'Cra the punch bowl and china. Morag MacKinnon and Alan were to have her sideboard. The list went on and on. In the end everything, from the stone girdle in the fire place to the broom in the corner, the pails and butter-bowl had been accounted for. Not that they were leaving everything! Sara refused to go to a new life in a strange land with only the clothes on their backs. The sale of the animals had given them some money, much more than many emigrants would think of having (even after settling accounts with the factor), so they were taking the applewood chairs, a fine little clock and two large crates filled with linens, tartans, and some heavy tweeds. In the center of the crate filled with textiles, Sara had placed her two pieces of Jacobite glass which had belonged to Duncan's grandmother, also her own mother's silver and some other small heirlooms. Sara had been born a MacLeod and the family had managed to prosper due to the clan's neutrality during some of the Jacobite trouble.

Of course there was excitement too over the wedding of Mairi and Seumais. Margaret M'Cra' accepted the sudden marriage of her son and his decision to embark for Canada...well, outwardly at least. Yet she did feel piqued that she hadn't been allowed to help toward a proper wedding feast. In fact, despite the fact that Duncan and Sara had a houseful of their friends and even 'though there were a few tunes on the pipes and some singing; even with the forced optimism of the guests, it was, after all, a sad gathering beneath it all. Duncan had suggested to Sara earlier in the day that perhaps it might be easier to leave the old place at night after people started to go home. He reasoned that it would be less painful to go away from the house during the dark hours than in the light of morning. Sara had said, "And leave my own home like a thief, or like one deserting an old friend? No, Duncan. I will leave this house when I can see it and it can see my going. Besides...no one will be going home. They will want to go with us to the bay and the ship." It was to turn out that she was right, for that is what many of them wanted to do.

"This is not a good way to start out a married life", Seumais was saying to Mairi. They found themselves alone for a few minutes at one side of the room. Seumais had suddenly felt awkward, shy even, at finding himself alone with her and he with nothing much to say at the moment.

"I don't see why not, Seumais,"She answered. "In a way it is the only thing that might give us a real start. Away from all of our memories, our past, we will be more forced to count on each other, won't we?"Seumais hugged her to him. "You're a grand, fine woman, Mairi!"

Alisdair Ruadh's brother Murdoch had come from Glennorriston with his wife, Elizabeth. Their aged father, old Christopher had wanted to see his grandson Seumais and his new bride-to-be, especially since they were "going to Carolina."

"No, Father. It is Canada that they are going to, not Carolina!" Alisdair told him.

"Well...the other M'Cra's, MacRaes and all went to Carolina. They would be going there too, I'm sure!"

"No, they are going to Canada."

"Canada,"the old man repeated after him.

"Yes, Father, to Canada."

"Well, what's the difference? They are all the same to me...all those strange places! They can't be far apart from each other. How far apart are they?"

"Oh,"Alisdair thought for a moment. "They would be as far away from each other as Scotland's length from South to North."

The old man looked at him for a long time, as if to see if he were jesting. When the expression on Alisdair's face remained unchanged through this inspection the old man answered. "Well, maybe so, Alisdair, maybe so, but then that seems an awfully big place to me!"

"Can I get you anything, Mrs. McPhee?"Morag was asking her. Morag had never seen her so quiet. Usually Maggie McPhee managed to conduct her own wee Ceilidh at one side of a room. This night she sat quietly listening to others, turning now and then when one or another spoke, but only as a measure of polite behavior rather than genuine interest.

"Oh, no, dear! No, I'm just fine, thank you."

"You are off and away from everything tonight."Morag persisted.

"Oh, aye. I suppose I am. To be honest, dear, I am afraid to say much of anything, for fear I'll start to cry."

"I know. Alan feels the same way. I can tell by looking at him! See him over there! Even when he laughs it's only for a flicker, then his eyebrows take on a hurt, worried slope that changes his whole face."

"Men cry too, dear!", Maggie McPhee said rather sadly." They hide their tears, or they think that they hide them. But men cry in their own way. To be truthful, I think that the way they hold in their grief is more heart-rending than is our own grief, when we can give vent to our feelings!"

Alan had turned from the other men when he had seen Dugall come up next to him. "It's a long hour since I've seen you, Dugall." he said. "Have I lost my helper, now that I am an old married man?"

"Och, no, Alan, but you'll want some time to yourselves. Ma and Dad said that I should give you and

Morag some time alone."

"Did they? Well, I think that is very kind of them, but I wasn't expecting you to sleep between us, was I now? Married or no, each day has its work that needs doing and Morag doesn't want my help in the house, nor do I want her to leave her work in order to help me to build the stone dykes!" He looked at the boy with affection although his tone had a jesting ring to it. Dugall looked toward the floor, a bit embarrassed but happy now that his place in Alan's life had had reaffirmation. As Alan looked at this young fellow who had been tagging around after him since his early childhood he noticed a glint of white high up on his chest where the neck of the lad's shirt had parted.

"Dugall!" he exclaimed. "You have a caberfeidh! Are you already that grown!" Alan reached his hand toward the lad's neck and gently lifted the deer antler cross toward him for a better look, then, as gently, tucked it back inside the boy's shirt and gave it a pat.

"Seumais gave it to me now that he'll be married."

"Aye, Dugall. That is the way of it. That was a fine thing for him to have done. You know, don't you, that it is an act of great trust and affection when a man gives his caberfeidh to another when he marries?"

"Oh, yes. I do know that. I'm very proud to be having it." The lad paused for a minute then blurted out, "Who did you give your caberfeidh to when you married Morag?"

"Aha," thought Alan, "so that is it!" Aloud he said,

"Well, you must promise not to tell a soul!"

"Very well."

"Do I have your sworn oath?"

"You have."

"Well," he bent close to Dugall and said, "I gave it to Mrs. McPhee!"

"You wouldn't have done that!"

"And why not?"

"A woman doesn't wear a caberfeidh!"

"Oh. I forgot that." Alan pretended to be confused. "Well, I didn't think of it at the time. I just said, "Mrs. McPhee, I would be pleased to have you wear my caberfeidh cross. Of course, she accepted it readily!"

"What did she do with it?" Dugall was smiling now, aware that he was being told a monstrous story and going along with the fun in it.

"Well, she took it by the thong, whipped it three times around her head sunwise and turned into a great grey seal! And this is a true story!" (Alan now was imitating Murdoch MacIan the story teller) "All of the rest of them is lies, but this one is true!" They were both trying not to laugh, but bursts of air and pent up foolishness kept exploding from their mouths, despite their efforts to hold everything in.

"What are you laughing at, the both of you?" Morag asked. She smiled despite herself, for such laughter is a terrible contagion. Her face, a blank with a question and a smile written on it made them both laugh all the more. She jabbed Alan with her finger in his ribs, an act of loving revenge, and he laughed harder still.

"Alan! Are the both of you laughing at me?" At this point Alan, shaking still with a boyish mirth and unable to speak, reached out to put his hand on his wife's shoulder. Morag ducked away, sliding easily out from under his hand with a grace that could have resulted from long practice, belying the short span of time they had spent together. As she did this she informed him in mock formality that he would be free to sleep all night in the byre and share his joking and laughter with the livestock.

Dugall, not quite sure of how serious or light the jesting and sparring of marriage partners is meant to be, explained to her that Alan had just been telling one of the 'old stories'. This attempt on his part to bridge any temporary gulf between husband and wife was immediately thwarted by his inability to keep a straight face. Although Dugall and Alan were still emitting the occasional bubble or eruption of a laugh, they started to come out of it slowly, wiping their eyes as they did so. For her part, Morag though, unable to keep a perfectly straight face, again shook her head in mock disbelief and moved away to talk to one of the ladies across the room, who hadn't had a clue as to what had been happening, but who had been smiling unconsciously at the three of them out of the sheer contagion of the whole thing.

Despite all efforts to press a mood of optimism on everything, the talk of the clearances kept surfacing throughout the evening, first in one small group and then in another.

"The hardest part of it all, Ross was telling me," related

Alisdair Ruadh to some small cluster of folk near the sideboard, "was that he didn't have time to let the cattle out! He could hear the cattle bawling in the byre and those men who were burning the cottages wouldn't let him go back to the byre to loose the cows! Can you even imagine such a thing?"

"Well, that would be heartbreaking to me, I'm sure." one of the group replied.

"What kind of mindless, soul-less men can those lowlanders be?" Alisdair asked again.

"The Lowlanders have always been like that! Aren't they the same people who sold their own King to the English and when they'd even'd out the money among themselves found it to be about a ha'penny apiece!" Another put in.

"Och, no, I canna believe that story, 'though I'm sure that I have heard it often enough in my life," said yet another.

"Aye, well...I believe it. There is no humor about the "Gallach". No heart. That's why they are keen to do what others would not do." On and on the stories went, although as bad as they seemed to be in the telling and the hearing, no one in the little house could possibly have known all that had been taking place. Here, they had been seeing waves of refugees moving toward the sea, yet there was no way that they could have known that what they were hearing and seeing was but the tiniest part of the whole. An entire culture was being torn up by the roots. People whose ancestors had been the first to make an area habitable, whose ancient right to the land had been beyond question, were now without a place to lay their heads.

"Have you given any thought to what we had been speaking of the other night, Alan?" Duncan finally asked. It seemed that each of them had been avoiding the subject. Finally, it had had to be brought up, and Duncan leaned close and asked,"What is your opinion?"

"Take the staff to America, Duncan!"

"You feel that I should not leave it in Scotland, then?"

Duncan looked deeply into Alan's eyes. "No, Duncan. There'll soon be no Scotland to leave it in. Take it with you."

"What do you mean?"

"I mean, Duncan, that Scotland is leaving Scotland! Och, man, it's only a question of time! I'll probably be joining you in the Canadian snow before we know it! It's finished for us here. The clans, the crofts, everything we have been, is for the story books that Englishmen read."

"Don't you think we'll take it all away with us, Alan? Put it all together over there on the other side?"

"Oh, aye! Aye...we're the kind of people to do that! We are given to sitting on rocks and dreaming of lost causes and great days that never were!" Alan lifted his head and stared past Duncan toward the chimney, but seemed to be looking past or through the stone, as if his eyes were fastened on some point on the horizon. "But, not all at once,"he said, as if thinking aloud. "Not all at once. Someday, though, little bits of it will begin to make sense. I really don't know, but it comes on me that maybe we'll have a nation now. We've never been a united people, but I think that the Scottish nation is being born. Why, (he looked suddenly at Duncan and laughed) "it may well be that the least of all Scots will be those who somehow will have managed to stay here. The Scots who stay in Scotland will have the ruins to live with, but it may well take a Canadian or a Yankee Scotsman's grandson to tell the folk back here what all of these things mean."

Alan looked away from Duncan and saw Dugall again. He motioned for the lad to come over.

"Dugall, I never told you what you wanted to know. The truth of the matter is that I lost my caberfeidh over the side of a fishing boat two years ago. If I had not done, and if you had a brain in your head rather than a clachmor, you would know this: that you would be wearing it now instead of the one you have." Dugall smiled in a very shy way. Duncan and Alan exchanged soft smiles.

"Thank you, Alan. I knew that it had to be something like that...but it is nice you told me. Thank you."

A bit later, just before the folk took ship for Canada, Alan did give young Dugall something of his own as a parting gift: a small brass compass. Years later, Dugall, even as an old man, still treasured almost above all of his possessions, the compass given to him when he was still a lad and Alan, his hero, a newly married man.

Prologue to
PART TWO

PROLOGUE TO PART 2

By Camus Clachan there is a sharp rise to a grassy knollwhich has some large granite rocks mostly covered with crotal, the blacklichen that is so greatly prized for the lovely

Orange-hued dye which can be got from it. There is also a great number of tiny flowering plants with incredibly delicate foliage and blossoms. Not until one climbs the knoll and moves toward and between the granite boulders is it possible to see the huge, very flat slab of granite lying on the ground. In this place, if one looks toward the bay, be will often have a great, free sweeping sense, or a sense of his soul sweeping, toward the sea, particularly if the wind comes to his back, as it often does there. It was on that rock that the staff of Comhghal (Cowall) had its last exposure to Scottish air and earth, for after he held it aloft, Duncan Gilcannon carefully wrapped it in his plaid, then taking his wife's arm headed toward the beach without a backward look. It was on that rock that a piper, wearing the MacKinnon tartan stood for hours in the sun and played his heart out to his departing friends, until at last, there were no more of the folk to be carried in the boats to the ship at anchor. Years later, another piper would stand in the same spot, unaware of Rory MacKinnon's having been there. Nor would the twentieth century American piper know what other sad piece had been performed for his own departing ancestors from that stone. Yet, the sweep of the land, the wind at his back would put flight to his fingers. After a couple of quick marches he would try a piobearachd, and would execute it well. And the wind and the chanter and the man would be one and the very notes would cry: "We shall return to Kintail...," but that would be years and years later.

From the ship there was scarcely a sound now. The crew hurried about, climbing, hauling, running, all of the carefully rehearsed and more carefully executed ritual for putting to sea. Among the passengers, most eyes were fastened to the great mass of rock and unbelievably bright green of Scotland's early summer shoreline. Ears strained to hear the notes of MacKinnon's chanter gliding on the wings of the wind out over the rocks, over the gentle waves of that day, sandwiched between creaks of spars, chain clinking, line whirring and hauser thudding. On the shore, every eye looked toward the ship. The tears were quiet ones now. Finally, after a very long time, Murdoch Donn, the tacksman turned toward the slope. "We may as well get back to our livestock. It is little good, our standing here any longer."

CHAPTER 1

PART 2

Kilduich, Upper Canada
Michaelmas, 1820

My Very Dear Morag and Alan,

It is so very hard to believe that we have now been in Upper Canada for a bit over a year. I know that I promised you that I would be a more careful correspondent, but it has been difficult getting settled here. As I told you in my May letter, we were still living with some people here as our house was not ready to be moved into. Well, that house is up now, and although there is much to be done to the inside of it before winter, we will be at home to anyone who might care to call, by this coming weekend.

Mairi has very a very lovely baby girl now. I know that Alisdair and Margaret will be glad to know that they have a grandchild. They have named her Margaret Jean. She resembles Seumais quite a bit in her coloring, and he dotes on her. This is not to say that he is not as much a father to young Duncan and Alisdair. He really is a good young man, and the lads seem to think the world of him. Mairi had a bad winter of it for a while, but after the baby came along she has come back to herself. It is Siubhan that we are more concerned about. I told you, I think, in my last letter that she has kept herself all locked up inside. Do you remember that young fellow who followed us home? I mean the one who was so stubborn and angry at the ministers. Ranald Dubh is his name. Well, he is Ranald Ross now that he is a Canadian. A customs man explained that the name "MacAindreas" is "Ross" in English, and that is how he is written down over here. Anyway, he is a madman for work. When we arrived last year he started right in clearing a piece of land. He built him a log house for the time being. He says that he will build a stone one later when he has more time. You can see the anger coming out of him when he chops wood or lifts stone. He seems to be very interested in Suibhan, but she doesn't seem to notice him. He is really a nice young fellow.

I miss the highlands very much. This is a cold and lonely land. It is pretty to look at, and I am sure that we can make a good living here, but I do miss the friendship of the old place. We share our work and we take meals together from time to time, but no one speaks of Scotland. If I mention home while we are either working or at rest, no one will answer. They will pretend not to hear. Do not think me to be a complainer, but I would be better gathering kelp and living in a miserable hut by the sea in Scotland, even though there is great promise here. It is when I look at the children that I know why we came across.

We see more and more of our fellow highlanders coming into this country all the time. The condition of men's minds back in Scotland must be terrible just now. How can anyone feel even the least sense of security? We met some people who had come out of Sutherland a while ago. They have been here for a while and are getting to be quite settled. A man among them told me stories that I could scarcely believe regarding the circumstances leading up to their embarkation. I worry for those of you who are still at home and pray that all will be well with you.

I will close at this time with my best wishes to all of you. Take my love and the love of us all to the friends of my youth and my life.

I am, as ever, your Duncan Gilcannon

Leachachan,
18thDecember, 1820

A Dhonnachaidh a Charaid Dileas,

We are in receipt of your letter of Michaelmas. What a stir your letter has caused! It is a surprise to me that it is not worn through with all of the handling it has endured. Alisdair and Margaret M'Cra' were elated at the news of the new baby, and it was an extra surprise for them when they had a letter waiting for them from Seumais in which he told them the same good news. It is probable that your letter and the one which Seumais sent out came over on the same ship. They needed some good news, I might add. Dugall and Murdoch are all that are home with them now and soon Murdoch will be gone as well. He has enlisted in the Earl's Regiment and must go to join the others next Monday. Margaret is very much the same as always, but Alisdair had a bad accident this last summer and has been brooding about. He doesn't seem to do much of anything save for what is absolutely necessary. We see Dugall quite often, but not as much as before. I am certain that he is picking up much of the load. It isn't like Alisdair to be so uncaring. Morag and I are quite concerned about him.

You mentioned in your letter that you would like to return to Scotland. As much as I would welcome that homecoming, I would be loath to see you carry through with such an idea. It is finished here. The life that we knew is over. The people who lived by the black cattle and what they could grow have been driven from many of the inner glens. Some have taken up a part of the kelping, for there is still a living to be madefrom gathering and burning it. The farmers of England like using the kelp on their fields as they have for so long now. Yet, many if not the greater part of the people who pass through our land are on their way to the ships that will carry them to America, or Canada more properly speaking. Things are every bit as bad asthey were. In truth, things are much worse than they were.

Now, for the good news. Morag will be giving us a child soon. In about three months, we think. She is taking good care of herself and the older women say that she shouldn't have a bad time of it at all. It isn't a good time to be bringing children into the world, is it? Yet, I suppose that there have been worse times. In any case, we are both very happy to be thinking of a baby. I confess that one side of me is worried. I can feel that we are being squeezed out of here. We may end all of this by coming to Canada yet. We shall have to trust in God and do what we can.

Take my blessing and salutations to all who are over there with you.

I am, as ever, your
Alan Dubh

Kilduich, Upper Canada
July 1, 1829

Dear Alisdair and Margaret,

Your very welcome package came to us on the day before yesterday. Iwas so happy that I cried. It seems so good to have something from home! I shouldn't say "home", I suppose, for this is home now. Still, a part of me will always be there among the rocks and heather. Oh, I miss the sight of those rocks and that heather! The sea is something that I never thought of missing, but I do long for the sight, the sound and the smell of it! Anyway, the box and the silver ladle mean a very great deal to us, all the more so because they were Seumais' grandmother's. I wish that you could see young Margaret. She is ten years old now and those who came across with us say that she does look a lot like her grannie Margaret. Seumais and the lads spoil her terribly. Duncan is the worst of the lot. He would always let her follow him about and now that he is soon to be sixteen he is less able to say no to her than when he was younger. He is more like an uncle than an older brother. Young Alisdair is a bit more wary of her wiles, but of course he is closer to her age.

We have a nice little house. It is made of stone, which isn't all that common here as it is in the old country. Seumais has done very well by us. He is now full-owner of the sawmill. Mr. Elphinstone's son went to New York State, having had no interest in the lumber business. He said that he could see no reason to keep any part of it, so he sold his share to Seumais. We hadn't expected that.

You have often inquired about Dugall, and I confess that we know little about him ourselves. He's off and away so much of the time. He was here at Easter time and has taken a post as a fur-trader. You know the company hires a good many Scots Highlanders because they seem to get on well with the Indians. He is up North of here by Rat Portage...or is it North-West? I can't keep track of this country. It is all so vast. Mr. Elphinstone was telling us that when the Red Indians first met with Highlanders they thought them to be distant relatives. It has something to with a way of thinking that Red Indians and we Highlanders have in common. I can't explain it all, although Seumais seems to understand.

I am afraid that we've had a bit of a "falling out" in the family. It is nothing too serious, I hope. When Dugall was here at Easter he had some man with him who is half French and half Red Indian. They talked of the trading and the Indian ways and we could see young Duncan really being taken in by it all. Dugall suggested that Duncan go up there with him the next time he comes down. Well, Seumais was quite put out by it. It isn't only that he could use the help in the mill, but we both want our lads to have good settled lives. Dugall says that we are silly to think like that and that the Indian is no different from the old Highlanders.

You asked about Duncan and Sara. They are doing well. In fact, they own a very great amount of land. Duncan has promised young Duncan and young Alisdair enough land for each of them to have a farm should they ever want it. Sara has changed, though. She drives everyone constantly... and Duncan's health hasn't been very good this past two years. He is still the same venerable, fatherly man that he always was. Everyone here seems to like him very much. Nothing is ever quite enough for Sara. She is very hard on the hired help and many people are just a bit afraid of her. Her inheritance was no blessing, either, for now that they own so much she is apt to play at being the great lady.

Suibhan is a changed woman now, but for the better. I told you in another letter, I am sure, how she suddenly pulled herself together two or three years ago. She and Ranald have two bairns now, both girls, called Martha and Jeanie. They live about three miles from us and we see them at least once a week.

I don't know why you both don't come over here. The boys have all gone in different directions. We have plenty of room and you are more than welcome. Seumais would like it, I know. By the way, I wrote to Morag and Alan MacKinnon quite a while ago and have had no response. I hope that everything is well with them.

I must close for now. Do write to us when you can. Please consider again Seumais' offer to join us. Seumais sends his. love.

Affectionately, yours,
Mairi

Balston Spa, New York
Sept. 29. 1838

A Dhonnachaidh a Charaid Dileas,

It is a long day since that hour, old friend! Anyway, here we are in America. I had expected that since we had to go that we would end our journey in Canada near you. I had no idea that we would be as we are, even now, a great distance apart. I could not pass by an opportunity such as the one I now have. A man on the ship with whom I had had many conversations ended by offering me a fine employment. I am now doing work on carriages andbuggies, also some sleds and sleighs. We make them from start to finish as well as do repair work. I am overseer of several men.

What has happened to the years? I have quite a family now. There is Helen who is seventeen, Flora, Fifteen; Lachlan, fourteen, Andrew, twelve and Ian who is eight. Then there is the "baby" of the family, Catriona. She is just turned five. Helen is being given quite a bit of attention by a young fellow from Albany. His people come from one of the New England States, Rhode Island. He is studying law and seems quite bright, but I hope that they are going to wait awhile before they think of marriage. He's a nice enough young man. His name is Richard Towner.

Morag got a letter from her mother a while ago. It read like a sheet of death notices. They are all either going or gone, Duncan. The folk that we knew will soon be no more and who is to remember that we were ever there ourselves? As often as I jokedabout Murdoch's old stories, how I would give a month's wage to hear one now! And Maggie McPhee's tongue will never be fluttering again, God bless her. Catriona has moved in with Margaret M'Cra' now that Alisdair has gone. She says that Margaret is just as active as ever, but her memory is starting to go.

We are spread all over the world. My brother, Rory, has been over for a while now and lives not far fromus. He has been teaching Lachie how to play the pipes, having no son of his own,

so it does seem that there will be a MacKinnon piper for one more generation. Morag's brother is on this side somewhere. The last we heard he was in Prince Edward Island, but we're not sure where he is now.

I wish that Canada was a bit closer. How I would love to see all of you! We'll have a good dram together when that day comes, and I am sure that it will come. Someday we'll singtogether again "Now That We Have Met."

Do take our love to all who are there. Tell Dugall to write to me sometime.

I remain as ever, your very good friend,
Alan MacKinnon

6 West Main Street
Galt, Ontario, Canada
August 19, 1863

My Dear Mrs. Towner,

This is in reply to your very kind and most welcome letter of August 6th. How very good of you it is to have written, although I wish that it had been under a happier set of circumstances.

Yes, I knew your late father and mother quite well. We grew up together in the same place in the Scottish Highlands. In fact, your father and mother had their wedding just ten days before I married Seumais McCrae. (We used to spell it M'Cra, but the immigration authorities changed the spelling, and now the name is even pronounced differently.).

I am saddened to hear of your mother's long illness before her death, and of your father's somewhat sudden death shortly afterward. I remember Alan and Morag very well! They were both fine people and I wish that we could have seen one another again. We always said that we would, but the day-to-day matters of life got in our way. There is a lesson in all of this. One must not keep putting off such important things.Perhaps you will come to Canada someday for a visit? I would love to meet you and Mr. Towner. I think that I remember being told he is an attorney. Is that correct? Anyway, I have plenty of room. I am an old lady in a big old house, and although my one son and daughter look in on me they never stay the night, so I have plenty of room as I said.

You mentioned having two sons in the Army of the Republic. My heart goes out to them and I pray that they shall return to you unscathed. Isn't that a terrible thing, to have a Civil war? My heart goes out also to the women of the States. Again, my thanks to you, and remember that you are more than welcome here.

Very Truly, your
Mary McCrae

Post Script: I almost forgot! Your father's concern over the staff surprises me. (He used to laugh at old Highland ideas.) There was a terrible fire here last year, and many of Seumais' things were lost, as were some things which had been in my first husband's family. We managed to save the staff of Cowall, or most of it. It had been in the keeping of my first husband's father, Mr. Duncan Gilcannon. Since his death it has passed into the keeping of my second son, Alisdair Gilcannon. My elder son, Duncan operates a trading post and he and his grandfather decided long ago that Alisdair should be the next keeper of the staff, his life being a bit more settled. Many "transplanted" Highland folk believe in its power to cure and bring blessings. In any case, it remains something of a link with our "old" Christianity.

M. McC.

INFORMATION NEEDED

RE. ancestors of Alan McKinnon, born Scotlandca. 1790
married Morag MacLennon (?),
settled Ballston, N.Y. ca.1825.
Anxious to meet descendants, will share information.
(Mrs.) Lillie Carson, Rte. #1, Athens, Ohio

2311 Carr Street
Niagara Falls, Ont.
April 3, 1972

Dear Mrs. Carson,

Your "ad" in the Highland magazine glared out at me like a neon sign! I couldn't believe my eyes. I have been trying to keep some of the family records together, and it seems that we must be interested in the same people. My husband is Andrew McKinnon and he is descended from Rory (Roderick) McKinnon who was the older brother of the Alan of whom you have made mention.

We really had almost lost track of the other side of the family, but a man was here about five years ago who is a descendent of Alan. He gave me quite a bit of information on the McKinnons, but mainly about the descendants of Alan. The greater number of them seem to be living in the States now, although this same man had been in Canada quite often as a child, even staying with us on the farm. We hadn't, in fact, seen him for about thirty rears. It seems that he lives in an area where there are quite a few people of Scotch (I should say "Scottish", I suppose!) ancestry. He plays the bagpipe, speaks some of the old Gallic (is that spelled right?) language, and even wears a kilt on certain occasions.

He mentioned that the McKinnons were very well thought of in Scotland, and that they had been forced to leave under rather sad circumstances. It might have been something like the potato famine in Ireland, but I don't know. I was never much on history, I'm afraid. I will give you his address, for I have been staying with my son this past winter and all that I wrote down is back on our farm near Brandtford, Ont. My health hasn't been too good and I couldn't face up to the winter on the farm this year. Anyway, his name is Robert W. MacKinnon and he lives at R.D. 1 Emporium, Pennsylvania. I really strongly suggest that you write to him. He appears to be the expert on such things.

I hope that you'll plan to come up to Canada sometime. I will be moving back to the farm next month. It's one of the old family farms and really quite lovely, although there's nothing "fancy" about it. If you write to me before May, I'll still be here.

Sincerely,
Mrs. Andrew (Ella) McKinnon

P.S. I notice that he spells the name "Mac" instead of "Mc.) It must be an older spelling of the name.

Athens, Ohio
April 8,1972

Dear Mr. MacKinnon,

It was suggested to me by Ella McKinnon that I write to you I had placed an "ad" in one of the genealogical sections of a Scottish-American Magazine and had a response from her. She says that you visited them many times when you were a boy and even stayed on their farm near Brantford, Ont. I should first introduce myself. My name is Lillie (MacKinnon) Carson. I am the second daughter of Robert Donald MacKinnon, who was the son of Lachlan James MacKinnon, the son of Alan McKinnon. It appears that you and I are descended from a common ancestor.

I was so excited to have word from Ella McKinnon, that I called her up immediately. She hadn't mentioned what her son's name was, but I narrowed it down with help from the operator (information), matching the last name with the street address. I must say that she sounded as pleased to hear from me as I was to have reached her! I hate to think of what my 'phone bill will look like!

From what I can gather, Alan and Morag MacKinnon had six children: Helen, Flora, Lachlan, Andrew, Ian and Catriona. You are, I understand, descended from Andrew, is that correct? I have no idea as to who the descendants of Andrew are, or even what his wife's name was. I would appreciate any help along this line.

My daughter, Helen, worked in Olean, New York for a time, which is not far from Emporium. She says that the region where you live is very beautiful, what with all of the hills, forests and all. Helen is also very interested in my "amateur" research project, and seems to have "infected" her cousin, Robbie with a desire to know more about our origins. It is Robbie who is primarily concerned with knowing about great grandfather Alan's Scottish background. He's been going to college here. His family and his grandfather, my brother Hugh, still live near Balston Spa. The family found that there was an easier way than farming to make a living in that part of the country. From the turn of the century on, the tourist industry seems to have been the source of most financial return. But Hugh still knows the old place that Alan and Morag built, and I am sure that he would gladly act as a "tour guide" should you ever choose to make the return trip, or "pilgrimage"", as my husband, Jack, calls it. Jack doesn't share our interest in "looking back". However, Jack does join me in extending to you a sincere invitation to visit us if and whenever you can. I am sure that we have much information to be shared.

Hoping to hear from you soon.

Sincerely,
Lillie Carson

This then, was the start of it: a reunion of people separated by time, circumstances and distance. It soon became obvious that there was a bit more to the exchange than a mere wish to fill out the missing blanks on a "family tree". What Lillie Carson had taken to be her "amateur research project", had, in fact, come about as a result of questions put to her by her daughter and nephew. She had really placed the "ad" in the magazine out of a feeling of "owing" it to them. After several letters in both directions, a phone call and the exchange of some photo copied pictures and documents, a meeting of sorts was arranged between the separated family members. Robbie MacKinnon was going to stop at Emporium on his way to a summer session at the College of Ceramics at Alfred, N.Y., and go on from there to his home in Balston Spa upon completion of the course of study. A detailed map of local roads, landmarks, complete with arrows and a large "X" marking the MacKinnon farm was sent to Lillie which she passed on to her nephew.

Years later, sometime before the turn of the 20th century to the 21st century, before all of the turmoil and the disastrous collapse of the older America, before the ruinous and costly wars in the Mid-East, in an age of computers and cell-phones and what would appear to be a technological continuity seemingly without an end in sight, in those better times, Lillie Carson's Nephew would stand on a rock-bound coast of the West Highlands of Scotland with his wife and their children and they would see with their own eyes that incredibly beautiful, heartbreakingly melancholy land from which his ancestors had taken their leave over a century and a half earlier. There would be no piper to greet them, to welcome them "home" as a piper had once played a sad lament to those others when they left. Rob MacKinnon would wonder why, upon seeing this ancient land, this particular part and place in that ancient land, he felt his eyes well up with tears. All of Scotland which they would have seen until this time had been stirring, interesting and very wonderful in so many ways, but here, in this particular place, something would have taken ahold of his very soul! He would feel, all at once: an elation, a sadness and also a deep-seated anger which he would have been unable to explain. He would have shocked his wife by his somehow knowing where to go, where things were: things and parts of that land he had never seen before in his life. Staring at the ruin of an old, tumbled and very weathered and vegetation claimed croft house, he would find a line of verse which he had read somewhere return to him: ".... Lone stands the house and the chimney stone is cold. Lone let it stand now. The friends are all departed, The kind hearts, the true hearts that loved the place of old."

CHAPTER 2

PART 2

Robbie hadn't really wanted to stop by on his way toward the college. Oh, he had been interested enough in the old lore, the history of the clans, their struggles and ongoing feuds with one another, culminating in the uprisings of 1715 and 1745 against the reigning royal house of Hanover. He had come in contact with the Highland version of history just prior to his going on to college. In his senior year of high school an English teacher had been discussing the romantic era of English literature and had spoken of Sir Walter Scott. Robbie's class had been assigned to read and report on any work done by Scott. Having put the assignment off until the "last minute", Robbie soon discovered that there wasn't much left of Scott in the local library, save for a book of poetry, which he felt to be long-winded and much too decorous in style. He had settled in to do the best that he could to salvage what he envisioned as a sinking English grade with the report due in only a few days. Unexpected aid was forthcoming, however, for on the following evening while stopping by his grandparents' home, he was able to find, not only a Scott novel, but quite a different slant on his own background as well. This is how it came to pass: His father had asked him to stop by his grandparents' to return a couple of borrowed seed catalogs.

It was the custom to stay a short time; long enough for a cup of hot chocolate or coffee and a bit of conversation. Robbie was "testing" some chocolate chip cookies in the kitchen and talking with his grandmother about various things. His grandmother steered the conversation toward school and asked if he was doing his best in his subjects.

"Oh, yeah. I guess so...If I don't flunk English over Sir Walter Scott!"

"Sir Walter Scott? What does he have to do with it?" His Grandmother asked, finishing the fork and spoon operation necessary to filling another cookie sheet with globs of the brown-spotted dough. She, opened the oven, then squinting against the heat, slid the sheet onto the wire oven shelf.

"Well, I have to read a book on Scott, well, one written by him, and make a report. The trouble is...there are no books left in the library but one on his poetry, and I can't relate to that at all!"

"Why does everyone today have to "relate" to anything and everything? Nobody cares if you "relate" to something! Just look at it, think about it and see how it affects you! I don't "relate" to nuclear devices, but heavens...I'd better know something about them." She poured herself a half cup of coffee and came over to the table, set the cup down and wiped her hands on her apron before pulling out a chair and seating herself. She looked at her grandson as he chomped down another cookie in record time, resting her chin on the knuckles of one hand, holding the cup handle with the other. After a moment of silence she said, "I know that with all of the books we have in this house, we have a Scott novel or two."

"Oh yeah?," Robbie answered as if with unsurprised discovery.

"Oh, yeah!," Allison McKinnon mimicked affirmation. "Hugh!" she called in toward the front of the house, "we have some Sir Walter Scott novels, haven't we?"

"Some what ?," came a reply from afar.

"Some Sir Walter Scott novels!"

"Yes." The voice came nearer, then from the kitchen doorway itself, "But what for? For *him*?" he indicated Robbie with pretended sternness.

"Hi, gramp!"

"Don't "hi" me! What did you do, smell those cookies all across town? How many dozen have you packed away?"

"I'm saving you the trouble of being tempted to eat more than is good for you."

"Well," Allison said, "neither of you need worry about that! They're supposed to be for the bake sale, so, Hugh... you'd better set aside a few before I put them away, and you, young Mr. Robbie Currie, aren't getting any more. You've had a half dozen if you've had one!"

"Not even one more?', Robbie teased.

"Well, maybe one more."

"Well, maybe one more, Robbie honey!" Hugh teased. "Boy! you'd better get what you can while you're still young and cute, too. Once you get a few years on you, these women get stingier than anything you ever saw!" Grandfather MacKinnon moved toward the cupboard and took a mug from the shelf. "I'll bet anything that she didn't leave any coffee in that pot!"

"There's almost a full pot, Hugh," she informed him.

"Oh. That must be left from this morning. She wouldn't let me have any all day."

"Do you believe him Robbie?" Allison feigned surprise.

"Grampa wouldn't lie, I don't imagine, Gramma." It was the kind of bantering and good humored teasing that went on and on among the MacKinnons. Robbie's father, was right at home with it too, despite the fact that he was married to a MacKinnon and not one by blood. Hugh sat down to the table with two cookies and his cup of coffee in front of him, reached over and took Robbie's cookie and popped it into his mouth.

"Gram'pah!"

"You don't, need any more. It'll ruin your complexion".

Robbie looked at his grandmother, who shrugged her shoulders, sipped her coffee before saying, "You like him so well, I guess you'll just have to put up with him."

"What do you need a Scott novel for?", Hugh asked suddenly.

"English class."

"Well, I've got one or two that belonged to my father. Trouble is I'll probably never see it again, if I loaned you one. Hell! your dad has had my seed catalogs since World War II."

"Hugh! Finish your coffee!", his wife said with feigned exasperation.

"I'll be right back. You just leave that coffee alone."

Robbie and Allison sat in silence, waiting. Robbie looked out of the kitchen windows of the breakfast nook at the bare trees and patches of snow. Did those trees really have leaves on them a few months ago, or did I dream that? those black limbs could be carved out of leather, or they could be black pig iron, or even if they are wood, they never could be other than what they are: leafless, dead-looking. In a few months they'll have leaves again. What if spring didn't come or what if it came and nothing happened? His eyes shifted to young shrubs wrapped in burlap, to mounds of leaves heaped up about rose bushes. How can anything be alive down under all of that cold, frozen earth?, he wondered. How much like his mother he looks, Allison thought. Sheila's hair and eyes, dark and sensitive in male form. Why is it that it's so often the boys who get the long, dark eyelashes? It just isn't fair! I am glad that he hasn't his mother's disposition! We spoiled Sheila. She has never had a care for anyone but herself. Oh, I know that that isn't quite true. She has been a pretty good mother. Rob and Carole are the living proof of that.

Hugh's entry into the kitchen brought each of them out of their private worlds. It was rather like being wakened suddenly from a deep sleep. The older people used to caution about waking someone too suddenly. It makes your soul snap back into your body too quickly, and it's bound to set you off keel for the whole day. Where did that old idea come from? Does the soul really wander or travel while we sleep? Tied to the body by an invisible silver cord, it can always find its way back. "Til the silver cord be loosed and the golden bowl be broken"

What does that mean? Where does it come from? Not where the quote comes from, but the idea. What did the ancients really believe?

"Here are two books by Scott," Hugh was saying. "I don't remember..." his voice trailed off as he looked inside the cover of the first one, then the other. "Huh! I thought that there'd be a name in there; in one of them, anyway. Doesn't that beat all?" He was really thinking out loud rather than talking. "Anyway!", his voice picked up volume, "they were either my father's or my grandfather's." He plunked them down in front of Rob. "The Waverly novels, Waverly" This other book is "Ivanhoe."

"I read "Ivanhoe" in my sophomore year, "Rob said. "What's the other one about?"

"It's about "the '45", Hugh said.

"The what?"

"The '45. Don't you know about "the '45?"

"No. I guess I can't say that I do", Rob answered.

"It's about the last great rebellion over in Scotland! In1745 a lot of the clans in the Highlands rose up in support of the Stuart cause. Prince Charles Edward Stuart, "Bonnie prince Charlie", the Highlanders called him, came to Scotland to raise support for his father, King James and to win back the throne for the Stuarts." Hugh stopped long enough to study Robbie for a moment. "Are you sure that you never heard of the rebellions? It's part of your heritage! Our MacKinnon ancestors supported the Stuarts. Some died in that year, fighting for King James Stuart."

"No, I never heard of it. Why didn't anybody ever tell me all of this stuff?", Rob asked.

"I don't know. I guess we just figured that you knew. Well, anyway, read "Waverly." Scott gets a little bit flowery in the way that he writes, but it's a good novel once you get into it", his grandfather assured him.

That is how it started. Rob glanced at the book, read a few words and didn't really open it to read in earnest until the following night. By the third chapter, he found himself unwilling to put the book down. After that on other visits he got his grandfather to rummage around until he found some other books. A two volume set of Logan's "Scottish Gael", very old and looking for all the world as if they had come out of George Washington's own library, it gave him more information about the clans, their tartans and origins. Rob was absolutely enthralled with what he could find about the old Celtic culture of his maternal ancestors. He pestered Hugh for stories and bits of history, growing a bit impatient when Hugh would dwell on family members and genealogical accounts. But he would wait, hoping that somewhere in the narrative another gem of "new" and fascinating history would emerge. One day during the summer he was talking with his grandmother in the back garden. He had been doing some digging for her and they were taking a "break" for some iced tea.

"My mother's mother, your great grandmother Barton, used to know the MacKinnon family very well. In fact, she knew old Morag Mackinnon. Of course, I imagine that everyone around here knew her. She owned a lot of property and was something of a tyrant."

"You mean that they were wealthy?", Rob asked.

"Well, I don't know that they were wealthy, really, but they were certainly well-to-do." Allison cocked her head a bit to one side and looked down out of the corners of her eyes. She often did that when she was trying to recall something. It was a little mannerism which everyone would remember. Age had only added to Allison's features a certain charm, a rather aristocratic aura. Not that she was, in any way, pretentious, for she was a very plain-spoken and uncomplicated person. It was just that her bright blue eyes and graying hair gave her otherwise fragile, doll-like appearance a certain vitality and grace which told the world that although this delicate lady might look like a fragile porcelain figure, she was very much a survivor. She went on: "There was a certain bearing about the MacKinnons. They were a proud people...not arrogant! But there was an almost royal dignity in those older people. They all worked hard. Even though they had hired hands they all worked hard. Your grandfather's great-uncle, Ian was alive yet when we were young. He was a fine looking man. He could still speak the Gaelic, and what stories he could tell!"

"The Gaelic." Rob interrupted. "That's that Strange Scotch accent with the rolling "RRRR's." The Robert Burns kind of Scotch accent, right?"

"Scottish, not "Scotch.", Allison corrected. "Scotch is a kind of alcoholic beverage. "Scottish" is the name given to a people...and no, Gaelic is a different language altogether. It is much more by far than an accent. When Uncle Ian used to visit he'd say to us, "Keemurra Hah Shee!" Does that sound like English?"

"Huh?" Rob stared and frowned. "What is it. I mean, what does it mean?"

"And we would say to him in reply, "Oh, g'mah. Keemura Hah Shee fane, Uncle Ian?" "Does that sound like English?"

"What does all of that mean, Gramma?"

"It means "how are you?", "Oh, good", and "how is yourself." That is all Gaelic."

"I always thought that the Scots all spoke English, but with their own accent on it."

"Well, they do...but they had this other language. It's very ancient; older than Latin!"

"So that is it! They kept using Gaelic terms and phrases in "Waverly," but I didn't stop to think that it was a whole different language. Well, yes, I knew that, but I didn't think that a lot of people spoke it, even now."

"Well, they don't"., his grandmother agreed. "Very few Scots would be able to speak any Gaelic nowadays. Either somebody told me, or else I read it somewhere, that there are more people in North America who speak Gaelic than in Scotland."

Rob sat back and turned his now empty glass in his hands, watching a small bead of reflected sunlight on the rim remain in the same spot as the glass moved in his hands; a slow circular movement. "It's too bad that they let it die out over there. I mean...anything like your own language is worth keeping, I would think."

"Would you like some more tea?"

"No, thanks. If I drink any more of anything I'll feel too bloated to work.." Then, continuing, he said, "I wonder why they let it all die out."

"Well..." the word came out almost as a sigh. "I don't think that they had much choice. Over there they had become part of the British Empire and it was important for people to learn English, especially if they wanted to get ahead. Over here, English was already the established language, but they clung to anything that reminded them of who they were. I guess that they were afraid of losing their identity in the "melting pot" that this country is supposed to be."

"But, we've lost it all, too, Gramma. We don't know much about the old highland past. Everybody is proud to be Scottish, but it ends right there."

"Well, life is quite a struggle in itself sometimes. People had to get on with making a life." Allison reflected for a minute, sipped her iced tea and squinted her eyes as if trying to remember something or else see something a great distance away.

"Your ancestors were all English and German weren't they, Gramma?"

"What?" Allison pried herself from her thoughts to face Rob. His words came together for her before he had to repeat them.

"Oh, no! My maiden name was Beaton, don't forget. That's a Scottish name. Of course, there was never a lot of mention made of it. And I had a great grandfather Galbraith too. He had come over from Scotland." Allison finished her iced tea and sat with the empty glass still in her hand, appearing again to be searching her memory. Without looking directly at Rob she went on.

"Something happened over there. It must have been something pretty terrible."

"In Scotland, you mean." Rob clarified the statement for himself.

"Yes. Those first people who came across never would speak of Scotland...not where they had lived nor what their lives had been before coming across the Atlantic. They kept their customs, language and all, but they dad an awful lot of bitterness about something. Yes, it must have been something pretty terrible. Anyway, that is something that we'll just never know, I guess. Whatever it was, it was their tragedy, not ours, and they died without ever letting on. It was almost as if a whole generation of immigrant highlanders had made some kind of pact never to reveal it to anyone."

"I don't understand that, at all. The Irish had the potato famine and came over here. They make no secret of it," Rob countered.

"Well, I'm sure that I don't know, and I don't suppose that we'll ever find out, do you?", Allison suggested.

"I'd sure like to try", her grandson said.

"Well, maybe you should then." Allison smiled at him. "There's probably material for a book in it somewhere."

CHAPTER 3

PART 2

The trip to his distant cousin's place in Pennsylvania meant his having to drive north from Athens on Route 50 and then North on Route 77 to Akron, then East on 76 to Youngstown, after which he would go into Pennsylvania on Route 80. Rob would find himself once again face to face to face with many examples of an "older" America, toe to toe with a rapidly changing society. At the beginning of what would prove to be a very long drive, he had felt a tremendous sense of freedom; a celebration of his youth and vitality, coupled with a spirit of adventure.. Simply to be just finished with his first year of college, out from under the load of coursework and all of the obligations connected with working towards that all-important degree. He had taken to the road with the same elation that he had experienced throughout his childhood once the school year had ended and summer vacation had begun. He had never outgrown that giddy feeling which comes at the end of each school year. In fact, given this same sense of freedom which he had always experienced, coupled now with the additional privileges of young adulthood, driving a car, a growing unfolding of his own identity and a certain amount of money on hand, he was the very personification of liberation. He had found however, that there is something very binding and quite monotonous about "thruways", four-lane highways, despite their often winding and cutting through some of the most scenic countryside. Theirs has always been "acquired", often stolen land, which at one time had been used for meadows, hayfields or cropland. Here and there along the way one could see the disowned barns and empty, forgotten silos: the silent, monuments to an American agricultural greatness which had been ebbing away for many years. Those years had slipped away unnoticed, without even having said 'goodbye'. On and on the road would wind through new seedlings, sloped and stone-paved sidings; trees in clusters and some singly, others legion, sufficient to cover entire hills, interrupted only by the exits with their large green and white signs; indicators listing the side roads by number, the conveniences and services listed at each exit in clusters on blue sign boards. Back of him and before him, the road seemed to go on forever. Trucks, automobiles from places as far away as California, Wyoming, Nebraska and even the Canadian provinces; some with trailers, others with luggage racks. There were campers and 'pick-ups' fitted out with caps which could double as temporary quarters. The campers, like the big Winnebagos, were often fitted out with some more personal signage, such as "Ed & Martha: the Tuttles", attached to the back of the vehicle. A somewhat beaten up old pickup truck wore a decal on the rear bumper:" Don't complain about Farmers with your mouth full" All can be interesting and amusing for a while, but there is so much to take in and the monotony of the road itself: the road ahead, the road in the rear-view mirror becomes pretty wearing. Rob felt himself becoming somewhat anxious, perhaps even trapped after a period of driving. He resolved to take the next exit no matter which one it was, or where it was, which roads connected with which others or what town lay beside it, just to take a break. "Might as well gas up and get something to eat", he thought. He moved into the right lane at the sign, followed the exit down and around…and around,…and around and There!: dumped almost in from of him, just across some county highway, he saw a huge black-topped area covering several acres of land, with all the look of a small air strip, at the far side of which were several low buildings of strand steel and brick. An enormous sign marked one of these as a restaurant and store. Just in front of it, on a small, round circle of grass in the middle of the black-top was a flag pole and one of the largest American flags which he had ever seen. The other buildings were obviously for the sale of gasoline or diesel fuel, tires or batteries and so forth. It was a truck stop alright! A huge truck stop; much larger than any of the ones which his family had sometimes patronized on a trip during their holidays when he had been a boy. He wondered for a moment or two whether he should cross the road and drive onto that expanse of black-top, or turn to the left or right and find a small diner or "hamburger joint" somewhere along the road., but since another car had come up behind him, he had to move immediately. His mind had been made up for him. He crossed the road, drove into the area and up to the building which looked all the world like a steel warehouse with windows, but which was labeled 'Restaurant and Store'.

Once inside the door the great expanse, the desolate feeling of there being too much space with nothing to break it up, disappeared immediately. A vestibule of sorts was lined with vending machines of every type: cigarettes, packaged cookies, cakes, candy bars, potato chips and corn chips, gum; anything that a person might think of to throw on the seat beside him to help break the monotony of a long drive. The entryway was separated from the main part of the building by two full length, heavy plate glass doors, each in turn flanked by a full, heavy glass side panel. Once inside this partition Rob could feel all of the closeness and clutter of a small, over-furnished room, but this room was, by no means, small. There was, at one end a very long, bent "L" of a lunch counter, behind which was a fortune in stainless steel and glass: coolers and pie cupboards with glass doors, coffee urns, mixers, blenders, stacks of cups and plates, bins of flatware and buckets of small packets of coffee creamer and sugar. It was readily apparent that a kitchen occupied another half an acre or so, Rob exaggerated in his thinking, behind all of this monument to the 20th century Americans' obsession for size, quantity and hygiene. There was a large number of booths, tables and chairs, as well as the stools in front of the counter, if one preferred to sit somewhere other than on one of those red-cushioned seats.

Rob thought at first to move up to the counter, but he had a wish to see the whole place and watch the goings on. He moved to a table which had been squeezed in a section of corner so that really have accommodated more than two patrons. He sat down in a chair which allowed him to look out and over the greater part of the building's interior. "My God!", he thought, "I must have died and gone to truckers' heaven! I can't believe this place!" . It would have been difficult for anyone from small town America, someone whose life was not spent driving loads of goods from one place on the map to another to comprehend. Half of the place consisted of counters, showcases, shelves and clothes racks. He sat there, taking it all in. Everything: the smell of cooking oil, coffee and pastries, mingled with that of stored leather and denim; the sounds of country music, clattering plates, knives forks, not to forget an electronic game of some sort being played in another corner. Yet, it was the volume of it all which he found to be almost overwhelming. Stacks of denim jeans and jackets competed with equally great stacks of western hats, baseball caps with logos, sunglasses on cardboard display units. Belts of all lengths and widths;

buckles in the shapes of eagles, guns, trucks, deer, emblems and insignia were all there, as if an army had to be outfitted at any time of the day or night. There were other things to take home as gifts for a wife or a child or a girlfriend: things such as wall plaques, many of which were religious in nature such as Durer's famous' Praying Hands' or of Jesus praying in the Garden of Gethsemane. Some of these would have small clocks or night-lights mounted in a corner. Rob remembered something from Tocqueville's "Democracy in America": "A Democratic people will demand an art-form that is useful." Rob was thinking:" Maybe we should have stayed with the Monarchy after all!", followed by a self-criticism:"Rob Currie, you are a snob!"

Continuing to take all of this in, seeing the people in the place and at very much 'at home' or comfortable with things around them they seemed to be, he invented a scenario in his mind. He thought that such merchandise must be sold in such places from coast to coast and that a trucker could get any number of things to take back home with him. He thought of a man returning from a very long cross-country haul:

"Here, kid. I bought ya this hat outside of St. Louis! See? It's a souvenir from St.Louis, and this belt buckle with the C.S.A. on it? It's from the South. I picked it up in Wheeling, West Virginia"

"Gee! Thanks, Dad!" Rob mused: Do kids still say, "Gee, thanks"? I'll bet that these guys' kids do!

He was aware that he was smiling to himself, an

awareness brought to his attention by a cold, blank stare from a thin, wiry young man, perhaps two or three years older than himself who sat a few tables away with a buddy. The wiry, blond guy said something at that moment to his buddy, whose back was to Rob. The man turned around to add his own expressionless stare to that of his friend. Both of them were, without a doubt looking directly at him. A wave of discomfort swept over him and he felt himself redden and he suddenly had a view of the young college guy sitting in his chair, the young man whom he might appear to be: Probably a bit pale, even too scrubbed perhaps and of all things, in a white shirt! The wiry fellow, though blond and of fair complexion, was grimy and tanned, his arm tattooed. Rob hoped that being out of his element wasn't too obvious, although he knew that he was not really "blending in". He also hoped that he hadn't turned a bit red-faced when the two truckers looked his way, although he had felt the blood rise from the neck of his white sports shirt. A voice at his side captured his attention:

"Well! The more they come, the better they look!" A waitress of about the same age as his mother was smiling down at him. What will you have, 'Hon? Coffee, maybe for a start?", she asked.

"Uh… yes, please! Coffee would be great!"

"Right, 'Hon! I'll get you a menu too. 'Be right back!"

The drivers a few tables away were back to their meal, no longer looking at anyone or anything other than the plate in front of each of them. In fact, all of the customers were quiet. minding their own business and generally quite polite. He noticed that they all wore their hats while they ate.

A man and woman sat down at the table next to his own. The man wore the usual jeans and work shirt, the woman wore slacks, comfortable-looking shoes and a light, pastel green smock-like upper garment. She looked to be perhaps fifty years old, the man a bit older. She was thin, gray and somewhat mousey looking, but hers was a kind and gentle face. The man was a bit heavy in build, showed the signs of a life of hard work, although he had a pleasant countenance. When they were seated, the man removed his hat and put it on the chair beside him. "They must be man and wife", Rob thought. It is the way he acts toward her. There was indeed a certain quiet respect, an ease of movement which he had seen in other, older people who had been together for a long period of time.

The waitress brought a coffee server to his table and filled his cup. She also laid a menu on the table. "Take your time, Hon'. I 'll go and see what these other folks are going to have".

Rob opened the menu and looked at a vast assortment of offerings. Most of the food listed seemed pretty down to earth, even what one might call "sensible", although there did appear to be a great many fried meals. There were other things such as 'Home-made Chicken and Biscuits', Liver and Onions', 'Pot Pie' and other home-style meals A sign in the corner of the menu proclaimed: "All of our Pies are Home-made".

"Oh, oh!", chimed the waitress to the man at the next table, "You have to behave yourself today! You 've got your wife with you!"

"Well, I guess that he better behave himself!", the wife said, brightening and smiling, having been given some recognition in this world of her husband's daily grind. The waitress handed them menus, joked about something or other in low tones and moved away as the pair were still laughing. She moved back to Rob's table.

"Hi again! See anything that you like on that menu, Hon'?"

"I'm not really sure. Tell me, what is "Mud Pie"? ", he asked.

"You've never heard of Mud Pie?" the waitress used the same tone as if he had said that he had never heard of the Viet Nam war or Christmas trees.

"I can't say that I have", Rob confessed. "What is it?"

"Oh, it is really *good*!", she exclaimed. "It's a big piece of chocolate pie with hot fudge and whipped cream with chocolate ice cream! It's a real hit here. You should try it!"

"I don't know if I dare!", he smiled up at her.

"Go ahead!, she replied, "Live dangerously!"

"Okay, I'll give it a try", he replied.

"One…mud…pie", she said as she scribbled on her pad. "I'll bring you a warm-up for your coffee too." She disappeared into the kitchen area.

Rob looked around the room again, although it wasn't

really a room per se, but rather more like a combination of lunch room and a bus depot, a slightly up-dated general store and roadside souvenir shop, all rolled into one. Everything in the place had a look of newness, as if there were no past to deal with nor a future to be concerned with either. It stood as an antithesis of the academic world from which had just come. In a college or university a great emphasis is placed upon the study of the past, and this pertains not only to the study of history alone. All disciplines have their backgrounds: the 'childhood' of Western civilization, the 'roots' of Greek art, the 'birth' of Psychology, the 'beginnings' of this and the 'causes' of that. From the very first week of the Freshman year, the need for a greater understanding of the cultural past has always been driven home. Professors emphasize that we must not think of history in terms of crumbling ruins or ashes of long-dead kings, heroes and builders, but as the steps to all that we hold sacred and of value in our own time. The American Bill of Rights had been inspired by the Magna Carta, signed as it was by a peevish English monarch on the Field of Runnymede in 1215, but even that document had been inspired by earlier Anglo-Saxon, Celtic and Roman forms of law. At the same time, there is a tremendous focus on "the Future": not only where the student him or herself might be going, but where is Democracy headed? What is the future of capitalism, socialism, human rights, feminism, cottage industries, cities, farms, villages rivers, jungles, marriage and the family, etc., etc., ad infinitum ? It occurred to Rob that here, in this world of country music and 'mud pie', time had become frozen and that he had stumbled somehow into a world where past and future were put out of mind: This was the world of 'now'.

In his mind he created a scenario, as if from one of those films on the television's "Late, Late Show". Not on a mountain top with lightening crackling all around him, but instead on a vast level area of asphalt, he, Rob Currie, in white shirt, tan slacks and having hair just a trifle too long for the taste of those who dwelt in the world where he now found himself to be, had discovered 'now'....or rather, "NOW"., as the heavenly voice thundered. "Will my hair be white when I leave here?, he asked. "But, 'now' is an impossible time period", he whined weakly in his drama to that voice of thunder, "for as soon as I have pronounced the very word, 'now' is already a part of the past". The voice of thunder did not grace him with an answer.

"Now", the waitress was saying, "Here's a warm-up for your coffee...and here's your mud pie. Enjoy!"

He was aware that he had been smiling to himself again. The wiry, blond guy was staring coldly at him. There was now a third person at the drivers' table: a thin, average-sized fellow of about seventeen or eighteen years, Rob figured, with a mass of fairly long, dark brown curls covering his head. This time, to Rob's discomfort, he saw that all three of them were looking in his direction.

"Thanks a lot!", Rob said to the waitress

"You're welcome, Hon' If you want anything else, just

give a yell, okay?, she asked with a smile.

"Right! I will", he promised.

The Mud Pie was a testament to the American love of plenty combined with the love of sweets. It was served in a deep soup bowl; the same kind of bowl which was being used to dispense Chili or the kitchen's home-made soup. The slice of pie itself must have been almost a quarter of the pie tin, covered with thick hot fudge, a huge amount of whipped cream, topped with a red cherry. Somehow someone in the kitchen had even managed to wedge into the side a huge chunk of chocolate ice cream.. "I must be out of my mind!", Rob's sensible, nutrition conscious self said, while the sweet lover in him was happily falling to the task of doing away with it.

As he ate, his eyes swept the store section with its wares and the different people who were looking at what was being offered there, then the restaurant section with the different types of people in various states of relaxation. A middle-aged man: tall, raw-boned and broad-shouldered, came into the restaurant wearing the apparent uniform of the day: Levis, work shirt,, wide belt with one of those huge buckles and a cap on his head with some kind of logo which served to advertise some automotive parts dealership. A boy of about fourteen moved with him in about the same manner, dressed very much like his senior. They both rocked from side to side as they walked, the man's movements somewhat smoother and more practiced than that of the boy's, whose arms, legs and feet seemed to be oversized, still awkward. "He'll be a big man if he ever grows into those feet!", the old-timers would say. That the kid was proud to be in the company of this older, experienced traveler could leave no one in doubt. Either his father or his uncle (there was no question of a blood relationship on seeing the two of them), the man had brought the boy out on a run with him and it would be difficult indeed for anyone to gauge which of them, the younger or the elder, were the more pleased or proud.

Turning his head and looking towards the end of the counter, Rob could see a waitress leaning back, her two hands behind her to serve as a buttress between her somewhat over-weight body and the stainless steel of a very large cooler. She had a pretty face and soft, kind eyes, blonde hair pulled back into a pony-tail which served only to emphasize the roundness of her head; a head which because of the massive body beneath it, appeared to be disproportionately too small. There was a look of such yearning, perhaps even some hurt, in her eyes as she smiled and listened to some story being told to her by a young driver, that Rob felt within himself a stab of compassion for her. His eyes moved to the object of the waitress' interest and concern. A medium-sized young man sat on a stool, hunched over the counter, his hands wrapped around a mug of coffee. "He really is a handsome guy, I guess", / Rob thought. The young driver was smiling and talking about something or other. When the driver looked down towards the counter and his mug, the girl's eyes would scan his face from his moving mouth to his hair line. When he would look up towards her, she would smile, nod her head in agreement, or look into his eyes. Rob thought:" No one should have to want somebody that much! Oh, well! What the Hell! She might end up with the guy after all! There's always a chance".

"Is that your blue Chevy outside?", someone was asking. It was the blond guy who had been a few tables away. His buddy and the young guy who had been sitting with him were a few feet from them..

"Yeah, why?" Rob's answer sounded as if he were asking which law he had broken.

"You going up to New York? We noticed the New York license plate on your car."

"Well, not right away. I'm heading for a place in Pennsylvania. Why? What's going on?", Rob asked.

"Nothing, really. You must think that I'm pretty nosey", the driver said. This was as close to an apology as the blond guy was going to give. Rob felt himself to be on his guard, out of his own territory; perhaps even a bit exposed to an alien world. He did not say that the man was nosey or that he wasn't nosey. The driver went on:

"Well, we picked this kid up on the road and out of the rain at about six, a.m. this morning. We aren't supposed to do that, but we felt kinda sorry for him. He says that he's headed for Binghamton, New York. That's why I asked you if that was your car and if you're headed for New York. They don't want people hitching rides on the four-lanes, and I wouldn't want a Smokey to pick him up for bumming rides. I'd hate for him to get picked up. I don't think that he has much money."

"Well, Look…, "Rob answered, I don't mind taking him part way. The fact is, I'm going across on Route 80, but I'm going just a few miles past DuBois, then I'll be turning North to a little above Emporium".

The Blond driver slid onto the chair across the table from Rob and motioned with his head to his buddy to come over to where he and Rob were sitting. The other guy and the kid came over to the edge of the table.

"Hi!", the other driver said to Rob.

"Hi!", Rob returned.

"Hey, Denny", the blond driver said to his friend, "This guy's going on Route 80 over to DuBois. If he took the kid that far, couldn't the kid go on to somewhere south of Williamsport and go north to Binghamton ?"

"Williamsport? Hell, no!, Denny reproved. "They ain't nothin' but woods north of Williamsport! He'd be better to stay on Route 80 'til it hitches up with '81, just below Wilkesbarre. Trouble is, he's still left on a damned four-lane!"

"Well, what else can he do?", the blond guy persisted," He won't get any rides stuck on some back road in Pennsylvania!" .

Denny pushed his western hat back and ran the knuckles of his hand across the faint crease mark high on his forehead. His reddish face turned to a very pale white above that line. "Well", he returned, being careful to avoid making his partner look bad, "I'll tell ya, Jimmy: If it was me, I'd go with this college boy here clear to DuBois and then take 219 north to cut into Route six, as I don't know that he'd get into any trouble with the cops. Not only that, but there are some really nice people up there."

"How did he know that I am a "college boy" ?", Rob wondered.

"And…., "Denny went on, "I'd follow Route Six east 'til it comes to Route Eleven, just above Scranton, then follow the few miles north to Binghamton".

Jimmy looked sideways towards his partner with an expression of admiration and pretended disgust. "Boy!", he said, "You really are a fuckin' know-it –all, aint ya?"

"No, I'm not!", Denny exclaimed. "I just know what I know, that's all!"

Rob, now getting into the spirit of the exchange, thought to make a suggestion: "What if he was to go with me clear to Emporium, go the few miles north to Route Six, leave Six at Towanda and go north to Waverly? That would put him on New York Route 17. He could follow that east to Binghamton."

"Waverly!?", both truckers exclaimed at once,

"I thought that you were from New York!", Jimmy said.

"Well, I am from New York!"

"You'd send this poor kid to Waverly?", Boy! Those smokies in New York are bad enough, but those local cops around that rotten little speed trap would have this kid for breakfast!", Jimmy said.

"Yeah", Rob admitted, "I've heard that they can be pretty bad! I forgot about that!"

"Okay!", Jimmy said, as if all had been settled, "Denny, why don't you get this guy a road map over there and we'll mark it out for him ?"

"Why, hell!", Denny protested, "There ain't nothing to remembering that!" Then, looking towards Rob in a quick appraisal, he conceded, "Well, I'll get a map and they'll have it in case they need it!" Having said that, Denny swung around and pushing the back of the young hitch-hiker's shoulder, they both moved off in the direction of the glass doors and the entry-way.

Jimmy turned in the chair to face Rob, but looking around, somewhat absently, taking in the ceiling fans, the activity behind the counter. His scanning stopped and his eyes crinkled at the corners and his face broke into a smile. Instinctively Rob turned to see what had caused this change in Jimmy's demeanor. He saw a man who was moving towards one of the stools by the counter. The man was grinning in return.

"You here again, or are you here *yet*?", Jimmy called over to him.

"Again! Definitely again!", the man called back. "Hey! I don't fool around, y'know? Places to go! Things to do!" He sat down, at the counter, a big man, maybe in his fifties.

"That's one hell of a man!", Jimmy remarked, a trace of a smile still on his face. "He has a wife who has been crippled for at least twenty years. Doctor bills you wouldn't believe!

Even so, if anybody ever is down on his luck or needs some help, guess who the first man on the scene would be! Boy! I sure hope that I can feel about my wife the way that he does about his, twenty or thirty years down the line!" He looked around for a minute or a bit longer in total silence, then turned to look Rob squarely in the eye, taking up the conversation again: "Life goes by so fast. I mean, everything happens before you know it. I got to thinking the other day: I'm pretty lucky to have a job and to be doing what I like to do, but at the same time, it's kinda scary. A couple of years ago, if I had a job,…fine; if I didn't, well, so what? Now I have a wife and a baby girl. Man! I'm scared out of my ever-loving mind to be out of work!"

"That would be pretty frightening, alright", Rob agreed. He felt that he needed to say something, although things were happening pretty fast for him as well at this time. It flashed through his mind that what Jimmy had described really did constitute a tremendous responsibility for a man who appeared to be not much older that himself. In fact an inner shiver or warning loomed up within him; a set of circumstances which he wanted to push away, far away, from himself for a few more years at least. Yet, he discovered that the feeling was accompanied by another, unexpected rumbling within himself which shadowed this momentary anxiety. "My God!", he thought, "am I experiencing some kind of envy? No! It couldn't be!" He felt as if he had been suddenly pulled under water, or that he had lost his balance and was kicking and struggling to get back on top of things.

Thoughts, feelings were coming too quickly. He had to turn his focus back to this young trucker.

"How old is your little girl?", Rob asked, thinking it to be a safe enough question.

"Eighteen months!", Jimmy replied.

"Really? How long have you been married ? I mean, you really are pretty young, you know?", Rob asked, already regretting having said something so 'dumb'. Yet Jimmy did not seem to take any offense. He was reaching around to the seat of his jeans with his right hand, slightly lifting himself from the chair. His hand came back into view with a wallet, which he began to open immediately.

"I'll show you a picture of my wife and little girl," he said, handing Rob a photograph of a girl who looked to be about eighteen years, maybe nineteen years old: a girl in slacks and blouse with long dark hair tumbling over her shoulders. She was an ordinary looking young woman, nothing really special about her, save for the look on her turned face as she looked, not towards the camera, but upon the child in her lap: a little girl with very blonde hair and who had a look on her upturned face and in her eyes which revealed immediately to the world just whose father's child she was.

"This may sound corny", Rob said, "But she really looks an awful lot like you! In fact, it's incredible!" . Again he felt something akin to a dull ache inside of himself. Envy? Fathering instinct? Whatever it was, he wanted it to go away!

"Yeah, I guess that there are some strong genes in this frame of mine!", Jimmy replied. "We've been married about two years now. The baby was on the way before we got around to it."

"Oh, I see," Rob answered, "I take it that you were living together for a while".

"Are you kidding? Her old man just about killed me as it was! We get along alright now, but it has taken him a while, believe me! He's Irish as Paddy's pig and Catholic and strict on top of that! Oh, no! He was pretty bent out of shape for a long time."

"Well, Rob suggested, "It seems to be getting more and more usual for two people to live together nowadays."

"Depends who you are and where you are", Jimmy countered. "Anyway, I figure that I'm pretty lucky. I know of a lot of guys who got their asses blown off or their legs shot to hell in Viet Nam before they were legally old enough to buy a drink in some states. Well, not a lot of guys that I know personally, but there were a lot of them!"

As Rob handed the photograph back to Jimmy, there was a quiet which had come over the place. Only the jukebox could be heard. A part of one of the selections had some bagpipes in the background and everyone seemed to be listening.

"Boy!", Jimmy said with a shake of his head, "Those bagpipes always do it to me!

"Well", Rob volunteered," Scottish Highlanders can be some pretty rough guys in battle!"

"No kidding!", Jimmy agreed.

"A lot of the Highlanders were driven out of Scotland years ago", Rob added. "Some to Canada, some to Australia, many to the 'States!"

"Yeah, I know", Jimmy said. Brightening up, he added, "Why hey! Even I have a lot of Scotch, or I should say "Scottish" blood! Highland Scottish, as a matter of fact!"

"Do you know which clan?, Rob asked politely. He expected Jimmy to say something like "I don't know, we're all Americans now!", and so forth, something like that.

"Well, if the name: James Simon Fraser means anything to you at all, which it may not unless you were to know, that's my clan and that's my name: Fraser!", Jimmy stated with pride.

"Oh, yes!", Rob assured him, "The Frasers gave the English a' hard way to go' for a long time! Still, without the Frasers, the British would never have captured Quebec!"

"You *know* about that!", Jimmy brightened. "Wow! You must have some of that Highland blood in you too!"

"My name is Robert James Currie", he said extending his hand. He and Jimmy shook hands before Rob went on: "Clan MacDonnell of Clanranald. Yes! Our ancestors fought on the same side!"

Rob found himself to be wondering what there was about all of this: these constant reminders of this other place across the sea, this faraway land from which the family had come. What about this trip itself: my willingness to go out of my way to meet some older relative who will just want to pore over some old pictures and written records? Why did I promise to do it anyway?

Denny came back with a map, the 'kid' on his heels. Seeing the smiles on the faces of both Jimmy and Rob, he looked from one to the other, but did not ask for any explanation. Some time was taken to clear the table and spread out the map, after which Denny made some marks here and there with a ball-point pen, indicating certain interchanges, sometimes also underlining the names of certain towns along the way. As it turned out, Rob discovered that the hitch-hiker did indeed have a name: "Paul"; "Paul King" to be exact, that he was making his way to Binghamton to stop at his mother's place there, after having been thrown out of his father's house. Rob reckoned him to be a somewhat superficial type at the time of this first meeting, yet Paul did not appear to be an angry or mean sort of guy in any way.

Once all had been figured out to Denny's satisfaction, Denny called Paul aside, moved away from Jimmy and Rob, turning Paul with him. Rob could see the slightest flurry of currency in the hand of the older trucker, which moved quickly to the shirt pocket of the young fellow. There appeared to be a protest on the part of Paul, who tried to step back, but Denny patted his back, turned away from him and moved back towards the table, leaving Paul to accept that which he had been given. Jimmy rose from the table and looking at his watch exclaimed, "Judas Priest! We've gotta get moving, Denny!"

Jimmy leaned on the table and asked Rob, "This is okay, taking him with you?"

"Oh, sure!", Rob assured him, "I could use some company anyway".

"Well, I hate just pushing him off and on you like that, but we kinda hated to see him stuck, You know?"

"Yes! Really, it's okay!", Rob assured him.

He could see Paul saying something to Denny, Denny then patting his back and shaking his hand. Paul then turned, moved over to the table to join Rob and sat down as soon as Denny and Jimmy said their goodbyes and headed in the direction of the glassed-in entryway. The waitress was back.

"How did you like your pie?", she asked him.

"You call that a pie? Hey! I'm glad that I hadn't had lunch first and decided to order it for desert! That was a meal in its own right!", he said to her, being sure to smile at the same time.

She laughed and said: "Yep! You are a male animal sure enough! Never satisfied! You're going to make some lucky girl very unhappy, but she'll love you for it! Can I get you anything else?"

No, thanks. Only the check, I guess."

"No more coffee?", she asked." I have the pot right here…"

"No, well…, maybe just half a cup, please" She poured some coffee into his cup, went off and was back in record time with his check, which she slid onto the table.

"Have a nice day, Hon'!", she said.

"You too", he replied. Rob drank his coffee, slid some quarters under the edge of his saucer, and said to Paul: "Well, Paul, we have a long road ahead! I'll pay up. We'd better get'er done!"

CHAPTER 4

PART 2

Rob did not return immediately to the four-lane highway when he left the Truck Stop. From that large parking area he had seen some wooden buildings and an old church steeple slightly visible among the trees in the near vicinity. An urge had risen within him to see what kind of a village had been left there; what manner of town and people had managed to withstand the march of progress and had stood their ground against modernization and the hurried pace of the 20th century. Perhaps it was such an interest or it might even have been simply a desire to observe something recognizably more "established," a glimpse of the fading, slower moving world that had been rural America. Rob himself quite possibly recognized that there may also have been a reluctance to return too quickly to the monotony of the expressway. In any case, and for whatever reason, as soon as the two young men had reached the car, thrown

Paul's single pack onto the back seat floor, and when the two of them had settled in for the long drive ahead, Rob heard himself saying:

"Are you in a hurry, a huge rush to get across Pennsylvania?"

"Huh?", Paul asked, surprised.

"I just thought that I'd check out this town over here!"

"Oh! Yeah!" Paul stammered." I mean, I don't care! It's up to you!" As a near after thought he added, "To tell you the truth, a rush is one thing that I am not in just now! I don't care how long it takes to get there!"

Rob backed the car out a bit, smoothly swung an arc and drove to the edge of the blacktop where it met a county road: pot-holed, weed-lined and abandoned by some yesterday's impatience to move on and away. The remains of one of those old "diners" sat among tall weeds on the other side of the road, the stalks of timothy, alfalfa and orchard grass coming up through the cracks in what had been pavement not long before. Windows broken, paint peeling, Rob could almost envision what it had been like. Probably more than one family had been supported by the place. Burgers and fries, black coffee; doughnuts and Danish pastries at breakfast time, although certainly the generous "Specials" of French Toast, Bacon and Eggs, or Hot Pancakes and Maple syrup. Always there would be banter and generous tips for the waitresses, a morning paper close at hand and never a lack of country music playing on the juke box.

Swinging the car now to the left and onto the county road and moving towards the village, the thought came into his mind that he was perhaps expected to ask his rider why he had stated no great desire to hurry the homeward trip. Certainly his newly acquired traveling companion, his "company" for the rest of the journey, had tendered his statement as if he had been inviting a request for clarification, but Rob felt a stubborn, resentment and a refusal to "care" rise inside of himself; an almost sadistic sentiment towards Paul himself, which he himself would never be able to explain. Rob did not care what the reasons may have been. He actually felt anger rising inside of him. It wasn't he told himself, that he had been maneuvered into taking on a passenger. That didn't bother him. He was even glad to have someone with whom he could share the time. He decided quite quickly, that it was Paul who bothered him. Here seemed to be a young man at the beginning of his life who invited pity! It was, Rob felt, as if Paul expected people to feel sorry for him. He expected it, waited for it and cashed in on it, wasting these good years of his life doing nothing save for garnering the pity of others That was it! Rob sensed that his traveling companion of the moment was far from stupid, and that he may have (NO! Probably had…) detected his own secret feelings, his own evaluation, of him. Nor was Rob any too happy with himself at the moment! He realized that he had done poorly indeed in the initial assessment of the truckers back there. He had somehow resented them also, after all, even perceiving them to have been hostile or threatening: men whom he had evaluated as cold and unfeeling, he had later found to be generous and kind. A lot of us will give of our money, after all. We do it all the time. We make donations to charities of every kind. Such donations can even be deducted from our income taxes! Parents shower their offspring with gifts; expensive gifts! Yet, the children know better. They are not stupid and know that money and "things" are a means of "buying them off", of postponing the real gifts of concern, shared interests, and time. The young know before having spent too many years in this life that the big gift: time, is too much to hope for, certainly too much to ask for. Rob thought of that: that the truckers, Denny and Jimmy gave of their time, to a stranger, and a good –sized chunk of it at that, despite the fact that their own livelihoods were super-glued to the movements of clocks from coast to coast.

The sign with its posted speed limit-30 MPH, itself going down for the third time in a swelling tide of weeds and choke-cherry bushes, marked the village line. Some local kids had obviously taken some of the tar from the road to make the 3 into an 8, as is so often seen on rural speed signs. The chances that some young guys in their cars or pick-up trucks might actually come close to the 80 mile posted limit on a Saturday night did not seem to be totally beyond the realm of possibility. A bridge of sorts, really simply a place where the road crossed over a creek, seems to have been the first actual structure of the village. Beyond that crossing was the remnants of a lawn and the first house. The street was lined with small houses, many of them being of the early 19th century style called "Greek Revival". Still, the thought came into Rob's mind: "Ugliness is often an idea of beauty which has never been attained, or else an idea of beauty which has been either carried too far or allowed to rot away." "Did somebody tell me that, or did I read it somewhere?", he was asking himself. "Probably Freshman Civ' Class!" In any case, at this time in the early summer of 1972, the houses were not nice. Once upon a time they would undoubtedly have been beautiful, but at this time they lay about like so many scattered toys left to the rain and the forces of gravity and wind.. Some of them actually looked tumbled towards their centers; others somewhat tilted to a side. The dwellings which bore signs of what lumber yards called "Renovation" were perhaps the saddest of all to behold. Someone had taken one of the little Greek Revivals, cut its windows down, fitting them out with tacky little plastic shutters and covered the house with metal siding. The porch had been removed and replaced with a concrete deck, which had been faced with that fake "stone" made of concrete. Aluminum scroll-work posts held up a turquoise translucent porch awning..Plastic toys of every color and size littered the front lawns which were really more given to pounded earth than to grass. There was a drive-way leading to a garage, the door of which being open to the world, revealed a couple of snow-mobiles. A motor boat was set up on some timbers beside the garage. "Ah, affluence!" Rob thought sarcastically, feeling just a bit ashamed of himself almost immediately afterward. Another house, probably once built of the same style, had been covered with some of that asphalt/asbestos stuff made to imitate brick. The imitation covering must have been applied several decades prior to this time, for much of this "improvement of twenty or thirty years ago was chipping or ripped away. A wooden porch dipped badly, the center almost touching the ground. A soggy-looking sofa sat on the curled floor boards of the porch, and a wooden box and a barrel at the side of the porch had a dog chained to each.

"This is terrible!", Rob said aloud.

"It's pretty bad, alright!", Paul agreed

Reaching a corner, there was a crossroad, an old church set back from the street. It was one of those once-charming Greek Revival structures with the addition of a square tower and steeple, so favored by Christmas card illustrators. The white paint was still in evidence, but the gray, weathered wood was beginning to win the battle for prominence. The original, large doorway with the wide, hand-planed heavy lintel (probably a true labor of love of some carpenter long retired from this earth) was still in place, but the doorways had been cut down considerably, hollow-core factory outlet doors with small rectangular windows hung inside of the much lesser portals. A hand-painted sign on plywood, not at all well done, was propped against the front steps of crumbling concrete, stating quite to the point: "Antiques... Bought and Sold".

"Let's see what they've got in here!", Rob suggested,

pulling the car off to the side, almost onto what had at one time been a lawn "Sometimes you can find some neat things in a place like this!". Paul made no reply, save for simply opening his door when Rob turned off the engine.

The first signs of life which presented themselves in the town came from the house just next to the church. The property had once been separated by one of those woven wire fences; the kind where the wire forms loops all along the top. There was very little of this barrier left standing, for it appeared to have been much leaned-upon, beaten upon, climbed over and ultimately walked over. There must have been rose bushes covering it at one time, but what little evidence they were able to still send forth suggested that any plant life had given up the struggle for survival many years ago. Too much metal, too much rust and too much human activity! A very large, over-weight woman on the house-side of the fence was yelling at two children who were climbing on a Thunderbird in the driveway, the car appearing to be receiving the attentions of someone with an idea towards its restoration.

"Get off that car! Junior will be mad as hell when he gets home!" She scuffled along like a rolling, wheezing, puffing machine: down the steps, of the porch, towards the two children, who were abandoning the car with squeals and laughter in record time. At that same moment, as the children left the vehicle, the cave woman added:" Who the Hell told you you could bring that T.V. table out here?" As she grabbed up a little folding stand with tube steel legs, its metal top painted with a scene of deer in a forest, she grumbled aloud, as much to Rob and Paul who were now nearby, as to the two young children: "Damn kids! A Person can't keep nothin' nice around here!". By this time the little boy and girl were off and away, scouting out other nice things to "get into" or destroy. The cave woman addressed Rob and Paul directly as they were nearing the edge of the church fence:

"You fellas wantin' to buy some of that hippie junk they got in there?" ("In there" was indicated by a show of a great, flabby arm and fist with a thumb indicating the church building). "I got a whole house full of junk that's as good or better than any of that Draft-Dodger shit in there…and I'd gladly GIVE it away as to see somebody waste his money on those kinds of people!"

"Well, we have to give them the benefit of the doubt!" Paul joked," Hey! You never know what you might find!" He was turning on his school boy charm and he knew it.

"That's for damned sure!" The woman laughed. "You never know what you might find! And maybe you just might not want to know, either!"

Rob gave her a shy and pleasant smile and said in a near whisper to Paul,

"Well, Always leave 'em smilin', right ?"

As they walked up towards the entrance to the old church building, a young woman of about 22 or 23 opened the door and looked out. She wore a long dress which almost reached the floor, a heavily embroidered blouse, filled with hours of someone's needle work in stitches, tucks and gathered fabric. Her reddish hair was very long and full, but quite straight, coming down around her shoulders, kept back from her face by a broad band of cloth tied about her head. Rob noticed that her features were smooth, almost too delicate, as a porcelain doll. She had a small nose and mouth, but her very grey eyes were most unusual. Rob had never in his life looked into eyes which appeared to be so totally devoid of expression. "Somebody's home, but they forgot to turn on the lights!", he thought to himself.

"Hi?" the young woman said, or asked, for it was as much a question as a greeting. Her voice had a tired, bored disappointed sound to it; crackly even, or hollow, like a pebble dropping into a well. She might better have simply asked them what they wanted. Rob looked down to her bare feet and long toes showing themselves from beneath her badly wrinkled floor-length dress.

"We saw your sign and thought that we'd like to look around. ….You know, your antiques or whatever!"

The girl continued to look at him as if she hadn't heard, then said,

"Well as long as you're looking to maybe buy something and not sell! We can't afford to buy anything for the store right now….so if you're looking to sell something in order to get some money, we can't help you." Just as suddenly, she stepped aside and motioned them into the packed and cluttered interior.

"We've got a little bit of everything", she whined, her

words almost a sigh or half-buried complaint; perhaps some hidden disappointments, real or imagined, to which she had allowed her self to be offered up as an enduring sacrificial victim.

A hopeless clutter, the large room was filled with the cast off items of mail order houses and three generations of impulse-buying, all come to rest in rows, stacks and hanging from hooks and odd pieces of wooden moldings which formed a part of the inner structure,. Every window-sill of the tall church windows was stacked with something or other as well. "God's living room sure is a pretty cluttered mess ", Rob thought. What he found to be amazing was that this great clutter was comprised of countless un-needed things; items which had no real use or function. So much of what was gathered in the old church had been bought as souvenirs, wedding gifts for friends or relatives, curios, decorations, sports trophies, and "things" which had fallen off of other "things". There were some votive candle lights and some brass holders for them which looked to have come out of some Catholic church. Religion was further represented here by some great, heavy brass-trimmed family Bible, some religious tracts and even some books put out by the Rosicrucians and also some books on Yoga. Oddly enough, every item did carry with it some pretense to "Usefulness". "The people of a Democratic Society will always require their art to be useful", Rob remembered from de Tocqueville's "Democracy in America". By and large, the so-called "antiques" gathered here rarely had an age which was beyond three decades.

"Do you want to buy a battery charger, by any chance?". The voice had come from behind a table stacked with dishes and lamp parts. Shifting his position, Rob could see a lightly bearded, blond young man in cut-off jeans, a bare and fuzzy chest and arms to match his heavily fuzzy legs, who was sitting on a small wooden crate. He had a lamp part or lighting fixture in one hand and a screw-driver in the other. His eyes were too full of mischief to be serious, for he probably wanted his question to come across in an earnest manner, but it would be very difficult to attach any complete trust to this guy. His eyes were quite expressive, evaluating and penetrating, but there was a dance of mischief in them. They turned upward at the outer corners, giving the fellow the time-honored caricature of the pixie or elf.

"Holy Shit!", Rob thought. "This guy looks like Jesus, but a bit too blond and not serious enough" Then contradicting his initial reaction:" Cleanliness is next to Godliness and this guy gives a totally new meaning to the word "Grubby"! He looks like a poster boy for a druggie too!"

"No, not really.", Rob answered somewhat absently, without stopping his eyes from moving over the tremendous acquisition around him, Finally, glancing towards the elfin fellow, he made brief eye contact and added: I guess that it might be a handy thing to have, but I don't need one all that much!"

"Well, that's too bad! I could give you a real eye-watering deal on a battery charger! I just got three of them in last week and they all seem to check out okay!" He tinkered for a minute more before asking "You looking for anything in particular?"

"Nah!" Rob answered with half a laugh. I just like to surprise myself with something that might turn up!"

"Well, hop right to it then! We sure have a little bit of everything, so look all you want!"

Rob was ready to leave already, but looked at a few more things in passing.. A couple of potato crates were filled with old 78 rpm records from the '50's, none of which seemed to have been too well cared for. Some boxes were stuffed with old pieces of heavy crocheted pieces which had been made to be runners for tables, or "doilies" or whatever. Quite a number of old oil lambs minus their glass chimneys were on hand, and there was an old pitcher and bowl set from some long-past farm house bedroom, no doubt, but both the bowl and the pitcher had been broken and very badly mended.

Paul had come up an aisle from the other direction and having reached the same table, he leaned over the boxes peering closely and occasionally lifting some article for closer inspection. It was at this time that Rob became fully aware of how badly his traveling companion smelled and found himself wondering why he hadn't noticed it when they were in the car. Of course, he reasoned, they had been farther apart in the car, not as close to one another as was now the case. Too, the windows of the car had been open. Rob could not resist an impulse to take the moment to further inspect his new riding companion, his "charge", even perhaps his "responsibility" Rob took in the thick, curly strands and clusters of Paul's unwashed brown hair as he leaned over the table, or his wrinkled, crusty-looking shirt which hung open part-way down his chest,; the filthy jeans, stiff-looking and too tight, and the scruffy running shoes on awkward feet. His mind, although he tried to shut the thought out, presented him with an imaginary X-ray of festoons of gray and filthy cloth loops which served as under shorts. "Gah! ", Rob thought. "I don't even want to imagine such a thing! Why did I think of that? Disgusting!"

Paul suddenly straightened up, turning in Rob's direction, he exclaimed (more of a horse whisper than an exclamation):

"Hey, check this out!"

"What did you find?" Rob asked, looking towards the object of Paul's interest: a "Peace" symbol (actually an anti-nuclear symbol) pendant minus a chain, left over from the sixties' beginnings of an anti-war movement.

Paul took the pendant in the direction of the elf-eyed one and asked, "How much for this?"

"Five bucks!" said the elf without looking up.

"What! Are you mad? Forget it!"

"Hey, man! It's worth it! It's sterling!"

"You wish!", answered Rob.

Instead of any response on his part, elf-eyes called out to the walls of the room:

"Hey, Marge! You got a customer here who wants to buy

one of yer goddam trinkets!" From the front entryway, a head appeared and a voice said,

"We'll take two dollars for it!"

"Do I get a chain with it?", Paul asked.

"What do you think this is, a jewelry store?", asked the tinkering elf.

"A chain will cost you a buck and a half", said the dead-eyed one from the entryway.

"Okay, I'll take it", Paul said.

"Just take a chain off'a one of those other things," the dead-eyed one commanded. "They're all about the same!"

By this time the woman had shuffled up to them. Paul handed her a ten Dollar Bill The woman looked at the bill and finally said,

"I can't make change for that". Addressing her tinkering mate she asked, "Rick, do you have change for a ten?"

"Nope!" came the reply. No pause in the tinkering, no looking up.

"Bastard!", the woman said just barely under her breath, then she said to Paul, "We can't make change for a Ten!" No solution was offered, nor was there any apparent great concern over the loss of a sale.

Back in the car, Rob started to turn around, being careful to avoid running over a wooden churn and a large, cast iron farmhouse bell, a stretch of iron railing and a badly broken rocking chair. The heavy, woman from the house next door was still making her appointed rounds, scuffing along the driveway of her villa again, still yelling at the kids:

"Get off that car! I'm not going to tell you again!" (mutter*, mutter*….Damned kids! Can't keep nothin' nice around here)…. "You wait until Junior gets home!", (etc., etc., waddle, waddle; scuff, scuff).

Rob found himself experiencing a sense of emptiness and disappointment as he swung the car up the ramp and onto the expressway. He wondered why he had decided to drive into the little town…or what was left of a little town, with its run-down houses and junk-yard church. "Who are those people? Where did they come from, or how did they slip through the cracks?" he was asking himself. The street had been lined with houses which had been built long before the advent of power tools, when carpenters were sawing boards by hand and built with timbers which had been hand-hewn and dressed. Some of the little details on those houses: the cornices and the lintels over the doors and windows must have taken a great deal of time to fashion, executed as they were solely by the use of hand-planes. The descendants of those builders, the great grandsons and grand-daughters of pioneers are too lazy to even slap a coat of paint on that which has already been made! "Yessir!" Rob thought, "You can't keep nothing nice around here!" Sheesss!

"Do you suppose that you and me will get to where we split by dark?" Paul asked.

"The way I have it figured, we should get there around four or five o'clock at the latest. Still daylight!"

"Yeah." Paul slid down on the seat and laid his head

back, his two knees high above his hands which he had settled in his lap. "No" he said, as if he were completing a statement which he had just made, "I'm not that anxious to get where I am supposed to be going".

Robbie thought: "Oh hell! Who cares!?", but pushing past his own stubborn reluctance to coddle his passenger, he brought himself to ask:" Why's that? Your mother will probably be glad to see you."

"No doubt! Her new husband won't be glad to see me. That much I can guarantee!"

"I take it that you and he don't exactly hit it off together" Rob turned his face towards Paul, then back to watch the road.

"You got THAT right! He hates my guts!"

"Maybe you just need to give him a chance. You know: sometimes it takes a while for a stepfather and stepson to accept one another."

"The only thing that he ever accepted from me was a chunk of two by four right up the back of his head!, and it wasn't because he wanted to accept it either!....the mean son of a bitch!"

Rob swung his head to face Paul, mouth agape, eyes wide, eyebrows high on his forehead and grinning in disbelief.

"You hit him with a two by four!? Sweet Screaming Judas! Why did you do THAT?" He was half laughing.

"Yeah! I did it! That's why he kicked me out and I went to stay with my Dad. That bastard needs to be killed!"

"Well, yeah", Rob reasoned, but what brought you to hit him like that?…and with a TWO BY FOUR!?"

"Oh, he came home one night, drunk out of his gourd and started giving my Mom a ration of shit, slapped her and got her crying. Then, he started in on my sister and my younger brother. He started calling my sister some really rotten names, slapped her around too, and I honest-to God think that he would have killed my kid brother! He had him by the hair and kept knocking his head against the wall, and all the time he kept yelling: "Hit me, you little faggot! Go ahead! Hit me! Just try it!" Then he punched him real hard in the gut and Lennie went down hard and couldn't breathe. He kept trying to catch his breath. The mean bastard was going to start kicking him, but that's when I saw that two by four leaning against the wall. About the time he drew back his foot to kick the poor kid, I had that piece of wood in both hands and I swung it like I was going to bat his head right out of the Ballpark! I guess that I hit him about three times, maybe four. I really wanted to kill him, I really did, but all three of them: Mom, my sister and brother were pulling on me, trying to get me away from him. He was laying there, out cold and finally my mom started to get him cleaned up."

"God!" was all that Rob could think to say. He felt a tingle run from the tips of his toes up to his groin at the thought of the pain involved.

"Yeah, well"…..Paul went on, "The next day he told me to pack some clothes and get out, so that's what I did. When

I went out the kitchen door with my bag, he was sitting at the table. I turned around and looked at him and said, "I'm going, but if you ever hit Mom or Lennie or Sue again, you had better be looking over your shoulder, because I might just want to be right there with whatever it takes: a piece of of pipe, a club, maybe even a twelve gauge shotgun!" He just snarled at me from behind his coffee cup: "Get your ass out of here!" That's all he said: "Get your ass out of here!" Anyway, I have a pretty good idea that he knew that I meant what I said. My Mom was waiting outside and she was crying. She hugged me and gave me ten bucks and a bag with a couple of sandwiches in it. Hell! She probably had to sneak that food and money past that stingy, drunken slob!"

Rob was silent for a short space of time before asking: "Well, why are you even thinking about going back there then? "At this point he was glancing back and forth between Paul and the road in front of him.

"Oh, I won't stay there! I'll stop and see my Mom and Sue and my kid brother, but I'll go on up to my Grandmother's place. She's always been great to me. She's my Dad's mother and she lives on a farm north of Binghamton, just a bit south of Syracuse. I can help out on the farm and stay there if I want to".

"You've been staying with your Dad, right? I suppose that you could always go back there", Rob ventured.

"My Dad is a great guy! He really is, and I really love him, but I can't stay there. He didn't really throw me out or anything like that. He has a real set of problems of his own.

The woman he married is okay. In a lot of ways she's a really good person, but she has some genuine hang-ups. See, she's a bit younger than my Dad, and about ten years older than me. Every time I turn around, she's there!"

"What, you mean she's always on your case about something?", Rob asked.

"No. I wish it was even that easy! She can't keep her hands off me, y'know? I tried to tell her. I said to her: "Hey, Linda, look: I love my Dad and I like you a lot, but we can't goof around, y'know? It's just not right!" She would go into a pout, start sniffing instead of talking, and Dad would ask me if I had said some thing to upset her. I couldn't very well tell my father that his wife wanted me as a boy toy! I would end up looking like the offender. He was working a night shift and she came into my room and started fooling around in a joking way. Before I knew what was happening, she was tonguing my neck and chest, telling me that she thought that I was beautiful. I tried to push her away, I really did! When I looked up, I saw my Dad standing in the doorway. The way I figure it, the way I had a hold of her arms, it may have looked like I was pulling her to me instead of pushing her away!" Paul paused for a short time and added: "Later on my Dad was crying out back of the house. I know he was! God! I felt sick to see him like that!"

"Did he ask you to leave then?", Rob asked.

"No, he didn't. I wanted to tell him what was happening, but I think that he really knew. I asked him if it might not be better if I left. He never answered me. He just grabbed me by the neck and pulled my head to his shoulder. I think that he was crying!"

"Sounds like this Linda might have a bit of a problem!", Rob ventured.

"Who knows? People usually make their own problems!"

The two young men rode on in silence for a distance. At length, Rob said, as if to himself, but loud enough for Paul to hear:" Boy! I thought that I had some troubles from time to time!"

CHAPTER 5

PART 2

By the time that they had reached the outskirts of Youngstown, Rob figured that he had been on the road for about five hours. Of course, he had not been driving steadily during that length of time, for a good hour or so had been spent at the truck stop and the "antiques" place. Paul was being quiet at this time,; sitting up, looking around but simply not saying anything. Rob broke the silence:

"Keep your eyes open for a sign for '80', okay? There's so much traffic right here that I don't even know for sure which lane I should be in!"

"I just saw a sign for the Pennsylvania Turnpike", Paul said.

"Yeah. That means that we're getting pretty close to our turn-off.", his words coming forth in a somewhat detached way.

"Oh! Wait! Here you go!, Paul exclaimed, followed by:

"Oops! Sorry! The sign says route 46 ....Austintown and Mineral Ridge."

"We should be pretty close now" "Rob said. "Route 80 has to be right up ahead." Under his breath:" Boy! Talk about 'defensive Driving'! This is beyond belief!"

"YES!! Here we are! Rte. 11 and 80! To Pennsylvania!", Paul proclaimed.

"Well, Hallelujah! We at least found our road!", Rob replied, and at that, he smoothly pulled the car into the lane marked by the great overhead sign marked "Rte 80 East. Pennsylvania". Rob went on:

"You know, Paul, it will only be about another couple of hours before we have to turn North. Two things: One, I think that we should stop down the road a little ways and get some supper before we split up, and Two: I have been wondering if it might not be a good idea if you were to travel north with me to almost where I am going. You'd only be about 25 miles from route Six. That's the road you should get on to go east in order to get near Binghamton. What do you think?"

"For my part, I don't see where it makes too much difference. I guess that I might as well stay with you as far as I can. I mean, what the Hell! At least this is a ride I can count on for as long as you're willing to take me!"

"Okay, That's what we'll do then!", Rob answered.

Neither of them spoke for quite a while. There didn't seem to be anything which either of them could think of to say. It was one of those times in life when, being somewhat unsure of new situations and people scarcely known, not knowing anything about the background or interests of another person, it is sometimes rather difficult to make even small talk. Men are much less capable of talking with strangers than are women. One more of those many, many unwritten, but carefully observed rules among men, even young men, is to "play it cool" and look to be minding your own business. Paul felt a bit awkward, in that he was accepting another's assistance or hospitality and he realized that it really might be a good thing if he could at least act a bit friendlier, more open, perhaps. He felt that he should be saying something, anything, rather than to simply fill up the passenger seat like a bag of dirty laundry but, there it was: He didn't have anything to say. He even wondered if Rob was wondering why he did not help to pass the time, even with useless talk, and this gradually led him to feeling something in the way of resentment. Paul was playing with his own thoughts: another of those "moth and flame" games with which we seem to often involve ourselves. He looked sidewise at his benefactor: this well-scrubbed, "wholesome", "squeaky-clean" and shiny-faced guy in a white shirt. He took in the profile and the neat hair of his driver; the shirtsleeves rolled half way up the tanned forearms, the strong, unblemished wrists and the pinkish knuckles gripping the steering wheel. "This guy is probably rich", he was thinking. "…a college kid whose father and mother are loaded! No scars, no blemishes, well-built. He probably works out and swims in his family swimming pool every day. 'Probably has used more talcum powder to dust his spoiled, rich little ass, than most people would use in a life-time!". Paul experienced a wash of anger sweep over him as a wave, the accompanying surge of envy and near hatred, to be as quickly followed by a sense of shame and guilt for having entertained such thoughts. It was a moment so tense, that the car somehow held the enmity in the air: as if he had actually given voice to his thoughts. It was also as if Rob had almost 'heard' his thoughts, for Rob turned his head to meet Paul's gaze, not slowly, but in a "double-take", a movement which betrayed a certain surprise or question on his part. It had been a contrived double-take; not one of total surprise, for Rob had deliberately used the gesture to ward off the close inspection to which he had felt himself being subjected.

"What's wrong?", Rob asked

"Huh?", asked Paul, taken off guard

"I asked, What's wrong! Is my nose on crooked or something?"

"No, why?" Paul asked guardedly.

"You were staring at me!" Rob kept his eyes on the road, not turning.

"Yeah, well….I guess I was thinking of something else and just happened to be looking at you at the time." Paul was truly embarrassed now.

Rob felt his fists tighten on the wheel. Continuing to keep his eyes straight ahead, he replied, "I'm not all that sure that I buy that! You know, some of us may have a certain perception to compensate for a lack of some kind of native intelligence!"

"Could you translate what you just said for me?"

"I mean that people aren't always totally stupid, or as dumb as they look, okay? Sometimes we can sense things!"

"Like what!?" Paul was feeling as if he were being backed into a corner.

"Like…" Rob said sarcastically, now turning to face him, "Like I can feel that something really bugs you about me! 'Care to tell me if I'm wrong?"

"What? Because I catch a ride with you we are supposed to be great buddies or something?"

"Hell, no! We probably haven't very much in common, but we can try to keep our little hostilities under wraps; not let them light up like a neon sign!"

"Excuse me all to Hell!", Paul snarled.. What the F___ difference does it make to you if I feel hostile or not? I'm just riding with you; not sleeping with you!"

"I can be eternally grateful for that, at least!", Rob fired back

"Okay, Okay, OKAY! Yeah! I suppose that I don't really like you! You've got money, an education, family, a future!... You've got it all! You've got everything that I don't have! You're a spoiled little College Boy …and I'll be shoveling shit!"

"Because I go to college, you think that I'm spoiled? You think that I'm *RICH*?", Rob asked with a slight, yet somewhat cruel laugh.

"Well, aren't you? Paul asked defiantly

"Hell, no! I'm going to be working in a Feed Mill this summer and driving truck part time! What! Did you think that I was going to spend the summer on a yacht?"

"Something like that, yeah!", Paul admitted.

"Well, I have to earn my college money, you simple jar of shit! My folks have two of us in college this next year. They help us somewhat, but they're not rich! I'm going to be paying on student loans 'til the cows come home: for years and years!"

Paul was definitely on the defense at this point.

"Yeah, well…." Paul persisted, "at least you're going to have a life!"

"And you're not?", Rob closed in on his argument.

"Sure! I'm going to own my own bank by the time that I'm thirty!"

"Well, buddy-boy, there's no anchor tied to your ass! You sure as hell can head in some direction and take it from there, right?", Rob persisted.

"Oh, hell, yes! Right!", Paul answered.

Rob felt himself losing patience. He had already had a sense that Paul invited pity. Something akin to anger was growing inside of him. At the same time he knew that a start in life had to be pretty difficult without some kind of family support, expectations aspiration; whatever. It must be pretty hard to get a job anywhere if you come from a family of losers…. And this realization in turn made him feel a bit guilty, for he knew that Paul was not completely wrong. But, hell! Why should a guy have to carry guilt because his family had worked for respect and admiration in the community, or that the family had done all that is possible to give a son or daughter a sense of worth, pride or whatever? He couldn't remember a time when his family had not supported him in his interests. True, his mother could be somewhat bothersome about table manners, introductions, neatness, promptness, and so forth, yet he knew that she was interested in his dealings with people; in his humanity. His father had always supported him too, but had pushed him to excel in whatever he had chosen to do. "No, Rob. I know that you don't like Mr. McIntosh as a swimming coach, but you signed on to swim and you'll stick with your team to the end of the season. A man is only as good as his word." Rob realized that his life had been geared toward doing something and doing it well. It was, he realized, the way in which parents gave their children the necessary tools for survival. There had been love in the house. He knew that his father had passed up a couple of opportunities to make a greater wage because he had opted to raise his children in a rural setting and had preferred to spend time with them. Of course, Rob had been aware of some tension between his parents from time to time. His mother would raise a fuss because his father would spend money on something for one of the children which she regarded as unnecessary. There had been quite a problem when he had come home with new skis or as happened on one occasion, a pony for Carole. Rob had heard his mom really sorting his father out:... "It must be nice to have so much money to spend! One of these days I may actually go out and spend some of this fabulous wealth on something for me!" ...and his father would always say, "Oh, Sheila. We aren't lacking for anything." Rob had philosophically decided early on that all families had such moments and had never doubted that his parents both wanted their children to grow into lives filled with meaning and value, harmony and contentment. All in all, he thought, it is the luck of the draw and I have been lucky. But, damn! Should someone else resent me for that? Probably. I mean, I don't know!

What Rob did know for certain was that he resented the thick, heavy awkwardness in the car at this moment. It was a tension between opposites which filled him with almost unbearable, suffocating discomfort. Even worse he found himself being steamrollered, buried, by the silent uneasiness of the stranger who occupied the seat beside him. He fumbled for the radio, turned it on and sought for a station with his right hand while continuing to steer with his left. He met with little success, which did at least give him a much needed opportunity toward breaking the silence.

"See if you can find something on this freakin' thing, will you, Paul?"

"Yeah, Sure." The relief in Paul's voice was plain to hear. "What do you want to hear?"

"Oh, I don't care. I can take just about anything but

elevator music. I can't stand the fakey, phony, syrup-sweet sound of that crap!"

"You mean you're afraid of romance?" Rob jerked his head sideways to see Paul smiling at him. Someone else had said something to him of the same nature and in almost the same words.

"Well, I don't know. I don't like canned, contrived romance. It makes everything so corny, so predictable, you know?"

Paul was moving the dial of the radio, catching snatches of car ads, a call-in show, an advertisement for a motel chain, a restaurant and a soon-to-be Blue Grass Jamboree. What music there was seemed to be mostly Country-Western.

"You're going to have to settle for "country," Paul said, leaving the dial at a station playing… "These Boots are made fer walkin'… an' that's just what they'll do. One o' these days these boots are gonna walk all over yew!"

The both laughed. It felt good to have the space again, the lack of anxiety, guilt; whatever else they had had riding with them.

"I'm going to leave this road up ahead and pull onto 66. It's supposed to be a beautiful road and it will take us up to route six so that you can go east on that."

"Yeah, but isn't it out of your way?", Paul asked

"Not Really. From where we part company, I'll just have to back track about thirty minutes."

"Well, I don't want you to go out of your way."

"Actually, this is the best thing to do. Really!" Rob turned to face Paul squarely to indicate his sincerity. "But", he went on, "when we pull off of this road onto 66 I want to stop for a break, okay?"

"Suits me. I'm just along for the ride."

"Well, that's that, then." And another voice from the radio twanged out a different song: this time it was "Crazy" by Patsy Cline.

The diner was one of those places that are to be found everywhere in the Allegany Mountain region, from South Western New York State down through Pennsylvania, West Virginia and into the Carolinas. Such places have a certain straightforwardness which is a reflection of the people who build and operate them. The walls are almost always of pine; sometimes 'tongue and groove' boards, but as often as not, wood from a local saw mill. Decorations are usually patriotic, sometimes backed by a religious theme. In this particular diner, the wall opposite the counter displayed a large American flag superimposed with an image of a plains Indian in full war bonnet. There were several amateurish oil paintings of various sizes, depicting forest scenes, streams, deer and woodland homesteads. Each had a price written on a gummed paper affixed to the lower right hand corner of the frame. At the end of the room next to a sign which pointed to the restrooms was a large slab of irregular wood, a cross-section of a tree, which had been given sufficient coats of Varithane as to give it the look of glass and mounted upon this or decoupaged into it was a picture of

Jesus praying in the Garden of Gethsemene, while a small clock had been set into the upper left side of the whole.

Rob ordered a coke and a cheeseburger and announced, "I'm going to go wash up", then moved toward the Jesus clock.

Paul ordered a milkshake and a "B.L.T."

When Rob returned, Paul said simply "Hold the fort", picked up a small plastic bag which he had brought into the diner with him, and moved toward the restroom.

Rob said to Paul, "You're looking for the door which is labeled "Bucks". The ones labeled "Does" are for the girls! Don't go into the wrong one or you're apt to be torn to pieces on the spot!"

Rob sat alone looking up at the oil painting of a deer among trees in the colors of autumn. The deer looked as if it had been cut out of a sportsman's magazine and pasted onto the backdrop, and not too straightforward at that, for it seemed to lean backward. The foreshortening of the animal's neck and face had fallen somewhat shy of what might be expected, giving the face a flattened, punched-in appearance. Yet the color of the painting was good, the treatment of the tree limbs and sky was quite fine. A price sticker had"$45.00" written on it.

"I think that that's my favorite of all the pictures that we have in here."

Rob looked up at the waitress who had brought their order.

"A lady near here does those paintings. You'd be

surprised at how many we've sold for her," the young woman went on as she placed his cheeseburger in front of him, then asked:

"Your friend is still here isn't he, 'hon'?"

"Yes. He went to wash up. He'll be right along."

"Well, I'll just put his milkshake and B.L.T here for him then." Straightening up she asked if she could get him anything else and when he said no, she tore two slips from her order pad and placed one of each beside his, then Paul's plate.

It was another five minutes or so before Paul slid into the booth across from Rob. Rob glanced up, then did a double take, this time, a real "double take", in total surprise.

"What? Is my nose on crooked or something?", Paul asked with a smirk.

"What did you do, take a shower, for God's sake?", Rob asked

"I just cleaned up, that's all", Paul shrugged.

"You shaved! You changed your shirt and jeans!", Rob accused him.

"Yeah. So?"

"In there?", Rob asked

"Better there than here, right?"

Rob just smiled, shaking his head from side to side.

"You're too much, Paul."

"Decorum in the face of provocation, College Boy!"

"Just eat your sandwich!", Rob ordered, shaking his head.

Rob couldn't believe how some soap, water, a comb and razor had transformed his travelling companion. In fact he felt that it was Rob Currie who now appeared to the world as the more crumpled and unwashed of the two. He had glanced across at Paul again only to catch Paul's eyes dancing with merriment straight at his own.

"You better stop looking at me like you just found sleeping beauty or everybody's gonna think that you're queer for me!", Paul wise-cracked.

"Yeah, Right! Just don't get your hopes up!" Rob smiled but felt himself redden somewhat.

"Naw! I'm not worried. Some college girl's sure to have already figured you for her future meal ticket. You're okay!", Paul assured him.

"Do you think that that's the only reason why a young woman would want an education? Maybe she wants to be her own 'meal ticket', as you call it.", Rob suggested.

"Yeah, well,…maybe. That seems to be the gist of what all the 'libbers' are saying. I'm not sure that I buy it. A lot of girls go to college and take basket weaving, but you don't see them hooking up with a guy who isn't into science of physics or something. They like to hedge their bets by making sure that the male partner is going into a high-paying job.". Paul opined

"Paul, I can now go back and admit that there really are some chauvinist pigs out in the world!", Rob jibed.

"Right! Stick with me and you'll learn a lot that you never knew before", Paul said.

The two of them continued to exchange mindless

remarks for a while, then having finished their meal began to exit the booth. Paul grabbed Rob's bill as well as his own.

"I'll take care of these!", he said."

"What are you doing?"' Rob asked.

"Let me do this, please.", Paul asked

"No."

"Screw you! I'm doing it! Pay the tip if you have to throw some money around! I can do this at least.", Paul stated flatly.

"Well, uh, okay. I'll get the tip. Thanks"…but"…, Rob stammered

"No 'buts'. You're welcome, by the way."

After gassing up and checking the oil and water, they headed North on Route 66 to Kane. The road had taken them through a section of the Allegheny National Park and the beauty of it all was almost overwhelming. Not much was said by either of them for each seemed to be absorbed by the wildly beautiful landscape, the little surprises at every turn. At Kane, Paul took his leave. He gathered up his bag, thanked Rob for the 'lift' and said "who knows? Maybe we'll meet again sometime." Rob watched him plant himself on the eastbound traffic lane side of Route six. Paul waved and turned Right onto Rte 321 and towards his MacKinnon Relatives. He judged the time to be about 4:30pm.

"What a strange day", he mused aloud, "what a strange guy! Why do I feel that I was supposed to meet that guy and why do I sense that we'll meet again?" Then, shifting his weight he said, "Naw! Sheess! I wonder what they put in that coke!"

CHAPTER 6

PART 2

Robert MacKinnon was on the roof of his house when his young kinsman came up the unpaved road in a cloud of yellow brown dust. He chuckled to himself, shook his head and continued to tighten down the nut of the television antennae brace. He worked the ratchet wrench back and forth until he could feel it tighten snuggly and went on to the next and last bolt and nut. "One way to get people to call or visit is to either go to the roof or the shower", he thought. He finished what he was doing and began to gather up his tools, below him a car door closed. A moment later the door knocker could be heard yet another moment and he heard his wife's voice and the voice of a young man. Again, the sound of his wife, Kathy, caught his recognition, "Funny how English sounds when you can't make out what's being said", he thought. "Must sound God-awful funny to a Greek or a Slav!...all of those sounds rising and falling,"

"Robert!", Kath's voice called up to him.

"Robert", are you almost finished up there? We have a real surprise down here!"

"Probably some guy with a new list of magazines he's trying to pawn off on people!", he thought,

"Be right down, Kath!", he yelled.

Kathy and the young man had moved around to the garden near the side of the house and were talking about superhighway traffic and the vagueness of some road signs when he stepped from the ladder to the ground. He went over to the garage and laid the tools on the bench far inside and came back out to join his wife and the young man. As they turned to face him, he felt himself start a bit. The young fellow could have been his own brother thirty years earlier. Kathy MacKinnon smiled broadly. Having anticipated her husband's reaction.

"If this isn't the damnedest thing!", he said without thinking.

"Doesn't he look just like Don? I can't get over it!", Kathy exclaimed.

"How do you do, sir? I am Robert Curie, a kinsman of yours."

Rob smiled as he extended his hand, feeling a bit awkward, yet grateful for the recognition as a family member.

"Well you sure look the part! My God! This is incredible!"

He took Rob's hand along with a strong sense of the

past. They shook hands

"I can't get over how much he looks like Don!", Kathy exclaimed. "Robert, doesn't he look like Don?" Turning to Rob she said almost in the manner of an interpreter, "Don is Robert's younger brother."

"It's incredible! Absolutely incredible!" He continued to stare while young Currie looked from one of them to the other, trying not to look embarrassed, trying very hard to smile.

"Well!", MacKinnon stammered, then started again, "Let's stop staring and have some coffee or iced tea or something. Come in, for heavens sake!"

"No!" Kathy blurted. "The house is a shambles. Sit here on the veranda, both of you, and I'll bring out some refreshment."

"I don't want to interrupt anything you may be doing", Rob said.

"Don't say that! I needed an excuse to stop work for a while", MacKinnon told him.

"Would you like coffee, iced tea? Could I make you some lemonade?" Kath asked. "I'm afraid we don't keep soft drinks like Coke or Pepsi."

"I'd love a cup of black coffee!", Rob said.

"I'll bet you're hungry after your long trip!" Kathy added. "How about a piece of pie along with your coffee to tide you over 'til dinner time?"

"Have you had any lunch?", MacKinnon asked.

"Oh, yeah! Yes! I stopped along the way at a truck stop

a while ago. I'm fine."

Kathy looked at him as if she didn't believe him. Rob glanced up, smiled and felt himself move his hands awkwardly. "Really! I'm fine!"

"Bring him some pie anyway," Mackinnon said.

"Well, I guess I could always eat a piece of pie," Rob admitted, feeling a bit more like himself; not quite a stranger. After all, these people were relatives; distant and never seen until now, but still relatives all the same. They moved to the porch and sat down a small table between them. They were both silent. Mackinnon looked out across the lawn with its carefully kept flowering shrubs, trees and ablaze with color.

"This place needs a full-time gardener," he said. "I can't keep up with it."

"It looks like you're doing a pretty fair job of it," Rob said in reply. "No joke! This is fantastic!"

"Oh, it's fantastic alright! A fantastic job of covering mistakes and things half-done."

"Well," Rob reasoned, "maybe that's what good gardening is all about!"

Mackinnon turned to look at him, half surprised at the directness of the remark.

"Robbie, young sir, your talents are wasted! You should be in the employ of the State Department, working in some U.S. Embassy behind the Iron Curtain! You're quite a diplomat, do you know that?"

Rob replied easily- "No, Dad says that it's, simply that

I'm more full of shit that a Christmas goose!"

Mackinnon turned and looked directly into the eyes of his young kinsman and saw the amusement there, half hidden behind a kind of almost quaint, "country" or small-town shyness; two brown-green eyes expressing both, a desire for acceptance and a boyish playfulness. MacKinnon paused then burst into laughter.

"I believe that your Dad isn't altogether wrong, Rob Currie, but I'm beginning to think that I like you anyway! Oh by the way, how was your trip out this way, did you have trouble finding us? and how long can you stay? The answers to these questions need not be in that order."

Rob smiled politely and said with a tilt of his head,

"Well, I wasn't planning to stay. I'm going on to Alfred and the College of Ceramics there. What is that, about three or four hours from here?"

"Something like that, I guess but you aren't getting off the place until you've had some dinner with us. Then we'll have to set around and catch up on family things. Hell! That could take 'till four A.M.! You have an appointment with someone there at some special time?"

"Oh no, not really," Rob Explained. "I just wanted to look the place over a bit. I may want to take some coursework there. In any case, I don't want to put you out."

"Well, you already have done that! Why worry about it now? I mean I could still be up there on that roof happily working away, cussing tools and pinched fingernails and roof tar; having a ball, if you hadn't come along when you did! I can hardly control my genuine disappointment."

The screen door opened and Kathy came out with a tray, pushing against the screen with the side of her arm and letting the door spring closed behind her.

"What are you saying about disappointment, Robert?," she asked

MacKinnon fished in his pocket for some matches and took a pipe from the windowsill behind him where he'd left it earlier. He poked around in the bowl of the pipe with a roofing nail he'd produced from somewhere before answering.

"Oh, I was just telling Robbie that a man has to live with a bit of disappointment; that I could have sworn that you had all kinds of money before I married you but found out otherwise much too late"

"Well, old man," she replied going along with him, "that makes two of us then, doesn't it?"

"Sounds as if you both haven't done too badly at covering your losses," Robbie said smiling.

"Well," MacKinnon told him in a matter-of-fact way, "what can you do? You just put a good face on things, that's all."

"Isn't that the truth," Kathy answered, "but," she explained to Rob "I've been so long with this would-be fortune hunter that a decent man would probably scare me off!"

"But I don't frighten you, do I?" Robbie asked her, his eyes dancing?

Kathy started at the directness of this youngster's humor, then laughed.

"No, you don't! I guess that more or less explains your level of decency, doesn't it? In time you'll be as corrupt and incorrigible as this relative of yours, I'm sure!" She put the coffee, lemonade and pie on the small outdoor table with bell-like, tinkling laughter, "Here," she commanded, "Eat your pie," she gave him a little swat on the back of his head. Robbie smiled at his kinsman.

"I told you she was mean," Mackinnon said.

Kathy sat down with them and sipped her lemonade while looking across the lawn. The trellis is in need of paint, she was thinking. Just when the roses look really nice for once. You can't very well cut back the roses at this time just to paint the trellis.

"I've been telling Robbie to stay with us a day or two before going on", Robert said

"Why, certainly!" Kathy agreed "Robbie, you weren't planning on leaving so soon after you just arrived here!"

Well, I really don't think that I could have come at a worse time. You aren't really expecting company in the middle of your busy summer. I have to go on home to Balston Spa and I wanted to stop and check out the Ceramics College on the way."

Bob MacKinnon turned toward Robbie with a questioning look. His eyebrows formed a frown but there was humor in his eyes.

"Do they have phones yet in Balston?"

A half laugh escaped from Rob.

"of Course!"

"Well, very good! I'll bet you might even be able to get through to your folks and tell them that you'd be a day or two late in getting there. As for the College of Ceramics, why I'll bet that that place might still be standing in another day or two."

"I would like to think so," Rob admitted with a grin."

"Very good. It's settled," MacKinnon declared "Now as far as your invasion of our time and space, let me tell you something. Our own kids are grown up and off into their own lives. We're still not awfully used to that. This place has changed from a hub of mindless, youthful chaos to an old folks' home overnight and neither Kathy nor I are all that sure that we want to spend all of our time being old folks! Just make yourself at home and I'll pull out some old family historical stuff for you to mull over or salt away in your mind."

"I'm really grateful but I'd feel better if you'd let me help you with something," Rob said.

"Like what?" MacKinnon asked

"Oh I don't know, but there must be something that needs two backs rather than one," Rob suggested.

"You mean Kathy doesn't have to plow by herself while you're here?", MacKinnon asked

"Something like that, yes." Rob Smiled

"Well, Rob, if it will make you feel any better, I really do have something that I could use help with, come to think of it!" MacKinnon stated.

Robbie ended staying with the MacKinnon's for close to ten days, at which point he had to leave or else lose an opportunity for summer employment back home. In the time that he stayed with Bob and Kathy he had helped take down some old and very heavy farm equipment from a loft in what had once been a horse barn. He had helped draw up rocks from the creek in back of the house for a low garden wall, then helped to lay the wall. He had mowed and trimmed, weeded and painted alongside of Bob and washed the outsides of the windows while Kathy did the insides. Each and every night they talked long into the wee hours. Bob always had maps and books, stories, songs and legends to share, and Robbie's eagerness to learn these things seemed to be matched only by Bob's willingness to share them. However, it wasn't until very close to the end of his stay with them that during evening talk Rob asked about the terrible thing that must have happened so long ago.

"You mean the Clearances," Bob said.

"The what?", Rob asked, obviously interested.

"The Clearances!" When Highland Scots were uprooted from their ancient lands and shipped across the sea." Bob explained.

"Well, I suppose that they needed to have a chance for a new life," Rob said.

"Horse manure! People rarely do that. That's a pile of garbage that they try to shove at us in school! Think about it. What would it take to make you leave America?"

MacKinnon asked.

"Well, a lot of Americans work outside of the country", Rob reminded him.

"Sure," the older man admitted, "They'll work outside of this country and for good pay. Still, they know that they'll be coming back here to live and die. It was different for our ancestors. They had no choice but to leave and they knew that they were saying goodbye forever."

"Yes, but it was still their decision to go," Rob persisted.

"No!" Bob stated with emphasis. "It was *not* their decision! It was *never* their decision! They had to get out. The roofs were burned from off the cottages and the walls were tumbled down to make them leave!"

"You're talking about just after the battle of Culloden, right?" Asked Rob, "When the Stuart cause was put to an end. I mean, when the Jacobite clans were defeated?"

"No! This happened about 80 or 90 years after Culloden!" Mackinnon said.

"But that would have been in the 19th century, the early 1800s. There was no trouble in the highlands at that time, was there?" Rob Asked.

"That was the worst time of all, Robbie! The very worst time of all!"

"I don't understand," Robbie said. I don't know how that could have happened so long after the rebellions."

"Okay," said Mackinnon, "I'll try to explain. Listen, for it is indeed an incredible story."

Bob MacKinnon set the book down on the coffee table

and settled back in his wing chair. He took a box of matches from his cardigan pocket, took a match and struck it, then slowly lit his pipe. He looked off toward a corner of the room as if he were going to read from the wall itself. Rob noticed for the first time how very grey the older man's hair was, in the glow of the match looking all the world like a golden aura around his head. His dark eyes were full of a rather deep sadness and yet a great softness and caring. Robbie listened with respect and gratitude and also with a degree of warmth for his older relative as Bob Mackinnon began to speak:

"Everyone who tries to run down anything regarding the clans comes to read about the Jacobite Rebellions, I suppose. I also suppose that unless they dig a bit deeper they get all of that rolled into one big battle and the great, lost cause: the destruction of the clans under "Bonnie Prince Charlie" at the battle of Culloden.

Actually, Culloden was just a part of the whole thing, for as little a country as Scotland is, and never having had a large population, nothing like England or France, Scotland's history is one of the most complex and difficult to understand as one could ever find. The Jacobite Rebellions were really the first time that some wild highland clansmen ever united for what they saw as a 'National' cause. Most of the wars in the North had been between clans and in the South between powerful families. There was a rebellion in 1688, the Massacre of the Glencoe Mac Donalds in 1692 by Royal troops, the rebellion in 1715 with the great battle at Sheriffmuir; a small, Spanish-supported rebellion in Glenshiel in 1719, some skirmishes in the 1720s in the West Highlands and then finally the landing at Moidart of Prince Charles in 1745. He raised his exiled father's flag at Glenfinnan and the clans started choosing sides. Campbells saw Mac Donalds flocking to the Stuart banner and swore allegience to the House of Hanover for a 5th or 6th time. Mackenzies tried to stay neutral and saw their clansmen trickling away to the cause of the young prince, Mackays couldn't decide at all. In the end there were fewer Highlanders actually committed to the Stuart Government, that is, or neutral. Remember that Scotland's largely lowland Lairds' Parliament had voted to Unite with the English Parliament in 1707 and that meant that the so-called "legal" government was London-based. The amazing thing is that the 1745 rebellion almost succeeded. The Stuart cause had won every battle and had even reached Derby, about 115 miles from London. King George had his gear packed and was ready to embark for the continent.

I'm sure you know the story and how when the clans finally stood to meet the Redcoats at Culloden or 'Drumossie Muir' that they were weakened by lack of food and sleep, scarlet fever and insufficient firepower. It must have been absolutely horrible: men with swords facing grape shot and bayonets, cavalry and cannon. After the battle was even worse. 'Stinking Billy', the Duke of Cumberland set his troops on the defenseless people and the burning, pillage and torture were beyond belief! Well, that is where the story usually ends in most people's minds. There is a shadowy century or near-century of time before our ancestors began flocking to America.

The fact is that no one knew too much about what was going on in Scotland at the time. There was war between France and England in the 1750s and 60s, rebellion in the American colonies in the 1770s and the French had a revolution of their own in 1789. Throughout this time, the Highland kilt had been proscribed by law, clan lands sold, the bagpipe forbidden and even the Gaelic tongue frowned upon. The Lowland Scots convinced the London Government that Highlanders were savages and could be brought into the civilized sphere only by renouncing Catholicism, Scottish Episcopacy and Celtic Christianity. The Church of Scotland, so-called (The Presbyterian Church), found itself as the guiding force in a Scottish Theocracy. But the English discovered at Quebec and the other battles of what we call the "French and Indian Wars" that these wild Highlanders could be useful to them as brave and loyal soldiers, especially if they could wear their kilts and play their war-pipes. So, by the time that Napoleon reared his head and all other heads turned to look at him, the recruitment of Highlanders became a very big thing. The Highlanders were also useful in England's wars in America, for English soldiers were not always over-anxious to kill other Englishmen who had crossed the sea. Scots had no love for Englishmen, whether at home or abroad. Their families were practically hostages and so their 'Loyalty' was on a pretty fair footing. It was probably a fine stab at genocide on the part of England's rulers, as well.

Actually, Scotland had known a certain prosperity. The potato, as in Ireland, had made it possible to feed more mouths while enabling families to sell beef and mutton. The wars had made the raising of beef and wool a very lucrative enterprise. Landlords could collect good-sized rents without squeezing the tenants too much and soldiers sent money home to better furnish the cottages of their families. The population of the Highlands is said to have doubled between 1780 and 1810. Still, there were other things."

Robert MacKinnon paused to reach over to the stand where he had laid his pipe and picked up the tobacco pouch which had been laying beside the heavy glass ashtray which had been holding the pipe. Robbie watched him somewhat absently, still letting the words of MacKinnon take shape in his mind, while his elder kinsman sank the bowl of the pipe into the pouch and began to push tobacco into it with his index finger. Robbie watched for a moment while MacKinnon clamped the stem of his pipe between his teeth and struck a match and then spoke to him:

"In other words you are saying that it was over-crowding which forced the Highlanders to leave", Robbie suggested.

MacKinnon was puffing on his pipe to get it lighted, sending up great clouds of smoke. He held up his hand as a gesture which meant "wait," continued to puff and billow smoke, then fairly satisfied that the pipe would hold its fire, he spoke:

"That was only a part of it and it could have been a blessing to the country in a way, for much of Scotland had never really been developed or even used. No, it was much more than that. Of course, later on, the potato failed them as it had failed their Irish cousins, but even that didn't really do them in, for the Scots had never become as totally dependent upon the potato as had the Irish. Really, I guess it was the failure of the old system and added to that, new ideas which were meant to bring Scotland into what they in London thought of as a great, modern age. For example, in the heyday of the clans, a man held land under a chief because of his ability to bear arms. The chief, on the other hand, held the land in trust for his people. When the clans were defeated, the role of the chief was changed by law. He could not pay men to act as soldiers, but had to list them as tenants. The government agents expected the chief to pay taxes which meant that a chief now had to collect taxes, find a source of money. Also, the chiefs had been required to send their sons south for education. A new breed of 'Landlord' began to spring up in Scotland where once chiefs had been. Their manners, outlooks, tastes and education were English. As a result, a wedge had been driven between clansman and chief. Many of the chiefs were now, themselves, poverty ridden while newcomers became owners of the lands once held for clansfolk. Scotland also was seen as a wild, story-book land, a hunting preserve for a new English upper class. There was no place in this scheme of things for the Highland clansman. The greatest blow came when southern developers and entrepreneurs were brought to the Highlands to tend the flocks of sheep that were fast replacing the people."

Robbie suddenly stood up, feeling anger. He was obviously shaken from some of his old, comfortable ideas about the Highlanders. He threw a hand out and then jerked it up to the back of his head where he roughly ran it through his hair.

"This doesn't make sense!", he said in near anger. "These men were supposed to be brave; fearless in fact! Why didn't they unite and drive the shepherds, sheep, new landlords, spoiled chiefs; whatever and whomever, right out of their country?"

"Hard to figure, isn't it?," Mackinnon agreed.

"Yes! I can't figure it at all!," Rob said. "The Highlander is known throughout the world for his bravery in battle. Back home, they even seem to make more mention of the Highland soldiers at Fort Ticonderoga than they do the Americans; this business about them chopping holes with axes in the French wooden bulwarks while under heavy fire. We also hear and read about them at New Orleans where the beaches ran red with their blood."

"Yes." Mackinnon nodded. "I've read where even the American defenders had tears in their eyes so as to make it hard to take aim, watching line after line of Highlanders fall to their musket and cannon fire."

"Why then," Rob Currie asked, "could they not stand up to being moved from their own homes? It doesn't make sense! My God! What had the British King's soldiers done to them in those years following the uprisings that they were so easily subdued?"

"Oh, they were subdued alright," MacKinnon said as he laid his pipe in the heavy glass ashtray beside him. He bent forward in his chair, forearms on his knees with his hands folded in front of him. "Robbie, what do you know of the "Kirk", the Church of Scotland?".

Robbie's dark brown eyes moved to those of his older kinsman, a question in his expression as if he hadn't heard correctly, or as if he had missed something.

"You mean the Presbyterian Church?"

"The same," nodded MacKinnon.

"Well," Rob ventured, "I know it is the state religion, national church, or whatever you want to call it."

"Alright." You are correct. What most people do not know is it wasn't only the Redcoats who made war on Highland ways as much as it was also the 'Kirk'. Oh, to be sure, the Highland garb and bagpipes were proscribed by law for about forty years, but that wasn't the death knell for the Gaelic or Pictish Scotland. No, not at all. The Church did it."

"You're not serious!", Rob said, somewhat surprised.

"Oh, yes!" MacKinnon went on. "You see, the London government could afford to ease up a bit on the Highlanders once they realized that the Lowland Scots clergymen would take up the 'civilizing' process for them. I don't even know if it was so much a religious difference as it was a cultural one.

You see, the Lowland families are not Gaelic or Pictish for the most part. There is the blood of the Angles, Normans, Northumbrians, Welsh, Danes and Flemings to be found there. The Lowland temperament can be quite different from that of the Highlander. Presbyterianism spread out from the Lowland cities and when it came to the Highland line it was at first rejected, except among some clans, such as the Campbells. The Jacobites, those Highlanders and others who supported the Stuarts, were more apt to be Catholics or Scottish Episcopalians. Then, of course, there were also the wild Western clans which held to the old Culdee scheme of things: the Celtic Christians. They were never Roman Catholic but they saw nothing that suited them in Calvinism either. They were, and are to this day, thought to be half pagan, druidic. In any case, once the Church of Scotland got the upper hand they began preaching against just about everything that the Scottish Gael stood for: bagpipes, fiddles, dancing, bare legs, colored woven cloth and especially the Gaelic language. They told people that what was happening to them was God's retribution for their former sinful, pagan way of life. They pointed out that you would never get ahead in this world or gain entry into the next if you didn't learn and use English rather than Gaelic."

"But," Rob persisted, "The Presbyterian Church is really into Scottish heritage. I remember that there was a big gathering of some kind near Schenectady and that they had a special church service, Presbyterian, and a "Kirking of the Tartans." That's a tradition, isn't it?"

"The older man continued to sit, arms on his knees, hunched forward, looking across the room. Without changing his expression he said simply, "No"

"But," Rob persisted "it seemed to be a thing that everyone took to be very ancient; something that's been going on forever."

"Kirking of the Tartans, Robbie, was begun in Washington D.C. and in this century, by a great chaplain and minister by the name of Marshall."

"Here? In America? Are you sure," Rob asked.

"Positively," Mackinnon said with finality.

Rob moved his hand again to the back of his head in the same, awkward movement that he had performed earlier.

"I am really confused," he said.

"Alright, son. Let's back up a bit," MacKinnon said. "Let me tell you what was told to me. I am a bit older than you by a year or two and I remember the Victorians. You know, the people who were born and spent a good part of their lives, or at least their young married lives, in the 19th century during the reign of Queen Victoria. Many of them were still around when I was your age and I guess that I was pretty lucky, because living as we did in the country and on a farm, we spent evenings talking and stories would be told."

"Oh!," Rob said with a note of discovery, "and these people had been born in Scotland. They were the ones who had been forced to leave."

"No. Not the people who spoke to me. They were

born here. But their parents had been forced to leave, and I suppose that sitting together during winter nights around an oil lamp in the middle of a table they had been told things, just as later, as older people, they told things to members of my generation". MacKinnon sat back and resting his head against the back of his upholstered chair, his eyes looking toward the ceiling of the room. He spoke very softly, as if he were looking into a scene and describing it as if he were looking over a wall, relating what he saw to one who was standing behind him.

"You know, Rob, it was rather wonderful to grow up on a farm without electricity, running water or radios, or television! We would gather around a table in the dining room. Someone might be reading or sketching something. My mother or grandmother might be knitting or darning. Ha! Darning! No one even knows what that means anymore!"

"Darning?", Rob asked.

"Yes. If we got holes in our socks, the women would take yarn, thin yarn, and a needle, and they would kind of weave a patch of sorts with the yarn so that the hole would be filled. We just throw socks away when they wear out nowadays." He thought about something without speaking, shook his head slowly with a light smile on his face, then continued,

"Anyway, the older people told us things about those first ones to come over the sea…"

"Just as they were told by their parents who first took

ship, I suppose," Rob put in.

"Well,… Not exactly…, and that's the strange thing about it." The older man's face took on a thoughtful frown as he moved his eyes to the left. He reached for his pipe and absently tapped it on the heavy glass ashtray.

"No," He went on. "The first ones, those who actually came across the sea, hardly ever spoke of Scotland."

"You know, sir, that is exactly what my grandmother MacKinnon told me and almost word for word! Yet, if that is the way it was, how did their children ever find out what had gone wrong?, Rob asked.

"Well, Robbie, I'm not sure that they ever did find out. Oh, certainly they learned the music, dances, some of the old language"

"The Gaelic!" Rob interrupted.

"Yes. The Gaelic. A beautiful Language. Very Ancient."

"Pardon me," Rob cut in. "but do any of the MacKinnons speak it anymore?"

"Tha Gaidhlig agam," MacKinnon murmured.

"What?"

"Hah Gahleck ahk' um," the older man said slowly.

"Is that Gaelic?", Rob asked.

"Tha (hah), I mean, it is!," Mackinnon said. "I said that I have Gaelic which means I speak it."

"That's fabulous! Fantastic! How did you ever manage to learn it?", Rob asked.

So it began. Robert MacKinnon spoke of his youth among older Scots. Canadians and Scots Americans in tiny towns and isolated farms where English was peppered with Scots Gaelic words and phrases, where men worked together throughout each day and took a dram together in the evening; where the lives of women took measure from bell like laughter and swinging screen doors as hens were chased from the path, strawberries were picked and cleaned, butter was made by paddling out the whey from the yellow mass in large wooden bowls. He told of a world of song; songs sung to make tedium a bit less heavy, songs sung to children and infants, to one another, with one another. Songs were sung in praise and songs were sung in joy.

Young Robbie Currie and the much older Robert MacKinnon would work during the day and talk when they rested and the talk would be taken up at night. Often Mrs. MacKinnon, Kathy, would sit in while she crocheted or worked on a piece of clothing. She would share in the stories and smile at things which she had heard dozens of times before. From time to time she would contribute a story or a bit of information which would get her husband going again. She would smile to herself when, looking over the top of her reading glasses she would watch the young man twist his hair around his index finger as he would be caught in the depth of a story being told; his brown- green eyes would be large and comprehending, his unblemished young face, still a blank page still unwritten upon by the lessons of life turned toward the carpet as he listened. The only movement from him at such a time would be the slow turning of his hair around his finger, almost as if the finger in turning was recording all that he heard, 'writing' it, in his head.

It was not as if he had the MacKinnons to himself for ten days. People would stop by, sometimes for a short visit, other times for the sharing of a meal. Whomever stopped and whether for a brief visit or one of several hours, no one left without having at least a cup of coffee or tea. What impressed Rob about the visitors was that each of them seemed to be quite proficient at some particular undertaking. He also noted that these friends of Robert and Kathy were articulate and well-read despite the fact that there was a great diversity among them as to the length or extent of their formal educations.

One evening a young man stopped by, a fellow, Rob noticed who couldn't have been more than twenty eight or twenty nine years of age. He was a well-built man of about medium height with hair so black that it almost had a blue-like tone to it, and eyes which were very penetrating, also quite blue, yet not in any way cold or distant. In fact, Rob could not help feeling a bit envious of the masculine beauty, yet the kindness, of the man's face. Rob had heard MacKinnon go to the door in response to a soft knocking followed by a turning of the door knob and the door opening about six inches. A voice called, "Hello?", but Rob could not make out the face in the opening. He was surprised to hear MacKinnon greet his visitor with a rush of what had to be Gaelic, and even more surprised that as the young man was steered into the room MacKinnon's hand on his shoulder he heard the older man say "We haven't seen you for a while, Father." MacKinnon then noticed his guest looking toward Robbie with curiosity.

"Martin, this is Robbie Currie, a distant kinsman of ours, and Robbie, this is my very dear young friend and kinsman Martin Craig. Martin lives a bit North of here." MacKinnon then briefly explained what he and Rob had been doing and what a God-send Rob's stay with them had been in regard to what they had been able to do together. Martin laid a book which he had been holding onto the coffee table and seated himself on the large footstool in front of MacKinnon, looking to Robbie and back again to the older man, smiling at the description of crippling work, near disasters and evening conversations.

"Well, Hey!" MacKinnon said suddenly. "I'll put the kettle on. You'll need a cup of tea," then to Rob he said, "Mart won't drink coffee, but he likes our tea."

"Bob and Kathy are among the few people who will still make a proper pot of tea," Martin explained. "You know: loose tea, boiling water in a pre-heated tea pot. The right way!"

"There is no other way, not if you want a real cup of tea", Rob agreed

"Where is Kathy tonight?", Martin Asked.

"Oh, a friend stopped by to take her to a budget meeting for the school. She expected to be home by nine."

"Pretty optimistic!" Martin said, "These budget meetings can turn ugly and go on and on and on."

The two sat in silence for a full minute. Finally Martin

asked Robbie, "How are you related to Bob?"

"Oh! Wow!" Rob brought his hand up to his head and feigned confusion." That's a rough question. Let's just say that Robert's great grandfather and my great, great grandfather were brothers."

Martin nodded without a hint of surprise about him.

"Well then, you are both members of the same Derbhe fine," he said.

"Dairvfeen?" Rob asked. "What is that?"

"It's a Celtic family unit in descent from a common ancestor within five generations."

"You sound like you know a lot about the old Celtic ways too; like Robert, I mean."

Martin smiled and reddened slightly.

"A bit here and there," he said. "Certainly not like your uncle, er he is an uncle, I suppose."

"More of a distant cousin," Rob Replied, "but I'd think of him as an uncle. Of course, he might have his own thoughts on that. He might think that I'm trying to make an old man of him."

"I doubt that, Robbie. He's pretty secure and he knows how really 'young' he is. He really is a very young-minded person, you know?"

"How long have you known him?", Rob asked

"Most of my life, I guess," Martin answered.

"He called you 'Father'. Are you a Catholic Priest?"

"You mean a Roman Catholic Priest?", Martin asked.

"Well, yeah. I suppose so", Rob answered. He wondered

why he had been corrected or whether Martin had qualified the term for some purpose.

"No, I'm not a Roman Priest. Bob calls me 'father' to remind me that I can sometimes be a bit too doctrinaire."

"Doctrinaire.About religion?", Rob asked

"Something like that. I have some growing to do." He smiled.

There was a genuine warmth in Martin's smile. He appeared to Rob to be a man who met the world head-on, unafraid of 'letting down his guard' or of not living up to the tough man image which boys learn to adopt at a very early age.

"Then, I shouldn't call you 'father'?", Rob asked.

"Only if it makes you happy, Rob. But I'd rather you call me 'Mart' or 'Martin.'"

Robert MacKinnon was back. As he entered the room, Martin got up from the foot stool.

"No. Sit where you are, Martin! I'll sit over here," Mackinnon indicated another chair.

"I'll go back and get that tea in a minute or so", MacKinnon said." I have also found a stash of Kath's cookies." Looking to Rob he asked, "How about you, young sir? Coffee?

"I think that I might try a cup of your famous tea."

"Fine!" MacKinnon got up and moved toward the door.

"Let me help you", Rob and Martin said almost in chorus.

"No, Stay where you are. I'm sure that I can handle this

little detail." Robert moved out toward the kitchen and his movements could be heard by the opening and closing of cupboard doors, pouring water and the clinking of cups and saucers.

"He is quite a man." Rob said to Martin.

"Believe me, you have no idea", Martin answered, and the answer was slow and steady, deliberate. "You can learn a lot from Robert Mackinnon. I assume that that is why you are here."

"Well, uh, no. Not really.", Robbie replied, "That is,…. I didn't think so when I arrived. I must admit that I have been learning a lot. Actually, I just thought to stop by for a few hours to learn more about my family background. A few hours! Now I've been here for days!"

"From what Bob was saying, Robbie, I guess that he appreciates the help you've given him. And if he didn't feel that he is meant to share such things with you, he would not have done so."

"What do you mean when you say "meant to share such things" with me?", Robbie asked

"Just a figure of speech", Martin smiled.

"Yes", Rob persisted. "But it sounds as if you mean to say that it is pre-ordained that he do this or that."

"Well? Perhaps everything is pre-ordained."

"What?" asked the voice behind a tray full of clattering and clinking china and spoons. "Are you preaching predestination, Martin?", Robert asked with a hint of teasing in his voice.

Robbie moved to clear a space on the coffee table, picking up a Time Magazine a candy dish and the book which Martin had laid there, placing all of these on another part of the same table. As MacKinnon put the tray down in the cleared area, Rob glanced at the book and noted the title: "The Winged Destiny" by Fiona MacLeod. Turning his head, he came into immediate eye contact with Martin who was sitting forward, forearms on his legs and hands folded together. On his face was an almost minute hint of a smile, aware of Rob's interest in the book's title.

"Well, I've made the tea and worked my fingers to the bone. I'm not going to drink it for you too! Help yourselves. And as I've said, I've even filched some of Kath's cookies for you", MacKinnon said before retrieving his pipe. He sat down and began to fill it from his worn leather pouch.

They engaged in small talk for the most part while they poured out the tea. MacKinnon was happy to see Rob pour the milk into his cup first, and the tea into the milk. "The only right way to do it", he said. The conversation moved to Rob's summer plans and then to where Martin had been, what he had been doing. He had been helping in the restoration of an historical Court House and then a church. It happened that he had some expertise in old style carpentry and cabinetry and had concentrated on re-constructing some very badly damaged wall paneling and wooden turnings in the case of the church steeple. It was not difficult for Rob to form a mental image of this rugged man in jeans and tee-shirt, perched on a beam with a heavy chisel and mallet or sweating profusely while shaping a piece of panel molding or turning a spindle on a lathe.

Kathy came in at about 10:00 PM and had a cup of tea with them and of course the topic turned to the happenings at the budget meeting, the fact that school taxes were going so far out of sight that people would be hard pressed to raise the money and that government mandates were the main cause of such high expenditures. When Kathy explained that she felt totally drained and felt the need for a shower and some sleep, Rob used her leave-taking as an opportunity to make his own retreat. Somehow he sensed that Martin might want to have an opportunity to speak with Mackinnon privately.

"I hope that you won't think me rude, but Robert and I have burned a lot of midnight oil these past few nights.", Rob explained "I'm going to have to beat a retreat to bed, otherwise I'll be useless tomorrow. I hope that I'll see you again, Martin. It's been good to meet you."

"I'm sure that we'll see each other again, Rob. I'm glad to have met you." His gaze was steady and his handshake firm.

Rob couldn't help thinking, "What did he mean when he said that we'll see each other again? The chance is one in a million. Unless, of course, I ever stop back here again," Rob picked up his cup and took it to the kitchen where he rinsed it and left it on the drain-board of the sink. On his way back to the stairway which was just outside the sitting room, he could hear MacKinnon and Martin speaking quietly. He was almost certain that he heard

Martin ask the older man, "You mean that he doesn't know who you are, what your function is?" MacKinnon's reply was inaudible. Robbie quietly moved up the stairs to the guest room. As he lay in bed he could hear a quiet exchange between the two men downstairs and although the words were inaudible he found himself fascinated by the rising and falling of tones. A short time later and he could hear only one voice, MacKinnon's, rising and falling and he imagined the waves of the sea coming and going, caressing the beach, and felt his own breathing and heartbeat to be a part of it all; the soft intonations, the ebb and the flow, the wind in the trees, his own heartbeat and breathing. It was all one. All of these things were together, were the same statement or manifestation of something else; something all-encompassing. He fell asleep, a vision of waves lapping the shoreline of his consciousness.

CHAPTER SEVEN

PART TWO

Rob woke to a sunlit room which smelled of old wood, and tradition; things carefully kept over the years, from the simple wooden chest and the dresser beside it, to the very coverlet on the bed. He may have slept longer had it not been for the persistence of one fly which had not taken the least bit of notice of the half-wakened waving of his hand, not to his turning over and away. In fact even when he had pulled the sheet up over his face, allowing only his nose to meet the air, the sheet being somehow wrapped around it, the dauntless fly landed on his nose and would have liked to explore a nostril. At that point he threw the sheet aside and swung his legs over the edge of the bed.

Kathy was picking up in the sitting room when he went downstairs. She looked up and smiled at him.

"Well, good morning! You certainly must have slept the sleep of the righteous!"

"I know. It must be late. What time is it?" Rob felt a twinge of embarrassment.

"Oh, it's not late. It's about 8:45", Kathy chuckled.

"How could I have slept so long? I went to bed around eleven last night."

"Well, I think that it was closer to midnight, Robbie. You needed your sleep, that's all. You and Bob have been keeping some pretty late hours." She emptied her husband's ashtray, the big heavy glass one, into a waste can, picked up a couple of books which had been laying there and stacked them neatly, one on top of the other, on the small table by the big overstuffed chair.

"Ready for some breakfast?", she asked.

"Oh, I know where everything is. I'll just get some cereal and orange juice", Robbie offered,

"Alright, young man! I'll let you do that. I'll join you for a cup of coffee in a few minutes."

She heard the cupboard doors and the refrigerator open and close, the sounds of breakfast. She found herself thinking absently "I wonder why breakfast sounds different from other meals. The same doors opening, the clatter of bowls or plates and silverware is the same as at any other time of the day, yet breakfast has a different sound somehow, funny. 'Never thought of it before." She finished tidying up, opened the draperies to let more sunlight into the room and walked toward the kitchen.

Rob was standing by the sink as if frozen. His half-finished glass of orange juice in his hand, his gaze out through the double window over the sink; all as if he had suddenly turned into a sculpture, made Kathy start.

"Rob? Is anything wrong?"

Brought out of what could have passed for a catatonic state, trance, whatever it was, he turned toward her, still only half, really focused.

"Uh, no! He stammered, "I just was looking at the back yard: the playhouse, that tree house up there. It seems like there are supposed to be kids out there. You must have watched your kids from this window a lot."

"Oh, yes!", Kathy agreed, "To me, I can almost still see them there sometimes. It all goes by so quickly, you know? Well, of course you don't know! And at your age you hear older people say that, but it really doesn't mean anything to you yet. But yes! Life moves by us quickly. She moved to the stove and turned the fire on under the coffee pot, then put a mug on the table for herself. Rob shook some cereal into his bowl, poured some milk over it and sat down.

"Where are all of your children now?", he asked.

Kathy poured some coffee into her mug and returned the pot to the stove before answering.

"Well, we only had two children, Rob", she said, sitting down. "Christine works for a law firm in Erie. She is married to a fellow who teaches High School 'Phys. Ed'. His name is Stanley Krupchek. He is Roman Catholic. Well, they both are now, aren't they? They have two lovely little girls: Paula and Marya… and just as blonde as blonde can be!"

Kath sipped her coffee and looked sideways out through the window before continuing.

"Our son Alisdair died in the Korean War." She fell silent, eyes still looking through the window. Was she looking toward the tree house? Her eyes grew misty.

"Of course, we still miss him, as much as ever, even after all these years.", she told him.

"Of course", Rob said quietly. "I am so sorry."

"Oh, nothing to be sorry about, Rob!", her voice grew soft, "There's no such thing as death. I know that. I know that when people leave us here and go their way into that great light that they still are with us. Yet, even knowing that and believing it as I do, I confess that I still miss him terribly." Moving her coffee to the table she sat down.

He said: "Well, he's your only son. I guess that I can understand in a way. I've never experienced it, but I think that I can understand it. I've never had a broken arm, but I have a pretty good idea what it would be like… except you're talking about a pain that has no end to it. I think that I can begin, I say 'begin', to understand how awful that could be." He spoke slowly as he moved his spoon in a pattern.

Kathy was looking squarely at him over the rim of her coffee mug. "Yes, Robbie, I believe that maybe you could begin to understand. Not many young people could, but I believe that perhaps you might have that ability. You know, you are very much like him in some ways. Not just your youth and your physical appearance, but your depth of understanding. Alisdair was a very kind, compassionate young man."

Rob felt his face redden a bit. Turning his spoon staring intently at the reflected light, the glow at the spoon's edge, he watched the glow grow larger in unfocused vision, as if daydreaming. He murmured, "Well, thank you, but if what you say is so, it is nothing for which I can take any credit. It isn't as if any compassion I might have is my own accomplishment."

"Of course, you can't, Rob. It's a gift, pure and simple. Even so, it's a gift I feel which you recognize and one which you'll put to good use! Now eat your breakfast, before your cereal turns to mush."

After a few spoons of cereal Rob asked, "Where is Robert this morning? I hope that he isn't out somewhere trying to do something that would normally require the strength of three or four men!"

"Oh, no! Not just now anyway!", she answered, "He took Martin up north a bit. There's a piece of equipment near Glen Hazel that he is interested in, Martin I mean. He's quite a character. Did you get to talk to him for any length of time?"

"I didn't.", Rob admitted. "I made my excuses soon after you took leave of us. After having burned the midnight oil so many times this week, I figured that going to bed at a decent hour wouldn't do me any harm." He paused for a moment, moved a couple of flakes which had beached themselves further up the inside of the bowl with his spoon, then added." I really thought too that Martin had something to take up with the man of the house, and that I'd leave them to it."

"Oh, that's too bad!", Kathy said it in the way that one remarks on having just missed a perfect score on a test or having lost a game by one point.

"Oh? Why do you say that?", Rob asked, surprised.

"Well, I really think that one of the main reasons why Martin has stopped by is to meet you."

"To meet me." Rob said it as a statement rather than a question, although it was an obvious request for clarification. "I'm surprised that he had even heard of me."

It's pretty difficult to keep any secrets among our friends and family. Nor do I mean that we're much given to gossip, for I can honestly say that gossip is not our way. Even so, the word gets around pretty fast." She stopped to watch his progress at his morning meal and said: "Don't you want a piece of toast and some jelly or jam with that cereal?"

"Uh, oh… no. I'm fine."

"Oh, you wouldn't admit it if you did!" Kathy chided, getting up, she opened the bread box and took out two slices of bread from a plastic wrapper, put them into the toaster. "I always used to bake all of our bread.", she said as she reached up to a corner cabinet and brought out a small dish, she then opened the refrigerator from which she took a jar of jam. "It just doesn't make any sense to bake bread anymore when there's just the two of us, but I always made our own bread when the children were home. I do make my own jams and jellies, though. She opened a drawer, took out a spoon and scooped some jam from the jar to the glass dish.

I hope that you like elderberry, for that's what I'm giving you." She put the dish of jam with the spoon in it on the table, then a small plate of butter, a knife and bread plate. Just then, the toaster popped up, presenting the brown toast which she put on the plate. "There! You butter your own toast, and while it's still hot!".

After breakfast. Rob went outside to finish up some work which he and Bob had started the day before. It involved the laying of a low wall of carefully stacked, but un-mortared stone. Rob figured that there was more a feeling of accomplishment in the laying up of the wall, but it occurred to him that it would be more useful to Bob to have a good supply of stone to work with. He hitched the small wagon to the garden tractor and made for the piles of rock at the edge of Bob and Kathy's property, the repository of many years of clearing rock from cultivated fields when the place had been a farm of two hundred acres. It wasn't until he pulled into the back yard with his third load that he met Bob and Martin getting out of Bob's 'four-wheel drive'car. He waved as he pulled the garden tractor alongside the stone which he had previously hauled up and unloaded. Bob walked toward him and Rob shut off the engine.

"What are you doing?", Bob asked him.

"Unloading stone", Robbie said simply, grinning.

"Well, I guess that I could have figured that out! Why didn't you wait for some help?", Bob asked him.

"Oh, it's not hard. Fact is, I enjoy it." Rob started throwing rocks from the trailer to the small pile of stone already on the ground.

"Well", Bob countered, "I'll bet that that one over there gave you something to think about," he said, indicating a rock about four inches thick, probably two feet in length and at least twenty inches wide.

"Yeah. I agreed that that one gave me a little something to think about.", Rob admitted, grinning.

"May I show you something?", Bob asked.

"Sure!", Rob replied.

"Okay!", The older man instructed, "Now don't just kill yourself picking that up. Listen to me and do what I tell you. First, put both hands on that big old widow-maker, like you're going to push it down instead of pick it up." To Rob's quizzical look Bob said evenly, "just do as I tell you!"

Rob did as Bob had instructed.

"Now, Rob, push it with all your might. Push it through the bottom of the trailer! Push it down!! Down! Push 'til you feel your arm muscles tighten right up."

"Okay, Okay! I'm pushing! So??", Rob asked through clenched teeth.

"Now! Right now! pick it up!"

The rock felt to Rob almost to float upward. He moved it, easily, from the trailer to the pile. His eyes were wide as he looked to Bob, then to a smiling Martin who had come across the yard to join them.

"God! I can't believe that! How does that work?"

"Oh, just accept that it works, Robbie," Martin said. Bob and Martin laughed at Robbie's still surprised expression which soon turned to a sheepish smile. Bob clapped his hand on Robbie's shoulder. "Let's go and get some coffee and", turning to Martin, "some tea."

After lunch Kathy announced her intention to drive down to the farm and garden center and told Bob that he might find it a good time to take the garden cultivator in for a tune-up. Robbie volunteered to go along in order to free Bob, but the older man informed him that he wasn't going to waste what little time Rob had left before his leaving them, adding that he had several other errands to run anyway.

"Martin", Kathy suggested, "Why don't you take Robbie up to the old home-place while we're gone? He hasn't seen it yet. It really is like a step back in time." Martin agreed that it might prove of interest and added that it was a good day for a walk, being not overly warm, yet sunny and the leaves and plants still holding their early summer gold-green of full summer. Robbie mentioned something about not being able to refuse after such a description of the prospect and there was a jest or two at Martin's expense, regarding his prosaic descriptions of just about any set of circumstances. He took it all very well and after Kathy gave them a verbal list of all that was available should he and Rob find themselves hungry, she and Bob got into the 'four-wheeler' and, in a cloud of dust, drove off for town.

Rob would look back on his walk across the fields and

through the woodlot to the 'home-place', time and again for the rest of his life. It was much more than a visit to the remains of a family farm. Rob would many times in later years, during the course of a conversation reflecting on his youth and young manhood, liken that short hike in the company of Martin unto a passing into, or through, a crack in time, a new world opening up to him; a spiritual and psychological awakening which would have been unimaginable to him a few days before. He would recall the quiet words, the penetrating eyes and smooth gestures of his companion and guide. Martin seemed to pour out the words and the logic, the explanations and the wonder, of Rob's own deep feelings and convictions; just as if he knew in advance all of Rob's unanswered questions. He would never forget watching Martin's touching the leaf of some plant or running his hand over the smooth form of a stone which he had picked up, as his soft voice spoke of the home-place and the MacKinnons; of the fold who were as members of an extended family, all of whom derived a certain strength and inspiration from the MacKinnons and their land.

"Who are you?" Rob had asked suddenly, and had felt awkward when Martin's face turned toward him with dancing eyes.

"You're a druid.. or a priest!", Rob exclaimed, "You're one of the half-Christian, half-pagan priests that Bob was talking about one night, aren't you? You're a Culdee!",

"Oh, but that's just a word, Robbie. A name.", Martin

said through a smile.

"Am I supposed to know you? Remember you?", feeling a bit embarrassed by his own question.

More important, who are you, Rob Currie?", Martin asked softly.

"You just said it. I'm Rob Currie."

"Ah, and that too is just a name. But who are you?", Martin persisted,... "Or rather, Who <u>are</u> you?"

"You're playing games with me, Mart."

"No. You are the one who is playing games!", Martin persisted. "I have seen you lose yourself in light reflected on the rim of a glass, on the bowl of a teaspoon. So? Why don't you walk into that orb of light someday and find out for yourself?"

Up to this point the two young men had slowed their pace while walking, but at this very direct line of questioning they came to a stop and having come to a section of mostly tumbled rocks from what had once been a stone wall, a part of that ancient barrier still intact for a length of about eight feet, they both seated themselves on the wall, side by side, not immediately resuming their conversation. All around them the fields with their hedge rows appeared to be returning to the wild state, the forests from which they had once been cleared. In fact, as Robbie was noticing, the hills were mainly covered by trees: forest-land, and what fields there were often appeared to resemble square islands in the midst of a sea of trees which seemed to go on forever. The Alleghenies are like that. The forests are always watching, waiting for a time when the fields will be under cover again. It is only a matter of time, after all. Even in places which once had concrete poured for a barn floor, with the help of winds which take a roof, rains which rot the timbers and frost which cracks the hard concrete surface, tiny shoots of grass and the odd sapling part away and break even the hardest material, returning everything to what it had once been. A stone wall seems destined to tumble the rocks back to the land and forests send out their young advance scouts: saplings which will soon grow into large trees. Robbie found himself to be thinking of all of this and broke the silence:

"In one of my courses we were reading Arnold Toynbee's book, "A Study of History", and in his discussion of untamed or hostile environments being a barrier to any 'civilizing attempts', or the attainment of civilization, he mentions the Appalachian region of the New World and how it beat back a people who once had known civilization to the point where they became examples of a superstitious and backward race. In other words, he was saying, or I think he was saying, that the natural environment of the New World was too much for those Europeans."

"More to the point, Robbie, I think that Toynbee was stating that the European had to cease being a product of the "Old World" and take onto himself a new identity with which he could live, create and find contentment, in a different environment which presented its own set of challenges. It seems that those who had not been able to adapt or 'reinvent' themselves in order to fit a new natural environment would sink to savagery", Martin said.

"You mean to 'go native'?", Robbie laughed.

"No, Robbie.", Martin explained. "After all, the Cherokees, Mohawks and such were not 'savages'. They had learned over a period of many generations to sustain themselves in this environment. The 'savage' is one who cannot survive in his natural surroundings because he lacks the skills. The savage is at the mercy of the world surrounding him."

Robbie smiled and then laughed a bit again before saying: "Like some of the Big City people who came up to the Adirondacks! They haven't a clue as to what life outside of "The Big Apple" is like. A simple task such as cutting some firewood, much less that of actually building a campfire, is so much a step back into the horse and buggy days for them, they scarcely know which way to turn. Even a farm is a mystery to them! I remember a lady who was supposed to be a Biology teacher asking me how the farmer managed to get his cows 'way up on a hill. I told her that the cows simply walked up there. She said, "Imagine that! Mountain-climbing cows!" I didn't really have an answer for that, so I just let it pass."

"She did that?" Martin asked with a smile. He shook his head and went on to remark: "Well, there is education and there is education. That lady is probably pretty good at what she does in her academic world. On the other hand, there is an elderly woman not far from here who probably never went beyond eighth grade in a one-room school, but her English is very good, almost poetic. She is well-read and knows just about every medicinal plant that grows in the area. I was talking to her one day, just off the roadway in the edge of the field and suddenly she stopped me short and said, "Oh! Don't back up, dear! That is a yarrow growing just behind your left foot! A wonderful plant, Yarrow! It will break a fever better than anything!" She told me that although we cannot give aspirin to an infant, yarrow tea will break a fever and is perfectly safe. Our local doctor, a pretty decent 'G.P.', has quite a bit of respect for her! Her name fits her too!: "Elsie Pettigrew". Now there is a name befitting a medicine-woman, if ever there was one!"

The two of them smiled and slowly fell silent, basking in the warmth of the late may sunshine on themselves and the land around them: trees, brushy fields and wild plants still coming into the life of impending summer. They felt also the good, quiet warmth of a possible friendship, itself also new but seeming already to be, like all else around them, ready to grow, perhaps even to blossom into something fine and beautiful.

Robbie turned his face towards Martin, absently studying the new friend's profile. Martin did not turn his head towards Robbie, seeming to have made his mind a guest house of the landscape. Still gazing towards some invisible vanishing point in the horizon he spoke:

"What, Robbie?"

"Well, I… I", Robbie stumbled over his words, taken by

surprise. "I was wondering if you are going to answer my question that I asked a while ago."

"Of course, Rob. If that is what you would like," Martin answered, still looking straight ahead.

"Are you a Culdee?", Robbie asked him straightly.

"The world would say that I am, Robbie"

"Well." Rob persisted. "Are you?"

Martin turned his face toward the other man. His eyes now quite serious, he answered.

"Yes Robbie I am a Céilede, a culdee, a Vassal of God. Does that worry you?", Martin asked.

"No, not at all", Rob quietly answered. "And who is Bob Mackinnon?", Rob asked

"Why don't you ask him?" Martin suggested.

"Who do you say that he is?", Rob persisted.

"I? I say that he is a' rememberer,' a keeper, one who sees."

"Okay. But, he is someone rather special, isn't he?", Robbie probed.

"We are all special, Rob. Maybe that is why your cousin, your uncle, is important to many people. Do you understand?"

"Not exactly."

"Well… let's just say that a man is wise until he thinks himself to be wise, at which time he proves himself to be foolish. Robert MacKinnon has a way of showing each of us how special we are. I suppose that we can feel special and highly complimented for a while."

"For a while…", Rob repeated. He waited for Martin's explanation, and on cue Martin answered.

"Until we realize that he has left us with a great responsibility, a commitment.. and that we have a lifetime of work ahead of us. His duty is to get us to do what only each of us can do and to walk in companionship with God. Robert MacKinnon is a Co-Arb."

"Now, what exactly is that.. a Co harb?", Rob asked, puzzled.

"A Co-Arb is a hereditary abbot or religious overseer; a person who is the living representor of an ancient tribal or clan saint", Martin explained.

"But an abbot is the head of a monastery, right? Robert is married, a father of two children, and he lives in an ordinary house."

"This is true. However it is the idea of monasticism which has become narrowed, Rob. We must think of monastic life as something not necessarily attached to what we've come to think of as the monastery: a group of buildings consisting of an oratory, dormitories, the cloister and so forth."

Martin explained that in the ancient Celtic Christian scheme of things a monastery would often be a cluster of small beehive-shaped stone cells wherein one monk or two students might have a place to sleep, to read and pray. There would be a chapel or "oratory" in the midst of such a collection of stone cells, and often a separate building for dining and/ or copying manuscripts, decorating pages and such. He went on to explain that many of the monks were, in fact, married men who would put in some time in "Retreat": work and prayer for a period of time after which they would return to working their own land or go out at the fishing.

Rob looked towards the ground, trying to comprehend this system of life so different from what he had thought monasteries to have been. Frowning in his attempt to understand, he looked towards Martin and asked

"They were 'part-time' monks then?"

"Oh, no!" Martin explained, "They were "full-time" monks right enough! They held to their rule of mediation and prayer wherever they chanced to be. The idea is to construct and maintain an on-going dialogue with the Almighty. The monastery is where a monk or student learns to find "sacred space", but this, once established, he carries with him wherever he goes, whatever he is doing."

Martin looked again towards Robbie and suggested: "We had better resume our walk or we'll be here 'til nightfall! We are pretty close to the old place now. It is not much farther."

Before long, Rob and Martin came to an unpaved section of road which was a driveway, and turning leftward they followed the driveway's two tire tracks divided by a ribbon of wildflowers and grass in its middle, up to where the roadway passed through a tall hedge of various shrubs. There were two stone columns on either side, and a pair of wooden gates pushed back, thus offering the world and a traffic which, by the look of things would have been somewhat rare, ready access to the hedged property. Passing through this gateway Rob found himself on a medium-sized lawn which formed a very slight mound, gently rising to a large wood-framed house. It had probably been built around 1850 and had the wide eaves, sophits and low-pitched roof of what had been a popular style called 'Italianate'. Shrubs and tall flowers obscured its foundation, many of them reaching sufficient height as to half hide the windows of the first floor. The same windows looked out at the surrounding countryside, their shutters fastened back on each side lending them the quality of a wide-eyed curiosity as if they were as interested in each visitor, as might the visitor himself be in the house. Certainly the old house, for all that it could have used a coat of paint and some minor repairs, held none of the sadness or hostility which sensitive people often perceive in houses which have been left behind unattended.

The two young men stopped and stood silently, looking at the large structure. Only a gentle breeze gave any indication of movement and sound. Otherwise, there was about the whole place, lawn, house, its staring windows and wide entryway, a sense of timelessness. Even a red squirrel which had been nervously and jerkily moving about at the base of a large ash tree had suddenly become frozen, staring and silent in keeping with the feeling of everything and everyone around him.

"What a great place!", Rob breathed out in awe, almost

a whisper.

"Ardachy", Martin said, still looking at the house.

"Ardakee?" What's that mean?", asked Rob turning to him.

"Ard-dachaid or Ardachaidh means 'high field' or it could mean 'our home' in the Gaelic. It's the name of the house and the farm."

"Ardahee" Rob repeated. "Nice name! Gentle! Not haughty or arrogant." Turning to Martin he met Martin's smile. "No, really! You know what I mean, don't you?"

"Oh, yes! I do know what you mean. C'mon. I'll show you around inside." His eyes danced with a quiet, friendly amusement.

It was very much like many old American farm houses. The smell of old wood, gentle aging and past wood fires had imparted sweetness to the air within. Here and there, floorboards had begun to turn upwards along their edges. Some of the plastered walls had developed cracks. All in all, the house looked to be well cared for: much of the furniture still in place and even a few things hanging on the walls. The dining room was somehow different: wooden paneled walls, a great fireplace at one end of the room. It possessed an almost baronial quality, yet it was not ostentatious or over-done as so many Victorian homes are found to be. Rob found himself a bit tense, uneasy. A heaviness was in his chest and yet it was not oppressive. Rather, it was akin to a sadness and a joy at the same time. A shiver passed over him. Looking sideways he caught Martin's eyes watching him. He even thought that Martin was about to ask him a question, but the other simply started moving slowly toward the living room and parlor of the house. Suddenly, Martin turned toward him and, as if he had just remembered something, he said to Rob"

"I have to go out and check the cistern and the spring. Why don't you just take a look around on your own? Feel free to explore the house. Robert and Kath would want you to, I'm sure."

"Oh! Well… I don't know, Mart. I'd feel like an intruder or something. It's not that I belong here. I mean… it's someone else's house, y' know?"

"You certainly have as much right to be here as anyone! You're home, Rob.", Martin said smiling. Then, he was gone out into the Kitchen. Rob heard a door open and close.

"Home? I am home here? What's that supposed to mean?"

There was a long, narrow room with empty bookshelves and an old melodeon, that small reed-organ of the 19th century, as its only piece of furniture. The parlor was large, light and airy, with many windows and wooden wainscoting all around it. Rob felt warm and welcome in this room and he noticed the shadows of tree branches playing brightly, breaking the light projected on the floor and the walls adjacent to the windows. It was a truly pleasant room, and despite the very few pieces of old furniture remaining, it could have been comfortable living space for the present generation, as it must have been for those of the past. He stood in the center for a while, turning and looking about him. Again, he suddenly experienced the same feeling which he had known in the dining room. It was by no means an unpleasant sensation, but unsettling all the same. It was as if some old memory lay deep within his being, knocking to get out, to be realized, revived. "Have I been here before?" He felt embarrassed, for he had spoken the words aloud. He hoped that Martin would not have heard him… but of course, Martin had gone out. Turning a brass doorknob he found himself in the front entryway, gazing at a beautiful staircase: probably the one part of the house which might have seemed 'over done', a bit too grand for the rest of the place. The turnings in the black walnut spindles were very well executed indeed, each of them rising to a taper which supported a rich-toned cherry wood railing. This looked as if it had been poured in place. How else, he wondered, would a carpenter or cabinet maker have been able to produce the beautiful curves and flow of the rail with almost invisible joinery?

He had hesitated to explore the upper rooms of the house and had thought to seek out Martin, but his looking up the staircase had revealed some old pictures in heavy ornate frames lining the stairwell and upper walls of the hallway. He began to ascend up the stairway slowly, studying each of the prints along his way. Most of them appeared to be 19th century lithographs: scenes of ruined castles and abbeys. There was an oil painting about halfway between floors, considerably larger in dimensions than the prints: a scene of lake, mountains and a small castle. It was obviously an amateur painter's work, but the composition and control of the medium seemed quite good. He didn't know why, but he felt that the scene was vaguely familiar to him.

At the top of the stairs he saw some large photographs of the type often found at auctions or in antique shops: large, heavy-framed and terribly serious. Suddenly, he caught himself staring in near shock at what appeared to be a photograph of himself in 19th century clothing. "My good God! It's like looking into a mirror!.. well… almost. No way would I be caught dead dressed like that!" Yet he continued to inspect the portrait and, looking into the silvered eyes, he perceived a hint of humor as if the subject was smiling at him. "Jesus!" He stepped back quickly and decided to look at the surrounding upstairs rooms. This he did by opening each door and looking in, not taking much time at all. Yet, before descending the stairs he could not stop himself from stealing another look at the photo of his look-alike.

When he entered the dining room he saw Martin by the fireplace on his knees and peering up the chimney. He spoke to Rob without turning his head and almost as if Rob had never been outside of the room:

"I think that something has built a nest up in here! I'll have to remember to tell Robert not to light a fire until we check it out."

Effortlessly, Martin sprang to his feet, wiped his hands of soot and dust and began slapping the dust from the knees of his jeans.

"Well! What do you think of the old place?"

"It's a great house. I like it… and wouldn't mind having a place like it someday.. but it does give me a strange feeling."

"Strange?" Martin asked. "Strange as in spooky or eerie, you mean?"

"No, nothing like that. I can't describe what I mean."

"Like you've been here before?", Martin asked.

Rob's head jerked around to face Martin as if he'd been caught in the act of theft. Martin's eyes were friendly but serious. Not a muscle in his face betrayed a smile.

"Yeah! How did you know?"

"Oh, just a lucky guess," Mart said with a shrug and a grin.

"Yeah, but it doesn't make sense. I've never been in this part of the country in my life," Rob stated.

"Maybe not in this life anyway," Martin said.

"What?" Rob asked, a bit of surprise in his question.

"Forget it. Hey! We had better start back. Robert and Kath are bound to have been home by now. I have to watch your Uncle like a hawk! He has a tendency to think that he's still 30 years old and he tries to take on too much by himself."

On the way back to join Kath and Robert, both of the two men were obviously deep in thought. Robbie was trying to piece together the different things which had presented themselves to him in the fine old house. He wondered why no one was living in the old place, although he had noticed that Martin seemed to engage himself in different ways which seemed to indicate something of an on-going connectedness with the house.

Martin glanced sidewise towards Robbie from time to time, wondering how all of this had registered with the younger man. In fact, Martin had been, despite his jovial comments and his outward acceptance of Robbie's discoveries and observations, quite unprepared for the inexplicable signs of the young fellow's apparent connectedness with the house. He found himself to be asking within himself: "Yes, who are you? What brought you here?" In any case, Martin had a sense that Robbie would indeed return to this part of his family; that he would somehow and in some way become an important part of who they were.

The two men stopped as if on a pre-arranged schedule and watched three deer trooping from one woodlot to another: one larger deer, still in the darker colored coat of winter, two smaller ones in much lighter hair. The deer stopped, looked towards the two men and slowly resumed their walk into the dense, newly leafing trees.

The two men smiled towards one another and walked on.

CHAPTER 8

PART 2

Kathy was about to put on water for tea and coffee. Robert MacKinnon smiled at Rob and Martin and asked:

"So, how did you like the old home place, Robbie?"

"It's a great house. It's full of charm, warmth and history," Rob answered.

"No ghosts?", MacKinnon asked with a laugh.

Rob was aware of Martin's eyes turned toward him, but as he glanced in the other man's direction, Martin was looking toward the carpet with only a trace of a smile on his face.

"I did have a curious feeling that I had been in the house before", Rob stated candidly. "I must also confess that I was a bit surprised to see a picture of a man in the upper hall who bore a great resemblance to myself."

"That would be the picture of Alan MacKinnon, Robert's grandfather." It was Kathy who spoke as she returned to the living room. She looked at her husband and asked... "and who was he always said to resemble, Robert?"

"Oh… well, the family always claimed him to be the spitting image of his uncle Lachlan. Lachlan would be your great, great grandfather, Robbie. By god, you do look my grandfather, now that I think of it!"

"That accounts for the resemblance, I suppose", Rob said, "but not for the strange feeling that I had seen the house before."

"Well, Robbie," MacKinnon replied, "none of us can know where we've been before… or what 'before' means, for that matter."

"I don't know what you mean," Rob replied

"Well, neither do I. Not really. But let me give you an example."

The older man picked up his pipe, knocked the ashes out of it and Reached for the tobacco pouch on the table by his chair. He began to fill his pipe by pushing it into the pouch on the table by his chair. He went on to strike a match and see the pipe well lit before continuing:

"We went over to Scotland a few years ago, Kathy and myself. We rented a car and had a heck of a time on those single track roads. My sense of direction was just about nil. Finally we got to a place where I just had to stop the car and get out. I told Kathy: 'I've been here. I know this place. There's a small hamlet just down the road and around that bend… and there's a burial ground just beyond that.' Kathy looked at me as if I'd taken leave of my senses."

"Well, I did indeed think that he had taken leave of his

senses!", she said. "He had me worried, I'll admit. But you know, we got back into the car and drove on and found the hamlet or what was left of a hamlet. There were ruined walls of houses… and further on, a burial ground, just as he had said."

Rob looked up at MacKinnon. The older man was puffing on his pipe, his head back against his over-stuffed chair; his eyes fixed on the ceiling, Kathy went on:

"The next day, we went back to the ruined houses and he took me for a walk along a trail, a heather track up the hill or mountain-side. We found a ruined cottage and byre up there too. He sat down by that ruin and he just sat there as quiet as he could be. I wandered off a bit, figuring to leave him alone to think his thoughts. I wandered up by a sheep field and stopped by a cairn. Then I picked some wild flowers. When I went back to where I'd left him I found him in the same spot. Tears were running down his face. I'll tell you, I was really frightened. I held out my hand to him and he took it and we walked back down to the road and the car where we'd left it by the ruins. Later on he told me that he had been overcome with a terrible sadness and an even more terrible anger. He couldn't explain it. Of course, I realize that nothing should surprise me about these Celtic people, having lived with Robert all these years!"

The teakettle whistled in the Kitchen and Kathy rose quickly from her chair.

"Kathy, sit still", Martin said. "Let me fix the tea and coffee."

"I have a better idea", Mackinnon said. "Mart, turn off the heat under that kettle and bring us some glasses. We'll have a dram."

"Not for me, Martin!", Kathy said. "Bring a sherry glass for me."

Martin shuffled out of the room, grinning.

The older man sat back looking at the ceiling, reached up and removed his glasses and rubbed his eyes. Carefully putting his eye glasses on the table he began to speak.

"Who knows what we are, what time is… or if it even exists? A thought that came into my mind when we were in Scotland was that someone, a long time ago carried the germ of my being in his or her body along those same paths, inside those ruins when they were homes. Fires were tended, children played on the floor, dogs barked, chickens scratched and pecked in the yard outside each house. Everything material in this world has been recycled so many times! Think of it: the atoms which make up the cells of our bodies have been a part of this planet since it became a planet! Now, if this is so, who knows about what happens to Spirit; human, plant or animal?"

"Are you talking about reincarnation?" Rob asked.

Martin re-entered, setting down three whiskey glasses and a sherry glass. Pouring the sherry, he handed the delicate wine glass and handed it to Kathy. He then half-filled the short, heavy dram glasses. He handed one to MacKinnon, one to Rob and picked up one for himself.

"Slaínte!" said MacKinnon as he raised his glass and

leaned forward. All four glasses met.

"Sláinte", said the others. They all sipped their drinks.

"Well, Robbie", MacKinnon finally continued, "to answer your question truthfully I would have to say that I am not sure. From everything that I've been able to gather, I understand that about 60% to 70% of the people of the world believe in some kind of life after life in the 'reincarnation' sense. Our own Celtic ancestors believed in the 'transmigration of souls' and from what I know of modern Highlanders, Irishmen and Welshmen, whether they are Catholic or Protestant, they tend to keep their options open on the subject."

"So, are you saying that perhaps I once lived in Ardachy in another life?", Rob asked.

"Is that what I'm saying? I don't know. It's possible… but first we have to have a better understanding of what is meant by the word 'life' or incarnation."

Looking at Martin, MacKinnon said to the dark haired quiet young man:

"C'mon, Mart. You're letting me do all the work here! Help me out on this!"

Martin set his glass down, rubbed his chin and seemed not to hear, yet he began to speak directly to Robbie.

"I can't speak for Robert. I can't speak for anyone, nor would I try to tell you what you must think or believe. Yet, let's think about some possibilities. Number one: yes, it's possible that you were here in another 'life' or incarnation. You may have been Alan or Lachlan MacKinnon, or a daughter, a son, a hired man who worked on the place. Number two: perhaps you are Alan or Lachlan MacKinnon in the sense that a part of you can return to being a part of either of them. Number three: maybe, just maybe, the spirit of a being is more tied up with the physical nature of that same being than has ever been realized. Perhaps we cannot separate the genetic memory from spirit memory as easily as we had thought. Even so, I have a very strong feeling that it all goes far beyond those three possibilities. What is most important is that we do 'leave our options open', as Robert says; that we do not 'paint ourselves into any corners'. For my own part, I cannot understand why people are so quick to close their minds to potential truths in light of the frequency of feelings, sensations or perceptions such as you experienced earlier today,"

"But, many people would question your assumption that there is such a thing as a spirit", Rob countered.

"Yes. Our technological upbringing has made greater savages of us than were our ancestors when they painted their bodies and ran naked into battle. We are savages in that we've lost control of our ability to live with our environment, our neighbors and ourselves. We are afraid to dream, we're afraid to die, we're afraid to go on living. We are dependent upon support systems which are beyond our individual abilities and comprehension, and that total 'nakedness', that vulnerability, make us the greatest of all savages:… because we are naked and refuse to admit it, because we are terrified of everything: sickness, fire, accidents, storms, physical death; everything!

As for 'spirit', whatever that is, or is not, think of this: four sons grow up in the same house under the same conditions with the same parents. They all have physical bodies and brains. We should be able to assume that all would be quite similar, but that is never the case. One becomes a 'workaholic', one becomes a mediocre but happy man, one is bone lazy and one is a born schemer, con-man and 'loser'. One of them may be a rocket scientist and one of his brothers a 'crazy' artist. There is something being carried by each of those guys which is beyond red blood cells, brain cells, and so forth."

"You couldn't say that this is, of itself, 'spirit' could you?", Rob asked.

"Oh, No! Not by a long shot! But it gives us a pretty good clue that each of these sons carry something which is not dependent on heredity or even environment, for that matter. There is some kind of 'inner direction' as opposed to tradition-direction or direction inspired by peers. This inner direction, 'drive', or whatever, gives some indication that there is an individual within the individual. Something very deeply his own, is feeding him with goals or ideas quite apart from the other members of his family. But again: this is only an indication that something is going on".

"And you are of the opinion that some of this is carried in us from another lifetime or incarnation?", Rob persisted.

"My opinion does not matter", Martin replied. "It would be silly to discount the possibility. We seem to carry hopes and fears from somewhere: hopes and fears which cannot be explained as a result of the experiences of this life alone. If life is something akin to a learning experience, a 'schooling', then it makes no sense to believe that we lose all of what we've learned the minute that we cease to breathe or when our hearts cease to beat."

The conversation went on for quite a while: about spirit, the impossibility of death in any final sense, about there being spirit in all things. At about nine-fifteen the phone rang in the study. Kathy rose to answer it and Martin went toward the kitchen mentioning that he would put water on for tea and coffee. Kathy picked up the telephone and could be heard to laugh and talk to someone about weather and then as her voice grew louder it was obvious that she was moving toward the living room door carrying the phone, its long cord behind her:

"Oh, no! You needn't apologize! No, really. It isn't late for us at all! Do you wish to speak to Rob? Well…, yes… he's right here."

Kathy held out the receiver toward Rob. He stood up and moved into the study following the cord back to the desk.

"Hello?"

"Robbie! I was beginning to worry about you!"

"Oh, hi mom! Why're you worried? I just called a couple of days ago!"

"Rob, you don't know those people well enough to impose on them in this way! Really! I sometimes wonder if you even think of how others may feel… and you still have to stop at Alfred and after that drive all the way here."

"Mom, it's okay! I've been helping out here and learning all about the family. Robert and Kathy are great and they regard me as family."

"Well, I'm sure that it's very interesting, although I don't know why you want to dig up all that clan stuff! Anyway what about your summer job?", she asked.

"It doesn't start for another ten days. I'll be there in plenty of time", he explained.

"Has it occurred to you that we may want to spend some time with you? There was coldness in her tone.

"Of course… but I'll be there all summer, mom!", He answered.

"As if that makes any difference! Oh by the way a young woman or a girl, has called for you twice. She said that her name is Lynn or Gwenn or something like that.", his mother reported.

"Her name is Gwynn", Rob advised her.

"Oh. Well… I can't help wondering what kind of girl she must be to be calling a boy's home like that", his mother remarked.

"She's a very nice girl, mother."

"When are you coming home?", She persisted.

"I'll probably leave the day after tomorrow. I've postponed my tour of the Ceramics College.", Rob said confidently.

"Rob!! That seems so irresponsible! Well…, we'll see

you in a few days. Here's your Dad,"

"Hi, Rob! How 's it going?"

"Great, Dad. I have a lot to tell you when I see you. I've learned a lot about Mom's family and about the Curries too! Did you know that they were a family of Bards and physicians?"

Rob's conversation with his father was so much more relaxed. He was glad to be hearing his voice and the tones of interest and understanding. His father ended by saying that he felt that he, Rob, knew what he was doing and that he looked forward to seeing him.

"Take it slow, Rob. We'll see you when you get here." In the background Rob's mother's voice could be heard: "Oh great! You set a wonderful example, Jim."

They were having coffee in the living room when Rob rejoined them and Kathy was shaking so much with laughter that she almost spilled the contents of her cup. Martin was grinning, shaking his head from side to side and MacKinnon was finishing a story:

"So the whole truckload of pigs that he'd bought, and the two goats as well, all got out and ran up the hill into the woods. Every now and then they descend on someone's back yard in the dead of night knocking over garbage cans and creating general havoc. Mrs. Spence wants the game warden to go up there and hunt them out.. but he says that he's damned if he's going to shoot any of Fred's pigs! That young police officer said that he saw the goats up in the old sugar house on Fletcher Prentice's place, but that he couldn't get anywhere near them."

"Fred's lost a lot of animals to that woods over the years", Martin ventured.

"Why I wouldn't doubt that, thanks to Fred, a person might find the long awaited Peaceable Kingdom on Earth up there!", Robert laughed.

"You're awful! Both of you… picking on poor Fred this way!", Kath said.

"Oh?" MacKinnon asked, "Well, that isn't stopping you from laughing, Kath! Neither one of us is holding his side and almost spilling his drink from laughing so hard!"

The three of them, still wearing broad smiles, looked up at Rob.

"Did I miss something?"

"Just people laughing at a man's misfortune," Kathy volunteered.

MacKinnon sat forward and indicated the tray with coffee and cookies. "Help yourself, young man. Fix it the way you like it."

As Rob poured out a cup of coffee for himself, MacKinnon asked:

"Your folks think that we're keeping you too long, Rob?

"Well, no but my mom thinks that I am staying too long and wearing out my welcome, I think.", Robbie ventured.

"You're doing no such thing!" Kathy quickly assured him.

"Thanks. I've really enjoyed being here. Still and all, I think that I should leave the day after tomorrow. I thought that maybe I could help Martin clean the main chimney at Ardachy before I go", Rob said.

"Oh! That's what I wanted to tell you, Robert." Martin said slapping his head. "Something has built a nest in the Dining Room fireplace chimney."

"Well, we have plenty of time before winter, Mart" MacKinnon assured him.

"Let me help with that before I leave", Rob put in. "You told me that I was, or seemed to be, 'at home' up there, Martin." And turning to Robert and Kathy he added, "Whatever that is supposed to mean. No one from my side of the family has ever been to Pennsylvania as far as I know."

"Not so, Rob. Not so!" MacKinnon told him.

"Oh? You mean that some of my family visited the Pennsylvania MacKinnons before me?"

"That is a story which needs to be told, Rob. Surely, you know! I thought that the main reason for your visit was to see the place built by your great, great grandfather! That isn't it?"

"I'm confused," Rob answered with a puzzled frown. "Your great grandfather, Andrew, built Ardachy. not my great great grandfather."

"Oh, no! Here: let me put it straight for you." Robert said. "sometime in the 1840s, I think it was, Lachlan and Ian Mackinnon came down into this area and bought a sizeable piece of land. They had about four or five hundred acres between them, which was just about two thirds forest at the time. It was a goodly parcel of land for those days.

Apparently old Morag MacKinnon helped them financially in the beginning. Their brother in Law, a fellow by the name of Jagger… I think he was called John Jagger, their sister Catriona's husband, was a Pennsylvania man. Morag wasn't happy about Lachlan and Ian leaving the Balston area, but she knew that their chances would be better elsewhere. Lachlan and Ian got into the logging and lumber business and did pretty well. Lachlan wanted to do something with the land, so in addition to the lumber business he built a pretty decent farming operation and he built Ardachy from the best timber around.

As it turned out, Lachlan's wife finally got her way. Síne or 'Jeanie' Morgan, her name was, she never wanted to come here. One day after her boys got to a certain age, she took them back to Balston. Her family had a lot of money and she missed the social life. Ian went west, then back to Balston as an old man. 'Went back there to die, they say. I guess that the heart went right out of Lachlan after Jeanie left him. He was a piper and a Gaelic poet, did you know that? They say that he never played his pipes after that nor did he ever write another poem. Sine was a Presbyterian of the old type. She saw sin in his music, his language and his poetry. He went back to Balston and later was killed years later by a runaway team after his own boys were married and she packed up his kilt and plaid and sent them to my great grandfather. 'Heathenish things', she called them. The reason why she sent them to Andrew, my great grandfather, was because he had taken over Ardachy. Lachlan saw to it that she never got a penny. At the same time, he had established a trust fund for his boys with Andrew. My grandmother, Laura Renfrew MacKinnon, always said that it wasn't the accident that killed Lachlan; that he died of a broken heart. People said that he was a fine, handsome man, very straight in the way that he carried himself. 'Uncle Lachie' they called him."

Robert MacKinnon was staring at the ceiling, his head back against the easy chair and he appeared to be lost in thought or somewhere back in his youth hearing the older folk recounting the stories of the family, Robbie broke the silence.

"Are any of Lachlan's poems around today?", he asked.

"Well, I doubt that there was much appreciation for Gaelic poetry in those days. No I think that they've been lost."

"Your Aunt Elizabeth said that someone had cut some of them up for dress patterns, for they were written several to a sheet on large pieces of paper", Kathy said to her husband.

"Oh, it wouldn't surprise me", Robert muttered, "God, but there are some ignorant people in the world! Aunt Lizzie was no mental giant, by any means!"

Robbie didn't know what to say. It all seemed so sad. A gifted and beautiful man had poured out his heart into a home and music and poetry and had lost all of his life's work. He saw, out of the corner of his eye, Martin sitting with his hands clasped between his knees simply staring at the carpet. One hand suddenly moved slowly up to his face and he wiped his eyes with his fingers.

"He lost it all, didn't he?" Rob asked.

"Why, no.", MacKinnon answered. "He left it for others. The house, the feeling.. and, well, you're here, aren't you? Why, I'll bet that a person would even start writing Gaelic poetry if he hung around for any length of time! No, Rob. I don't think that anything was lost; not the poetry or music, not the place and certainly not Lachlan himself. He's around here somewhere."

"Speaking of which…", Kathy put in, "I got those pictures out of the chest in the spare room. You were going to look at them sometime before Robbie leaves. He might want to see them."

"Kathy", her husband grimaced, "Young lads don't want to look at old pictures! Seeing all of those ancestors will probably scare him off forever! He'll go and join the French Foreign Legion, where they'll take a man 'no questions asked', no prying into one's background."

"Oh, I don't think that Rob would feel like that", Kathy persisted.

"I really would like to look at some of them, Rob agreed."

"How about you, Mart? MacKinnon asked. Are you game for this too?"

"I think so. I still have a lot of catching up to do. I'm sure that I've already seen a lot of them, but I'm just as sure that there are many more which I haven't seen", Martin said.

"Well, let's move into the dining room and we can

spread these out on the table. The you can tell us all what each of them are or who they are."

The four of them brought chairs together on one side of the table, seating Robert at the center of the tableside, Kathy to his right and the young men on his left. Martin insisted that Rob sit next to MacKinnon. Two thick albums and a small cardboard box were set down on the cleared table. MacKinnon set the box to one side and opened one of the albums. He then turned the page and stopped at the first large photo: a seated woman and a man standing at her side.

"That's my father and my mother. This was taken during their wedding trip to Niagara Falls." Turning the pages he indicated other family members, close relatives and friends of other generations.

"Well!", MacKinnon said. "I'd forgotten this one! This is an old one! 'Probably should be in that other album. Look here, boys. This is a group picture of the six of them: Helen, Flora, Lachlan, Andrew, Ian and Catriona."

"They appear to be in their 30's or 40's, Mart observed.

"Yes. Probably taken at a reunion somewhere? Yep! Here it is: the photographer's mark: Stuart, Balston Spa, N.Y." Robert continued to stare at the photograph. "Well, they're a tough looking bunch, aren't they?"

In the second album there was a photograph of a very old lady with a late-middle-aged woman standing beside her. The elderly lady had on a white head-covering and her right hand rested on a cane before her.

"There's the old Matriarch, the old tyrant herself!

This is our common ancestress, gentlemen: Morag MacKinnon. She lived to be close to a hundred years of age! This was taken about 1890, I expect." Turning a few pages they came to a small silvered photograph of a man in the uniform of the Army of the Republic: Ian MacKinnon. The pose was stiff, the eyes defiant. It was really rather comical; almost Napoleonic.

Robert turned pages, named the images of people long gone on: merchants and their stylish wives, army officers, little girls in white dresses and sashes, their curling hair either tied back or cascading over their shoulders.

The cardboard box was more a collection of photographs in embossed matts or tintypes, each of these carefully wrapped in tissue paper. There was no order to this collection. All generations were represented. There were several photographs, still in frames, of World War II soldiers, officers, a navy pilot, a young woman in a WAC uniform. MacKinnon identified them one by one. He came upon a picture of a young man in uniform, hatless and smiling, leaning against a jeep. Robert and Kathy said nothing, but both of them as well as Martin looked at the photograph without saying a word. Rob glanced at the three of them expecting to hear a name or some identification given. There were tears in the eyes of Robert and Kathy.

"He really… hem… was a fine-looking lad", Robert said with a break in his voice. Kathy's hand went up to her face, covering her mouth.

"Did you ever remember him, Martin?", Robert asked.

"No. I've seen pictures. In fact, mom has one fairly similar to this one. I wish that I had had a chance to know him."

"This is Martin's Dad... our son Alisdair", Robert said to Robbie.

"He went off to Korea in 1951 and we lost him."

Robbie started in surprise. He looked from Kathy to Martin, then to Robert. "Then, you mean... Martin is your grandson?

"Why, yes... of course", Kathy said.

"I didn't realize. I... thought that he was just a close friend!"

"He *is* a close friend!" MacKinnon said. "He's also our grandson! I thought you knew."

"No... I guess that it got by me... and the fact that he calls you 'Robert' and 'Kathy', Rather than grandpa and grandma, or whatever. I missed the connection altogether!"

"Why,... I was sure that I'd identified Mart as our grandson." Robert said absently, as if half speaking to himself.

"We had always been very close to Martin", Kathy added, "and our friendship and our casual attitude toward Mart, and his to Robert and me, has always been more or less taken for granted."

MacKinnon sat back in his chair, leaving the photograph of Alisdair in the center and on top of several others.

He frowned slightly, reaching back in time as he began to speak:

"Alisdair went off to the Korean War.. 'Police Action', they called it…, shortly after he and Charlotte were married. Well, it wasn't immediately after they were married, because Mart here was probably close to two and a half years old when his father was called up, and closer to three when he was shipped out. Anyway, Alisdair came home to us in a box not long afterward. Mart's mother held it all in. She just didn't speak, she didn't eat. We were really worried about her. One night she and little Marty were here she began to help Kathy pick up after dinner. She went to get the mop from the kitchen closet, and the next thing we knew she was sitting by the closet door, right on the floor… crying and sobbing and she had Alisdair's red and black check hunting shirt in her two fists and just beating it against her own chest. She just kept sobbing and crying 'Damn you!', over and over. I guess that the sight of his hunting shirt hanging there in that closet just set her off. I guess that it was what she needed, though. Not too long after that she came by for Sunday dinner and told us that she was going to work in Bradford and that she and Mart would be leaving the following Saturday. It was pretty tough on us, but Kathy and I both knew that it was pretty hard for her too. Even this house had too much of Alisdair in it, and here was this girl at what should have been the beginning of her adult life, already a widow with a boy to raise!"

"So, you see, we didn't see much of Martin or his mother after that", Kathy put in. "Then, when Mart was nine or ten, Charlotte remarried… and he certainly is a wonderful man.

He took to Marty from the start and we couldn't ask for a better human being to be stepfather to our grandson!"

"He really is a fine man", Martin confirmed.

"…And, you know?… Well, this is the kind of man that he is,…" MacKinnon added, "When he went to legally adopt Mart and give him his name, he came to see us… and wanted to assure us that he did not want to separate the boy from his father's folks, but that he did want to have Mart carry his name, 'Craig'. Yes Danny Craig is a thoughtful, good man. It meant a lot to us that he would consider our feelings in that way."

The MacKinnons and Martin, taking turns in the long explanation, seemed to be using the moment for the purpose of divesting themselves of all the things which they had wanted to share for years. Rob learned that Martin had not spent too much of his childhood away from his paternal grandparents; that his mother and step-father saw to it that he spent some of his summer holidays at this place. He had had a horse when in his 'teens and used to ride 'hell-bent for leather' through the pastures surrounding Ardachy.

Apparently, it had been Alisdair and Charlotte who had been the last to live in the 'home place'. It is there that they had intended to raise 'Marty' and whatever children they might have had. Charlotte loved Ardachy and as Alisdair was handy with tools and also in possession of good sense where carpentry is concerned, they did a lot towards renovation and repair. After Alisdair had gone to Korea and had been killed, Charlotte could not bear to live in the house. In any case, Martin held the connectedness with the place and it was expected that he might one day take over the house and land himself.

It was a perfect way to end his stay with the MacKinnon relatives. That last night, Rob realized, brought so much together: things, people and events which had served to give proof to an inextricable bond: a powerful reminder of generational and familial things; traits and personalities which demonstrate a remarkable continuum, a rich culture and an ever-present meaning.

"So", Robbie thought, "We have simply found our place in all of it! I have to return to this place, to these people!"

Rob took leave of Bob and Kathy MacKinnon, but only after a promise to stop by on his return to Ohio in the Autumn. Kathy had packed him a lunch as well as having filled a small box with cookies. Bob had insisted on Rob's taking five books on loan. MacKinnon had jokingly told his young kinsman that the loaned books would act as a guarantee that there would be a reunion at the end of the summer. Rob had assured him that he need have no worry in that regard. In fact, during this brief conversation something had come up quite unexpectedly which Rob would remember for the rest of his life. This is the way that it happened:

They were gathering Rob's things in the front hallway at the foot of the stairs and feeling the customary awkwardness of such leave takings. We say our goodbyes many, many times in the course of a human life, yet we never seem to learn how to span the very few minutes of such an occurrence without a sinking feeling of loss, some embarrassment or a sense of a lack of our own decorum.

"I will definitely stop by on my way back to Athens," Rob had said." We have so much left to talk about, that is,… if you feel like putting up with more of my questions!"

"Well, Rob", Kathy informed him, "Bob and I feel that there is a reason for our being brought together. Perhaps we may have to wait a few years to discover that reason, but it is somewhere." Mackinnon had smiled and nodded in agreement.

"I'm afraid that you'll have a hard time getting rid of me now. I want to stay in touch with this part of my family, now that we have met.", Robbie assured them.

MacKinnon's eyes had opened wide, a look of surprise and something remembered transforming his fade.

"Nise bho na thacair sin!", MacKinnon exclaimed. "That's it!"

"What?", Now it had been Rob's surprise.

"Nise bho na thacair sin! Now that we have met! Yes!"

MacKinnon explained that it was a Gaelic poem written by a John Macrae in the 1700s. A song, really. He sang the chorus:

"Tha tighinn fodham, fodham, fodham.

Tha tighinn fodham, fodham, fodham.

Tha tighinn fodham agus fodham.

Tha tighinn fodham, eirigh…"

He had laughed a short laugh then, clapping Rob on the shoulder.

"Yes you'll be coming back alright!"

With freshly laundered clothes, Bob's books, Kathy's cookies and some plants for his parent's garden, Rob had seen reflected in the rearview mirror the two gray-haired people waving until he rounded the bend in the driveway; until the curtain of now heavy green foliage obscured their forms. He thought with a slight embarrassment that he must almost have looted their place.

CHAPTER 9

PART 2

Driving Northwards up Route 155 towards Port Allegany, Rob was deeply impressed by the natural beauty all around him. This particular road winds through a part of Pennsylvania's Elk State Forest. Back at Emporium, when Rob had stopped to 'gas-up', he had been told that it is a very beautiful drive and that one could expect to see deer, even elk and the occasional bear. The lady at the register in the store had told him: "It's also great rattlesnake country, so if you get out to walk around, just be careful to watch the ground! They're most apt to be where there's rocks where they can shade up!" She shuddered and went on: "Ooh! I hate snakes! My husband and our boys hunt sometimes up there. Not me! I won't go where there are snakes!"

"Snakes or not," Rob thought as he drove along, "It is an incredibly beautiful land!"

It suddenly occurred to him that he was, once again,

totally alone: no one to share the ride, mess with the radio or talk to him. His mind conjured up an image or Paul and Rob wondered how his former passenger had made out for the rest of his trip. He found himself also remembering how this one guy, in such a fairly short period of time, had brought out so many conflicting emotions. There had been some grudging compassion, not just a little anger, plenty of judgment, but also some real liking for his crumpled rider. "What a nut-job!" In an instant, a voice in his mind begged the question: "Nut-job? Who? You or him?" Rob smiled at this mind-game but answered back: "Both of us, I guess!"

He had initially planned to stay in New York's Southern Tier for a couple of days, but when he reached Alfred, he found a quiet, neat little village which was almost devoid of human beings. The academic year had ended and all but a very small number of graduate students had left for the summer. He had been directed to Binns-Merrill Hall, where the College of Ceramics was located. This place too looked to be quite deserted. Signs of cleaning up and clearing out were to be seen everywhere. In the kiln room the great brick kilns stood cold, empty with blackened mouths open to reveal the emptiness within. Kiln carts stood empty, scattered here and there. He saw piles of broken ceramic test tiles and discarded clay pots, waiting to be shoveled up and trucked away.

Rob glanced up to a railed corridor on the second floor: a balcony of sorts overlooking the Kiln Room. Two men in work clothes were having a cigarette break, talking and leaning on the top steel tail. He decided to find the stairwell and go up to talk to them. He located the stairs, walked up to a landing and then onto another few steps, here he found himself looking straight down the balcony area. He walked up to the two men.

"Hi!", he said. "How're you doin'?"

"Not bad", the man nearest to him answered, "How about yourself?"

"Good!" Rob answered.

The second man, a small, wiry guy, spoke:

"Okay. Now what did you forget or need keys to? You must be another person who left something or who has something locked up somewhere."

"Uh, no", Rob said, "I'm not a student here. I just stopped by to check this place out. I may want to come here in future."

The man right before Rob, a taller man with humor in his eyes and a great jutting chin said to him: "Well, hop right to it! All of the main areas are open and unlocked. All but the offices, that is!"

"You mean I can just look around this whole building?", Rob asked.

"Sure! Why not?", The smaller man said, "You might find the odd graduate student at work, but you won't bother anyone."

"Thanks a lot!", Rob said and started to tour the College of Ceramics.

Later, he decided that he had managed to have a fairly

good look at the facilities and a sufficient quantity of works in progress or left behind by graduating students and underclassmen to allow him to form an opinion of the College. It all had seemed fairly impressive in his mind.

Robbie had decided to head on towards his home and family in Balston Spa rather than to stay overnight in Alfred. He figured that if the driving became too tiresome, he would stop at some motel and continue on the following day. It was already midafternoon, after all and another six or seven hours driving to his home even without stopping for dinner.

He got in his car, took another look at the road-map (probably the fourth time that he had done so since morning) and headed towards Corning. He realized that by the time he reached that city, the famous glass center there would be either closing or closed for the day. Another of his planned visits would have to be put on hold.

Driving on through hills covered with forests, along the river now and then, he thought again of the beauty of the land. Steep hillside fields were to be seen, dotted with grazing animals, hip-roofed barns with their silos and nearby wooden farm houses, some of which appeared to be quite old. When he came to the Village of Bath he was impressed by the neatness of the town. Two really outstanding churches pointed heaven-ward with their steeples: one of them a well built, stone Episcopal church with the usual red doors; the other a strong, fortress-like Presbyterian church with an almost Germanic steeple with small facets and gables.

"The Kirk!", he said aloud. "The Kirrick o' Scotlan'!" He chuckled to himself. Each denomination had brought the old countries with them! The English Anglicans (later to be styled 'Episcopalians' after the Revolution) always seemed to construct houses of worship as if they were in an English county. The Presbyterians built strong, no-nonsense 'statements': "Ye'll preach nae mass in ma lug!!" (you'll preach no Mass in my ear!) He found himself thinking of his own mother and father. His mother had had exposure to the "Old Way", the Celtic Christian faith, while his father's folk had followed the Presbyterian traditions of his own forebears. Yet, it was his father who was more easy-going, less doctrinaire. His mother thought the 'Celtic' path to be too "Airie-Faerie", too much in keeping with the old nature spirits and ways of the clans-folk. It was Sheila MacKinnon Currie who would have been closest to the teachings and scorn of John Knox. Jim Currie would have been recognized as a "back-slider", one not strong in the tenets of the Kirk. Rob had always felt closer to his father's approach to belief. Suddenly it occurred to Rob and he spoke aloud to the car and himself: "Wow! Dad is a closet Celtic Christian! How about that? He doesn't even know it himself!"

Rob decided to drive on through Corning and the Elmira area, following Rte. 17 to Binghamton, from where he could take Rte 7 North to Schenectady. He did manage to get as far as Horseheads, between Corning and Elmira, before he felt the need for something to eat. There, at

Horseheads, he stopped when he saw a diner. He wanted to have a quick bite to eat and a cup of coffee and be back on the road towards home.

Inside the diner he went to the counter and took a stool rather than to sit in a booth, figuring that it would perhaps take less time to be served.

A motherly sort of woman was behind the counter and asked him: "Would you like a menu?"

"Uh, no. Thanks", he responded.. "I just want a cheeseburger with fries and a cup of coffee please."

The lady wrote his order on her pad, tore the order sheet from the pad and laid it on a window sort of opening behind which was the kitchen. Pouring coffee into a mug and setting it before him, she said: "It will be coming right along, hon! Anything else?"

"No, thank you", he answered.

"Let me guess!" she said." I'll bet that you are a student on your way home for summer break!"

"How did you know? Does it 'show'??", he smiled.

"Well, yes it does, hon'. Your good manners and looks are what 'show'. Of course, I've seen some pretty rude College kids too! Some of them are real jerks! Your folks can be proud of you, and I mean it.", she said.

"Wow!" Rob blushed a bit "Well, thank you!"

The lady went to the register to accept payment from some customers, took a few orders to some tables, "rang up" another customer, and then provided Rob with a paper table mat and some flatware, immediately following these with his order.

When he had finished his meal, he left a tip under the edge of his plate and went to pay his bill. Pleasantries were exchanged again and the lady told him to drive carefully and to not even think of having so much as a beer. She assured him: "They'll nail you for sure, hon'!" He knew that by "they" she was referring to local police.

"Thanks", he said. "You take care."

He decided to top off the gasoline in his tank while in Horseheads, and it was there and at that time that he discovered that Paul had left something in the car when he left him and was off to try his luck at hitch-hiking on Rte. 6. Rob had just come out of the service station and he opened the passenger side door to open the glove compartment. There, on the floor, partially under the seat, he noticed a flat, blue canvas case or packet. It was the kind of case such as one might use for the keeping of notes or documents, perhaps even a journal or writing kit.

"Oh, great!", he said aloud. "Now, what do I do with this?"

Around the booklet-like case there was a wide, strong rubber-band. Rob thought briefly about taking off the rubber-band and opening the case. He considered that looking into someone else's personal property is a bit unethical. Yet, perhaps inside there might be some address, some indication as to how this lost property might be returned to its rightful owner.

Opening it, he found that there were some notes or

writings, two badly soiled letters in envelopes, a couple of small photographs and a ball-point pen. There were also some official looking forms of some kind as well. In a side pocket of the kit he found what appeared to be Paul's birth certificate with a letter of recommendation from some teacher or school official.

He couldn't help feeling like a sneak, looking over someone's personal property, but he thought that he might at least find an address or some clue as to where the forgotten case might be sent. Nothing! No address card, no name, nothing of help.

He started the car, leaving the case on the seat next to him. He pulled onto Route 17 and saw the sign for Route 13 to Ithaca, on and up toward the Elmira turnoffs. As he drove along, it suddenly came back to him that Paul had said something about going to his grandmother's. It also registered in his mind that one of the letters had a woman's return address in the upper left-hand corner. He drove on until he found a place where the road had a very wide gravel shoulder, but didn't like the fact that he was moving upward on a hill. He crested the hill, found that there was still plenty of shoulder, so he flipped his right turn signal and pulled well off of the highway and stopped the car. With the engine still running, he reached beside him and picked up the canvas case. Opening the case, he took out the letter with the lady's return address: Mrs. Carol King, R.F.D. #1, Tully, N.Y. Again, feeling as if he had suddenly been left in charge of another's very personal matters, he opened the envelope and pulled out the letter. He turned to the last of three pages of neat hand-writing and read the letter's ending: "Paul you know that you'll always be welcome here, so stop by when you can for as long as you like. Love, 'Gramma.'"

Ron paused, reading the sentence over twice more, "Yep! This must be 'Gramma,'" he said aloud. "Maybe Gramma has a phone. I'm sure as hell not going to drive up to Tully on my way home, wherever 'Tully' might be."

Nor did he drive on up to Tully not right away, anyway. He did, however, stop at a diner and telephoned an information operator, and he asked if there was a listing for a Mrs. Carol King in the Tully area. He was told that there was, then he was given a telephone number which he jotted down on a corner margin of the road map which he had taken in to the diner with him. He got himself a 'coke', putting off the call as long as he could. He even decided to see if the list of towns on the reverse side of the map might indicate a geographical connection; a place actually on the map. True enough, there was such a place and it was a bit south of Syracuse. "Oh, hell! Here goes nothing!" He rounded up his change and was pleasantly surprised to find that he had a pretty fair amount of money in the way of quarters, nickels and dimes. He hated to ask anyone for "change for a dollar for the telephone." No cashier ever seemed overjoyed at parting with their register's coinage.

Using the number which he had received from "information", he dialed the home of the woman whom he hoped might be the grandmother of his recent passenger.

The phone rang several times and he was about to hang up the receiver when he heard a response at the other end: a woman answered, seemingly out of breath from having rushed to the phone from some distance.

"Is this Mrs. King?", he heard himself ask, feeling himself to be sounding stupid, child-like.

The voice replied, "yes?" (an implied question in the response)

Rob asked if she were the grandmother of a young fellow called Paul King and received another "yes?", this one more of an interrogative than the first.

"There isn't anything wrong, is there?" she asked.

"Oh, no! Not at all, Ma'am. My name is Rob Currie. Paul travelled with me from Ohio into Pennsylvania and I realized some time later that he had left some of his things in my car. I'd like to get them to him some way. He had mentioned that he might be going to your place... and ... I thought that I might find him there."

"Oh. Well, that is very kind of you, I'm sure. No, I haven't heard from Paul, but isn't this the strangest thing! You know, I was out in my garden and suddenly I got to thinking about him. I wondered if I shouldn't put a pie in the oven or make up a stew of some kind. I simply had the strangest feeling that he would be coming to see me! Oh, wouldn't that be wonderful! Paul is really a very special person once you get past that wall that he's built up around himself! Well, would you be coming up this way?"

"I am headed up toward Albany, then to my home

in Balston." He found himself putting, as if it were, a questioning form to the name of his town."

"Up North of Albany", Mrs. King stated as fact.

"Yes, that's right!"

"Well, Tully isn't far from Route 20. Route 20 goes directly to Albany. We're about 10 miles at most from Route 20."

Rob was back behind the wheel of his car, having back tracked to Route 13 and was heading North toward Route 11 and Tully. "I must be out of my mind! How did I get suckered into this? It will make me about God knows how late getting home! I will probably find myself in some hill-billy shack surrounded by hunting dogs and toothless relatives of this Paul character! Sheess! What an honest-to-God jerk I am! I'll get there and these documents of his will probably not amount to a damn!" He turned on the radio, laid his arm on the sill of the door and drummed his hand in time to the music.

He finally found Tully. It was typical of small towns in Upstate New York: There was much that was drab, much that echoed a quiet beauty. He found himself wondering again as to how people had found their way to such and such a place, what had made them stop there, build there, settle there. Why not another place farther west, or north or south; why in such and such a place? The countryside was, he admitted to himself, quite beautiful. He pulled into a gas station to ask directions to the King place. A man behind the short counter was talking to another man. Both were in oily work clothes. The one behind the counter wore a baseball cap which had borne witness to many an oil change and lube job.

Rob waited patiently for the men to finish their business, his eyes taking in the air-fresheners, candy bars, potato chips, coke machine and such. There was the usual garage calendar on the wall: a picture of a seductive woman with her swimsuit, the swimsuit on a sheet of clear plastic which of course could be raised to see the woman totally without clothes. While he stood there, he felt the grip of a hand on his shoulder. He jerked around to see the smiling face of Paul King.

"Damn! I knew it, College boy! Ever since I cleaned up and got pretty you just can't stay away from me! What in the Corn-bread hell are you doing here?"

Smiling broadly in spite of himself Rob replied "Looking for you, you forgetful, stupid no-brainer!"

"See! What did I tell you? You can't go on without me!", Paul smirked

"You wish!" Rob parried. "Look I'm glad that I didn't have to chase you any further. Did you know that you left some of your stuff in my car? Some papers, documents, or whatever?"

"Oh shit!! I need that stuff! But how…?"

"Look! I saw your grandmother's letter to where she signed "gramma" and I remember you telling me that you might go there… to her place. Anyway, I telephoned her. I got her number from information.", Rob explained.

"Great! Damn!... You're a regular detective, aren't you? So… you talked to her, my grandmother?", Paul asked, obviously surprised.

"Yes. She says that she is expecting you. 'Sounds like she's started cooking up a storm for your return from the jungle!"

"Yeah! That's her to a Tee. You can never surprise that old girl. She always seems to know when I'm coming to see her! Anyway", he paused and looked toward Rob's car, "So c'mon with me and meet the best person in my family! Probably in the world!", Paul said.

"Oh, hey! Maybe some other time. I've really got to make tracks for home!", Rob explained.

"So? You'll only be an hour or two later than expected! It's no big deal.", Paul suggested.

"Really, I can't. I have to move on."

Yet somehow Rob gave in. He couldn't have explained it. Of all of the family, he was always reckoned to be the most stubborn. His refusal to alter a course of action was legendary among the Curries, yet here he was: driving the extra miles to accommodate this guy for whom he had entertained a near loathing not long before. He drove onto a back road listening to Paul and looking at the different things that Paul would point out to him. Paul was actually quite animated now; a far cry from the sullen shabby passenger he had first appeared to be.

Rob was somewhat surprised on seeing the place where Paul told him to turn in: a neat little white Greek Revival farmhouse with a wide, deep front lawn and well-kept foundation shrubbery. A small, many-windowed addition on the side of the house had been carefully planned and executed so as to enhance, rather than detract from, the architectural purity of the original building. The drive-way extended beyond the house toward some out-buildings: a large barn and milk house, a carriage shed, and what appeared to be a stone spring house. It was of picture post-card quality: nostalgic, simple, and very well kept-up.

As Rob pulled the car up into a siding at the back of the house, an older woman appeared in the back doorway: smiling, waving with one hand and wiping her eyes with an apron corner. She came forward and waited for Paul to exit the car, whereupon she hugged him, laughing and saying over and over, "for Heaven's Sake!" She then swiped him across the back of the head with one hand.

"You scamp! I've worried and wondered about you! I knew that you'd come along and all, but I've wondered all the same." Then pushing him away she looked him up and down.

"Those clothes will walk to the creek themselves for want of water!" Turning to Rob she asked "And who is this fine-looking young fellow?"

Paul made the introductions.

"Oh you're the man who called me on the phone a while ago! Well, isn't this nice? You must be a very kind person, I must say." She was a bright, blue eyed woman with white hair, her glasses resting on a small nose. She looked at her grandson, then at Rob, back and forth twice or three times then said: by the time that the two of you wash up, I'll have something on the table for you to eat. You must be starved." Again, Rob's protest and expression of urgency was vetoed. Mrs. King told him that Balston couldn't be more than three hours away, that he'd get home well before dark, that he'd do better to have a decent meal (implying that restaurant food, although fit for consumption, could never sustain human life), and that she wasn't about to waste what had been prepared. She was not prepared, however, to debate the matter.

Paul took Rob up a narrow stairway into a hallway carpeted with hand hooked and braided rugs, tastefully decorated with off-white walls and an earthy-red woodwork, then into a bed-room which was not large but very comfortable and neat in appearance, the far ceiling of which slanted downward under the roof. Age, dignity, and pride was the very hallmark here.

"This used to be my dad's room. It's mine now whenever I want it. I've always liked this room", Paul was explaining. He turned to see Rob looking at the books in a group of built-in shelves.

"Yeah." Paul said. "we can read."

"Have you read these books?" Rob asked with unconcealed respect.

"I've read quite a few of them. Why?"

"I'm impressed!"

"Well, most of them belonged to my dad, some he gave

me, some I got here and there. Do you have to use the bathroom? I'm going to take a quick shower."

Rob sat down in a chair with a book relating to the Lewis and Clark expedition, thinking: "books. Well, well, well! You can't tell a book by its cover, after all." He looked up toward the shelves again and several titles took him by surprise: "Waverly", "The Life of Rob Roy", "The Scottish Gaël" in two volumes. He replaced "Lewis and Clark" and took out "The Life of Rob Roy". As he was reading it, Paul came back into the bedroom, glistening with water, his hair wet, and wearing a towel.

"Did you find something of interest?"

"Yeah. Rob Roy," Paul murmured.

"No Kidding! We're somehow related to him. The Kings are MacGregors… you know: clan Mac Gregor… Scotland." Paul was rubbing his hair with his towel as he spoke, unconcerned as to his nudity. He opened a drawer, pulled out some underwear, and socks, closed it and took a striped cotton shirt and a pair of jeans from another. All of these he threw on the bed. Robbie had glanced in his direction and felt an instant pang of envy. Paul really had a good build. In fact, he seemed to have the look of a real athlete. He realized that Paul had seen his glancing, for he instinctively turned away to pull on his undershorts. Robbie felt himself redden with embarrassment.

"Go ahead and wash up, Rob."

"Oh, now I'm 'Rob'! What happened to 'College boy'?"

"Dunnoe! Maybe its' because we are sharing an

intimate moment!"

"To hell with you, you closet queen!", Rob bantered as he got up to move toward the door and the bathroom.

"Don't ever call me that!" The voice was low, steady and threatening. "Never!"

"Hey, Paul! No offense. Why are you so up-tight?" Rob felt confused, somehow wounded.

"Yeah, okay. I'm sorry. I guess that I over-react to some things. Sorry. Honest!

Rob washed his hands and face and went back to find Paul dressed and looking like a new person. On their way down the stairs, Paul paused and asked:

"Still friends?"

"Yes, but… try to lighten up a bit, ok?"

Mrs. King had cooked for the two young men as if they had been making hay all day. It was only about 4:300 PM but she served them a great stew, scones, rice pudding blackberry pie and had complained that young men no longer knew how to eat enough. When Robbie commented on the Scottish books in the house, she said that the family actually had two buttons of silver which were once worn by Rob Roy Mac Gregor. She also told him that her father-in-law had known quite a bit of the family history and that he had been a bagpiper. She also said that Alan King had always maintained that the sur-name 'King' had been used by many Mac Gregors from the time when people of that clan were forbidden by law to use the name ' Mac Gregor'. Robbie found Mrs. King to be very well-read and quite articulate. That she cared a great deal for her grandson was there for all to see. She didn't hide it.

"Paul has always been very special. I don't think that I ever, in all my life, knew a child who was more giving, more concerned for others than he was. Of course, I may be prejudicial, I admit."

Robbie glanced at Paul and saw him shrug his shoulders and without looking up he said "Boy, I sure got her fooled! Right Rob?"

Rob mentioned his having been to see a relative in Pennsylvania to find out more about the MacKinnon ancestors. He was surprised to find that Mrs. King knew a few things about some fairly obscure points of Scottish history.

"Your own name, your father's people were a pretty important family in their own right", she told him. "You know, the Curries were called Mac Mhurrich (Mac Vuric or Moc Wuric) in the old language. The chief of that clan was always the clan Bard for the Clan Ranald MacDonalds."

"Really?" He wanted to know how she knew that, for he had never heard any mention of such a thing, but he held himself in check. After all, Mrs. King simply put the information forward with such ease and with such conviction that her word could scarcely be questioned.

"I don't know how she remembers all of this stuff.", Paul said.

"I remember it because my mind isn't taken up with television and all of that kind of nonsense!". She grew thoughtful for a moment, then went on: "My husband William, Paul's grandfather, had a long illness before he died. I used to spend quite a bit of time reading to him. For one reason or another we both became interested in exploring the contents of a few of these many books which he and his father, Alan King, had acquired or inherited. Ever since he passed on, I find myself still exploring, still reading. It's silly, I suppose, but it's almost as if he is still here when I read them. He was a wonderful man. Paul is quite like him in many ways."

The meal finally ended, Rob took leave of the Kings but not without a bag of mincemeat cookies and some scones which Mrs. King had insisted that he take with him.

"You be sure and come back sometime, Robbie." she said, "We'd like to see you. We can talk some more about Scotch things and I'll rummage around and see what I can find. I'm going to try to talk Paul into staying through the summer to help on the place."

"Thanks for everything, Rob", Paul said. "I'm sorry if I acted like a real pain in the ass sometimes."

"I guess that we all do that, Paul. Take care of yourself and this wonderful lady here."

The next thing he knew, he was heading east on Route 20, trying to sort out all that had happened in such a short period of time.

CHAPTER 10

PART 2

Rob reached his home at about eleven thirty. The family had been watching television and about to retire when he drove in. His mother acted somewhat coolly toward him, but was happy to have him home. They wanted to know all that had taken place, all about the MacKinnons, and they were surprised that he had detoured to meet Mrs. King.

"It all fits!" He was saying. "All of it! It is exactly as if everything that happened on this trip was meant to happen."

Jim Currie spoke up, "Oh, no! Now Robbie, you're not going to accept the belief in predestination, I hope." He was smiling, playing 'Devil's Advocate'.

"God! I hope not! Even so, it was amazing: the truck-driver talking about Clan Fraser, the Piper on the Television, this guy who looked like the worst down n' outer imaginable turning out to be part of this Mac Gregor thing and even hearing about the Curries from his Grandmother!

How do you explain something like that?"

"I wouldn't even begin to try", his father said. "Yet, like a new word one learns: you may never have heard it before, but as soon as you learn it, it keeps cropping up all around you! The information you heard on this trip was always around you, but now you have a focus. You're really hearing it for the first time."

"Yeah, maybe. Still and all, it's pretty strange! And this Robert MacKinnon! I learned more from him in a few days than I've learned in a whole semester at Athens."

"Well, perhaps we should send tuition money to Robert MacKinnon", his father said.

"So, do you think that you'll ever see these people again?", his mother asked, not without a bit of anxiety which Rob was able to detect.

"Most definitely! I want to see all of them! There's so much that I don't know!", he said eagerly.

"Well, Robbie", his mother warned, "that is certainly true, but your priority has to be working toward you degree. I'm just afraid that my father and mother have put you on a wild goose chase! This family or clan stuff or whatever it is, will be a great hobby for you in later years, but you're a young man, a college student! All of that clan stuff happened in the past. We're not living in the 1700's or the 1800's!"

"Well, wait a minute, Sheila", his dad put in. "Maybe he's cut out to be a history major! We don't know. There's certainly nothing wrong with that!"

"I don't suppose that there is anything wrong with that", Sheila Currie sniffed "and I don't suppose that there's anything wrong in finishing what a person sets out to do before casting in every direction for new paths to follow."

Rob could sense that things were about to get out of hand. He had learned at a fairly early age to divert the conversation or else suffer the consequences of his mother's displeasure, her sense of being outvoted, the absolute surety that her opinions were being disregarded, considered to be of no value in the eyes of the males in her household. This mild paranoia on her part should inevitably lead to her having a severe headache and a quiet chill would settle on the house which could last for days.

"Hey! Whoa! Stop! Everyone stop!!" Rob exclaimed, "I'm not changing my major! I am following a path! A am not too young to have a hobby in addition to my other studies and everything will turn out fine. I promise!"

"Well, I think that I should call my mother and tell her what I think!" Sheila said as a parting salvo.

"I really wish that you wouldn't.", Rob said, "I would be terribly embarrassed if you did that, mom." He then rose and turned to the door. "I guess I better get the rest of my stuff out of the car."

As he carried two bags up the stairs he was aware of his mother and father sitting very quietly. His father had finished saying something in hushed tones. His mother sat there stony-eyed, her mouth in a thin line.

"How the hell has he been able to put up with her all of

these years?", Rob asked himself. "When in God's name has she ever been happy about anything? I sure as hell don't remember!"

Later, he had a cup of coffee with them, during which time, he told them of some funny happenings on campus. His mother brightened up and even laughed. Rob could sense his father's gratitude.

"Well tomorrow is a big day", Rob said. "I'll go over to the feed mill and ask when they want me to start."

"I don't know why you want me to work there instead of architectural drawing for Howie Kemp", his mother said.

"Because", Rob explained, "I am young and vain and need to keep my muscles toned up. I'd get fat and lazy at a drafting board!"

"Oh, you!" His mother laughed. "You will never be fat and lazy!"

"Leave 'em laughing", he thought. "At least she's laughing."

"So I'm off to bed!" He bent over and kissed his mother, hugged his dad and went up the stairs.

After he had stripped down to his undershorts and slipped between the sheets. He was certain that he would fall right off to sleep. He didn't. Instead he lay on his back in the darkened room with his eyes looking up toward the ceiling all the time, watching the events of the last week and a half roll through his mind. Oddly enough, his thoughts kept bringing back the images of the Greek Revival farm house at Tully, the white haired, bird-like lady whose eyes sparkled behind her crystal-like glasses as she spoke and laughed; of the transformed young man in a towel, of the intensity and humor in his eyes. When he saw again the nude form turned from him, his hand went to his own chest and abdomen. "Why can't I be built like that?" He found himself to be surprised that the Kings occupied so much of his mind. There had been some wood carvings. I'll have to ask Paul about them. Ha! I'll probably never see him again!"

He slept later than he had intended. He had hoped to be up and over to the feed mill by at least 9:00 AM. It was already 10:15 and that meant that he would not get there much before 11:30. A fine way to start a summer's job, he thought. Of course he would be 'checking in' as it were, for he wasn't really to start the job until Monday and this was Wednesday. It isn't as if I told anyone that I'd be checking in today. Perhaps it might be better to simply take a day to unpack and wander around. Yes. Tomorrow would do as well…, still enough time in advance to show interest in the job.

He looked out of the window. Raining again. "We sure have been getting our share of rain these past few days!" he thought, "Alfred was one ducking in and out of the rain after another. Tully looked like it was about sodden. "Sodden". Great word. I wonder if anyone uses the term, word, adjective. Anymore. Too much in the way of old books. I'm already out of touch with the "real world". Oops! There's another one: "Real World"… a term used by disgruntled bored College Kids from the big city who feel that they're trapped in a small town. "Can't wait to get back to the 'Real World.'" Right! And do what? Hang out in the neighborhood? Watch the pimps and the hookers? Get mugged? Play catch in the street? 'The Real World'!"

On Thursday, Rob went to the feed mill in fact he went in about 8:30 and talked with the owner-manager, Buck Watson, a man known by Rob's family, his own people having been in the area from long before even the MacKinnons and Curries had settled there. He was a thick-set, not overly tall man with close-cropped reddish-grey hair, large glasses resting on a red nose that came out of a face that could have been roughly sculpted of red rock. What neck he had, for there wasn't much neck in evidence, was like old leather, deeply lined with creases which extended up to the base of his skull. His eyes were large slits which turned up, not down, at the corners and their greenish focus seemed always to weigh every word which a person might be saying. He would fix his eyes on the face of the speaker, pause a fraction of time to make certain that all had been tallied up in his mind, then nod his head… but never would there be more than one, quick nod. He was a representative of that old American stock which wanted things to be put forth clearly, briefly and above all else, honestly. Honesty was a desperate creed of his, he being known to back-track with his truck for twenty five miles if he had found himself to have over-charged someone even as much as fifty cents on a four hundred dollar order. He would neither over-pay an employee, nor would he underpay. He believed in the letter of the law and the printed word, whether in the Bible, the Law of the Land, or the Department of Agriculture Guidelines. Satire or wit would not only be wasted on him, it would also be most unwelcome. A thoroughly good and decent human being to be sure, and Rob was already wondering how in Heaven's name he would be able to last out the summer working for this fine, honest and totally uninspiring man.

"We open up at eight AM; not seven-thirty, not eight-thirty, but eight o'clock", Buck was saying. "Now that means that we have to get here by seven… well, 'seven' most days! Sometimes we have to get some grinding and mixing done, 'er load some trucks, and we might have to get around some and be here around six." Buck paused. "Can you handle that? I'm as much for young folks havin' a good time as the next fella, but if a young fella wants to rip and rare around all night and sleep 'till all hours, this is not the job for him. 'Way I see it, you was always a pretty decent kid, got good folks n' all, 'n the way I figure it, you're the man for a man's job. Now if you don't let me down, I sure as anything won't let you down! How's that?"

"Sounds pretty fair to me", Rob said, smiling.

"That's as fair as I can make it! So! That's that then! We'll see you Monday morning." Buck paused for a minute as if deep in thought, then said, "Right now I've got another situation that needs some thinking on. A friend of mine, Johnny Silvernail needs to get a horse trailer clear over to Cazenovia… about two and a half hours west of here. 'Trouble is, he promised a fella' that he'd get it over there by tomorrow evening so that he could use it bright and early Saturday morning. Besides that… as if that isn't enough; it's got to be back here over to Johnny's by Sunday night. Johnny's tied up. I thought that he could help out, but Stan Sicora got hurt yesterday and has his arm in a cast. Stan's the one I was goin' to send out for Johnny. The fella who's returnin' the horse trailer is willing to pay $100 for the driver to take it out there, wait over until Saturday night or Sunday morning. They need the trailer all day Saturday, y'see. Horse people! More money than sense, some of them!"

"Well, I could drive it out there, if you trust my driving. I could use the extra money", Rob ventured.

"Oh, I don't know", Buck mused, "I figured you'd rather get settled in, have a couple of days to get caught up before starting work. Besides your mom probably plans a big dinner on Sunday for you… 'kind of home coming celebration an' all."

"I could be back by mid-afternoon, couldn't I?", Rob asked.

"Yeah but Sunday's the Lord's day. I don't like to ask a man to work on a Sunday."

"Well", Rob countered, "What was Stan going to do?"

"Oh, Stan!", Buck chuckled. "The church roof would fall in if he went to church! He's s'posed to be Catholic."

"Well", Rob said, "Tell you what. I'll run it by my folks and get back to you within an hour or two. I already visited my grandparents yesterday… They'd be on hand for Sunday dinner, and I'm sure that they'd not feel offended if I came home in mid-afternoon of Sunday. But to be on the safe side, I'll run it by my mother and get back to you."

"That would be a load off my mind, I admit" Buck said. "Still and all, I don't want you to feel that it's something you have to do. I admit that I don't feel that it's something you have to do. I admit that I do feel a little bit guilty even considering you doing it."

"Well, I wouldn't mind at all! Like I said, I'll get back to you in an hour or two", Rob promised.

Rob had already known what his mother's reaction would be. The complaint and objection began with, "Oh, Robbie!" and then went into a litany of reasons beginning with a Saturday evening together, Sunday breakfast, Church (especially church! The "What am I supposed to tell people?… Everyone knows you're home from college and even wondered why you weren't there last week!…), Sunday afternoon Dinner with the family, everyone going over to Grandma and Grandpa's,…etc., etc. From there it went into the 'kind' of job it was when it could have been a nine-to-five draftsman's job. Rob wished that he'd not mentioned it until the following morning. Now it would be a "cold shoulder from mom to all concerned", evening.

"Well, grandma' won't mind", Rob suggested, "if I don't spend the whole afternoon over there. I'll give her a call. Anyway, Mr. Watson looks to be a fair-minded boss and I'd like to help him out."

"Help him out!" Sheila Currie snapped, ""He could go into any tavern and find himself a dozen men who would drive a pick-up and horse trailer to Cazenovia!"

"Probably he could, mom. But he trusts *me*! I'm going to do it!"

His mother didn't respond. She had been folding laundry and the 'snapping' of pillowcases and towels as she snapped and folded intensified to the point where Rob was sure that the articles would be separated from their hems. Every injury or questioning of her opinion, real or imagined, had to be neatly folded, saved.

Rob called his grandmother MacKinnon and explained the situation.

"Well, why don't we simply plan to have Sunday dinner at six o'clock then?", his grandmother suggested. "It will give me more time anyway." She paused then added, "I'm sure that your mother isn't entirely in agreement!"

"Oh, well… you know her better than I do, Gram."

"Indeed I do!", she agreed, "Well, if she never has any problems any greater than this, she'll do well indeed! Anyway, your mother cares for you very much, son. You must remember that."

Rob called Buck Watson and told him that he'd be able to take the horse trailer to Cazenovia, Watson was clearly overjoyed.

"That's a load off my mind!", he said with more enthusiasm than his usual composure would allow. You know, I hate to go back on my word, especially to Johnny.

He's got me out of more than one bind. You are a God-send pure and simple!"

He told Rob that he'd have the pickup and trailer all hitched up and ready to go, with a full tank of gas, and that it would beside the feed store first thing in the morning. He added that he would give him some travelling money since it would mean his having to stay over at a motel for a night or two.

"You just stop in here and I'll give you the keys and some money. I won't forget this favor!", Buck assured him.

Later, Rob was thinking about what he would do in Cazenovia for a day and a half and he took out the Road map. "Yep, right on Route 20! No problem." He started to fold the map up when the phone number which he had written in the margin of the map caught his eye. He thought "why not?" and called Mrs. King.

Mrs. King answered with her usual questioning sound "Hello?"

"Mrs. King, this is Rob Currie. I was at your place a few days ago…"

"Oh, yes! How are you, Rob?"

After some polite exchanges he asked if Paul were in the house. She said that he was out under the hood of her car, but that she would call out to him. There was a pause.He heard her voice calling out in the background, some sounds of walking, then Paul's voice.

"What do you want?", Paul asked flippantly.

"What do you mean 'whaddya want'?" Is that any way

to answer the phone?"

"Normally, I'd be polite, but I knew who it was."

"Well, thanks," Rob went on to tell him that he would be driving a pickup and horse trailer to Cazenovia the following day and that he would have some time to kill. He was about to ask him if they could meet for a few hours when Paul interrupted.

"Cazenovia? No kidding! I'm going to be in Cazenovia tomorrow afternoon. In fact I'll be there from about ten o'clock on.

"Well, why don't we meet for some lunch or something?"

"When do you have to go back to Balston?"

"Well, that's it. I have to bring the trailer back Saturday night or Sunday morning, so I'll have plenty of time to do just about anything."

"I've got a better idea," Paul said. "Why don't you meet me and after I've finished my business in Cazenovia we can come back to the farm? Now, I know that our accommodations may not be like what you'd get at a five star hotel, but we can put you up and give you a meal or two."

"Oh, I wouldn't expect anything like that… "Rob began.

"Wait a minute…", what, Gramma?" There was a pause and some dialogue at the other end of the line Paul was speaking to Rob again.

"Rob? Gramma says that she won't take 'no' for an answer. I don't particularly care if you come here or not, but she wants you to, so I guess that that decides everything."

"Thanks, Paul, but that would mean an extra trip to Cazenovia and back for you, so I don't think so."

"No it doesn't! I'd bring you to the farm. How you get back to Cazenovia is your look-out, not mine!, "Paul said.

Rob could hear Mrs. King scolding Paul in the background.

"You are one hell of a kind, generous and compassionate guy!", Rob said, laughing.

"You've noticed that too, huh?", Paul joked, then, adapting a more serious tone he said, "No. I'll see that you get back to pick up your wheels. I wouldn't leave you stranded. Besides, you'd probably decide that I didn't like you or something."

"Well, you don't like me, but that's okay. At least I've won your gramma over!", Rob laughed.

"Yeah, Well", Paul countered, "She has a kind heart and despite her age she's pretty naïve."

Rob was smiling when he hung up the phone. "What a jerk that guy is!" There is no doubt that he was very much looking forward to seeing the Kings again.

CHAPTER 11

PART 2

As it turned out, Rob was not expected to leave both the pick-up and the horse trailer. The man in Cazenovia had his own truck and preferred to hitch the trailer to that, so Rob had a vehicle at his disposal, after all. In fact, he had thus incurred a responsibility, for he felt that he would not want to leave the pickup in town overnight, even locked, while he was at the King farm. He drove to the place on the outskirts of Cazenovia where he had been told to take the trailer, and after a short time, the trailer was hitched to the other truck in the drive and barn yard where the man's truck had been. The owner, a Mr. Kavish, had a 'big-city' accent and although the grounds of the farm were beautifully kept the place lacked the life and spirit of a working farm. Rob told him that he would pick up the trailer on Sunday morning, and Mr. Kavish requested that the pick-up time be no earlier than ten a.m. Rob assured him that that would be fine.

Having not known much about Cazenovia, he had told Paul that he would meet him at the post-office, wherever that might be, at some time around noon. It was about 12:30 by the time that he found a place to park, also the location of the post-office, and walked to the front of that building. There was Paul, his back against the building, standing on one foot, the other leg bent with the foot flat against the wall. He was smoking a cigarette and at that moment his attention was riveted on a young woman who seemed to be having a very difficult time with two very small rebellious, half 'tamed' children.

Rob couldn't get over how very different Paul looked from when he had first seen him. The stringy, dirty hair was now wavy and full, somewhat reddish tints glinting from the dark brown of it all. His features looked sculpted and polished from fine stone: above all, clean! Paul swung his head in Rob's direction, his eyes looking farther down the street past him, before coming to focus on Rob's features and the recognition coming into them.

"Hey! How y' doin'?" Paul asked, dark hazel eyes dancing.

"Not bad. You?", his own eyes meeting the challenge.

"Decent!", Paul exclaimed.

"You've never been decent! Rob countered.

They were still in the stage of friendship between males wherein a certain "sizing up" takes place, each one evaluating the other in terms of strength, outlook, trustworthiness and such traits as are important to a sex which has found it necessary to select carefully those others who might be counted upon in life. 'Male bonding' has become the standard parlor joke in an age of feminism, but it is nevertheless a tool for survival which has been in place for a few thousand years at least… and one which will be with us for many years to come, or so we had better hope. In the case of Rob and Paul, they met under circumstances which had initially made each somewhat antagonistic toward one another. What each of them had become as a result of his experiences, aspirations and family expectation, had placed them in opposing camps. The possibility that each might see a potentially valuable friend in the other, forced both Rob and Paul to question their own initial judgments; possibly to even question personal loyalty to the ideas and ideals which they had believed themselves to represent. For many such reasons, each of the young men felt a need to proceed with caution.

"Where's a good place to eat?", Rob was asking.

"The farm. Gram's expecting us."

Rob explained that he would have to follow Paul out there, that he did after all, have a pickup which, because it was another's property, he couldn't leave in town. Paul was of the opinion that it would be 'alright' to leave it locked and parked, but Rob explained that if he left it, his time at the farm would be ruined by restlessness and concern. After a few more comments, Paul agreed and said that he could understand the feeling of responsibility. Paul indicated the grey car he was driving and Rob went around for the truck and positioned himself to follow him. They took Route 80 just a bit out of town which went southward and then looped over toward Tully; all in all, a distance of about 20 miles. Once at the farm, Mrs. King seemed truly glad to see Rob again, one of her great farm lunches meant to feed haymakers, ready for them, and they sat down together at somewhere between 1:30 and 2:00 PM; a late lunch and therefore all the more welcome to them both.

Part way into the meal, Mrs. King asked:

"Paul, did you say anything to Robbie about your plans and your reason for going to Cazenovia?"

"No, I didn't. 'Truth is: I didn't have any chance to say much of anything to him yet.", Paul said.

Rob paused to look questioningly at Paul, then at Mrs. King.

"What have you been up to, Paul?", he asked, his dark eyes, wide with curiosity and amusement.

"Applying for work as a male stripper in town."

"Yeah, okay…, but who'd pay to see your chicken breasted, bandy-legged form?", Rob asked.

"Boys! You are terrible! Both of you!" Mrs. King exclaimed with feigned indignation. She went on:

"Will you tell him, Paul, or shall I?"

"Oh…", Paul said. "It will just feed his madness! He'll think that it's his great example or something!"

"My great example!", Rob mused aloud. "I've got it! You're going to study for the ministry!"

"Yeah, right!" Paul murmured.

"Paul has applied for College!", Mrs. King said with pride and great happiness. "He really did! 'Went in today to talk to a faculty advisor! All I can say is: it's about time!"

"No kidding!" Rob stared, wide eyed at Paul, his mouth open in mock surprise, but he was indeed surprised. "That's fantastic!"

"Well", Mrs. King went on, "He has always done well in school... and his writing has always been superb!"

"His hand-writing?"

"No, Robbie,... his ability to write, and write well... of all sorts of things! He paints pictures with words such as I never read in my life! He's really very good!"

Robbie didn't know what to say. He simply continued to stare at Paul, nodding his head very slowly, as if deep in thought. Finally, grasping for something, he exclaimed:

"Yeah! It figures, yes it truly all adds up! A real artist, anyway, he sure looked the part when I first met him!"

"Okay! Okay! That's it! I am a person! I have feelings and the two of you don't have to talk about me as if I were an object, or a pet chicken or some such thing!" He smiled sheepishly and Mrs. King and Rob exchanged smiles as well.

The rest of the meal they spoke of courses of study, some possibilities in the field of liberal arts; literature and cultural anthropology in particular. Mrs. King could not have been happier if she were to find herself sitting in a great salon with celebrated members of the intelligentsia at her table.

After lunch, Paul took a bucket of table scraps, peelings and other such things out to the hen house (people who live on farms are not apt to throw away those things which an animal or bird can use), while Rob helped in the clearing up.

"What made him decide to do that?", he asked Paul's grandmother.

"Well, Robbie, I can't be one hundred percent certain, but I think that you may have had something to do with it."

"Not I!" Rob protested. "He made it very clear that he hates what I stand for!"

Mrs. King didn't respond immediately, but her mouth had a hint of a smile and her eyes glittered behind the lenses of her eye-glasses.

"You think that, do you?", she asked somewhat cryptically.

"Well, I got that impression. Y' know, ma'am, our trip up here from Ohio wasn't all that joyful at times. We said some pretty rotten things to each other", Rob confessed.

"Perhaps so. Perhaps things needed to be said." She looked out toward the barn, pointed and went on:

"That old hand-pump out there: You could go out and pump that handle up and down from now 'til doomsday, but it would not give you so much as a drop of water. It needs to be primed first. If, on the other hand, you were to take half a bucket of water and poured it into the top in order to fill the casing and wet the valve, you'd only have to pump that handle up and down about four times and water would come forth to supply your needs for the rest of the day. People are a bit like that, I think. Sometimes they need a bit of priming to get them started. Paul is stubborn, left to fend for himself and more than just a touch "testy". He can be downright bitter! He has reason to be bitter. But, Rob you have been that half bucket of water which he has been needing. You got him going!

"Mrs. King, I am not at all sure that Paul even likes me, to tell you the truth!", Rob said, feeling himself to be turning a bit red through embarrassment.

"Well," the elderly lady persisted, "He admires you. He has talked about you quite a lot since you were here. It may not mean that he ' likes' you", she chuckled," but it is a pretty good substitute. In any case, you managed to get his attention!"

Rob felt an uneasiness wash over himself: a strange feeling, certainly not elation, but rather something akin to a wave of fear of some kind, yet a giddiness too. He sensed that something was required, expected, of him which was far beyond his capabilities.

At that moment they both looked towards the opening back door and stared at Paul as he came into the room, bucket in hand. He stopped, looked at both his grandmother and Rob.

"What!" he said, as if it were a question and an accusation all in one word.

"Nothing.", his grandmother said. "Do you think that you are the only one worth looking at around here?"

Paul put the "chicken bucket" back under the far cupboard, saying over his shoulder, "…And yes, Gramma, I remembered to rinse it out." Then, as an after-thought, "By the way there was a dead hen out there!"

"What did you do with it?", she asked

"Took a spade and buried it in the midden", he replied simply.

"Thank you, Paul", she said, then as if thinking aloud: Dear!" I hope that we are not having trouble with some animal such as a 'coon or a weasel!"

Paul and Rob spent what was left of the afternoon working on the farm tractor: an old Allis-Chalmers D-17. It would be needed if and when the rain ever stopped for more than a day at a time to start the haying season. There weren't many animals on the place since Paul's grandfather had died a few years before, but Gramma King said that she could not bear the thought of the fields going unmown and growing up with brush and honeysuckle after their having been taken care of for so long a time. She had held fast to a hope that her younger son, Paul's Uncle Art, might want to work the place after he got back from Viet Nam and the war. She knew that it didn't seem to be too likely. He had done two tours of duty over there and there was every indication that he was pretty "messed up". Even so, Mrs. King continued to hold onto the idea almost as if it were a life-line thrown to her. Paul had talked briefly about his uncle to Rob and had mentioned that he was a beautiful singer, that he had written some songs and that he had been in a 'group' before he had been called up for military service. According to Paul, Art's last furlough at the farm had been cut short; that the few days that he did stay on the place saw him sitting up night after night with his guitar; drinking, crying and trying to sing. "Art needs help!", Paul had said, then dropping the subject (although Rob could swear that he had heard Paul add almost inaudibly: "What am I talking about? I am about as messed up as he is!") Rob had let it drop without question, comment or a request for clarification.

After dinner the three of them sat in the living room of the old farmhouse, talking of the Viet Nam war, how America seemed to have been losing balance somehow. So many questions had arisen since the eruption of violent protest everywhere in the country. Both Paul and Rob had fairly high numbers for the draft, but in the background there always lurked that possibility of being called into the military service.

"I have always loved my country", Mrs. King was saying "Our family have always paid our dues to this nation. Even so, I can not get it through my head that this war is getting us anywhere or that we can even hope to win it. I can't bear the thought of young fellows like you going off to that awful place! I won't rest 'til Art is home for good, safe and sound!"

Arthur's name came up several times during that conversation, but Rob could not help noticing that at each time that his uncle's name was mentioned, Paul would become very quiet, neither adding to the conversation nor even looking up. He would instead simply listen, keeping his head and his eyes lowered. Rob had a feeling that he had somehow been introduced to some rather private family matters which did not really concern him, nor of which he had any right to be a part. He was relieved to find the topics changing to those of familial matters of days gone by: clan and family histories; ancestral connections pertaining to the clans of the Highlands of Scotland, a subject which they all held in common. At one point, Paul's grandmother rose up and went into another room and brought back a small wooden box. In a reverential manner, she lifted the lid of the box to reveal a faded and folded piece of tartan woven in silk. This she unwrapped carefully and exhibited upon the tartan of silk two metal buttons, each about the size of an American nickel coin. She explained that these two buttons had once been worn by Rob Roy MacGregor. The two buttons had each of them the symbol of a Lion's head with a pointed medieval crown. The MacGregors had always claimed to be heirs to the ancient kingship of the Dalriadic Gaels. Indeed, their motto has been "S'rioghal mo Dhream" ….Royal is my race".

"These are about two hundred and fifty years old", Mrs. King explained with a certain reverence. "Maybe even a little bit older than that" Looking up towards Rob, she asked, "Are you familiar with Rob Roy MacGregor, Robbie?"

"Every one of Highland descent has heard of Rob Roy, Ma'am", he replied. He felt a great awe and a sense of humility come over him in the face of these two pieces of silver, these pieces of a distant past. He found himself to be wishing that Robert MacKinnon could have been present.

At the same time he realized almost immediately after having had that thought that Robert MacKinnon would have been impressed but certainly not overwhelmed. To his older MacKinnon relative, "things", although interesting, were not, in and of themselves the true mortar which held together the structure of tradition. The living memories of people, their refusal to forget who they are and how their families have been as a part of each block of time: such is the binding force after all. Even so, the evening and the sharing of information and stories in the farmhouse living room; the discussions fueled by coffee and cookies, not to mention Mrs. King's undisguised pleasure in the company of the two young men, made for a memorable and most warm occasion which would be remembered throughout Rob's life. He would remember the feel of the place, the scent of an old American farmhouse: its smell of wood and smoke, the sense of tradition and family connectedness: warm, secure, contentment of the most basic things. This is what America was once about and he knew it and without him really understanding a gnawing inner feeling, he felt that something in all of this was slipping away from his people and his nation.

Grandmother King looked across at Paul and said to Robbie: "You know, come to think of it, for all of this talk of Clan MacGregor, my late husband's clan, Rob Roy and such, I am not all that sure that more of Paul's really deep Scottish roots aren't from his dad's grandmother King, my mother in law! She was born a Gilcannon. She was half Indian as well!

"Really?" Rob gave a small, delighted laugh. "So THAT explains how taciturn and very into himself Paul can become from time to time!"

"Okay! Knock it off!" Paul ordered, with a slight smile.

"Oh, yes!, Mrs.King went on "Paul's grandmother, Mary Gilcannon and her brother Jack were born 'way out in British Columbia. Their father, Duncan had left Ontario and gone out to the Canadian west, working for the Hudson's Bay Company. The Native folk seem to have trusted Scots, especially Highland Scots. Anyway, Duncan ended up marrying a Native girl named Ellie Whitewolf. So, you see my mother in law and her brother, whom we always called "Uncle Jack", were "half 'n half as it were!"

The grandmother fell silent and seemed to be contemplating something or other, a slight frown drawing her brows together, her eyes narrowed. As if to herself, she said: "I wonder where the staff is now".

Paul spoke up immediately: "Yes! What was all that about, anyway? What was that whole business about some sacred stick ?".

"Oh, Paul!", his grandmother said, sending a weary, sidelong look his way, "It isn't a 'sacred stick', but a very ancient Scottish relic; the pastoral staff of some saint who lived centuries ago!"

"How did they end up with that?", Paul asked.

"They didn't "end up with it", at all! The Gilcannons had been entrusted with the care of that staff centuries before they ever came over to Canada!", she corrected.

"It's still in the family?", Rob asked.

"Oh, it must be!", Mrs. King said. "It had been entrusted to Duncan, Paul's great great grandfather, but when he went out west he left it with his brother, who was called Alisdair. According to what my mother in law told me, Alisdair passed the staff on to Andrew, who was his eldest son. The last anyone in the family knew anything at all about the staff, it had been passed down to Andrew's nephew, Charles. Andrew never married, you see, so it was passed to the eldest son of James Gilcannon, who was Charles. Charles and his wife Elsie lost their oldest boy "Alec" during World War II. He was in the R.C.A.F. and was shot down over the Channel during the Battle of Britain. He was a beautiful lad! He was so polite and truly a kind young fellow!. They never really got over his having been killed".

"Oh!", Paul said in surprise, "Did you know them personally?"

"Why, yes, Paul! Your great grandparents were still closely connected to the family members still in Canada. Your grand dad and I went up to see them quite often. There were three children. Alec was the eldest, then his brother James and their sister Debbie. The children would have been cousins of some kind to your grandfather, but Elsie and Charlie had taught them to call us "Uncle Bill and Aunt Carol". I am still "Aunt Carol" to them, I'm sure!" .

"Have you ever seen the staff, Gramma?", Paul asked

"Oh, yes!", she exclaimed. "Several times! I do not think that the family ever really made a "muchness" of their guardianship, although they did take great pride in the fact and they took their duty quite seriously."

"So, the staff is still with Charles Gilcannon", Paul suggested.

"Oh, for Land's Sake! ", his grandmother exclaimed. "Charlie died before either of you boys were born! Elsie went to live with Debbie and her husband in Cambridge. Well, It's called Cambridge now. It used to be called Galt. I don't know if she is still living or not". The elderly lady had tears in her eyes and seemed to have again gone deep into thought. There was a faint, wistful smile on her face as she looked to the table top at nothing in particular.

"The staff probably went to Alec's brother then", Paul said.

"What's that, Dear?", Mrs. King asked, her reverie having been broken.

"The staff", Paul reminded her.

"Oh, Yes!", she replied. "The staff is probably being taken care of by Jimmy! That's right! Jimmy is Alec's brother".

Grandma King spoke a bit more about Canada and the relatives there, of visits and reunions, of how much more "British" Canada had been up to and throughout the war years.

"The King and Queen came to Canada in 1939: that summer just before Britain, and Canada, both went to war against Nazi Germany. Up until that time, the world had never seen anything like the British Empire! Speaking of Scottish things: Canada has more Scottish regiments than

Scotland! As a matter of fact, Jimmy Gilcannon, Alec's younger brother, had been too young to go into military service during World War II, but he enlisted in the Argyll and Sutherland Highland regiment for the Korean War! Poor Elsie! She was just about fit to be tied! It had been pretty hard on them to have lost Alec in the Battle of Britain and the thought of possibly losing another son in Korea almost killed her. He managed to come home in one piece, Thank the Good Lord!"

The three of them sat quietly for awhile: the white-haired elderly woman of many winters and the two young men of not even twenty summers. Grandma King held her coffee cup in both hands, elbows on the table before her, seeming to be again deep in thought. Finally, she spoke as if recalling something almost lost in time:

"You know, I was just thinking about Jimmy Gilcannon. He married Ruth Reid and I am almost certain that someone said that they had moved into the farm where Charlie and Elsie raised those children. Jimmy and Ruth have a boy and two girls" Barbara, Douglas and Emily. Now, I'm pretty sure that someone told me that Doug had gone to Viet Nam! I can not figure how that could be!....unless Doug had come over to the 'States from Canada! After all, Canada had the good sense to stay clear of involvement in this terrible thing!" She paused for a moment, put her cup down and then continued:" Barbara, That is the older girl, is pretty close to the age of you two boys by now!"

"Is she good-looking?", Rob asked with a smile.

"Never mind that! Paul exclaimed. "the question is: does she have a good car and a good job?"

Mrs. King stood up, feigned disgust and waved the two of them away.

"What difference would it make? She asked the two smiling young men "She's certainly too smart to hook up with either of you! I'd be the first to personally set her straight!"

CHAPTER 12

PART II

Rob had enjoyed the conversation, the friendly banter and joking and found himself to be quite impressed by Mrs. King's readiness to join in to such open humor. It was obvious to him that she was one of those older people who, rather than harbor ill-feelings or an awkwardness in her dealings with younger people, actually enjoyed their company.

Later, when everyone seemed to be preparing to settle in for the night, Rob asked Paul if it would be possible for him to have a shower. This was as much in the way of asking where he was to sleep as anything else.

"Oh!", Mrs. King exclaimed, having overheard the question, "My goodness! We haven't even got your things into the house yet from the car, have we?"

"Yes, Gram!", Paul put in, "I did that when I went out a while ago. I put Rob's bag upstairs."

"I hope that you don't mind bunking with Paul, Rob", Mrs. King said. "Art's room is a disaster! I wouldn't dream of having you spend the night in there!"

"Fine, I guess!", Rob replied,", If Paul can put up with me, I can probably put up with him!" . At this same moment, his thoughts sped back in time to the Paul whom he had first encountered in Ohio: stringy-haired, filthy in clothes and body. Glancing over at this Paul who stood here clean and fit, a bright face surrounded by a mass of wavy brown hair, his bright hazel eyes clear and merry, he saw that this Paul was a very different man altogether. Here, on his home ground he radiated a confidence, an identity impossible for anyone to have foreseen, anyone who might have seen the drab hitch-hiker at the truck stop anyway.

Once upstairs, Paul showed Rob into the neat bedroom tucked under the roof of the old house; larger than one might expect and very "homey" with simple wall paper, a few pictures and some posters which Paul had put up on the walls. There was a regular-sized bed of the style which is called a "sleigh bed", with outward curving headboard and footboard, The quilt on the bed was obviously a hand-made patch-work quilt, probably already a family heirloom. Rob was impressed by the simple, orderly beauty, the sense of simple and contented living which the farmhouse presented. He unzipped the canvas carry-all which he had brought with him, dug around until he produced a shaving kit and towel He turned around to see Paul coming into the room from the bathroom.

"There is a bath-sized towel and washcloth laid by the tub for you, Rob", Paul told him. That is a pretty-old-fashion shower in there, but if you just make sure that the shower curtain is tucked into the tub all the way around, you shouldn't have any trouble".

Rob murmured his thanks and moved towards the bathroom.

When, after a quick shower he re-entered the room, he saw Paul propped up on two pillows, looking at a magazine by the light of the bed-side lamp on the side table on his side of the bed. Paul's bare shoulders, chest and arms rose up from the bed clothes of the bed. Rob was wearing sarong-like, the bath towel which Paul had given him, holding the towel with his right hand.In his other hand he was carrying the toiletry kit and the clothes which he had been wearing. He turned his back to Paul, dropped the towel and began to step into a clean pair of undershorts. Paul glanced up from the magazine only to be confronted with Rob's bare buttocks as he pulled on the shorts.

"Well!", Paul wise-cracked, "at least you're going to wear something to sleep in! But, what? No Pajamas?"

"No. Undershorts are fine," Rob said, just a touch embarrassed, but then said, "But hey! I don't see you wearing Pajamas, so what are you talking about?"

"You don't see me wearing anything at all", Paul returned.

Rob stopped all movement, suddenly wide eyed and staring. "You ARE wearing shorts, right?, he asked, arching one eyebrow.

"I usually sleep in the raw" Paul informed him.

"Usually", Rob repeated, "but not now, right? I'm not getting into that bed if you're naked!"

"What difference would it make?", Paul asked. "Like you never sleep in the nude!"

"Well, yes. I do sometimes sleep in the nude, Paul, but not with another guy, I don't!"

Paul continued to look up at him, half-smiling. Suddenly, Rob lunged forward and grabbing the bed-clothes, whipped them off and away from Paul, with Paul yelling, "Hey!", to find his intended bed-partner to be sitting there in his jockey shorts.

"You crazy bastard!", Rob half yelled, and pulling a pillow from his side of the bed, began to pummel a cringing, laughing Paul.

"Had you worried for a while, didn't I ?", Paul laughed, trying to regain his speech between "AAh's" and "ouches" and more laughter.

"You silly, sick sack of puke!", Rob said as he pulled the bedding back in place, slipped into bed onto his side, his back to Paul. Still, he could feel a shaking beside him followed by a burst of near-hysterical laughter from Paul. Rob turned onto his back and turned his head to watch Paul, who seemed unable to stop laughing.

"Oh, that's funnier than hell!" Rob said sarcastically. "Okay, Paul! Just turn out the light!" Paul raised himself slightly on an elbow, reached over and the room went dark.

Rob was reminded of camp-outs and wondered to himself why it seemed to be that the sounds of the countryside aren't really heard until all of the lights are out. Through the screen in the bedroom window he could hear crickets signalling one another, a distant owl, the breeze through the tree limbs and twigs near the house. Everything was so totally dark, and yet one's eyes became adjusted to such darkness rather quickly and all of the senses are sharpened:smell, even the taste of the air and most certainly the hearing. After a while, laying there and thinking about the day and his present surroundings, Rob broke the silence:

"Paul?", he asked in a low voice, almost asking if this other young man were still awake.

"That's my name!" Paul answered sarcastically and obviously still quite awake

"Paul, I've been wanting to ask you something that I have been wondering about. I noticed, first in that Hippie antique place and again, just a little while ago when you were sitting up in bed. What is that carved white pendant or whatever, that you wear on that leather thong around your neck?"

"Why?, Paul asked. "You think that it looks kinda "witchy", "voodoo or something?"

"No", Rob answered, "In fact I think that it looks pretty neat! What is it?"

"Caberfeidh", Paul answered, rolling onto his back, "Crois Caberfeidh".

"Cobber fay?" Rob asked." What is that?"

"It's an old Scottish Highland kind of thing; a cross carved from deer antler", Paul told him." There are no two alike in the world".

"Where did you get it?", Rob asked, rolling on his side to face Paul.

"I didn't 'get it' anywhere!", Paul answered a bit impatiently. "You'll never come across one in an antique store or junk shop. Someone carves it by hand and gives it to some younger guy. It is a Christian symbol, but has some of the older religion mixed in. Actually, it is something of an honor to be given one. It means that the guy who wears it has been given some kind of respect; that he is someone who can be trusted, even with deep secrets".

"Really!", Rob exclaimed, awe in his tone.

"Yeah, Really!" Paul answered somewhat testily. "Who ever would've thunk it? And here was you, thinking of me only as a genuine dirt-bag!"

"Come on, Paul! I didn't think that!", Rob said

"Give me your hand", Paul ordered. He took hold of Rob's hand disregarding his protestations and hesitancy, raised his hand and laid it on his own chest in order that Rob's fingers were in contact with the carved piece. "Leave your hand there for a minute or two"

Rob was aware of his hand on another young man's bare chest, for the first time ever in his life. He felt the warmth and smoothness of the skin, but also his fingers began to feel the carving: a cross shape with the usual circle associated with the Celtic Cross. Moving his fingers to the back side of the carved form he could feel s raised design, but could not identify it. He started a bit as he was certain that he felt a single pulsing from the object. It happened a second time and he quickly pulled his hand back as if he had been shocked.

"Did you feel it? You did, didn't you?", Paul asked

"YYeahhh!", Rob breathed out. "How did you do that?"

"You dork! *I* didn't do it! Sometimes it just happens like that", Paul said.

"Has it ever done that to anyone else?", Rob asked impatiently.

"Not to any other guy. No guy has ever touched my chest before tonight, except maybe my dad when I was a kid. Normally, I don't like to be touched. For some reason I wanted you to feel that caberfeidh, rather than to just look at it."

"I am honored", Rob said with a bit of embarrassment.

Paul began to laugh to himself and turned to face Rob. "There was this time that I was with a girl", he related. "We were in the haymow of the barn and it was really warm up there. We still had our clothes on, except for the parts that needed to be undone. Anyway, there I was, banging this girl and my Caberfeidh slipped out of my mostly opened shirt and plopped on her breast! She freaked! She said that I had to take it off and I told her that even the coach in school could never make me take it off. I always had to tape it to my shoulder when I was playing a game. She wouldn't have anything to do with me! Man! I went home really hurting that night! It had really scared her!" After a short pause, he added, "Y'know, I think that this Caberfeidh did me a favor that night, We weren't using any protection and I have a feeling that if we hadn't stopped, I would have made her pregnant! Somehow, I just know it!"

Rob had been smiling in the darkness as the story was being told, but he suddenly said to Paul: "You do know that it is really just an object without life. It's a 'thing', not a living organism. I think that you are ascribing some pretty great power to a piece of deer horn"

"You aren't all that bright for a College kid, are you?", Paul asked." There is 'life' in everything you come across in this world. Science talks about "organic" this and "inorganic" that, but in every stone or grain of sand there are all of these tiny forces at work, spinning around, doing their thing. Without them, there would be no stone or grain of sand. Plants have an ability to sense the world around them. Life is everywhere!"

"Wow, Paul! You are beginning to sound like one of these "Back to the Earth", Nature-worshipping hippie types!", Rob countered. "What are we doing here, going into all of this "New Age" stuff?"

"Well, Robbie honey", Paul stated with sarcasm, "You may know a lot about some things and you have had some what they call "Higher Education", but what do you think all of our ancestors back in Scotland were all about? This is what our Old Way, what the world calls "Celtic Christianity" has been all about! It's the celebration of life: the life you've been given, the life all around us in land and trees, plants, the seas, mountains, rocks. All of it! You know, this is one thing that has made me question going back to school. There is a lot that a guy can learn, but he can also get pretty contaminated with skepticism too. Look at some of these professors.! I know that you must have a few of them: this half-smirking sense of "knowing" that nothing really exists unless it can be weighed, measured, X-rayed or broken down to some formula! Just look at their faces! They seem to be proud that they and they alone have all of the answers; that everything is to be refuted, doubted or made fun of. They spend their lives teaching you that there is no magic in this world, that 'magic' is all "smoke and mirrors ". Our ancestors took the tack that there is nothing in this world that is *not* magic!" .

"Yeah, Paul, but our ancestors believed in Faeries, the Forest Lord, and all of that happy horse shit!", Robbie reminded him.

Paul was becoming irritated and asked: "…and you don't? These things were ways of explaining some forces in nature! For God's sake, Robbie! If this sort of thing is beneath your consideration, then please be so kind as to leave us poor, unlettered peasants to our age-old superstitions! Go and live in that wonderful, brave new world with its sterile architecture, meaningless painting and sculpture and check-out counters in supermarkets filled with cardboard food!"

"I am much reproved", Rob countered. "However, you forgot to mention this great new Age of Aquarius with its reefers, Anti-war ballads and free love! You might as well sentence me to those things as well! Paul, I am simply asking you to be objective!"

"Rob, you are on the way towards being educated, but it remains to be seen whether or not you will know anything. Can't you see that you are already beginning to close your mind? What kind of a husband and father will you be? My dad has let me down in a great many ways, but I will say this for him: he taught me how to dream and hope and see good all around me despite some pretty grim realities!" After a pause he said, "Let's get some sleep!"

The next morning at breakfast Grandma King noticed the absence of the usual banter between the young men and that such had been replaced by a sullen silence. She wondered what falling-out there might have been to so alter their outward expressions. She went on about the business of setting things out, chiding them for not eating enough: the usual things that mothers and especially grandmothers do. She moved towards the back door and turned to them.

"You boys eat up now and don't let anything go to waste! I'm going out to clean out the strawberry beds"

"Okay, Gram'!", Paul answered. "I am going to rebuild that one section of fence today, over by the west pasture".

"Oh, That would be great if you could do that!, she answered.

After she had gone out of doors, the two of them ate

silently. Rob finally spoke:

"I'd probably better go back to Cazenovia today, Paul".

Paul looked up at him and asked, "Why?"

"Well, I feel that I have pretty well screwed things up here. I was a real jerk last night! I really feel more than just a little embarrassed, to tell the truth", Rob confessed.

"Well, I didn't exactly end the evening on too happy a note either. One could say that I was also a bit of a pain in the ass! I have to say 'though that you sure acted, what's the word that I want? Pontifical ?"

"Pontifical?" Rob asked, smiling. "Good word!, but I doubt that any pontiff would have said what I did. No, I was just being a smart-assed shit!"

"So? Don't go, Rob. Stay until you have to go back. Please? "

Rob smiled shyly, then said:" You just want me to help you build fence!"

"Yeah! That too! We need to rebuild a fence, but not *between* us, okay?" There was an almost childlike plea in Paul's tone. "Whether you like it or not, Rob, I want to be your friend."

"Boy! You don't know what you're letting yourself in for!", Rob replied. "Ooookay! Let's get'er done!"

Throughout the day the two of them worked on the fence. Even with gloves, the barb wire would manage to leave some pretty nasty scratches and cuts. As wire goes, it seems to have a genuine vendetta against anyone who would work with it: curling up unexpectedly, springing back to catch an arm or leg, ripping a shirt sleeve or a pant-leg and leaving a bleeding scratch in the skin beneath the torn fabric. Then too, rebuilding fence is more difficult than stringing a new one. Fence staples do not enter easily into wooden posts which have dried and seasoned in the weather. Wire has to be spliced and new tension given to it by ratcheting up on a 'come-along'. It is hard work, true enough, but rewarding in its own way.

People who work on the land learn early on in life that the earth has her own creeds and the man or woman who would live close to nature must learn to dance to the creeds and the rhythms of those creeds. The city woman cries out for "equality". She wants to make history as a man makes history. The country man knows that he can help make history, but come what may, the female *is* that history and all that it can ever be. The land is the eternal feminine and the farmer knows it, just as the sailor knows that the sea is a grand feminine entity. "Learn to love the sea!", the older sailor says to the young crewman, "and she will be more kind to you! She knows that you love her sister the land more than you love her. Learn to love the sea!" The earth is our mother. We are walking parts of her, but we all initially came from out of the waters: from the sea itself, and each of us from the waters of our mothers' wombs. All of it, the entire planet and the countless other planets and suns of our universe, are filled with the "magic" of which Paul spoke to Rob. Rob knew it, felt it, but needed to be reminded. Throughout our world, all peoples of the various cultures stand upon the earth and look upwards, away from the planet beneath our feet. Are they looking towards some "Sky Faerie" sitting on a throne on a piece of real estate in the sky? Are they not perhaps looking out and somewhat instinctively towards the center of a vast intelligence of which each of us is but a very tiny part?

It may have been on this day, the first day that the two of them had actually worked together on some project, that they began that long process of building a friendship which would endure over the years ahead. It takes a long time to build a friendship, after all, nor is friendship to be confused with an acquaintanceship or experiences shared with even a friendly co-worker. A friendship is something akin to a marriage of souls and requires time, tests of one kind or another and the gradual building of mutual trust and respect. Rob and Paul would have a long road ahead of them and would see something very important in their nation and their society slowly slip away. Each of them already had a sense that something was happening which would change their world forever.

The two of them would see one another and work together on several occasions during that summer. From time to time, Rob could take a weekend from the feed mill and go out to the King farm. Paul would also meet Gwynne during that season and they would come to like one another very much. Rob's mother could never understand that Gwynne did not try to rein Rob in more, to try to keep him to herself; why she did not object to his going to the farm from time to time, but Gwynne was very secure in her relationship with Rob and she was mature far beyond her years. Perhaps she sensed that both she and Rob needed time of their own in order for their own bond to have greater meaning for each of them as individuals, for both of them as a couple. When he would return from the farm she always wanted to hear all of the details: what they did, the stories and snippets of history which Grandmother King might have brought forth; even what they had for their meals. At the same time, Gwynne did not simply sit in Rob's shadow. She was a very talented young woman in her own right. She acted as a tutor for a couple of children, she was involved in summer theater and was called upon as a window-dresser for one of the better shops. She had her stories to share with Rob as well and he would laugh himself to tears upon hearing some of her experiences, for in her way, Gwynne was also an excellent story-teller: a natural mimic who could make her stories come to life. Local dialects, foreign accents, were very easy for her repeat in order to fill out some related event. When Rob listened to her tell of an exchange in a shop between two older women, he told her that she really should consider writing such stories down; that she was a natural anthropologist. The one story which brought him to say this involved a discussion between two women in regard to pregnant women staying away from dangerous farm animals, even a nasty rooster, for if the mother-to-be had a bad fright from a mean animal it might leave a mark on the unborn child. Gwynne had been relating the story:

"Well", the one woman said, "I told her to stay clear of the barnyard, that she was too close to her time! Well, she went down there, don't you know (don't pay any mind to anything that *I* might say!), and this terrible, mean rooster came tearing across the ground from out of nowhere and jumped right up at her, just a clawin' and a peckin' at her 'til she was scared to death almost! Well, when that child was born, it wasn't too long, once he started walkin', that he moved jus' like a chicken! He'd even bob his head whilst he walked, just like a chicken! I told Irene Baxter: That child was marked for a chicken by that nasty rooster, pure and simple!"

Robbie liked to tease Gwynne about her chocolate fudge. She was a pretty good cook, but for some reason, whenever she made fudge it would never set properly and they would end by eating it as "hot fudge" on ice cream. If she tried to cook or boil it longer it would be as hard as a rock. To Gwynne's credit, she took his kidding her quite well. He might get socked in the arm, but she took it well.

On one occasion Rob took some soil sampling things from the feed mill up to the King farm and he and Paul took soil samples from two of the former hay fields to find if they needed lime or nitrogen. Paul had never done this before and Rob gained some added respect in his eyes. They had been making some hay as well and their bodies had taken on good tone over the summer. Certainly they had acquired very tanned faces and arms, which were always considerably more tanned than backs and chests on farm workers. Putting up hay is not the kind of thing that would lead to one's being comfortable with hay bales' sharp stubble scraping across his bare torso. After a day of "haying" they would come into the mud-room before entering the house, in order to take off their shirts and socks to empty them of hay chaff. Sometimes there would be enough time before supper to grab a towel and head out to the farm pond, just beyond the lawn, for a quick swim. Grandma King would smile and shake her head at hearing the shouting and laughter borne on the summer breeze of early evening. "Boys!" . She said aloud to herself on one occasion upon hearing the male voices and laughter, "Men somehow never stop being boys!", then somewhat more solemnly:" Rejoice in your youth while it is with you!"

She opened the oven door, squinted and poked a Johnnie Cake with a finger to see if it was done and she found herself humming a fragment of an old Scottish song which her mother in law used to sing which had just come back to her at that time:

"The bairnies cuddle doon at nicht wi' mirth that's dear tae me,

For soon the grit warld's cark and care will quaten doon their glee...."

She stopped and stared at the stove-top, as in a day-dream. "Now, I wonder why or how I came to remember that! Hmmm! For that matter, I do not remember that I ever really learned it! 'Osmosis', I guess!" At that moment she resolved to say something about her late husband's family to the young fellows after the evening meal. She had set herself to some gathering of family records, old photographs and the odd letter, not to mention an old dirk and a wooden box which contained a few odd pieces of jewelry. Having noticed that Paul had become quite interested in the history of his family, a fire which had started as a tiny spark and fanned by Rob's search into his own past, she had also, through the offices of the Mormons' familial records, been able to find some, although by no means all, of the missing pieces.

The men had decided earlier in the day that they would drive into town that same evening, maybe take in a movie and get a few beers. Since it was getting well into summer and they had been working pretty hard, they thought that it was time for a "night out" on the town, not as if there was ever really all that much going on in such a small town. Of course, Grandma King did not know of their having made any plans, she mentioned to them during the evening meal that she had some more things to show them after the kitchen had been cleaned and the dishes were done. A look was shared between the men that signaled, "We'll just go out a bit later".

What she had set aside to show them and the things which she would have them read seemed to affect Paul more deeply than either she or his friend could have believed possible. He would sit motionless and study with great intensity a paper or an object in his hand as if he were actually drawing its essence into himself; his face serious, his dark hazel eyes wide and staring. All that he touched he handled in an almost sacerdotal, priest-like manner Finally, Mrs. King unfolded a large paper which appeared to resemble a chart of some sort.

"This is where I've stopped so far", she explained, "This is the genealogy which I have put together. Here! Let's spread it out on the dining table where there's better light and we can all look at it".

They three moved to a side of the dining room table. Like all country homes in America's rural parts, there is usually a well-appointed dining room which displays familial heirlooms and where the wood is always well polished and glowing. Somehow however, rural Americans often use their kitchens as a modern day version or adaptation of the old "keeping room", where families often spent a great part of the time. Even families which inhabit some of the truly great houses or mansions often may be found following this practice. There is often a tea kettle or coffee pot at the ready on the stove top. Families often move to the dining room if they need a table in common for study or such. This is especially true in the Northern states which have cold winters. It is the kitchen where the greatest supply of heat is ever present, but the dining room is often more formal, and as stated, more useful for studying charts or such.

"Now, this is all about the King family, right?", Paul asked while looking at this spread sheet of data and names.

"Well, a lot of it is", his grandmother answered, " but, and if this isn't the strangest thing!, once we get back to your great grandfather Alan King, the bulk of the information goes back through Alan's wife's family. Alan's wife was your great grandmother Mary Gilcannon. I know that I have mentioned her before, and there seems to be much about her family. I think that there must have been some kind of terrible trouble! Rob, you may be able to fill in some of these gaps for us. Maybe Mr. MacKinnon, the man you told us about who lives in Pennsylvania? He may know something about the background history of it all. Mary, my own mother in law, used to say something about what she called the ' Red River Rebellion', but that was supposed to have happened up in Canada. Well, anyway! You can't prove it by me, one way or the other!"

Later that same evening, Rob and Paul got into the pick-up and went into town for a few beers. They stopped at a tavern which would have been called a "Beer-joint". The place was terribly crowded, small and very noisy, a situation which was made even worse by everyone almost shouting at one another in order to be heard over the general noise and other shouting. To compete with the general noise, the Jukebox against a side wall not far from the front windows had been "cranked up" to a sizeable volume of its own. People were two and three deep in front of the bar and even the business of getting a couple of draft beers was difficult enough without ever hoping to find a stool. The few tables and chairs in the place were fully occupied, so Paul motioned Rob over to a wide ledge beneath one of the large front windows, where the two of them could at least sit on that edging which was just barely able to accommodate them. Rob remembered his father talking of "narrow-assed Presbyterians" and considered himself to have benefitted from his mother's Presbyterianism. He made a mental note that he would have to mention this experience to his father. Both of them sat simply "people watching" since it would have been pointless to try to carry on any kind of conversation.

A girl in her early twenties with tight blonde curls, a small form and an almost too-delicate face walked past them, glancing sideways. Without stopping, she swung by them in short-shorts and a blouse which was tied by the shirt tails at her waist. With only a trace of a smile she spoke:

"Hi, Paul!", still moving towards the juke box, a glass and a cigarette in the same right hand.

"Hi, Wanda", Paul replied

"A friend of yours?" Rob asked

"Kind of a sad story!", Paul said. "Kind of a sad story. Poor Wanda. I don't know if she has any friends or even wants any friends, but yeah, I know her and have never had any problems with her. She has her own share of problems".

Wanda made a "production" of looking over the selections in the clear plastic housing of the Juke box before finally pushing some buttons. As a tune began to belt out she came back towards Paul and Rob, swaying to the rhythm and melody of her chosen selection. Still clutching her glass and between two fingers, her cigarette between two fingers of that hand, she bobbed her head and swayed her hips to the beat of the tune. Swinging and bobbing she came up to face Paul.

"You back here to stay for a while, Paul?, she asked him. "Christ! If I could once get out of this berg I'd just keep going!"

"Well, I don't know, Wanda. I have kinda come back to gather my resources, to 'regroup', y'know? I might be here for a while. I'll just have to see what happens", he explained.

"So! Who's your friend?", she asked as if not even hearing his answer to her question. She was obviously appraising Rob.

"Oh!," Paul said, somewhat taken off guard, "This is Rob Currie. He lives over by Albany".

"Hi, Rob Currie! I'm Wanda. At least I think that I'm Wanda. I'm pretty drunk right now, in case you haven't noticed".

"Hi, Wanda! ", Rob replied. "Glad to meet you!...and No, I hadn't noticed".

"Well, I sure as hell am!" She paused for a moment, looked at Rob closely and then went on: "God! You're gorgeous! Rob Currie, You are absolutely gorgeous!"

"Knock it off, Wanda!", Paul ordered sternly.

"Okay, Okay, OKAY!", her voice loud and shrill, "I wouldn't begin to try to come between you two! He's too pretty and good to be true anyway!" and with that she wandered off, moving and bobbing to the music.

Rob watched her move across the floor, weaving between people and going up to the bar. He felt a kind of pity for her. She then seemed to be having some kind of angry confrontation with the bartender.

'What was that all about?', Rob asked Paul.

"Who Knows?", was Paul's answer.

"No. I mean, what did she mean by that remark?"

"How the hell should I know?, Paul answered somewhat impatiently.

But, Rob could not dismiss this somewhat angry and defensive tone in his friend's voice. Rob drained his glass.

"Want another?", he asked Paul.

"Nah! Let's blow this pop stand and go somewhere else!", Paul growled.

"Suits me, Bwana!", Rob said simply, at the same time studying Paul's face, looking for some clue as to what had come over him, for it was quite obvious that something had triggered a definite mood change: some sort of darkness having come into Paul's features and demeanor, as if a cloud had come between his face and all light. Rob almost asked Paul if he was 'alright'; if anything was wrong, but he caught himself before the words had been formed. Still, he felt a deep concern.

On the way towards the door a man who appeared to be in his late twenties collided with Paul, which resulted in the other man dropping his car keys.

"Sorry about that!" the man said as he stooped to recover the keys, then, he looked upwards at Paul and a look of recognition came across his features.

"Paul! Is that you, kid?," he asked, smiling, at the same time grabbing Paul's forearm in his hand. "How the hell are you?"

"Just peachy keen!", Paul answered somewhat dryly, with only the slightest smile.

"What do you hear from Art? Will he be coming home soon?"

"Well, I couldn't really say", Paul answered coldly. "Art is Art. Does anyone know what he might do next, or when he might do it? Of course, you already know that, don't you?" Then, after a very brief pause, Paul went on: "Hey! Gotta go! 'See you around!", disengaging himself and moving towards the door, leaving Rob to nod to the young man and then follow Paul out of the bar.

They got into the truck without either of them speaking. Rob found himself reminded of the first time that they had been riding in the same vehicle, back when he was driving from Ohio into Pennsylvania. He turned on the windshield wipers, for once again a drizzling rain was falling like an unending haze of mist and water. As they pulled out onto the street, they were as a moving part of a gigantic light show: streetlights, neon signs, traffic lights and every color of light imaginable were all playing on the wet pavement all around them.

"Where do you want to go?", Rob asked, trying to control a mixture of helplessness and rising anger inside of himself.

"Oh, I don't know", Paul answered. "Go on up a couple

more blocks. There's a place on the corner" Paul was aware of Rob's frustration, but could not seem to pull himself out of the black mood which had enveloped him.

Slowing the truck, Rob peered through the heavier rainfall towards the various lighted and colored beer-ad displays in the windows of the place on the corner and asked, "Is this the place?"

"Yeah, fine. It should be less noisy in here", Paul told him.

Rob stopped the truck by the tavern, but had to drive a few spaces further in order to park the vehicle. He pulled into a parking spot and they exited the truck, heads lowered and shoulders hunched up, running through the rain which was really pelting the earth and pavement now. They entered into the tavern, stamping their feet and shaking their heads in the entryway, throwing sprays of water around them.

Looking up, Rob noticed an atmosphere quite different from the other place. There were probably no more than a dozen people in the tavern, most of them being middle-aged locals. Four men sat around a table, playing cards. There was no shouting, save for a triumphant sound or a groan of disappointment from one of the card players. Others were by the bar talking quietly and although there was a juke-box in the premises, even that was sending forth a song at a fairly low volume. As they approached the bar, Rob noticed a thick-set woman with heavy cheeks and very little evidence of a neck at all. As the two young men moved towards her, the woman's features, which had first appeared to be sullen and heavy, came to a transformation of brightness and life.

"Hey!", she exclaimed, looking at Paul. "I know you! You're Dave King's kid, aren't ya?" Her smile revealed that there had been a very pretty woman here not too many cares, disappointments and burdens in the years before.

"Guilty as charged, Ma'am!", Paul grinned shyly, trying to lighten his demeanor to match the occasion.

"Well, Hon', I'll tell ya: You could be guilty of a lot worse things than that! Your dad is one very fine man, a truly good person! After he was made, they threw the mold away! How is he doing? Do you ever see him?"

"Not as often as I'd like to, but we manage to keep in touch", Paul answered

"Well, I hope so! I really do! Boy! He always thought the world and all of you!" after a pause, she asked: "So what can I get you two half-drowned rats tonight?"

"Could we have a couple of drafts?", Rob asked her.

"You can have anything in the place that you're old enough to have, Hon', but first I have to see some 'I.D'!"

Rob fished out his driver's license from his wallet and handed it to her.

"Robert Currie", she said upon close inspection of the card, I deduce from this that you are 19 years of age!" Turning to Paul she said, "Now, don't try to kid a kidder, Hon'! I know that you aren't 18 yet!"

"C'mon Louise!", he said in a tone of disbelief. "I'm

almost 20!"

"Yeah, right! I just turned 28 myself too!", she replied

Paul shook his head, smiling weakly and presented his driver's license.

"Well, I know that you are Paul King and this is Paul King's license and this license says that you are 19! Now, how about that? It isn't possible! I must have missed a couple of years somewhere."

"Turning to Rob, she said, "I can't give you any draft beer, Hon'. I'm having the whole system cleaned out. Bottled beer is the best that I can come up with!"

"No problem, Ma'am! Just give us a couple of Budweisers, please, Rob said.

"You got them, handsome!" She turned to the cooler and brought back two bottles, and swept two glasses from the back-bar in one movement and set them before him. Paul had gone over to the cigarette machine.

Rob slid onto a bar stool and began to pour his beer from the bottle into his glass, tilting the glass in order that the beer would slide down the side and make for less foam. Paul slid onto a stool beside him, tearing the cellophane from the top of his pack of cigarettes. He also poured his beer into the glass and they both raised their glasses towards one another, basically saying "cheers". Paul then tapped the bottom of his cigarette package, forcing the cigarettes to make themselves known, He held the pack towards Rob, offering him one. Rob simply shook his head in refusal, so Paul took a cigarette for himself and struck a paper match to light it. Louise had moved down to the far end of the bar where a middle-aged couple were sitting. They looked as if the clock had stopped for them in the mid 1950's by the way they were dressed. Louise set a couple of refilled glasses in front of them and began what would be a long conversation with them. The young men sat quietly hunched over the bar for a while, simply enjoying the relative peacefulness of their present surroundings. Rob studied the back-bar and some of the old photographs: a U.S. Navy Destroyer, A faded black and white picture of a young sailor in uniform, another photo of a sailor receiving some decoration from a man who must have been President Truman. He turned to look at Paul who, as if on cue, turned his head to return his look and face him, as if to say, "What!", but there was no sound, just his face expressing the same question.

"So! 'Mind telling me what it is that got into you back there in that other place?", Robbie asked.

"What do you mean?" Paul asked defensively.

Rob reached over, took the cigarette from between Paul's fingers, took it to his own lips and inhaled deeply before blowing out a great cloud of smoke. He handed it back to Paul, who stared at the cigarette in awe.

"You just about took my whole cigarette in one drag!", Paul marveled. "I didn't think that you smoked!"

"I don't!", Rob answered simply. "So, are you going to answer my question?"

"Nothing is wrong or was wrong! Why does something have to be wrong? Can't I change my expression without there being something freaking wrong?", Paul spat out.

"Ooookay!! Forget that I asked!", Rob replied.

"Oh, Christ! Now you're pissed off at me!", Paul sighed. Rob did not answer him.

"I mean, it's not like you have to watch over me or some damn thing, Rob! Sometimes things just get to a guy, you know?"

Rob remained silent.

"Oh, Piss! Now I've gone and hurt your feelings! C'mon, Robbie! It has nothing to do with you! It is not you! It's me! I'm the one who is screwed up".

"Nah! Really?" Rob asked, looking at him with exaggerated, comic surprise.

They sat there for a few minutes in silence until Paul suggested:

"Let's get a couple more beers and take them to that table over there. Let's talk, okay?"

Rob nodded his agreement and waited for the bottles to be set before them. Paul insisted on paying this time around, leaving a couple of bills on the bar as a tip. They moved over to table at the side of the room which was quite apart from any other occupied space.

"It's certainly more relaxed in this place, isn't it? That other place was a mad house! ", Rob said.

"I should never have taken you there", Paul said." I don't know what I was thinking of. All of those people, trying so hard to act like they are having a ball, when nobody can even hear the person next to him! I can't take that sort of thing: places where everyone is trying to show everybody else that they're having a great time! When I was a kid, someone would take me to a carnival, figuring that I would love it. I had to pretend to be grateful. Truth is that a carnival would make me really depressed! The smells, those carneys who all looked like they hadn't any idea of what a bath or shower is all about; but most of all, the cheapness of the place and all of these people trying to be happy for a while. I can't explain it, but carnivals always ended up leaving me depressed as hell. That bar back there: everything that is wrong around here, the most lost people in the area, can be found there, all trying to out talk the person next to him". Paul looked to see Rob looking at him intently, studying his face.

"You are a pretty sensitive guy after all, Paul. Most people would not be able to see what you were seeing or share your feelings", Rob told him. "But, I know exactly what you are saying. Not only do I know, but I understand completely. Such places have always had a negative effect on me as well. Maybe I am just sneakier than you are. Maybe I have simply learned how to hide my feelings from the world." Now it was Paul who was studying Robbie.

Noticing Paul watching him, Rob said: " In the word of a friend of mine who wants to know what is going on: "What!"

Paul took out his package of cigarettes again, smiling to himself, and once again held the pack towards Rob and somewhat to his surprise, Rob took one of them. After they' lit up', Paul said: "You are some piece of work, Rob!"

They went on to speak of other things, of funny happenings, of experienced joys and near-misses, mistakes and observations. Rob was talking about a girl he had been seeing back in High school, before he had started going out with Gwynne. She had taken up with another guy and "dumped" him for this other fellow who ended up going to Viet Nam a year later.

"So, I was home for Christmas break and one night Gwynne and I went to a party and this other girl started acting as if she and I were still going together. I asked her what the story was; that I thought that she was still going with this other guy. She told me that she wrote to him and broke it off; that she couldn't spend the best years of her life waiting for some guy who might not come back and who was probably cheating on her anyway. I didn't know what to say! I just looked at her Then, I see Gwynne just a little bit away. She wasn't acting jealous or upset; nothing like that. She just seemed to be waiting for me, as calm and as unruffled as anyone could be. I decided then and there to myself: That is the woman I want to spend my life with!"

"Gwynne is a lucky girl", Paul said softly

"What?" Rob asked, turning his face towards Paul. He felt a sudden breeze-like sensation pass through himself for he realized that Paul had been studying him very intently while he had been speaking. He felt himself flush with a bit of embarrassment, picked up his glass and finished his beer.

"Come on, Paul. Let's drink up and go back to the farm".

"You don't want another beer?", Paul asked.

"I'd better not. Not while I'm driving someone else's truck. It would be hard to explain if I were to get a ticket or if I had even a slight 'fender bender'. If you want another, I don't mind staying here a bit longer talking with you."

"Good point! It's kinda "iffy" when you're driving someone else's vehicle. That's for sure", Paul agreed. "Let's saddle up!"

Getting up from the table, Paul called over to Louise: "You have a good night, Louise."

"You too, Hon'. Come back and see me, and you too, Rob Currie!"

When they arrived back at the farm the house was darkened save for a light which had been left on in the kitchen for them. They quietly raided the refrigerator, had a cup of warmed-up coffee and headed up the stairs, being very careful to avoid making any noise. Of course, as usually happens in such cases, one of them stepped heavily on a squeaky stair tread, which managed to get both of them laughing.

Once in the bedroom, Rob pulled off his still-damp shirt and sat down on the bed to remove his shoes.
"I hope that you will not think that I'm a scrounge if I come to bed without taking a shower tonight". He said to Paul.

Paul sat down next to him and, at first, said nothing at all. Rob could sense that there had been something on Paul's mind and that he wanted to speak about something; that he had almost begun to say something, but he thought it better not to ask him at this time. After a difficult silence between them, Paul began to speak:

"Rob, I know that I've acted like a real bastard tonight. I want you to know that I am really sorry. I really value your friendship. I am just getting to really know you and already I'm afraid that you will give up on me and simply walk away….or just tell me to "piss off"!"

"No, Paul", Rob protested. ". Why would I do that?"

"Well, Just hear me out, okay?", Paul asked with great solemnity "I have something that I want to say, or have to say, and then you do whatever you think you should do"

Rob sat very still, looking down at the carpet beneath his feet and waited for Paul to begin. It seemed to him to be a very long time before any words came forth, and when they did so, it seemed that the words were spoken with great effort on Paul's part.

"You know, Rob,…. My life has been like a roller coaster: the highs, the lows, and the long, sweeping little ups and downs between those highs and lows are almost too much sometimes. I haven't always been a very good person, but I don't think that I have ever really intentionally hurt anyone." He paused and looking downward, smoothed the small wrinkles in the coverlet as if he were also attempting to iron out his own thoughts. After a pause, he went on:

"You are the kind of friend I always wanted to have, but never did. I like everything about you, but now I am not sure that I am cut out to hang onto a real friend. Maybe I like you too much. What are the limits on something like this?", Paul asked searching Rob's face with his eyes.

"I'm not sure that I know, Paul. Hell! I am pretty new at this game of life myself. Maybe what you are afraid of is that we could be building a friendship. If, as they say, friendship is a marriage of souls, that implies a hell of a lot of work, and probably some fighting along the way. Hey! I'm game if you are!I hear women talk about how easy it is for males to "bond". I guess that after about 30,000 years of hunting side by side, watching the back of a fellow warrior or such in battle, we are bound to pick up some bonding skills. Let's go for it, and stop worrying about who is going to be scared off. I think that we are both honest enough and stubborn enough to want to get into the other guy's face before simply running off."

"You are great, Rob!", Paul said

"You noticed! See? You're getting smarter already!", Rob laughed "Well. Paul, for what it's worth, I want to see where this friendship goes. I rather like you too! "Let's get some sleep!"

CHAPTER 13

PART II

Back from his trip to Cazenovia and the King farm, Rob left the pick-up at the back of the Feed Mill and walked the few blocks to his grandparents' house. Not only had he arrived there in good time before the planned dinner, but even before his parents' arrival at the house.

"Oh!", his grandmother said, "You didn't stop off home first?"

"Well, no, I didn't", he replied. "I figured that everyone would have already gathered here by now. Truth to tell, I expected to come in to be greeted by some accusing stares from my mom!"

"How was your weekend?", his grandmother asked him, ignoring his remark, although she knew what he meant right enough. Her daughter Sheila did not overlook the little things by any means.

"Really good!", Rob stated with enthusiasm. "It turned

out to be pretty interesting: more Scottish connections, in fact". He picked up their copy of the Sunday paper and sat on the couch, looking at the front page with detachment. "I'll tell you all about it", he added.

"Tell us all about what?", his grandfather asked in mock gruffness as he entered the room.

"Hi, Gramp!", Rod said, rising to hug his grandfather

"Sit down, sit down!", his grandfather ordered. "You don't have to make a fuss over me! I haven't a dime to my name, I have just been kicked out of my own kitchen and I'm cutting you off without a cent anyway."

"You mean *MY* kitchen!", came a voice from the dining room.

Hugh MacKinnon sat down heavily in his chair, both hands on the front edges of the heavily upholstered arm rests.

"So, what's all this stuff about your stopping off to see the stump-jumpers in Pennsylvania to learn of your family? I meant to ask you about that before. Going down there to get your head filled with a bunch of old Gaelic lies! You don't have to go to Emporium to hear tall tales. I can tell more stories and make up more nonsense as I go along than anyone, and right here in Balston".

"Isn't that the truth!", came the voice from the kitchen.

"Don't pay any attention to her", his grandfather advised with a wave of his hand." She's back there trying to cook something or other".

Rob smiled at the on-going playful sniping between his

grandparents. They had always been like that, obviously truly comfortable with one another.

"No, Gramp, Mr MacKinnon seems to know a lot!"

"Well, he's supposed to! That's his job", Hugh stated as a matter of fact.

Rob's confusion was very evident by his facial expression. Frowning, he asked:

"Do you know him?"

"Well, yes! "Hugh answered his grandson." Of course I know him! His great- grandfather and my own grandfather were brothers! Of course, I haven't seen him in years; not since we about your age, I suppose".

"But Aunt Lilly just found this guy through some lady up in Canada,", Rob protested.

"My sister Lilly", Hugh pointed out," is a sweet, thoroughly good woman, who has about as much retention as one of your gramma's kitchen sieves! Of course, she is a bit younger than I am and may not remember some of those folks. For my own part, I hadn't seen or spoken with a member of that branch of the family since before World War Two, until the other day when I talked to Robert".

"Just the other day", Rob repeated, asking as it were, for clarification.

"Why, yes! The old stump-jumper called me on the 'phone just a couple of days ago".

"Robert MacKinnon", Rob said, seeking some affirmation.

"Isn't that who we've been talking about?" Hugh leaned

forward as if to emphasize what he was saying, then went on: "'Told me that he felt like a damned fool! He said that he realized that you are descended from Lachlan MacKinnon and that you are from Balston, but not until after you left did he put it all together that you are my grandson".

"Well, that rules out any possibility of any further visits to the wilds of Pennsylvania, Robbie", his grandmother said, coming into the room. "Your reputation is dusted now! Anyway, the real reason that I came in here is to tell you two that I need the dining table leaves put in and the table pulled more to the center. You strong, Male-hero types can fulfil a useful function at last".

"Well! If I had known that I would have to work for my meal, I could have gone down to the diner for a hamburger!", Hugh groused as he winked at Rob

"Great idea! Why don't you just do that?", his wife asked.

"Easy for you to say, Allie! You've managed to gold-dig me out of all my money and I am broke! 'Might as well do this lugging and hauling, I guess". Allison left the room, shaking her head and smiling.

As Hugh and Robbie were seeing to the table leaves and moving the table, the front door opened and Rob's mom and dad came into the house. Hugs and kisses were exchanged, followed immediately by Sheila's account of how no one knew that Rob would already be here; how they waited and waited and finally set out by themselves; that families moved around like Gypsies anymore rather than as settled families; No, Carol wasn't with them and that she would be coming later bringing her young man with her, whom she took it upon herself to invite without consulting anyone or without even considering how others might feel.

"Your mother could probably use some help in the kitchen, Sheila", Hugh said flatly, after having stood there as if in disbelief and a growing impatience with her ramblings. He had spoken with a finality which Sheila had rarely heard expressed by him in all her years as his daughter. He brought the palm of his hand to the back of his neck as he looked downward, shaking his head from side to side as Sheila made for the kitchen.

"Let's get those table leaves taken care of", he said.

After seeing to the table leaves and its extension and centering in the room, the three men went into the living room and sat down. Hugh had turned off the television, its having been tuned down so as to be almost inaudible anyway.

Rob turned to his father and told him:" Grampa was telling me that he knows Robert MacKinnon, Dad, and that they are some kind of cousins. Here I was thinking that Mr. MacKinnon was somebody discovered by Aunt Lilly".

"Well, in a way, she did discover him, Robbie", Hugh explained "If I had known that you wanted such information or to meet him, I suppose that I could have made the introductions, but I didn't know"

"How is he related to you, Pa?", Jim asked

"Well, as I was just telling Robbie, his great grandfather and my grandfather were brothers, Hugh explained

"What I do not understand", Rob said, "is why he would have been going up to Canada so often as a kid and a young man. I thought that.the MacKinnons had mostly lived around here."

"Well, yes. Most of the family seemed to be here, but we had close ties with Canada and our Canadian relatives there. We would go up there for reunions and such, and of course to the Canadian Highland Games. As I recall, my grandfather's Uncle Ruaridh went up to Canada with some people that they all knew. They had come over from Scotland together. Ruaridh had been here for awhile and then went up to help a friend with a saw-mill operation. If memory serves me, I believe that the man's name was Gilcannon. Anyway, the man had a saw-mill. I suppose that in time Ruaridh, or 'Rory' just stayed there, married a girl and got a farm started. Now, somehow, Bob MacKinnon's family always had kept in touch with Rory's family. In fact, Bob's grandfather, Alan, married a girl from up there. It is funny though, when you stop to think of it: the family having gone down into Pennsylvania".

Hugh stopped and squinted his eyes as if trying to remember something, soon to raise his hand in a gesture which signaled "wait", and then, nodding his head, resumed his explanation:

"Lachlan MacKinnon, my great grandfather, built the farm and that big old show-place of a house not too far from Emporium and then he came back here. His brother Andrew bought the whole thing from him for a pretty good price. Yes, Andrew was my great-grandfather's brother, you see. Lachlan's wife, Jean Morgan is said to have been some piece of work from what we've been able to gather. Sine Morgan. She was Hell-fire and damnation Presbyterian of the old school. She had all of the MacKinnons figured for soul-less pagans; no use whatever for the Old ways, the Highland ways."

"The Culdees?", Rob asked.

"Well, I guess so, although that word has been tossed around quite a bit. There is a fair-sized load of nonsense in print about the Culdees", Hugh advised.

"Whoa! Back up! I am missing something here!", Jim put in. "Who or what were the Culdees?"

"Well, Jim" Hugh said, turning to him," It's probably the term which is throwing you. If I had said "Celtic Christians", you would have known right away".

"Oh, of course! You are Celtic Christian, Hugh. I do know that: No doctrine of Original Sin, confessing to a Soul Friend rather than to a priest and so forth".

"Wait a minute!" This time it was Rob who needed an explanation. Looking to his grandfather, Rob asked, "*You* are Celtic Christian, Gramps?" He stared in disbelief; his mouth half opened and his brows knit in confusion.

"Always have been!", Hugh answered simply.

"But, you don't even go to church, Gramps!"

"Celtic Christians don't go to a church, Robbie. They carry their faith in their hearts and use their homes for gathered worship", Jim explained to his son.

"Why didn't anyone ever tell me, or teach me, anything about this?" Rob's voice registered disappointment, perhaps even betrayal.

Hugh and Jim exchanged embarrassed glances

"What! Is it a great, dark secret or something?" Rob was becoming increasingly agitated. He looked up to see his mother entering the room. Rob's dad and grandfather exchanged a slight smile.

"Whatever you three are arguing about, you'll have to wind it up soon. Dinner is about ready and we will begin as soon as Aunt Harriet arrives", Sheila announced.

"Harriet?" Hugh asked. "I didn't know that she was coming!" .

"Dad!", Sheila admonished, "You know that Aunt Harriet always joins us at family dinners. Carol and Henry will be here at about the same time, I should imagine".

Rob wanted to ask his mother why she had never mentioned Celtic Christianity to him or that her own parents had kept the ancient faith, but at that precise moment he caught his father's eye, and as if Jim had read his son's mind, he frowned and shook his head, the word 'later' silently with his lips. Just at that moment, a silhouette appeared outside the side-lights of the entryway. Aunt Harriet had arrived.

"Open the door for Aunt Harriet", Jim instructed his son.

"She entered the room as a gust of wind from out of the west and immediately filled the room with her presence, her rapid-fire explanations for her supposed tardiness. A flurry of handing a box and a shopping bag to Rob as she kissed and hugged him, bubbling with laughter.

"Hello, Jim!" She gushed, kissing him on the cheek. "Nice to see you! You're working too hard, I can see that! You can't burn the candle at both ends forever, you know!" Turning to her brother:

"Hughie! Well, here's a man who knows how to take it easy in life!"

"Nice to see you too, Harriet", her brother said, kissing her cheek.

Turning towards the dining area and kitchen, she called out to the women:"Halloooo??

Am I too late to help? I hope so!"

At that moment Rob glanced up to see his sister Carol and Henry, her "B.F." as Robbie called Henry, coming into the living room. He hadn't seen his sister since Christmas and they had always been quite close.

"Here are Carol and Henry!" he announced, going towards them. Carol looked to be very happy, prettier than ever. Her dark hair was fluffed out in a short but attractive cut, framing her delicate, doll-like features. Her eyes appeared to be more darkly brown than even he had remembered. He took her up into his arms and squeezed her to himself in a great bear-hug, his cheek pressed to hers, lifting her off the floor as he did so. "I have….missed you… so much!", Rob expressed, as if too were being squeezed.

"You are such a hunk!", Carol said with pride, as if he

were her own product, which in some ways, he may well have been. Certainly she had guarded him, watched over him, read to him, had been vexed by him time and time again, always to have forgiven his transgressions. To her, he had always been her 'baby brother': vulnerable and beautiful, capable of saving the world.

Rob released his grip, set her down and kissed her cheek, ceding her to their father and grandfather. Turning to Henry, he took his hand firmly in his own, with his left hand grasping Henry's upper arm just above his elbow, the same warm form of greeting being given to himself by this young man whom he had come to like very much.

"Henry! Good to see you again! How are you doing?"

"I am doing fine, Rob! How about yourself?"

"Not too bad! I'm hanging in there!", Rob said, grinning.

Henry nodded, returning Rob's smile. His light brown hair with tight curls made a halo-like effect around his head in the afternoon sunlight. His very grey eyes crinkled in merriment and his full mouth held an open and sincere smile above a square, cloven chin. He was a well-built fellow, perhaps an inch or two taller than Rob. Despite the warmth of the day, he was wearing a tie over his crisp short-sleeved summer shirt. His liking for Rob was very open and quite genuine. For his part, Rob instinctively approved of this man who had become such an important part of Carole's life.

"Well, are you wombats going to stand here, or come

into the dining room and have some dinner?" It was Grandpa, standing in the doorway in a pretense of stern scolding. He pecked Carole warmly on the cheek and gave her a great hug. He then took Henry by the hand as Rob had done"'Good to see you again, Henry! No doubt you have met my son-in-law, Jim"

"Yes" Jim laughed. We've been introduced! "With his left arm around his daughter's waist, he shook Henry's hand warmly.

After all the greetings had been shared and expressed with and to all present, they went to the table. The places had been set by Sheila and Rob noticed that Henry and Sheila were placed opposite, across the table from one another. Rob had been seated next to his sister, which was indicated by a glass of milk at his plate. He would be the only one having milk at the meal, he knew. Rob picked up the milk and moved to the other side of the table, opposite his sister.

"What are you doing, Robbie?", his mother asked.

"I am changing places with Henry ", he said simply "I have already hugged and kissed Carole. I am not going to be elbowed by her throughout the meal as well". Turning to Henry he said, "You like her so much, let her elbow you, rather than me!'

"Well,", Henry told him, "At least, next to her, she won't be able to kick me in the shins under the table". Carole flashed Rob a look of thanks.For her part, Sheila simply moved her eyebrows up and down with a "so that's that!

Whatever!" gesture akin to a shrug of the shoulders.

Hugh asked the blessing before the meal and took hold of the stem of his wine glass.

"That was a very short Grace, Dad!", Sheila admonished

"Well, Honey, the Good Lord who hath of His bounty brought forth this wonderful meal has also bestowed upon me a powerful appetite. I'm hungry! Anything else which any one of us might add to what I said, the Lord will hear". Raising his wine glass, he went on: Good health to all and may we meet often in the future".

"Dad", Jim put in, "I think that we may have something to add, perhaps even another toast." Everyone turned to look at Jim at the other end of the table from Hugh. He smiled and looked towards Henry and Carole and said: "Henry, the ball is in your court now!"

Henry stood, looking down at Carole with a face so filled with love that it caused Rob to stare in awe and almost tearful admiration.

"I have asked Carole to marry me, to share my life and she has agreed and wants me to share her life as well", Henry announced.

"Excellent!" Hugh's face was a broad smile. He rose from his chair, walked around and put his hand on Henry's shoulder. "I was afraid that she was going to be on our hands forever!"

"Oh, Hugh! You old fool!" Allison said, tears of joy in her eyes, "Isn't this wonderful?"

"So, everyone, A Toast!, " Jim said, raising his glass, "to a long and happy marriage!" All glasses were raised and, at this time, drained. Henry took a ring from his pocket and slipped it onto Carole's finger. They kissed and everyone applauded. Allison, Harriet, Sheila were all wiping their eyes and smiling.

Henry resumed his seat next to Carole and the rest of the dinner was greatly devoted to talk of the future wedding, of plans of every sort regarding two young people embarking on a long life together.

"Will you be married here, at the Presbyterian church?", Harriet asked. The question was followed by Henry and Carole looking at each other and a brief period of silence, which was broken by none other than Sheila:

"Carole and Henry will be living according to the faith of our future son-in-law, so as I understand it, the wedding will be the starting point of this connectedness in the same faith as well".

"Oh!" Aunt Hariette said, unable to mask her confusion. "Are you Catholic, Henry?"

"No, Ma'am", Henry answered. "I am Jewish".

"Oh dear!" It was Allison, her hand over her mouth. Everyone looked at her in surprise that she had registered such a tone of despair.

"Mrs. MacKinnon", Henry said to her softly, "I hope that this will not be a problem for us. I do love Carole very much and my family have come to think the world of her".

"Oh, no, no! For Heaven's sake, no! That is not it at all!" Allison waved her napkin almost as a signalman trying to avert a disaster. She explained: I had no idea that you are Jewish, Henry! I should have made certain, had I known, that we did not set a table with foods which would have you violate your dietary law: Meat and cottage cheese, milk, all at the same meal! Oh! I wish that I had known!"

"Mother, What on earth are you talking about?", Sheila asked, not comprehending the cause of her mother's distress.

"Jews are not to have meat and milk dishes at the same meal", Allison explained.

Henry smiled warmly at the older woman and told her:

"Mrs. MacKinnon, It is wonderful that you would concern yourself about such things, but we are not Orthodox Jews. Now, we do not eat ham or pork or shell-fish of any kind, but we do not strictly observe all of the old dietary laws. We have some leeway in our lives!"

"Are you sure, Henry?", she persisted.

"Absolutely! My mom's dad, my grandfather, is a Rabbi!", he explained.

"You really do not look Jewish at all, Henry!" It was Harriet, as if it were time for some comic relief.

"Harriet, you always manage to say a dumb thing at a smart time, or a smart thing at a dumb time!", Hugh said.

Everyone laughed and Aunt Harriet wore a little girl's mischievous smile which made Rob wonder if Aunt Harriet was as "dumb" as she might pretend to be.

"Well, Ma'am, you aren't the first person to tell me that I do not look Jewish, whatever that means. In any case, I feel myself to be Jewish", Henry said with a smile.

"If I were a Jew", Rob put in, "I would want to go for the whole nine yards: the tradition, the Kosher meals, all of it!"

"You think so, do you? It takes a lot of money to run an Orthodox household: two sets of china: one for meat dishes, the other for milk dishes; strict observance of the Sabbath, and think of it, Rob, your sister would have to cut off her hair before the wedding!", Henry explained.

"Goodness!" Aunt Harriet exclaimed. "You don't have to do that do you, Carole?" At the end of the table, Hugh rolled his eyes.

"No, Aunt Harriet! I will be pretty much left in tact", Carole laughed

Rob was looking at his sister with an expression of great love and deep approval, then his eyes met those of Henry, who was mirroring Rob's expression, but towards his future young brother-in-law. Rob then spoke in a very matter of fact manner:

"I can not believe that none of you knew that Henry is Jewish! I have known that since about the second time I had been around him!" .

"Oh? How did you know that?", Sheila asked.

"We went swimming one day. Who ever saw a cross hanging from a chain around a guy's neck that is shaped like a six-pointed star ?", Rob asked.

"Rob", Henry laughed, "I am going to love having a brother like you!" .

"Don't be so sure, Henry! I might make your life really

interesting! I never had a brother to fight with, or borrow his stuff….or blame things on! Wow! There are some really great possibilities here! Yessss!", Rob ended with two thumbs up.

"See what I mean?", Henry asked all present, "I rest my case!"

"Oh, No!", Jim Currie intoned, "My son the Jewish Lawyer! What could be worse?"

"A son in law who is a Catholic priest living in sin with a daughter who is a nun, I should imagine", Hugh said. Everyone laughed. Sheila smiled, looking sideways towards her husband. Rob wondered how long it had taken his dad to get his mom to accept the occasion at hand.

After dinner, having instructed, Jim, Henry and Rob to follow him, Hugh led them into the living room. He opened the leaded glass doors of a built-in cabinet, from which he brought forth heavy, dark and long-necked bottle. From a lower shelf he produced four short, heavy drinking glasses, which he then set down on the marble-topped coffee table. He then began to open the bottle.

"I have been saving this single-malt Scotch for a special occasion", he explained to them, " and it would seem that this evening has given me that long awaited reason. This is the occasion." He poured the glasses to about one third full and then handed one each to his son-in-law, to Henry and to Rob. Raising his own glass he said:

"To a great future for us all. For harmony and peace. Slainte!"

"Slainte", the men replied, although for Henry it was a strange new word:"Slahnjj", but he repeated the sound which had come to his ears. The glasses clinked together and the four men sipped their drinks.

"Henry", Hugh explained to him:" That is a Scots Gaelic word and it means "Health". ". In deference to your tradition, we'll toast again". Hugh raised his glass. "Le Chaim!", he pronounced and all repeated "Le Chaim",:" To Life"..Again the four glasses came together, after which Hugh said:

"Now, men, let's take our drinks, and this bottle, and go out to the back terrace and let the women worry about what we might be discussing!"

On the way to the back door, Hugh asked Henry if he was satisfied with the single malt and if he were wishing that it had some ice in the glass.

"No, Sir, no ice" Henry replied, "perhaps just a drop or two of water to release the full flavor".

"Aha! You really know how to drink a good single malt!", Hugh said to him, then turning to Rob he asked him to snake in past the women in the kitchen and put a bit of cold water in a small cream pitcher and bring it out to them. Rob handed his glass to his father and went into the kitchen. When Rob returned with the pitcher of water he heard Henry saying:

"Mr.MacKinnon, as much as I really like this Single Malt, I must not drink too much tonight. I have to drive after I leave and I would hate to be pulled over by a cop! My motel is on the other side of town".

"Motel?", Hugh asked him, "What for? You are going to stay here tonight! Where are your bags ?"

"In the car, but…", Henry began.

"Well, that's that then!", Hugh stated. "We have a spare room and we even have indoor plumbing with hot and cold running water! I won't take 'no' for an answer! Now, perhaps you should go inside and call that place and tell them that you've had a change in plans so that you won't be owing anything for that room. We'll guard your drink while you're gone….for a while anyway!"

Rob felt so proud of the way in which his elders were taking Henry into the family and had never before now sat with his father and grandfather as another adult male. He loved the banter and pretended bluster of his grandfather and he admired deeply his own father's rather quiet, caring strength. He rather supposed that he would himself probably become more like his father and that seemed to him to be a very agreeable prospect, for Jim Currie was highly regarded in the community as a good, fair and honorable man. That he would be a good father-in-law to Henry Rob had no doubt whatever. Rob felt good! He rejoiced in his own youth and it occurred to him that it was a gift to him that he could realize, while young, that he could appreciate what he was experiencing. "Know what you have when you have it!", so went the old expression which he had heard so often.

When Henry returned to join them in the settling

darkness of the evening, the men on the terrace having become moving, speaking silhouettes, only the glasses on the table reflecting some light from the kitchen window. Hugh was speaking in a low voice, telling of a happening from his much younger days:

"….this fellow sounded like he had just got off the boat! What a thick Scottish burr he had! My father asked him where he had come from in Scotland and he told us that he had come from a place near Glasgow. I thought that he said that his name was Robin or Robbin. He said,"It's nae ROBIN! it's Rabin!" I asked him if that was an English name and he said: "Ahm Nae English! I'm a Scot! Not a Lawlander, not a Haelander. Ah'm a Jew, a Scots Jew!" The fellow was one of the most nationalistic Scots I've ever met! He went on to tell us that his ancestors had moved into Scotland in the 1200's, when there were terrible pogroms in York, where they had lived for some time. Apparently King William the Lion had much earlier welcomed England's Jews, for Scotland had no real mercantile or banking firms of any note. At that time. Anyway, the fellow went on to tell us that Scotland is the one land which had never persecuted Jews. My father said to him:" Well, the clans in the north were feuding, the Border clans were too busy stealing English cows and the Lowland Lairds were involved in their great intrigues as well. After that, Protestants were too busy sacking and burning Catholic churches and abbeys to the ground. They just didn't have time to persecute Jews!" The fellow laughed at that and admitted that he had never thought of that." They all laughed.

"Hey!", Henry put in, "if Carole and I have a son he may well be called a Scottish Jew! I certainly would expect him to want to wear his mother's clan tartan".

"Or a Jewish Scot!", Rob suggested. "Yes, I would want to see him wear Currie tartan from time to time. Well, actually we wear the MacDonnell of Clan Ranald tartan, Right, dad?", he asked, turning toward his father.

"There is a Currie tartan, but most clansmen wear MacDonnell because the Curries have been the hereditary bards of the MacDonnell chiefs. We also have a Chieftain of our own. He is the hereditary bard ", Jim explained. "Another thought! Carole and you and your children will be keeping the same Sabbath as my parents-in-law! How about that, Pa, ?" Jim asked Hugh.

"What? What do you mean?. Now I'm confused!", Henry exclaimed.

"Well, Yes, Henry ", Hugh admitted. We keep the same Sabbath as you in this house. The lady of the house lights the candles, the man of the house reads scripture and leads in prayer. Of course, I do not wear a yarmulke. We are Sabbath-keepers too: Friday sundown 'til Saturday sundown. We follow the ways of the very ancient church."

"I was thinking that you would be Presbyterians, like the Curries!", Henry said, somewhat perplexed.

"Actually, Henry, I am not Presbyterian either.", Jim told him. "My wife is committed to that church and of course I attend service with her. We all went as a family to church there when the kids were home.", Jim explained." I was brought up Anglican. As a matter of fact, Rob was baptized Anglican!"

"Wow! This is too much!", this time it was Rob who registered confusion. I always thought that both you and mom are Presbyterian, Dad! And how did I come to be baptized Anglican?"

"It's a long story, Rob", Jim said. "When your sister had been baptized four years before you came along, there had been a minister there who went on and on about Original Sin and such nonsense at Carole's Christening that I decided that I had had it!.Anglicans have the doctrine of Original Sin too, but usually soft-pedal the whole idea. Any way! Enough of this! We are supposed to be a welcoming committee, for pete's sake!; Not to scare Henry off!"

"Believe me", Henry assured them, "In no way am I being scared off! I must admit though, that I think that we would have been ahead of the game if Carole had experienced the Sabbath of her grandparents. I would really like to know more about your faith, Mr MacKinnon. Really!"

"There will be plenty of time for that, Henry!" Hugh assured him

"Well, now that I have reached the so-called age of reason, I am not going to wait, Gramps!", Rob put in. "You can expect company at your next Sabbath. Don't worry! I won't destroy my Mom's grand plan or drive her to distraction. I will attend church with her and Dad on

Sundays, but I need to know more about what really should be our ancestral church!"

Henry looked towards Jim whom he could vaguely see through the darkness. His future father-in law smiled, tilted his head to one side and shrugged his shoulders.

"So, Mr. MacKinnon", Henry persisted, "What is your branch of Christianity called?"

"Well", Hugh told him, "When I was a boy, folks just called it ;'the Old Way' or the 'Ancient Faith'. I see that today we are being referred to as' Celtic Christians ', which is pretty much who or what we are, I suppose. Even so, when people refer to the Celtic Church or write about us, they seem to speak or write about us in the past tense, unable to believe that our church is still alive to this day".

"Is it a branch of Catholicism, or is it a Protestant denomination?". Henry asked, seemingly truly interested.

"Well, Henry", Hugh answered," it is not Protestant, for we were never Catholic in the first place, so did not break from the Roman Catholic Church. We, that is, Celtic ancestors first heard of the message when some people who actually had known Jesus brought their teachings to some Welsh-speaking Celts of Southwestern Britannia. That is reported to have happened sometime around 37 A.D. The very first Christian "above ground, out-in-the open church was built near Glastonbury in 63 A.D. The Roman Church even accepts that Britannia was the first Christian nation." Hugh paused and looked squarely at his future grandson-in-law before stating: "The main thing is this: If my granddaughter has decided to support her husband in Judaism and raise whatever children you may have come into your lives in the Jewish faith, you will both have my full support and I think that I may speak for Jim and Rob as well in this".

"You'll have my support, Henry, ", Jim said, "I sure expect to attend my grandson's Bar Mitzva, however! "

Rob simply smiled his approval and the three of them sat quietly for a while. In the still of the evening children could be heard playing and a dog barking off in the distance. The air was still and from time to time the night sounds of crickets as well as the odd insect hitting against the kitchen's lighted window glass were the only sounds near to them, although before long a distant adult neighbor's voice could be heard:" Time for you kids to come inside now and get washed up!"

"Was he talking to us?" Hugh asked." Well, It must be time for last orders. Let's have another dram and head on into the house! Besides that, the women are probably as nervous as a witch in church!", he chuckled..

"Why do you say that, Grampa?", Rob asked

"Well, the way I figure it, Hugh explained, "they would have sent Carole out here to get us before this, but they think that they have to let us find out whether we, in this family are going to accept Henry, or whether Henry, having met us, is going to head for the hills!"

"What do you think of that, Henry?", Jim asked with just the hint of a smile, "You going to hang around this looney bin, or escape while you still have a chance?"

"Oh, I don't know", Henry said, as if in speculation, "It looks rather interesting; maybe like a study in tribal customs and Anthropology. I guess that I am curious to see what else might happen, so, yes! I will stick around and no,. I do not plan to run off just yet!"

It was two days before Rob went back to his grandparents' house again. Curiosity had been eating at him and he wanted to get his grandfather to one side and ask him more about this part of his heritage which had been kept from him. He felt that he had been able to do this very thing, but just as they were settling in for some conversation, an elderly neighbor called to ask if Hugh could help him with a dysfunctional lighting fixture. Rob asked if he might go along and perhaps be of some help, but Hugh told him to stay and visit with his grandmother, explaining that he did not expect that there was any major problem at his friend's house. Mr. Wilson, the neighbor, lived alone, having lost his wife to cancer two years previously and Hugh believed that any problems which he might have were probably more due to a need for some company, as much as anything else.

Allison had taken a pitcher of iced tea to the table on the back terrace, expecting that the three of them might have a visit together, When Rob mentioned that his grandfather had been called away by Mr. Wilson, his grandmother expressed her sadness for the poor fellow. She said that he had not taken his wife's death well at all and seemed so often to be somewhat lost without her.

"Men are not as capable of being the surviving spouse as are women", she said. "Heaven knows that it isn't easy for anyone, male *or* female, but when it comes to suddenly finding oneself to be alone, women seem to fare better somehow. Of course, I really question whether I could really go on with my life without your grandfather's constant teasing and smart remarks! What ever would I do without that mean old cuss?"

They joked about such things for awhile. Finally Rob got right to the point:

"Gram, in all the years that I have been in this family, no one ever told me that you and Grampa practice Celtic Christianity. Why is that, anyway?", he asked.

"Oh, Robbie! I don't know. Perhaps no one ever thought that it mattered".

"Gramma, I don't buy that for one minute! Looking back, I see now that Mom never wanted me to come over here on Friday evenings. She always said that that was your and gramps' quiet time, and that Carole and I had to leave you alone!"

"Yes," Allison said, tilting her head to one side in that way of hers which had become so familiar to him. She looked down at her glass, pushing the condensation on its surface with her thumb. "Yes. I suppose that she might have said that, and of course it is indeed our 'quiet time', But…", she raised her eyes to meet those of her grandson, "Good Heavens! We would not have wanted you to stay away!

Surely you must know that you would always be welcome at any time at all!"

"But why would she have put it like that?", he persisted.

"Well! Look at that!", she said, ignoring his question and motioning to a large crab-apple tree, "Those Blue Jays are terrible! First it's the Red Squirrels causing so much trouble, then the Jays!"

Rob did not look away. He kept his eyes on her face, wanting her to know that he was waiting for an answer to his question. Without looking away from the tree Allison spoke to him:

"I heard you. It's difficult to know why your mother reacts as she does. She sometimes seems to have so much anger in her! I have asked myself over and over: just what I did, or what her father did, to fill her with such antagonism. Maybe she thought that we loved Denny more than we love her. I really don't know". She looked down to her glass again, raised her eyebrows to two fine high, rounded arches and continued: "Maybe we did. I don't know. But if we did I do not think that we were aware of it. Of course….", she took a sip of her tea, …"Denny was so loving, so caring. He was an easy child to raise in that respect. I can not remember him ever showing any sign of rebellion at all, not ever, until this Viet Nam war. It was as if he had been saving all of the rebellion in his life for this one great issue! Strange.".

They sat there in silence for awhile, Grandmother and grandson, for what seemed to Rob a very long time. He knew that his grandmother was thinking of the tree house at the edge of the garden with children still playing there, of his own mother and other little girls playing in the well built, still brightly painted playhouse not far away. Somewhat slowly, Allison pushed up her glasses and wiped her eyes with the thumb and forefinger of her right hand: a gesture which Rob calculated to pass for a rubbing of tired eyes.

"Do you hear from him very often?", Rob asked.

"What's that dear?" Allison looked up, her expression somewhat conveying surprise.

"Do you hear from Uncle Denny? Does he write?"

"Oh, yes! Yes, we hear from him frequently. Your grandfather has been renting a post office box in another town and he goes there once or twice a week to see if there's anything from Canada" She took of her tea, pursed her lips and frowned slightly before continuing: "I'm sure that we're not fooling anyone. Everyone knows. Mind you, a number of people stopped speaking to us after Denny decided to go to Canada".

"That must have hurt!", Rob said to her.

"Well, not really, Robbie". I suppose that it did make us a bit disappointed,.perhaps even a bit angry at first. But in this life one learns to live with some disappointments from time to time. Your grandfather stopped going to his Veterans' gatherings and I dropped out of my Early American Heritage group. No loss, Robbie! No loss at all! Some people felt that we weren't being good Americans, supporting a son who refused to go to war. It seems to be all

"Love it or leave it!", "America can not possibly be wrong!" . Your uncle Dennis didn't see it that way. He truly believed that this war is morally wrong. Well, we have had soldiers in Viet Nam for over nine years now, twice as long as our involvement in World War Two, and we seem to be no closer to ending this terrible thing than ever we were".

The two of them sat quietly for a few minutes, simply looking at the back garden, enjoying the peace of the afternoon. Glancing toward his grandmother, Rob's eyes stopped to take in her face as she looked out across the lawn. He noticed a rather wan, perhaps tired half smile come to her face. He would remember her as she appeared this day for many, many years after she had gone: the gentle half-smile, her right hand holding her glass as it sat on the table, her left hand spread out over her upper chest. Despite that hint of a smile, her eyes had in them a strong hint of some unexpressed fear. He would remember that at that moment, he had seen that his grandmother MacKinnon had become an old lady, without his ever had any prior warning.

"How old is Uncle Denny now, Gram?", Rob asked, breaking the silence

"He will be twenty-eight. Oh, No! He is already twenty-eight now! My goodness!"

"Oh! I didn't realize that he is that much younger than my Mom" he said, a bit surprised.

"Well", His grandmother explained, "He is almost ten years younger than Sheila".

"Do you and Grampa see him often?" Rob was finally

able to learn something of his uncle and was hungry for every detail.

"We go up to Montreal a few times each year, Robbie. As a matter of fact, Canada has become our "vacation land". We were with him in April. Your granddad and I went with him to Quebec City, and then the three of us went up to Baie St. Paul. It was a wonderful holiday for us! Old Quebec city is marvelous and Baie St. Paul is like stepping back in time! Heavens!, she laughed, "Come to think of it, we probably see more of our adult son than most Americans do!"

"Do you think that he will ever come home to the States?", Rob asked.

"I really don't know, Robbie", his grandmother said thoughtfully. "He has been building a life for himself where he is. With his degree in engineering, the firm that he is working for snapped him right up! He seems happy with his job and they seem to be glad to have him. We met his "boss" and he couldn't have praised him more! Also, Dennis has met a very nice young woman. She is French, by the way; a really fine girl. Her name is Madeleine de Veau. Now, there's a good French name if ever there was one!"

"Does Uncle Denny even speak French?"

"Well, he certainly does now! He took French in High School, but now he reads and writes in French all the time as well as speak the language!"

"Wow!", Rob said with awe,"That's great! I studied French for three years as well and will be able to stumble through some of the language with him!"

"Well, Robbie", his grandmother said, tilting her head towards him," The chances that your grandfather and I may be seeing some French-speaking grandchildren before long are not that remote!"

They both laughed, neither of them at all adverse to the idea.

CHAPTER 14

PART II

Rob would not see Paul again until later in the summer, when he would be accompanying Gwynne and Rob on a day trip to Fort Ticonderoga. Summer is busy at a Feed Mill or any farm supply business in the summer months, and this had been a busy summer indeed. Rob found himself to be working longer hours, yet he managed to spend as much time as he could with Gwynne in the evenings. He and Gwynne had come together towards the end of their Sophomore year in High school. They had been in some of the same classes before then, but the unrest of the times is what really brought them together. There had probably not been a time in the history of the country when rebellion was so wide-spread among the nation's youth. On May 4th of that year, after two days of protests against President Nixon's decision to broaden combat activities to include Cambodia, Ohio National Guardsmen had opened fire on a group of students at Kent State University, killing four students and wounding nine others. As a result of this action, demonstrations and protests which sometimes escalated to near-riots took place on College and University campuses across the country. Considering the age, before the widespread use of the internet, when television and radio were the sources of news, it is a source of amazement even yet, how quickly the news had spread. The photo image of a teen-aged girl kneeling, screaming, her arms thrown into the air as she lamented over the prone, lifeless body of a male student was a photo which was seen throughout the world in record time and a photo which would win a Pulitzer prize for the photographer. Many, many forces in small college towns prepared for the worst. Some Presidents and University trustees simply locked their institutions. Others simply left town for a week, hoping for things to "cool down". The Viet Nam war was, by this time, becoming increasingly unpopular and President Nixon was becoming the target of an intense hatred by the young people especially. Truth to tell, he was not enjoying great popularity among older people either as more and more of them came to question his policies and what had come to be called "the Imperial Presidency". In any case, the turmoil and anger of youth is what brought Rob and Gwynne to become truly acquainted for the first time; one of those things which somehow simply "happen".

There had been a discussion among some students during a Social Studies class which was carried on by them even after the end of the class and the school day itself. Some of the male students had taken the side of the government, having relatives serving in the military and perhaps feeling that they themselves might be "called up" in a couple of years' time. One of the girls had been particularly outspoken, even a bit nasty in her responses in opposition to the war She called the boys out on this, her parting shot being: "Right! You guys probably can't wait to get your rifles and grenades and all that great stuff! You can be baby-killers too, right?" Gwynne had spoken up in a very calm and mature manner and asked the girl if she really believed what she had been saying and went on to explain that her own brother had been in that war and that he had come home deeply wounded in spirit, as he had been wounded in body. After the students ended their discussion and started going their separate ways, Rob stopped at his locker to get his books prior to going on to Swim practice. On his way through a lower, back corridor, he saw a girl sitting on a broad window ledge, hunched over and she seemed to be crying. He had stopped and slowly approached her. He then realized that the girl was Gwynne! He moved to her side, knelt down on one knee and gently pushed her hair back from her face.

"Hey!, come on", he was almost whispering. "Please don't cry! You don't have to cry, Gwynne". He put his hand on her shoulder and quietly asked her: "Take a walk with me, okay?"

"No, I'm alright", she said, her voice still breaking as she spoke.

"No, Gwynne. You are *not* alright", he answered her directly.

She raised her head to face him and he could see that her eyes were red and tearful. He reached in his Shirt pocket and produced a white, folded handkerchief and handed it to her.

"Don't worry!", he said playfully, "I haven't used it!"

She accepted the handkerchief, a weak smile on her face from his remark, she asked him:

"Aren't you on your way to a practice?", she asked.

"Some things take precedence over others ", he replied. "The coach knows that I am pretty faithful to the team. He will understand if I tell him that something came up. C'mon, Gwynne. Walk with me".

They walked together. They walked past mealtime. Sometimes they stopped here or there and listened to one another. Rob liked her company, her wonderful, feminine way of seeing things. For Gwynne, Rob was almost overwhelming: kind, considerate, somewhat needy, but oh, so masculine! He appeared to be both: a little boy looking for acceptance and a man ready to take on the world! She felt a blush of shame when she found herself wondering what he would look like naked, yet in a way, she thought that perhaps she already knew.

Finally, in front of her house, he asked her if he could see her again. He gave her a kiss: a somewhat self-conscious kiss, as if he were not really sure of himself. Gwynne answered that she would hope to see him again and she thanked him for his concern, his kindness and his having reached out to her. Later, in her room, she realized that she still had his handkerchief and she remembered how he had taken it from his shirt pocket. She drew it up to her nose and found that it still carried his scent, a scent that she found to be agreeable: the smell of a very sweet and kind boy, the smell of a good man who had shown genuine concern for her.

"Rob Currie", she thought to herself, "I could happily spend my life with you and go with you to the ends of the earth! I never knew that a boy could be so beautiful!"

In the following two years they were building a rather special friendship. Considering their ages and relative inexperience, Gwynne and Rob shared something very special, even a rather amazing relationship. Simply put, they were comfortable together. They did not crowd each other or "cling" to one another. They allowed one another his or her "space". Gwynne was to Rob so many things which his own mother somehow could never be. Gwynne did not make expectations or mentally write a script for him to follow She was that very rare girl who had perhaps displayed the qualities of a mature woman. She was not "cute" in the Hollywood sense of the world, but with her soft grey eyes and dark blonde hair, her quiet, accepting demeanor, she was nevertheless very striking. The other students too seemed to respect something about her. There was indeed something quite special about Gwynne. She did not resort to those signs of possession in front of others To her, Rob was bright and beautiful and strong in her eyes. He sensed this and felt it and loved her deeply in return. He respected her, and felt no need to exhibit or assert any of the masculine dominance which seems to have been the general rule at that time. The two of them actually seemed to somehow liberate one another from the deeply cast role playing of the age in which they found themselves to be living. After all of this, by the time that Gwynne had completed her Freshman year at Syracuse University, she and Rob had already established a relationship where they not only loved one another, but one in which they had found that they truly 'liked' one another very much.

"Yes, I want him!", she explained to her room mate one day, "But I don't want him as a trophy to show to the world. I do not want a "boyfriend" to show the world. I want him to be the father of our children. I want to share his life and I want him to share mine". When asked how she could be so sure, Gwynne explained: "because he is a boy.....No! because he is a man who is beautiful inside and out! You should see him with children! He is so tender and caring! God! When I see him interact with a small child, I feel my ovaries leap inside of me!" Her room mate looked at her long and hard and told her that she was convinced that Gwynne was totally "hooked"!

It is not that they did not experience some real questions regarding that "dance to the earth's (and biology's) desperate creeds"! When the two of them would come into a deep kiss, it was as if two halves of some thing had discovered each its missing part. When they kissed it was as if they could not pull apart. It was difficult for both of them, for they wanted deeply to melt, one into the other. They had gone "skinny dipping" in a lake or pond in the night and felt the warmth of one another's bodies in the cool water. On more than one occasion, while swimming and playing games in the water, Rob's body would glide by, next to, or over Gwynne's own body and she could feel that he was aroused. On one such occasion, she laughed and asked him:" How can you be a swimmer when you have a rudder such as you seem to have? Doesn't it slow you down in the water?" He laughed and told her that if, when he was racing, she had been in the same pool, he would have lost a meet hands down. Yet, they were careful about sex. She had told him early on that she did not want to have him wear some latex thing if and when they made love; that she wanted to feel *him*, his body and its member, and not some balloon-type thing in her body. This naturally complicated things somewhat. Somehow, they managed to express their love one for the other without getting too carried away by their urges and drives. It had not been easy for either of them.

It might be well to mention that Rob's mother, Sheila, was not particularly won over by her son's young lady, although she was indeed quite capable of using Gwynne's name and person for the purpose of argument from time to time. One example of this was a Friday of the last weekend which Rob had spent at the King farm. His mother had, after all, been violently opposed to his going there.

"And what about Gwynne?", she had asked. "If she is so special, how can you leave her sitting by the 'phone while you traipse off to some farm out in the boondocks? It's pretty hard for a girl to wait next to a telephone, hoping that some boy whom she happens to love, may get around to call her whenever he gets damned good and ready!"

"Sheila! Stop it!", his father had put in. "Gwynne knows how to use a telephone, I'm sure!"

"Right!", Sheila fired back. "That's another thing! What kind of family permits a daughter to chase after boys, calling them at their homes?"

"We are good friends, Mom! Why shouldn't she be able to call me?", Rob asked. "As for this other thing, the farm: Gwynne thinks that I should go there if it is important to me."

"Well then", came his mother's parting salvo, "one might be excused from wondering just how important *you* are to *her*, if she does not care one way or the other!"

"Right!", Rob said wearily, and turning while also raising his eyes heavenward. His eyes then met those of his father's and Jim's somewhat sympathetic but also amused expression.

Rob had come to an understanding with his father regarding Sheila at an earlier time when Rob had been the recipient of one of his mother's verbal artillery. He had made so bold as to ask Jim a question which had been in his mind:

"Is she like that with you all the time too ?"

"Where the hell have you been for nineteen years, Rob?", Jim asked. "Are you deaf, dumb and blind?"

"Why is she like that?", Rob persisted.

"Because", Jim Currie explained as if speaking to a very slow student, "your Grandpa MacKinnon, who by the way, is one of the most intelligent men I have ever known, had a blind spot where your mother was concerned when she was a girl and into her young adulthood. She was" Daddy's Little Princess". She was a spoiled brat, pure and simple! I was attracted to her because of her 'spunk', or what I thought was ' spunk'. Your Mom never lacked for anything. If there was anything she felt she wanted, her father would get it for her. Hell! Even after we were married, she *had* to have new Living Room furniture! I couldn't afford it at the time. We were young; just starting out! The next thing that I knew, a delivery van showed up and two men carried a couch, two chairs and an ottoman into the house. You can imagine how that made *me* feel! Life went on like that for a while....until your Grandma MacKinnon put a stop to it.".

"How'd she do that, Dad?", Rob asked with a faint smile.

"Well, Rob, she came over here and gave me a piece of her mind. I will never forget it! She said, straight out: "Jim Currie, you're a good man, but you are a damned fool!" As you know, she can be pretty direct when the mood strikes her. She told me that I should go over and tell my father-in-law to either back away or else take his daughter back. She said that my young wife was an expert at playing one end against the other, and that unless I wanted to spend my life, dedicating my life, to a child in a woman's body, I had to put a stop to it."

"Wow! Did you do as she said?", Rob asked.

"I thought about it for a while; really "chewed" on it. What she had said made me angry, but I realized that your grandmother MacKinnon isn't apt to act "the busybody" for no reason at all, and that what she had said made sense. Anyway, I got up my courage (I don't think that I had been that scared even during the war!), went over there and I talked to him. I was surprised! He acted almost as if he had expected me to talk to him about it. He admitted that he realized that he had not been helping our marriage in the long run". Rob saw his father stop, as if in thought, and smile to himself for a moment before going on:" Ever since then we get along very well. I can say in all honesty that I truly love my father-in-law. He is a good man".

"Well, Dad, from everything that I have seen and heard, he certainly seems to think a lot of you as well!"

"Yeah! I know! ", Jim laughed," Now he gives stuff to me all the time instead of to his daughter!" He then turned to Rob with a more serious face.

"Now!", he began emphasizing what he was about to say with a finger at his son's chest: "Hear this! Your Mom can be a pain in the butt. I know it, you know it. But she is my wife! When another man, even if he happens to be my son, criticizes MY wife, that man is asking for trouble! Do you catch my drift? So, Back Off! I do not want you to criticize your mother again. For all of her faults, and we all have faults, there is a very good, caring and loving human being in that woman, and she has been a good mother to you and to your sister. That's it! I have said all that I am going to say!"

They looked at one another for what seemed like a long time. Rob could feel his cheeks to be a bit flushed. Finally, Jim said to his son:

"C'mere!", and stretching forward he hugged Rob to him, holding the back of his son's neck with one hand, he kissed his forehead. "Okay?"

"Okay", Rob responded, his voice low, "I really do love Mom, Dad, but somehow I am never able to please her".

"It probably seems like that sometimes, Rob, but sometimes love gets translated into caring too much about someone, not wanting that person to fail or become disappointed in life. It's not hard to get our feelings mixed up, or our priorities somewhat tangled in the process. In the end, your mom loves you and is terribly proud of you. Yet, she is your mother and you are her "cub" She would give her life for you without even stopping to think about it".

"I know that", Rob replied hoarsely, "but I wish that she could maybe just ease up a bit and cut me some slack, you know? Dad, sometimes I think that Mom and God must have one hell of a time keeping us all in line!"

Jim's laugh followed a near explosion of air from his mouth. He shook his head and said: "Sorry to remind you of this, Rob, but the apples don't fall far from the tree! You are a lot more like your mother than you will ever know!"

"Really? Is that what you think? Give me a break, Dad! I don't get all bent out of shape because someone isn't living up to what I have decided he or she is supposed to do or be!"

"Well, yes, Rob. You do." His father said, looking into his son's eyes. "In a way, we all do this. You may show your disappointment in different ways, but you somehow manage to get your point across".

Rob looked downward, smiling a bit shyly, maybe even a bit slyly, as if he had been found out.

"Not meaning to change the subject", Jim said, "but in any case, changing the subject, when do we get to see your young lady?"

"Oh! Well, you have already met her, Dad! She is the girl that I took to our Senior Prom".

"So, *that's* the girl!, Jim said, remembering. "You mean Owen Williams' daughter! Why didn't you say so?"

"You know the Williams family? ", Rob asked, somewhat surprised.

"Well, yes!", Jim replied. "I do not know them well, but enough to exchange small talk from time to time. Owen is in the Insurance Business and I have attended some County meetings with him now and then". Jim smiled, obviously thinking of something, then continued:

"Bring her to the house sometime, Rob, perhaps for a dinner with us. Your mother and I would be glad to see her again". After a moment's pause, he continued: "...and Rob, you may be surprised to find how sweet your Mom will be to her!"

Rob paused for a moment and decided to broach another subject, something of which he had been considering for some time:

"Dad, I was wondering if, when we go to Vermont over the Fourth of July weekend to see Grampa and Gramma Currie, we might be able to take Gwynne with us. I know that you run the trip into several days, but I'm pretty sure that Buck would have no problem in giving me a couple of days off. Would Grampa and Gramma be able to put her up, Gwynne, I mean, at the house?"

"I feel certain that they would have no problem with that at all, Rob", his father replied. "In fact, They would be happy to be included in that way".

"Will Mom be alright with it?", Rob asked.

"I will see to it myself, Rob! Trust me".

A few days later, when Rob had come home from work, Sheila asked him to help her to move some large planters on the back deck. He readily agreed and stopping in the kitchen for a tall glass of cold water, he joined her on the back terrace, Something inside of him told him that this was his mother's way of taking him to one side to discuss something or other. When he joined her, he saw her standing with her hands on her hips, looking towards the trellis in the back yard.

"Just look at that!", she remarked. "That Wisteria at the side of that trellis has really taken over! Look at how it has actually pulled the whole thing off kilter and to one side!

Why didn't I have the sense to plant another Wisteria on the other side ? At least the two plants would more or less have to compromise somewhat and leave the structure level".

"We could straighten it, Mom", Rob suggested, "but we would need a "come-along" and ratchet it up straight. Of course, there is a danger that the trellis might actually break before the vines eased up. We would also have to be careful not to get too carried away or aggressive, and pull the plant from the ground or hurt the root system".

"Well", she replied, turning away and towards the planters, "I will just add that to a list of things which I have for you and your father to do". She moved towards the first long planter.

"Mom, Leave the planters for now ", Rob suggested at seeing their size and thinking of their probable weight. "When Dad gets home in a while, let the two of us move these big things!"

"That sounds like a good idea, and I will let you two strong male hero-types do that", she said. Turning towards her son, she went on: " By the way, Robbie: I understand that your young lady may be going with us to Vermont".

"Her name is Gwynne, Mom", Rob replied." I would like it very much if we could include her, take her with us".

"Well, I think that before that time, we should have her over to dinner with us, don't you agree?", his mother had suggested quite openly and without even a hint of sarcasm. "Besides, after she is here with us she may decide that spending several days with your family is absolutely out of the question! We may frighten the poor girl to death! Anyway, I will be able to call her by name once I have really met her!"

"That would be really great, Mom!, Rob exclaimed.

"Ask her if she might come to dinner on Saturday evening then", Sheila said.

When Jim came home from his work, he and Rob moved the planters as Sheila had requested and after the evening meal the two men, father and son, went again to the back terrace to enjoy the closing of the day. It had been a fairly clear day after many days of rain; not really ever a pouring rain, but rather an incessant drizzle, The air still felt a bit heavy and the warm scent of damp earth was very noticeable, even after the day of sunshine.

"Humid, isn't it?", Jim asked as he settled into a chair.

Rob leaned against one of the supporting upright timbers which held the projected roofed area over the patio. Looking towards the sky, he said:" It has been pretty soggy alright. Still, I have heard that the Southern Tier has had a real beating from all of the rain".

"Yes", Jim agreed. I have been reading about that! There has been genuine flooding all west of the Susquehanna. Elmira actually had cars and mobile homes floating down some streets and Corning has been a good share of it under water".

Suddenly Jim slapped his hand down on the arm of his lawn chair and said"

"Oh! Before I forget! I called your grand dad and

grandma this afternoon. They are really looking forward to seeing you again. I told them that you might be bringing a young lady with you and they are really anxious to meet her. Dad said that there would be no trouble at all in putting Gwynne up in a spare room"

"That's great, Dad!" Rob said happily "of course, it depends on whether she can get someone to fill in for her for a couple of days".

Where or what is she working at over the Summer break?", Jim asked. He reached into his shirt pocket and pulled out a pack of Pall Mall cigarettes, tapped one out and put it between his lips, then glancing towards Rob he asked, "You don't use these things, do you?"

"Not regularly", Rob answered. "every once in a while I will smoke one".

"Do you want one now?", his father asked, the package still in his hand.

"Sure! I'll smoke one with you!", Rob replied, taking a cigarette from the proffered pack. He put the cigarette between his lips as his father returned to package to his pocket and then struck a match.

"These things will kill you", Jim said as he lit their smokes. "I should quit. I keep saying that I will do just that if cigarettes ever get up to fifty cents a pack! I would probably be better to smoke a pipe anyway!"

"Well, it's like a guy from way out west said one day: No matter whut, we all gotta git day'idd sometime 'er other!", Rob twanged.

"Anyway", Jim said, "you were about to tell me what Gwynne is working at".

"Oh, yes", Rob replied. "She is working as a nurses' aide at the hospital. She seems to like the work and dealing with people. She was telling me about a young couple who were in a bad accident and they have a very young baby. The wife is mending, but the husband is still in a coma. The lady was quite worried about the baby, since they are Catholic and I guess the baby has not been baptized. That was really bothering her, for I guess that they believe that if the baby were to die without baptism, he or she would not be able to get into Heaven. One of the nurses brought the baby and a priest who was on hospital visitation into the young mother's room and the baby was baptized then and there. From what Gwynne has been told, the baby isn't in any great danger and the mother is going to be alright. It is up in the air as to how long the husband's coma might last." Stopping for a moment, Rob then asked his father, "Do people really believe that about unbaptized babies? It seems kind of harsh!"

"Oh, yes!" Jim nodded. I do not know if your mother really believes that, although she was hell-bent on having you and Carole baptized"

"That's right!", Rob stated with triumph, "Carole is a baptized Presbyterian and I am an un-cut, baptized Anglican!"

"Rob", his father reminded him, "When you came along, I put my foot down! I said, This little boy is One: going to remain intact, uncircumcised, and Two: he is Not going to be baptized into hard-bitten Calvinism! So, here you are, as far as I know, still uncut and a baptized Anglican!" .

"Wow!", Rob was laughing, "EeeeeHaw!! I am almost perfect!: right up there with that statue of David by Michelangelo, and a Baptized Anglican to boot! How about *that*!?"

Watching his son's over the top laughter, Jim felt himself being drawn into the same craziness: "Well, Good Lord, Rob!", he laughed, "I didn't think that you would come unhinged!"

Sheila appeared at the kitchen door, drawn by the sounds from the deck.

"Are you two *alright*?", she asked. Have you been drinking? You sound like a pair of lunatics!" .

Jim wiped his eyes, still chuckling. "No, we haven't been drinking, Sheila. Come to think of it, that's not a bad idea, and I did pick up a couple of six packs! Turning to Rob he asked:

"Rob, 'want a beer?"

"Is the Pope Catholic?", Rob asked.

Sheila turned away and back to the kitchen, shaking her head, smiling to herself. The thought then hit her: Rob was smoking! She shook her head again, still smiling. Smoking was still a social grace in 1972, after all.

CHAPTER 15

PART II

On Friday, the 30th of June, in the late afternoon, Jim, Sheila, Rob and Gwynne, headed off to spend what was meant to be a Fourth of July with Jim's mother and father in Vermont. After it was realized that the Fourth of July itself would fall on a Tuesday, it would not be feasible to stay that long in Vermont for the holiday itself. After all considerations, and all employers telling everyone to go ahead and take the extra day, Monday the 3rd. and return on July 5th. This was to make their stay longer than they had planned.

It was a good day for the somewhat long drive: up through a section of the Adirondacks on Route 9N towards Crown Point, then to continue on to where that road could connect with Vermont's Route 17. These were unbelievably scenic roads; almost too much to take in. They were to go on to St. Johnsbury in Vermont's North East Kingdom. This is all subject matter for avid photographers, for magazine and Calendar illustrations. Gwynne kept pointing things out to Rob: a country church, a beautiful farmstead, often with the farmhouse a series of added on sections which had spanned the centuries, split rail fences as well as stone walls and fields which traveled up and down over hilly landscape. Gwynne herself felt comfortable enough with Rob's family, but still harbored a bit of apprehension at the thought of meeting her boyfriend's paternal grandparents. She wanted very much for them to like her, to accept her. Rob sensed her uneasiness and tried to divert her attention to a host of other things as they moved along. She would discover that she needed not have been concerned.

The elder Curries had a modest but well-maintained old house of the post and beam style, its barn-red clapboards and broad upright end –pieces neatly painted, the windows sided by neat, dark gray shutters. An old stone springhouse stood near to the house and the other out-buildings seemed to have been placed here and there as their functions had been decreed over the years. There was an amazing array of flowers and the shrubbery was well trimmed and neat. It was one of the prettiest farms Gwynne had ever seen.

As soon as Jim turned the car into the driveway, two white-haired, smiling people were coming out of the house's side door, Jim's mother wiping her eyes with the corner of her apron, crying tears of great joy. There were soon hugs and kisses all around, nor was Gwynne to be left out of all of the joyful greetings, for Jim's father stepped aside from the knot of reunion and spoke out directly to the young woman in their midst: even before Rob had been able to make the introduction.

"This has to be Gwynne!", he said, smiling broadly." Well, we've heard some good things about you! Welcome to the North East Kingdom!"

"Welcome, Gwynne!", Grandma Currie said, giving her a hug. "We're so glad that you could come to see us! How do you like our part of the world?"

"Oh! It is breath-taking!", Gwynne exclaimed. "Everything is so beautiful here!"

"Well! Let's go on into the house!", the elder Currie said. Then turning to his son he said, "Let me help you unload your things!"

"Rob and I can get the bags, Dad, but here, you can take all of the goodies!", Jim said, handing his father a full shopping bag and a box of baked things.

"Well", his father exclaimed, "You gave all the goodies to the right person anyway! All of these things should last me a couple of hours at least!"

The days were filled with activities of every kind. Rob and his father helped his grandfather to trim some brush and repair an arbor out back of the house, paint up an old, one-horse "Democrat" wagon which Donald Currie had beautifully restored and Robbie even learned how to make "Buttermilk "paint, which had been in use on Early American wooden cupboards and such from before the Revolution.

"Now, in your art classes, "Robbie, this type of paint would be called "Casein", for it is, after all, a milk-based, or casein-based paint", his grandfather explained. "It is water-soluble to a point, but once really dry, it sticks like snot to a hair-lip! There's nothing you can buy that will remove it easily!"

The women did gardening, weeding and Grandmother Currie even taught Gwynne how to card wool and later, how to spin it into yarn by means of a spinning wheel. Gwynne was absolutely intrigued by these traditional crafts: this knowledge from another time which some folks had kept alive into the present. In the afternoons, Gwynne and Rob would have a swim in the farm pond. Their laughter and Gwynne's screams could be heard down to the house. Even Sheila smiled and shook her head. It was youth, she realized. Puppy dogs, kitty-cats, calves, lambs, goslings, all played games and made noise: wonderful games, joyous noise, a celebration of life: Beautiful, really.

The evenings were given to board games, sometimes a bit of television, although not much, for there were stories to tell, news that needed to be shared. On Sunday night Rob was telling them of how much he had been learning of their Highland forebears. He mentioned how as one thing would be made known, something else would seem to present itself; how one door seemed always to open into another area and another door to be opened. He mentioned that Hugh MacKinnon knew the Gaelic language and that Gwynne's dad had recently given him a Gaelic-English Dictionary; that he had also found some information about the Curries and the War Hero Chieftain of the clan.

"Your Grandma Currie knows the Gaelic!", Grandfather Currie told him.

"You know the Gaelic, Ma?" Jim swung his head to ask his mother. "I remember that you used to hum and sing some old songs and such, but you can actually speak the language?"

"Oh, dear!" She answered modestly, "There was never any real reason to mention it! Besides, I am not as "fluent" in the old tongue as I would wish to be. Remember that I grew up on Prince Edward Island in the Maritimes! We all spoke the Ghaidhlig (Gaw'lick, she pronounced it) at home most of the time. My own grandmother refused to speak English! If one of us acted up at table or showed a lack of good manners, she would say to that child: "Cha n'eil anad ach Sassanach!", which means:"There is nothing in you but English!", and believe you me, we would straighten right up!" They all laughed at that. The elderly lady was smiling, a bit tearful and for a moment, a far away look in her eyes. She was wondering if there were any of the folk left there: those as she had known in her own youth. Her brief reverie was interrupted by a somewhat excited Robbie:

"Gramma, could you help me to learn some Gaelic?"

"Oh, Robbie!", she replied with a little laugh, "I could help you with the sounds and the pronunciation, but I would not know how to go about trying to read or write a word of it! We spoke it at home, but not a one of us ever learned to read and write in anything but English. There was never a reason or cause for us to read or write in the Gaelic".

Here again and once again, another door had been opened, another possibility had been presented. From that time Rob began pestering his grandmother for words and phrases. She told him that he was becoming a real pain in the neck, but it was quite clear that she enjoyed tremendously this interest in the old language, the language which she had spoken as a child and which she had supposed would die with her when she herself would pass. Jim quietly observed that his mother was well pleased and that there was a new life in her. Donald Currie had the same feelings and shook his head, smiling to himself. He had "flash-backs to his brothers-in-law when they were young, cursing one another, insulting one another playfully in Scots Gaelic as they went about their chores on Ellen's family farm. He liked hearing the sounds again, even if the words were few as they were being taught to his grandson.

On the last evening of their stay everyone gathered in the living room or 'parlor' of the old farm house. Gwynne noticed the various framed photographs of young men in uniform, Bridal couples, children and grandchildren, all watched over by two very old sepia tone Photographs in ornate frames on the wall by the fireplace: Ellen's mother and father. Older people tend to fill their living rooms with a myriad of pictures of family and friends, as if a means by which all of these people of various ages may be kept alive in their hearts and memories. Donald finally said to his wife:

"Ellen, why don't you sing us one or two of the old

songs ? Robbie and Gwynne would like to hear a song in the Gaelic, I'm sure!"

"Donald!", she protested, "I am not at all sure that I could anymore!"

"Come on, Ma!", Jim urged, "Sing for us!" Everyone else joined in, requesting a song from her.

The elderly lady took her glasses from her face and held them in her lap, closed her eyes and tilted her head back. She began to sing and beautifully, for despite her age, her voice was still strong and quite melodic:

"O, Chi, Chi mi na Morbheanna,

"O, Chi, Chi mi na Corbheanna,

"O Chi, Chi mi na coiregann,

"Chi m na' Sgurrain bho'n cheo….."

She sang through several verses with the refrain after each of them Finally, she simply stopped, opened her eyes and smiled shyly. The room was absolutely silent. The awe expressed by everyone by the silence was finally broken as Gwynne almost whispered:

"That is the most beautiful song I have ever heard! Really!"

"Really!" Rob breathed out in agreement.

"It's called "The Mist-covered Mountains", Ellen Currie explained, "It is about someone coming home to the Highlands. Oh, we used to sing all of the time! We sang when we worked, at ceilidhs, for any reason at all! Mind you, there was no television or radio back then. We had to make a game of our work and we had to make our own entertainment."

She was called upon to sing another song, then another. Everyone was captivated by the rich sounds, the melodies and by the quality of her voice. Soon thereafter, the women produced coffee and tea and a large, very 'chocolaty' cake.

"Now, Gwynne made this beautiful cake!", Grandma Currie announced. "Isn't it beautiful?"

"Oh! Don't tell them! What if is a flop?", Gwynne asked.

As it turned out, everyone said that the cake was as delicious as it was rich and fine to behold. Rob felt a surge of pride that his girl had made this contribution to the family's last evening together. He squeezed her hand and smiled at her, but he could not resist turning to Gwynne and whispering in her ear: "How come this cake is so great, but every time that you make fudge we have to end up by eating it as a topping on ice cream?"

"Shut up, Robbie, you rotten creep!", she whispered in reply.

The leave-taking on the following morning was a scene of familial partings throughout rural America and Canada for decades upon decades. Vehicles have to be repacked in order to accommodate the foods, baked goods and canned goods which are given by family members remaining in the country to their children and grandchildren who live in towns and cities. The older generation seems often also to bring some cherished item from storage which is passed on to a younger generation. In this case, Ellen Currie had brought out a hand-crocheted lace tablecloth which her own mother had made and had it all wrapped for Sheila. Sheila looked upon it as something terribly dear, almost sacred.

"Oh, Mother Currie! I can not take this!", Sheila protested.

"Well, we do not have occasions to use it any more. What do you want me to do with it, give it to the Salvation Army?" Ellen asked. "It was made by Jim's grandmother, my mother… and you should have it in your house!"

Sheila hugged her mother–in-law and said:" I will cherish it!"

A similar scenario had been presented a bit earlier, when Donald Currie came out of the house and motioned Jim and Rob to one side. He had a somber, though furtive look on his face and was carrying a rifle. He presented the weapon to Rob with both hands. Rob stood dumfounded, staring at his grand dad's Winchester 30/30.

"Are you going to take this thing or not?" Or maybe you just want me to keep holding it out on display!", the older man asked with exaggerated sternness.

"Grand dad! That's your Winchester! I can't take that!", Rob protested.

"Well, I want you to have it! I don't need a rifle anymore. I have my shotgun in there and a Bird gun. That's enough weaponry to defend the chicken coop or to shoot predators. Besides, I want you to have it. I know that your Dad has taught you to be responsible and that you will use it wisely and well. After all, you're my grandson, aren't you?"

Rob's eyes looked from the rifle to those of his grandfather. He lunged forward and hugged the older man. It was a tearful moment for all three of the Currie males.

"I will cherish this rifle forever!", Rob promised.

"I know you will, son! I know you will! That's why I want you to have it!", his grandfather replied.

Jim had asked Rob if he would like to drive part of the way home and Rob was very willing to do so. Jim had asked Gwynne if she would like to sit in the front seat with Rob and told her that he would sit in the back seat with Rob's mother. Sheila looked surprised when Gwynne said that if it was alright with them, she would prefer to sit in the back seat with her, and that Rob's dad might want to sit up front and act as navigator for his son. Jim instinctively glanced at Sheila to see what her reaction might be, only to see her breaking into a broad smile.

"That's a great suggestion, Gwynne! I would like that very much!, We two can simply take it easy!" Sheila said.

Rob and Jim glanced at one another. Both had one eyebrow cocked up to indicate personal confusion, as Jim slid onto the seat next to his son.

The men in the front seat were aware that the women in the back were talking, although little could be heard of their conversation, the road noise and such as it was. In any case, Sheila and Gwynne seemed to have enough to discuss. Gwynne had remarked to Sheila that the elder Curries seemed to have been such kind and wonderful people and a couple who had obviously grown quite close over the years.

"It can't have been easy", Sheila was telling Gwynne, "My father-in-law came back from World War Two a pretty confused man. He must have been harboring some terrible memories! He had been in the Normandy Invasion and later, the Battle of the Bulge, and on into the thick of it all. I guess that mother Currie had her work cut out for her!"

The two women had no trouble in talking with one another. Finally, after a couple of short stops, they returned to Balston Spa and left Gwynne at her house. Rob got out of the car and walked with Gwynne to the front door of her parents' house. Sheila moved to the front seat next to her husband, who was now in the driver's seat. She watched her son and Gwynne lean in close together until the two figures in the shadows blended together. Sheila thought to herself and asked how all of this could have come together so quickly and without warning. She saw that her boy had become a man, a man who had found a mate. A shiver went through her, but it was not altogether disagreeable.

Once home, and into the house, Sheila sank into a chair and waited for the two men to unload the car. When all was accomplished and Jim and Rob came inside and closed the front door for the night, Sheila said to Rob: "You have found yourself a very fine girl, Robbie! Don't you dare let her go, for this girl loves you beyond belief!" Jim and Rob exchanged glances, as if to enquire of one another: "What on earth brought this on? How on earth did Gwynne get through to her and win her over?"

Two weeks later, in mid-July, Paul accompanied Rob

and Gwynne to Ticonderoga and the old Fort just beyond the town. Rob had promised Paul that he would show him the old bastion, which like many others in the northeastern part of the country, had been first French, then English and finally, American. The outpost was made quite famous by the action of the Royal 42nd Highland Regiment, the "Black Watch", during the French and Indian War. There had been an occasion at one of the after-dinner discussions at the King farm when Rob had told the story:" Ticonderoga", made famous by Robert Louis Stevenson: something of a' Ghost Story', which that author had set forth in the form of a lengthy poem. It is a story which is based on a true experience of a Highland chieftain and his family. The tale had its beginnings in Scotland and was to meet with its strange conclusion in the wilds of North America.

Gwynne had hinted several times that she wanted to meet Paul, this young man whom her boyfriend had spoken of so often; sometimes with admiration and at other times with a heavy frustration. In any case, it was evident to her that Rob harbored a genuine affection for this fellow whom he had first encountered as a "grubby, stringy-haired loser"; a hitchhiker whom he had prepared to dislike intensely. Gwynne had listened to Rob's accounts of farm-work, evenings spent discussing history or poring over old articles and letters at the King house. He had spoken of Gramma King's home-made breads, "Johnny Cake ", pies and rice puddings. Gwynne felt herself often to be sharing her boyfriend's enthusiasm, if even in a second-hand manner.

At the same time, she often felt the need to beat back or keep at bay a certain disquietude deep within herself: something unsettling and perhaps even menacing. Was it jealousy? No. Was it fear?, Not really, yet certainly it was apprehension. This other young man who had somehow been fired up by Rob to attend college, to rise from a tragic boyhood to claim a life of meaning, a life of service to others was a tremendous enigma in human guise, He had as yet not been seen by her in human form, but rather a faceless name who was only in stories She wondered if he could be a friend to her as well as to this young man for whom she felt so very much love.

Paul got out of the old grey car and walked slowly towards them as they moved forward to meet him as well. He was grinning like a mischievous school boy, his expression carrying a message such as: "Here I am, you lucky people! Aren't you glad to see me?" Rob was smiling brightly back at him. For her part, Gwynne could sense, almost feel, Rob's pleasure as he stood close to her. Paul looked at her without losing even a touch of his smile, yet as he looked into her eyes, she was surprised to see, or she felt that she could see behind that smile, a plea for her acceptance. Rob's arm came around her waist, almost a primitive gesture of protectiveness, or even possessiveness, but that would be out of character for Rob, wouldn't it?

"Gwynne, this is the crazy I have been telling you about!", Rob said in the way of introduction, "and Paul", he went on, "This is a very wonderful and long-suffering young woman whom I am glad to have in my life: Gwynne"

"Hi, Paul!", Gwynne said brightly, "I am glad to meet you at last!"

Paul took Gwynne's hand, still smiling, he said:" I'm glad to meet you too! "Then, glancing towards Rob, he said, "I can tell you right now: You are too fine a girl for Robbie!"

Rob staged a look of shock and laughed. He said:

"You Snake! One introduction and you're making moves on my girl! I can not believe this!"

Gwynne had taken the remark in good humor, but she could see that Paul's attempt at levity had backfired in his own thinking and he seemed to feel that he had embarrassed himself. They spoke together briefly about his trip from Tully and agreed that it would not be a bad day after all for the trip north. Paul asked if they should take his car.

"No. We're all set, Paul" Rob told him. "As a matter of fact we had just finished stowing some food and stuff into my dad's car. Mine is in the shop, by the way, so we're taking this one".

"Oh! Well, okay. I will put Gram's to the side then, to make sure that it's not in anyone's way. By the way, Gramma sent some stuff along for our trip. I'll move the car and bring the food".

As Paul turned away from them towards the car he had been driving, Gwynne took Robs hand in hers and said to him:

"Good Lord, Rob! You never mentioned that he is so good-looking!" she exclaimed in a near whisper. "All of that dark honey-colored and wavy hair and those incredible eyes! I have never seen eyes that color: dark hazel, like polished gem stones!"

"Do you really think that he is that good-looking?", Rob asked, feeling a sense of embarrassment (or was it envy?) sweep over him.

"Absolutely!",, she stated. "Now, don't tell me that you never realized it!"

"Well, yes", Rob conceded, "I guess that he is better than average where looks and all might be concerned, but as a rule, guys don't go around, checking other guys out, you know?"

Gwynne shot him a look of unbelief, rolled her eyes heavenward, and shook her head in mock exasperation.

When Paul was coming back from moving the car, carrying a small box and a metal cookie tin: his grandmother's contribution, he was smiling at the two of them. He told them that they looked like "a couple" right enough, like the leads in a "surfer" or "Beach Boy" movie. He handed the box and tin to Rob, who put them onto the back seat of his father's car. Paul looked at the back seat filled with things and before he could ask or say anything, Rob told him that they could all sit in the front of the car. Rob opened the door on the passenger side and held the door until Gwynne was inside and had slid over to the middle. Rob left the door open and moved around to the driver's side as Paul slid onto the seat beside Gwynne, pulling the door shut after him. Once the three of them were in place, Rob started the car and backed out of the driveway. Gwynne felt secure, protected even, sitting between these two young men, both of them so well-formed and handsome, only to feel, almost immediately, a bit of self-criticism for having allowed such a "sappy" sentiment to wash over her. Rob usually drove with his right hand on the wheel and his left elbow on the ledge of the rolled down window. Paul allowed for a cramped position for a while, but soon put his left arm up on the back of the seat, behind Gwynne's shoulders. For his part, Rob simply glanced sideways at the movement, yet seemed not to feel himself threatened or challenged in any way. Even so, his momentary reaction did not escape Gwynne's notice. She smiled to herself, took her small handbag in her right hand and placed her left hand on her boyfriend's leg, just above his knee. Rob smiled at her. He appreciated her reassurance while feeling a current of momentary excitement run through his entire being at her touch. She felt it too as she smiled at him in return. In their time together they had found that they often communicated without speaking, a rare gift, for many couples may spend a lifetime together and fail to reach that one-ness, that coming together of spirit which had already, in their very young lives, come to be such a great part of their time together.

The three of them had a good day. Paul found the Fort to be extremely interesting and the fact that at this time restoration was still underway, diggings revealing long forgotten artifacts, gave the old outpost a sense of something still being developed, rather than simply a tired monument to a set of military engagements which had taken place two centuries back in time. They pored over the exhibits of bits and pieces of old weaponry, charts and lithographs and took their time in what had been the main center and inner parade and muster area. The stone buildings and the arched entry to that center gave a hint of something which had been picked up in Europe by a giant hand and set down on this rise above the lake in a wild, forested and untamed New World. To them, there was nothing really strange about this still somewhat unconquered natural environment, for they were themselves, products of this land and had sprung from this same world. To think of the Adirondack region as ever being truly subjected to human domination was something which would be incomprehensible to them. Long after the Western expansion, the Federal wars against the plains Indians, the railroads, the near annihilation of the plains Buffalo herds and the rising of cities in California, the Adirondacks had remained, in many ways, as the first French, then British explorers had seen them to be. So anxious had been the New Englanders to push west, they had almost by-passed upstate New York on their way to Ohio and beyond. Fort Ticonderoga also stood, somewhat hard to find, as a mere attempt to build a temporary campsite in the midst of a vast wilderness. The forests are patient. They wait. Ultimately, they reclaim the cleared areas of human progress: slowly, a sapling here a shrub there, but in time the hills are forested again. To the three young visitors to the fort, this all seemed to be as right as rain. They were products of this land as well.

They also filled out their day with clowning, laughter, photographing and good-natured banter. Rob was happy to see that Gwynne and Paul seemed to accept and like each other. In fact, Gwynne somehow managed to bring Paul out of his usual reserve which was so much a part of him when he found himself among people whom he did not know. He realized that up until this day he had never known Paul to really laugh and that he could be very entertaining and very pleasant company. He noticed too, that his feelings for Gwynne were deep, even beyond what he could have imagined. At the same time, it occurred to him that he had never in his life felt such a strong attachment for any other guy as he felt for Paul. A flash went through him at that moment: the remembrance of a lecture on the Arthurian legends and the underlying message:" What happens if there is an excess of love? Can there be such a thing? For Arthur loved Gwynevere, and he loved Lancelot. Gwynevere loved Arthur and she loved Lancelot, and finally Lancelot loved Arthur, but he also loved Gwynevere.". A flash had gone through him and he tried desperately to distance himself from that thought: how an excess of love had actually been the undoing of a whole noble purpose and a way of life! Rob shook it off as a crazy, stupid analogy.

On the way out and away from Ticonderoga, heading back to Balston Spa, Rob pulled into a gas station, mentioning that he had to "gas up" and also check the oil. His father had told him that the car had been burning oil and that it had to be watched carefully. Rob exited the vehicle, lifted the hood of the car and began to check the oil level. At the same time, Paul got out of the car and took the nozzle from the pump, unscrewed the gas cap of the car's tank and began to pump gasoline into the tank. When he saw that he had pumped ten dollars' worth of gasoline, he replaced the nozzle to the pump and replaced the car's gas cap. Rob had gone into the station and returned with a quart can of oil, which he began to pour into the cars engine. He looked up at Paul and asked how much gas he had rung up. Paul told him and said:

"Don't worry about it! I'll go in and pay for the oil and gas! Don't say no!"

Rob refused, reminding Paul that it had been he who had insisted on paying for their admissions to the fort, that it had been stated as Paul's "treat" and that he would pay for the travel expense and not Paul. Paul shrugged his shoulders with his characteristic grin and Rob went into the station to pay for the gas and oil.

Rob was gone for quite a while as Paul and Gwynne waited. Paul moved to the passenger side of the car and spoke to Gwynne through the window opening, resting his arms on the ledge. For a while they exchanged small talk, until quite suddenly Paul directed a very pointed question to her:

"So! Are you going to marry this guy, or not?"

"What?" Gwynne was taken completely off guard. Her

face registered great surprise.

"You and Robbie. Are you going to get married?", he asked.

"Well, we're both young yet! We've talked about it in an off-hand way, but I'm afraid that we would have to wait for quite a while yet", she replied

"Yeah, well, I suppose that that might be true enough," Paul said, "But I'll tell you one thing: you'll never find a better guy than this one that you're with right now! I know that I have never seen any other guy like him! I'll tell you another thing: he sure thinks the world and all of you!"

"Well, Paul, in case you haven't noticed, I think quite a bit of him too!", she replied. "I do wonder sometimes however, if I can ever really be a match for such a boy, such a man! But, how about you? Do you have someone special in your life?"

"No. No one in particular", he replied. "I guess that I am kind of shy or something, you know?"

"Paul", she replied. "Some girls might actually find that to be attractive! It certainly is nicer than all of this "macho" boasting, posing and role-playing that we see all of the time!"

"Do you think so?, Paul asked. He was looking into her eyes now, his eyes moving back and forth, looking into each of her eyes, from one to the other. Still she realized that in this he was not being flirtatious, but instead desperately seeking reassurance, acceptance. How like a little boy he seemed to be!

Rob returned to the car from the station. He glanced

at Paul and at Gwynne and walked to the driver's side of the car. Putting some bills into his wallet he said as if to them both:

"Boy! I cannot believe how hard it is to get change for a twenty!" Glancing toward Paul, he said:" C'mon, Young hero! Saddle up! We're moving out!"

Back in Balston they all had a rather late evening meal at Gwynne's parents' home; a simple meal, really, consisting of some potato salad, hamburgers and beans which had been left-overs from a picnic which the Williams family had had earlier in the day with some neighbors. Gwynne's mother came into the kitchen from outside, where she had been sitting on the back deck with Owen, Gwynne's father.

"There is both: ice tea and lemonade in the 'fridge, Gwynne", she said to her daughter, "and maybe the boys would like some fruited Jello. There is an awful lot of it left!" She turned and smiled towards the two young men and asked, "Did all of you have a good day?"

"Well, I think so, Mrs. Williams", Rob answered. "I know that I certainly enjoyed it!" He then stopped and said rather awkwardly, "Oh! All of my manners are bad ones! I should have introduced you to Paul. This is Paul King, and Paul, this is Gwynne's mom, Mrs. Williams".

She smiled, and taking his hand, said: "Hello, Paul. I am glad to meet you! We have heard a bit about you".

"Wow! I'm busted! That can be scary, Ma'am", Paul said, half rising from his chair.

"Well, I wouldn't worry too much if I were you", she

assured him. "Thus far we have heard good things!"

Gwynne's father came into the kitchen from the back deck. Pulling the screen door hard behind him. "Those mosquitoes are getting wicked out there! They come at you with a real vengeance!", he exclaimed. Turning to Rob, he said, "Good thing you got my girl back here in decent season, young man! I was about to call the County Sheriff!"

"No, sir! It wasn't my fault! It's Gwynne who kept us out so late!", Rob exclaimed with a smile, looking sideways towards Gwynne, who rolled her eyes and shook her head.

"Yeah! Well, that figures!", her father replied'

"Mr. Williams", Rob said, "This is my friend, Paul King". Paul stood to greet him.

"Glad to meet you, Paul", he said shaking his hand. "Are you a classmate of Rob's?"

"No, Sir. I'm a guy that he once gave a ride when I was hitch-hiking", Paul replied.

"Hitch-hiking!" Owen repeated, "You don't see many hitch-hikers any more! Back when I was in the service, the roads were full of them! It was a very common form of transportation, especially for servicemen!" He then abruptly turned to Rob and said" Oh, Rob! Before I forget! I found something in a used book store which I thought might interest you. I thought of you when I came across it and it was only a buck and a half. Wait! I'll go and get it!"

"Now, what could that be?", Gwynne asked, looking towards her mother.

"I haven't the foggiest! Your father is a man of many

surprises", her mother replied.

Mr. Williams came back into the kitchen holding a hard-bound, green covered book in his hand. He gave it to Rob, without speaking, waiting for Rob's response. Rob looked at the binding, opened the book and read: "Gaelic-English and English- Gaelic Dictionary". Rob looked up with a look of amazement which turned to a broad smile.

"This is great, Mr. Williams!", he exclaimed," There is a pronunciation key, plus every word is followed by a pronunciation! Really! This is wonderful!"

"Does this mean that I will have to learn to speak Gaelic?", Gwynne asked, looking over his shoulder. She turned and announced to her parents: "We found out when we were in Vermont that Robbie's Grandmother Currie speaks Gaelic. She sang some songs for us and it is a beautiful sounding language!"

"I hope that it is not as difficult as Cymric…Welsh!", Mr. Williams said. "My grandparents spoke Cymric and it certainly sounds to be a challenge!"

"Your grandparents spoke Welsh? Fantastic!", Rob exclaimed.

"Well, now!" Owen Williams said, assuming a Welsh accent, "You Scots think that you are the only Celts to be found, do you?" He went on: "Anyway, you may not decide to sit down and learn the language ever, but you'll at least be able to look up meanings and pronunciations of place names and such. Oh!" (another thought obviously had come to him) He turned to Rob and went on:" And guess what! When I was in Albany, I had an opportunity to meet a man who knows the chief of the Curries!"

"I didn't know that the Curries had a chief, other than the Chiefs of the ClanRanald MacDonnells", Rob said

"Well, I certainly couldn't tell you about that. We didn't have much time to talk during lunch because we had a very important afternoon meeting to attend. In any case, this gentleman seemed to be quite knowledgeable. I took down his name, address and a telephone number. I had told him that my daughter has been keeping company with a young fellow who is very interested in his Scottish heritage. He seemed to be impressed with that and mentioned that yours is a very ancient line, apparently going back to somebody called " Neil of the Nine Hostages". He did tell me that you should get in touch with him, that your chief is something of a war hero!"

"This is all so great, Mr. Williams! I will sit down and write him first. He sounds to be an interesting man.", Rob said.

"Well, I certainly found him to be an interesting man", Williams said "Well, anyway, sit down and eat! I have some work to do in the study. By the way, stay clear of the Three Bean Salad!' Worst concoction to have been put together, EVER!" Turning to Paul, he said, "Nice to meet you, Paul". Paul expressed his pleasure also and they shook hands.

"Three Bean Salad", Gwynne intoned." I take it that Aunt Lucy was at your picnic, Mom".

"Oh, my yes! With bells on!", her mother answered.

"Not only had she brought a huge bowl of her salad, which your father is convinced is the Protestant equivalent of "Mortification of the Flesh" for any and all who might ingest it, but went on, text and sermon about your having driven off somewhere with, not just one, but *two* …count them… *two* (!!) young males! Whatever will people think? Gwynne, I just know that I will not be able to hold my head up or show my face in this town!" Her last sentence had been uttered with a Southern Belle accent and they all laughed. Paul was very much taken with the sense of humor which seemed to be so much a part of Gwynne's mother, and that she seemed to truly enjoy the company of young people. When she asked them about their day and what they had done, they really did not hold back one bit, but went on to discuss each detail. At times they would laugh hysterically, such as when Gwynne began to recall their having stopped for some cokes at a small restaurant:

"The woman behind the counter was talking to some locals about her husband's recent surgery". Paul then chimed in: "An' they took out a length of his bowels about two foot long!". He mimicked the scratchy voice and dialect almost perfectly For his part, Rob could not believe the change in Paul.: the theatrics, the humor and his ability to pick up on every detail.

"And then", Gwynne laughed, wiped her eyes and went on, "and then, while all of this description was taking place, of cut up bowels and such, this little waitress brought a huge plate of Goulash to a man who was seated very near to us, and we all looked at each other, and at the goulash, while all of this talk of cut up bowels was going on!" They all started laughing hysterically.

"What's going on? Did you all get into my liquor cabinet or what? You sound like a bunch of nut cases!" It was Owen Williams who had appeared at the doorway.

"Oh, these kids!", Marge Williams laughed, "These kids are making me sick!"

"And that's funny?", Williams asked with a confused smile, at which point they all started laughing again. Owen shook his head, smiling, and moved back towards his study. Paul took in this familial scene with great interest: how Robbie was treated as a member of the family, of Mr. Williams' good humor and his wife's obvious ease among young people. "Rob could not find a better family", he thought to himself. "It is as if they already think of him as a son! Beautiful!"

Despite the occasional laughing as they moved about, they started clearing the table. Mrs. Williams had begun to run the water to wash dishes and the young people carried the plates and flat ware to the side of the sink. As she started to wash dishes and rinse them, she placed them into the dish rack. Paul took down a dish cloth and began to dry them, one by one.

"You are going to make someone a great husband, Paul!", Marge Owens said to him.

"Because I dry dishes?, he asked with a touch of puckish impudence.

"That too!", Marge said to him, "Although I feel certain that you have many other attributes as well which would be cherished by some young lady."

"I certainly hope that you are right, Ma'am", he replied.

"Okay! Enough of this!" It was Owen. He had returned from his study. "Anyone care for a beer ?", he asked. "You are all old enough, right?"

"We are all old enough, Sir", and ready and willing too!", Rob said.

"I don't know if I should, Rob" I have a long way to drive tonight", Paul said quietly.

"You aren't driving home tonight, are you? How far do you have to go?", Mr. Williams asked. When Paul told him, Owen said to Rob, "Robbie you can't let him drive that far tonight!"

"Well, I would not want to have my grandmother worrying. I have her car and I've been staying with her at the farm. She worries about everything".

"Give her a call on the' phone!" Williams suggested. "She will rest easier knowing that you are staying 'til daylight anyway!"

"Yes, Paul!, Rob put in, "Give her a call and stay at my house tonight! You can drive home tomorrow. On a Sunday the roads will be much less busy anyway. You don't have to work or anything, do you?"

"No", Paul admitted.

"Well that's that then!, Williams said. "The phone is right around the corner!"

Paul made the call and soon thereafter Marge and Owen Williams left the younger folk to their own company, having extended the invitation for another beer. Owen had suggested to Rob that two beers should be his limit since he would be driving. Gwynne, Rob and Paul moved out to the back deck and set their bottles and glasses down onto the round outdoor table. The night was warm and still, the sky clears, save for a few wisps of clouds. Save for the distant barking of a dog from time to time and the occasional sound of a car motor, it was an unusually still night. They elected to sit it the darkness, save for what light shone out from the kitchen window, which casted a somewhat mystical and other-worldly ambiance. Certainly there would be less problem with flying insects!

The conversation among them revealed much of their hopes for their futures, what things in life they most wanted to avoid: hopes, aspirations, even fears. It was serious talk in which they revealed their dreams for a better society. They soon found themselves to be discussing the war and, for Rob and Paul, the possibility of being "called up" for military service. Paul mentioned his uncle Art and how messed up he had been since his tours of duty in Viet Nam.

"Why would guys want to go to war?" Gwynne asked. "I just don't understand it at all! I simply can't understand it and I refuse to even try to understand it!"

"No one wants to go to war, Gwynne", Rob told her. "Sometimes you just have to go. It isn't like we have a choice in the matter".

"That doesn't answer the question", Gwynne insisted. "Why does a young man have to go to some foreign land to kill someone, or be killed by one of the people he is fighting, or have his arms or legs blown off and maybe be killed in his very soul?"

"It's always been like that, Gwynne", Paul put in. "Young guys have always been expected to go to war and defend their country. You know that".

"Oh, Right!" She spat out, "And Viet Nam poses a big threat to our country! Is that what you are saying? You guys are so *dumb*! You make me so damned mad! Look at my brother Evan! He acts like a mindless zombie half of the time. We don't know where he is, whether he's even alive between his visits. My Mom is worried sick about him and Dad doesn't say much, but I know that it is almost killing him!" She shook her head as if to clear it of all thoughts of Evan and said," Let's change the subject! I can't talk about this any more!" The boys fell silent.

They tried to talk of other things: everything and anything else that they could think of, yet somehow the whole mood of the evening had changed. The side-splitting laughter had given way to an awkwardness, something heavy and dark and sad inside each of them personally and over them collectively as well. The war had come very close to them, here in the stillness of a beautiful night in a small town in America. The two young men felt its nearness, sensed its coming ever closer to them each and every day. What else can a guy do? He can't run and hide, although some men had tried to do that. Some left the country, knowing that they might never be permitted to return. Some others tried to relocate themselves into a remote rural area or in the crowds of a big city. Initially such men had been held in contempt by the majority of people, but the mood was changing. Public opinion had begun to waver, if not turn around. By this time there had been so many scenes on television of police and swinging clubs against not only student protesters, but against men who had actually been to Viet Nam, some disabled or in wheelchairs. The police, the dogs, the tear gas the swinging clubs made no distinction. All of this had begun to weigh heavily upon the national conscience, and with that, something of a national near-nausea, perhaps some shame. Above all, there was in the land an impatience with a war which had dragged on for over nine years with no clear goals and with no sign of any progress, much less a hope of victory. The words which had accompanied the photograph of the teen-aged girl kneeling over the lifeless form of that young male at Kent State two years before seemed to linger in the minds of many young people:" Oh, my God! We are losing a great country!"

It was a bit past One in the morning when Rob and Paul returned to the Currie home. The house was silent and dark save for a lamp which had been left lit on an end table in the living room, and since it was one of those 'three-way' lamps, it had been turned to the lowest setting. There was really only a sufficient amount of light in the room to keep one from colliding with, or falling over the furniture.

Upstairs in Rob's room they both went directly to bed as quietly as possible. Showers could wait until morning. Neither of them wished to make the noise, much less take the time. They stripped down to their undershorts and got into bed. Rob turned out the lamp on the bed-stand beside him and laid on his back with his hands under his head, staring into the white-speckled darkness above. He thought of the night, of Gwynne's reaction to talk of the war. He was aware that Paul was also lying in the same position as himself, also quite far from sleep. He spoke without turning his head:

"So, what do you think of my girl?"

"I like her! I like her because she is down to earth, honest, caring and because she is not "bitchy" in any way like so many girls you see", Paul responded.

""Yeah", Rob answered, "I gathered that you like her. She likes you too. She told me as much when I was saying goodbye to her....And, you know?...You're right about her being forthright and not all caught up in what you call "Bitchiness" or whatever. She likes being a woman and she likes men for who each of us are. Do you know what I mean?"

"I know what you mean", Paul said as he turned his head to face Rob in the darkness. "You two are both so great together. You're both good-looking and really seem to make each other....I don't know, *complete* or something! I was wondering..."

"Wondering what?", Rob asked, turning his face towards Paul.

"Well, did you ever, have you ever…done it with her ?, have sex?", Paul asked".

"Done it with her? Rob asked, irritated. "What kind of a question is *that* ?

"It's just a question", Paul said smoothly, calmly. Yet he was persistent, "Well, did you?

"I don't think that it is any of your freakin' business, do you?" Rob asked with rising anger. Things could only go just so far, he thought and before long, just as his attitude towards Paul had softened and he had taken him as a friend, this could-be hippie farm boy from the "boonies" had to say something dumb, crazy and stupid!

"Don't get pissed!" Paul said, still unruffled." I just asked you a question, that's all!"

"Well, the answer to your question is "no". We haven't 'done' it, Paul! In fact, I've never 'done' it with anybody!"

"No kidding!" Paul's voice registered surprise. Whether it was genuine surprise or not, Rob could not tell.

"Yeah!, No kidding!", Rob mimicked. "Am I a traitor to my generation because I'm not caught up in the Sexual Revolution?"

"Most definitely! But, hey! That's your choice.", Paul explained," It's just that you and Gwynne are both so good looking, so perfect together and all….."

"That we should be groping and grinding and ripping each other's clothes off at every opportunity", Rob finished.

"No, I didn't mean that!" Forget it. I shouldn't have asked".

"Right! You shouldn't have asked". Rob stated flatly. He fell silent and then spoke again: "So, to one of your vast experience, I am a real jerk, right?"

"My vast experience?", Paul asked.

"Yes! What about you? Obviously you have 'done ' it", had sex, maybe you'd even say that you have "banged" somebody!" Rob wanted to be hurtful now, to hit out.

"Yes", Paul replied just above a whisper, "I have had sex., but nothing that I would choose to call a cherished memory. In fact it was pretty awful!"

"Oh…", Rob answered softly. This guy! Why do I have to end up feeling sorry for him?, he thought to himself, but Rob's own inner monster surfaced (we all have one, after all) and he went on: " "Paul, whenever you look at Gwynne I do not ever want you to even *think* of sex!"

"I don't do that! I would never do that, Robbie!", Paul responded as if wounded. "I know that you two belong together. I would never try to beat your time! I have more loyalty than that!"

"Loyalty?" Rob asked cynically, "To me? Why, for God's sake?"

"Because whether you like it or not, I am your friend!" Paul answered. "I like you very much, I respect you. I am your friend! I never asked or expected that you had to reciprocate and return that kind of feeling"

"But, Why, Paul? What reason have I ever given you to

care about me to that extent?"

"You know, for a bright College Kid, you are a pretty slow learner after all, Robbie!" Paul turned his back to Rob and said:" Let's get some sleep!"

When Rob awoke the next morning he found that he was alone in the room. He looked out of the bedroom window and saw that the grey car was gone. Paul had left early.

CHAPTER 16

PART II

In the second week of August of 1972, Rob headed back towards College in Athens. His parents had persuaded him to follow the same course of study for at least another academic year If, at the end of that time, he still wanted to transfer credits to another College or University in order to change his program, it was agreed that they would make no attempt to dissuade him from doing so. He had decided to leave a few days early so that he could spend some time with Robert and Kathy MacKinnon. Of course, this idea had come under fire from his mother who had employed every weapon in her fairly well-equipped arsenal, but Rob had come under fire so many times during the summer with his wish to transfer, his trips to the King farm, and his spending what could have been "family time" with Gwynne and his times with Paul, that he was in no mood to make even one more concession. He had simply told her 'flat out' that he was going to leave early, stop at the MacKinnons and that nothing was going to change his mind. At the same time, he did realize that his mother had really softened her tone quite a bit during the season, especially where Gwynne and Paul were concerned.

He had called the King farm on two occasions since Paul's visit, in hope of speaking with Paul, but on each occasion Paul had not been on hand. Mrs. King had seemed truly glad to hear from him and had also told him that Paul was indeed planning to attend college, but that he had to go to talk with a Selective Service representative about his Draft status. During the second conversation with Mrs. King she seemed to sound as if she were a bit upset. It seems that Paul had gone to see his mother, regardless of what reception he might receive from her husband. She went on to tell Rob that Paul had called and told her that he would be back at the farm before the time for registration for his College courses, but that she had not heard from him since. She admitted to Rob that she felt a bit worried and asked him if he could find the time to stop by the farm on his way back to Ohio. He came very close to telling her that it would be nearly impossible, but sensing the urgency in her tone, he told her that he would manage to stop by for a short visit.

Rob had also spoken to Kathy MacKinnon and she was delighted that he would be visiting them for a few days. She told him that her husband had amassed a veritable mountain of articles, books and old letters which he wanted to share with his young kinsman and that she would be happy to have one corner, at least, of the study back in use…something which could not become a reality until Rob visited and helped to do his share of "sifting" with Robert and Martin. She mentioned that the timing was perfect for another\ reason: Martin and a young lady whom he had been seeing would be on hand, an engagement party having been planned for one night of that same week; right during the time of his visit! He was anxious to see Robert and Kathy again and he hoped too, that he would have an opportunity to speak with Martin. Rob realized that with the engagement party and Martin's fiancée on hand that it might prove to be a bit difficult to spend even a short time with him. At the same time, anxious as he found himself to be to see the Pennsylvania relatives, he strongly felt that he had to take the time to stop at the Kings'.

True to form, Paul's grandmother was not taken off guard by Rob's arrival. She had had one of her "feelings" that he might be coming and was prepared to meet his visit with a table laden with the fruits of her labors and long experience at cooking and baking. He had been received with a great hug as well as a scolding for not having been by more often, but overall he received a welcome as sincere as it seemed to be indicative of her wish to speak to him very earnestly about some matter.

They spoke initially of how the summer had progressed, how badly the war was going. As they sat at the kitchen table she asked about his family, his returning to school and other simple things. Finally, they got around to the subject of Paul.

"Is he still visiting his mother?", Rob asked.

"Oh, no! He is back now. I'm afraid that things did not go any better than ever, although Colleen's husband has apparently been less of a problem. Well, for one thing, she finally got an order of Protection and a Restraining Order. If he shows up anywhere near her, he can go to jail. That keeps him away from her and the children, right enough, but he isn't helping her out financially in any way either, and, well…Colleen has never been much of a manager where money is concerned. Believe me, young man ", She looked sternly towards him," If you find a wife who can manage your money, you won't have to make a lot to live well. But if you get a woman who can not manage, no matter how much you may earn, you will always not have enough!"

"So, you say that Paul is back ?", Rob asked. "Where is he now?"

"He went into town", she replied. "He should be back before nightfall".

"How is he doing? Really. Is he alright?"

Mrs. King took a sip of her tea, looked out through the window, her cup in her hand for a moment before returning it to the saucer. She frowned to herself and then answered him:

"I am not all that sure. He was very quiet for a few days after he came back from your trip to Ticonderoga. I asked him about his visit with you and he said that it had been a great day, that he had met your young lady and found her to be quite nice. Other than that, he didn't really say all that much. I wondered if something had happened, since he was so quiet and into himself for a few days. After that, there was a great mood change. He started digging into work, looked into his preparation for school, Draft status, and then all of a sudden he decided to go and visit his mother. It was as if he was trying to get all loose ends tied up, if you know what I mean".

As Rob listened to her, he felt a sadness, perhaps a feeling of regret tinged with some kind of inexplicable guilt welled up inside of himself. He toyed with a half-eaten muffin as she spoke and he decided that he would not mention Paul's very early departure, his having left before ever meeting the Curries; before anyone in the house had wakened.

"It's hard to tell", Rob said. "Paul is sometimes so easily hurt. I have just recently become aware of that. He always puts on such a 'tough guy' act; appears so often not to care, yet he is very complicated really. For all of his outward nonchalance, he feels things very deeply".

"He has always been like that", Mrs. King agreed," Even as a little boy, he might suddenly disappear. He didn't want anyone to see him if something was bothering him. We might find him sitting off by himself in the corner of the parlor on the floor or maybe on a step in the stairwell". She wiped her eyes with a paper napkin, pushing the corner of it under her glasses, first one, then the other and continued:" He was such a beautiful child! What a tragic boyhood he has had!"

They continued conversing for a while longer, although Rob was listening for the most part as Paul's grandmother spoke of a family torn apart by the erosion of traditional values, of a foreign war that had transformed one of her sons into a man pursued by the demons of his terrible memories, unable to escape the on-going nightmare of that war; of a rebellious daughter who had been too pretty for her own good and who could not wait to leave the farm and a sometimes vicious small town.; of a son who had been all that any set of parents could possibly hope for, yet the victim of a bad marriage, and that same man's son, Paul, who had been swept into a life of run-down apartments, his mother trying to cope with poverty, working long hours for little pay. When Colleen, Paul's mother finally divorced David King, she soon afterwards married a truck driver who chased around and who showed a very abusive personality early on.

"When our youngsters were growing up", Mrs. King explained, "we thought that we had it all! Mind you, we never had a lot of money, but we didn't really need it. I am pretty good at sewing and I made shirts, dresses and such and the children always looked scrubbed and tidy for school. My husband was a wonderful man: an excellent father and a hard worker. Goodness! We would sing together, all of us-, by the piano some nights. We all pitched in together on the farm, had picnics, the kids had ponies. It just seemed that we could not possibly have been any better off. Martha loved the farm, but she was just too pretty and too bright for her own good! Some of the townsfolk seemed to have it in for her. She got tired of it and when she graduated from High School, she just couldn't pack her things fast enough!" After a pause, she added, "You know, Robbie, I think that after all, the most important thing in life is to know what you have when you have it. No one can tell when such good times may end".

The sound of a car engine and the crunching of the gravel in the driveway caused them to turn their heads towards the side window.

"Now, who could *that* be?", Mrs. King wondered aloud. She got up from the table and peeked out through the window. "Oh! It's Paul! I didn't expect him back for a while yet!" Moving to the stove, she said: "I'll just heat up this coffee and set a place for him".

Paul came into the kitchen carrying two bags of groceries, which he set down on the dry sink by the back door.

"Why, Hello!", he said to Rob. "What brings *you* to the Boonies?"

"I'm on my way to Ohio", Rob replied, getting up from the table. "So, how are you, anyway? ""He smiled at Paul and moved toward him.

"Oh, Just peachy-keen!" Paul answered, moving aside toward the sink, avoiding Rob's hand poised to grab his shoulder. "Just peachy!" He spoke to his grandmother, past Rob, "Here's the check-out slip from the grocery store, Gramma", handing her a long, curled paper slip.

"Sit down and have some lunch, Paul", his grandmother said." Robbie and I were just having ours".

"No Thanks, Gramma. I had a cheeseburger in town, so I don't need anything".

"Well, can't you at least sit down and have a cup of coffee with your friend?", she asked. "We won't be seeing him for quite a while".

"Yeah! I guess that I could do that", he replied. Still, the tight smile.

"Are you all set to start your first semester?", Rob asked, trying to initiate a conversation.

"Ready as I'll ever be, I guess!", Paul replied curtly.

Rob felt his throat grow dry He was hoping that his embarrassment was not too obvious to Mrs. King. For her part, she was pretending to be busy, fussing around the stove. She moved quietly and somewhat self-consciously, wishing that she could somehow break this silence and relieve some of the tension in the air. No one spoke until the sound of a dog's barking came into the kitchen through the screen door.

"Do you have a dog now?", Rob asked.

"Someone must have dropped off a dog by here", Mrs. King said, grateful for a chance to break the silence. "People have been known to leave a dog by a farm, figuring that the people who live there will take it in. Anyway, this stray showed up at our back door one morning. She's a nice little dog, very affectionate. She looks like a Border Collie. She's a pretty little thing. We named her 'Lorna".

"Well, a farm isn't a farm without a dog", Paul put in.

"Could I see her?", Rob asked.

"Sure! Come on out back", Paul said somewhat lifelessly.

The two young men walked towards the mud-room. Mrs. King turned and watched them push the screen door open and exit the house. They walked around the corner of the house to a small enclosure, maybe four feet high. Inside was a very bright-eyed and lively black and white sheep dog. Paul unlatched the gate and the dog, as dogs seem always to do, squeezed through the opening before the gate was completely opened. In a flash she was all over Paul, jumping up and down, turning about and lunging at him repeatedly. He squatted down and she was nipping at his hair, licking his face and all but knocking him over. He shrugged back, hunched up and laughed while fending off her amazing affection. Rob squatted down next to Paul and allowed the dog to smell his hand, then began to stroke her fur.

"Are you going to tell me what's wrong, Paul?", Rob asked.

"Whatta ya mean, wrong?", Paul asked, still playing with the dog's ears and nose as she licked and gently mouthed his hands.

"Something seems to be wrong", Rob said quietly. "You left my house long before any of us were up. You never did meet my folks. I have called here twice and you have not, even once, returned my call, and now you act as if I were the alien invader or some damned thing!"

"Well, I have had a lot to do. If you remember rightly,

413

I had really planned to leave right away and not spend the night anyway. I just figured that I should get an early start", Paul told him.

"Oh, I see!...and your telephone line fell down after each of my calls, right?

"Hey, listen, you stupid jerk-off...!", Paul snarled, jumping to his feet, now looking down upon Rob, "I don't have to answer to you or anyone else! If you drove all of this distance and out of your way to lay a guilt trip on me, you can just forget that happy horse shit right now!"

Rob arose to face Paul. He tried to put his hand on Paul's shoulder. Paul pulled away.

"Paul! Paul! Come on!", Rob said questioningly. He forced his hand on Paul's shoulder this time. Paul's eyes narrowed, his teeth showed.

"Take your freakin' hand off me or I'll smash your face!"

Rob's hand slid away as he stood open-mouthed, staring at Paul.

"Can't you at least talk to me? I have a right to know what I did to make you so angry!"

"There's nothing to talk about, Rob. You are the way that you are and I am the way that I am. End of subject!", Paul stated with a shrug of his shoulders.

"Tell me, Paul! Please!", Rob asked again.

"Let's go back to the house! We can at least put on a good front for my grandmother!", Paul said coldly.

Rob wouldn't let it go. "Paul, you told me that you are my friend!"

"I *am* your friend, Robbie! I wouldn't let anyone hurt you or harm a hair of your head,….but you aren't *my* friend. I don't know if you are anyone's friend! I can't stand to be around you! Still, that doesn't mean that I don't like you. I like you more than I should, maybe more than you deserve!"

"Paul, this doesn't make any sense! I thought that we all had a great day when you came out to see us. What did we do wrong?"

"What do you mean, *'we'*? What! Are you a king….or are you pregnant or something?", Paul asked sarcastically. "It isn't "we" who did something wrong. It is *you*! You might ask, "What did *I* do wrong" to be more accurate!"

"Okay! Then what did *I* do wrong, Paul?", Rob asked.

"Forget it, okay? It's all over and done with!"

"Look!", Rob was persistent, "It has finally been narrowed down that something went wrong….and that *I* did something wrong! I have a right to know what it is!"

"You don't have to know anything that I don't want to tell you!", Paul said through bared teeth.

"Bastard! Why are you doing this,?", Rob insisted.

"Okay, okay, OKAY! "Paul threw his arms in the air, palms towards Rob. "Here's a situation for you:" He started walking slowly as he spoke. Rob fell in by his side. Paul continued: Let's suppose that you found that you really liked someone, even loved that person; that you loved that person more than you ever dreamed you could care about anyone ever"

"Alright", Rob breathed out," and…?"

"But as much love that you felt for this person, you could never tell anyone about how you feel. You couldn't even let that very person know about your deep feeling. It would have to be a secret and remain a secret. You could never express your happiness because this person smiled at you, or your sadness if he or she sometimes acted as if you did not exist. Can you even imagine such a situation?"

"Well, yes", Rob conceded, "I guess so. Like I had a crush on a woman who was married or something like that, I suppose".

"No!", Paul said loudly, emphatically, "It's more than that!"

"What are you getting at?", Rob asked, studying Paul in order to relate what he was saying to what might possibly have gone wrong when they had all been together at Ticonderoga and afterwards at Balston Spa. Suddenly, Rob felt his face become a mask of surprise. "Wait a minute! … Gwynne!"

"What about Gwynne?", Paul asked.

"We had been talking about whether or not Gwynne and I had ever 'had it off'!", Rob said.

They had reached the barn in their walking. They stopped and Rob said: "It's Gwynne! You have a 'thing' for Gwynne! You got pissed at me when I told you not to ever think of sex when you look at my girl!"

"No, Robbie!", Paul spat out, "I got pissed off when I offered you friendship and you brushed it aside. You don't *feel*, Robbie, and because you don't feel you can't imagine that other people feel!. I like Gwynne. She is about the nicest girl whom I have ever met. I really like her, but I like her for who she is and the kind of person she is. I don't *want* her in the way that you think. I *can't want* her in the way that you would want her!"

"Well, then…who are you….talking about?", Rob's words trailed off as he slowly turned his head to face Paul and to see the tears in his eyes; tears of anger, hurt and longing, realizing that he had not really taken the time to know him at all. "Oh, God, Paul! You don't really mean what I think you mean!"

"Yes, Robbie! I see that you now catch my drift!", Paul conceded.

Rob fell silent, slumped his right arm and shoulder against the wall of the barn. "I can't believe this!", he half whispered.

"So, you see, Robbie? I don't want to be around you. I don't want you near me, I don't want to see you, hear you, smell you. I just can't deal with it! So, now that you know my deepest, darkest secret, you can get into your car, head out for Ohio and chalk all of this up to one of life's interesting experiences. It might even give you something to talk and laugh about with your College buddies!"

"Is that what you think I might do, Paul?", Rob asked sadly.

"How the Hell should I know what you find to be funny?", Paul whispered.

Rob gave no answer. After a moment, rocking himself forward from the barn with his shoulder, he moved silently, slowly towards Paul and almost as a sleep-walker, put his hand behind Paul's head and put his other arm around Paul's shoulders. Pulling Paul's head to his own shoulder, laying his cheek against that of Paul, he hugged him for a very long time.

"I am…so…sorry!", Rob whispered." I am so very sorry! I did not mean to hurt your feelings…or act like a jerk, but, how could I have known that you feel this way? I didn't plan it or want it". He withdrew his hand and pulled his head back, then, with his arm still around Paul's shoulders he said, "We'd better sit down".

The two of them moved to a low, flat-bed wagon and sat on it. Neither of them said anything for quite a while. Finally, Paul broke the silence.

"I guess that I can't really blame you, I know that. But, I have felt so much for you since the first time I ever met you. I realize that that is my problem, not yours. You aren't about to be able to love another guy!"

"But, I can and I *do* love you, Paul!", Rob told him. "Maybe not in the same way, exactly, but I know the feelings of love, and yes!, those feelings are in place! I have missed you! When I woke up and found that you had gone, I felt like hell! I couldn't think of much else for days! First, I'd say to myself, "screw him!" Why should I care one way or the other?, then I would find myself asking what I had done to make you disappear. Each time that I called the farm, my heart was dancing,….then you weren't there! I have told myself at least ten times that I wouldn't stop by here, but I knew inside of myself that I had to". He paused, played with a stalk of some barnyard plant, paused again, then went on: "I don't know for sure if that's the kind of love that you expect, but for what it's worth, it's what I feel. It's deep and sometimes it hurts. 'sure seems to be like what I know of love. I have discovered that you mean a lot to me…and…I do not want to lose you. I can't give you more than that; I can't do anything, you know….physical or 'sexual'. He laid his hand on Paul's knee and raised his eyes to meet Paul's. There was a questioning in Rob's eye, almost a plea. He then asked: "Could you still value my friendship and my kind of love without feeling that I was taunting you or 'dangling' myself before you and saying:" Ha, ha! You can look, but you can't touch?" Could you do that, Paul?"

"Robbie, You already have my friendship. I told you that. I feel deeply for you and sometimes wonder what you might be like, I admit. Still what if I am a 'homo'? Will you hold it against me?"

"Hold it against you? Not in your dreams will I hold "it" against you, Paul!", Rob wise-cracked, trying to wedge some levity into their discourse. No! Even if you are queer, which I doubt, I won't hold it against you if you don't hold it against me that I'm, as far as I have been able to tell, "straight", okay?"

Getting off the flat-bed they stood, looking squarely at one another.

"Friends?" Rob asked.

"Friends!", Paul answered. Taking a few steps, he halted. Rob stopped also, waiting, looking at him.

"But, how can I be sure?", Paul asked, obviously embarrassed...."How can I know for sure that you will still trust me? Especially now that I've told you?".

"Well, Paul, I guess that I'll trust you to care enough about me to never expect me to do anything that would make me feel rotten, guilty or ashamed of anything, right?"

"It might not be easy", Paul admitted. "I do sometimes wonder about things like that when you're around".

"Of course not!", Rob agreed, "If I woke up one morning and saw somebody as beautiful, well-built and such as I am, lying next to me...why, I'd never get out of bed! I'd be all over... that...person....and..."

Rob never finished the sentence as Paul let out a growl and rushed him, knocking him to the ground. They wrestled and laughed, Rob laughing so hard that he could not defend himself. Paul sat astride his chest, grabbed his ears and knocked his head against the ground. Rob laughed: "See?....see? See what I mean?"

The dog suddenly appeared, jumping into the mix of human activity, jumping and barking. They pulled her into the mix and she was hysterical with joy; squirming, nipping, licking faces, arms and trying to escape her confinement while reveling in it. Finally, the two young men sat back, smiling and catching their breath. Paul had both arms wrapped around Lorna who was licking what part of his face he could not pull far enough away from the reach of her tongue, Rob reached over and stroked Lorna's fur saying "Good Dog! You saved me from this mean guy, didn't you? He was trying to knock my head off, but you saved me! Good, good girl!"

Rob ended up staying for dinner. Grandma King would not take 'no' for an answer. She had first heard the barking and laughing and then witnessed the wrestling and flurry of activity out by the barn and felt a relief and happiness come over her which she had not felt for a long time, save for when Robbie had been with then before. She had come to believe that this boy, or young man, held a certain magic, a joy which he brought into Paul's life, and no, not Paul alone, but into her own life as well. She prepared one of her "simple farm meals" which could rival the offering of a four star hotel or, if she had been running a Bed and Breakfast place, would see it booked up for months in advance. On this occasion she had put together her locally famous Chicken and Biscuits, mashed potatoes, glazed carrots and a wonderful salad. There was also some not too hard apple cider, with just enough alcohol and "fizz" to serve in place of what would have been, in Europe, a good table wine. This meal she topped off with a Blackberry pie and coffee. Of course, at the end of such a repast she would scold the boys for not eating enough "to keep a bird alive", which if one considers it, is no small amount, since a bird is reputed to require an amount of food equal to its own body weight per diem.

After their dinner, Rob helped to clear the table of dishes and flatware, putting the left-overs to one side to be stored in the fridge. The plates and cups neatly stacked by the sink, Mrs. King began to wash the dishes. Paul had taken up the scraps into the "chicken bucket" and went out through the mud-room and towards the hen house.

"I am just so happy to have my two boys back again! I could just burst!", Paul's grandmother confided to Rob. "The two of you seem to make everything just so much better!"

"Thanks, Mrs. King", Rob said. "That means a lot to me!" He picked up a dish cloth and began to dry plates.

"And", she continued, "I want you to call me Gramma King! That's what I'm known as and that's what I want you to call me!"

"I consider that to be an honor", he said, looking at her, "Thanks, Gramma!"

"There!", she smiled. "Now, that wasn't so hard, was it?" As she continued washing dishes and putting them into the rinse water she went on:" You are like a tonic for Paul. He is just another person when you are around. He loves you so much, Robbie!"

Rob felt himself start a bit and without turning his head, looked towards her from the corner of his eye, but Carole King had simply made a statement, revealed an observation with which she seemed to be quite comfortable.

"Well, Gramma, I like Paul… an awful lot too", he conceded.

"Oh, I know that!", she answered." I'm pretty sure

that Paul knows it too, although he doubts his ability to hold onto anyone. I guess that every time he has ever felt anything really, strongly, for anyone, that person has gone on and out of his life. It's sad, really."

The back door opened and Paul came back into the kitchen. Both Rob and Gramma turned to look at him at the same time, both silent. Paul froze, bucket in hand and stared back at the two of them'

"What!" It came forth sounding like a statement, while really being a question.

"Can't the cat look at the Queen?", Gramma asked him. From behind her, Rob caught Paul's eye and smirking wickedly, moved his eyebrows up and down. Paul rolled his eyes upwards and shook his head as if to clear it.

"You did it again!", Rob said quickly to cover himself. "You always think that you are the only person worth looking at!"

Paul put the bucket under the old dry sink by the back door, hung his hat on a hook and moved over to the table and sat down. His grandmother placed an ashtray on the table in front of him. He glanced up at her.

"I know that you smoke, Paul", she told him, "Go ahead and smoke if you want to".

"Mom always told me that you don't like people to smoke, Gramma"

"Well, Paul, I am old fashioned! I don't like to see *women* smoke!....especially if they have young children. Men are different somehow. Male animals, whether stallions, rams, bulls or human beings, seem to need something to keep them calmed down. If tobacco works for a man, well then… let him smoke!" She stopped and thought for a short while and went on, as if recalling an important event or series of events, then said, to no one in particular.:" My father always smelled so good to me as a little girl.! I would sit in his lap and he smelled strong and warm and kind. He smelled of horses and hay and tobacco!" She chuckled. "He smelled like a man! Pa was good! He was a wonderful person!" Then, as an afterthought she added:" When I became nine years old, Mother told me that I was too big to sit in my father's lap. I cried that night."

Paul took the pack of cigarettes out of his shirt pocket, took one of them and tapped the end of it against his thumbnail before putting it between his lips. He lit it with a match and took a drag of it pulling the smoke into his lungs before exhaling it in a cloud. The dishes being dried, Rob sat down at the table with him. Neither of them said anything, seemingly each in his own thoughts. Gramma King had gone into the other room. After a minute, Rob reached over, almost absently, took Paul's cigarette and took a long pull of it into himself.

"Geez, Robbie! You did it again! You always hand me back a butt that is so hot that I can hardly put it to my mouth! For a guy who doesn't smoke, you sure make up for it when you do!"

"Just bitch about it, why don't you, Paul?", Rob asked sarcastically, playfully, "Go ahead: piss and moan, piss and moan!"

Not long afterward, Rob told him that he had really better be heading out, that he had a long drive ahead of him and that he had really expected to get back on the road long before. Paul felt that he should try to dissuade him, to tell him to stay the night and start out in the morning when he would have some light. At the same time, after what they had been through and the revelation that he had made, he didn't want to push things. When Gramma King heard of his plan to leave, she would not hear of it. She told him everything which Paul would have said. Rob realized that it really would be more difficult at night and he also thought of Paul's "confession". He might be, in Paul's mind, showing a reluctance to stay because he harbored some misgivings on that account. He wanted to shore up what he had promised Paul and not simply "beat tracks" out of there so soon after dinner. He was therefore surprised to hear Paul explain to his grandmother that perhaps he, Rob, really had to leave that evening instead of in the morning. Paul was giving him an "out". Rob decided to stay until morning.

The three of them visited in the living room, looked at a few more books which had been found tucked away in the house, and ended by watching the Eleven o'clock News on the television: usual footage of student demonstrations, some stories from Viet Nam, followed by the local news and weather report. After Gramma asked Rob what time he wanted to leave in the morning, he rose from the couch and gave her a hug, followed by the same from Paul and she went on in to bed. Rob then took a few notes and some sources from books' bibliographies. Paul announced that he was going up to take a shower.

"Me too", Rob said absently." I'm almost done here. You go ahead and I'll be up shortly."

Paul turned off the Television and headed out back to check on the dog. Rob heard the back door open and close and not long afterwards, the same sound repeated, then the thudding of Paul's feet up the stairs. A bit later, when Rob entered the bedroom, he saw Paul sitting up in bed, reading a book by the light of the bedside lamp.

"What are you reading, Paul?", he asked.

"The White and the Gold", Paul answered. "It's about the French colonies in Canada and the 'States. Ever since Ticonderoga I've been interested to know more about that".

"Okay if I take a shower?", Rob asked.

"Don't even ask! You know where everything is, right?" Paul laid his book down beside him on the bed and continued:" You know, after what I told you today I don't want you to feel awkward or anything. Would you rather sleep alone?"

"On the floor, or me in bed and you on the floor? Hell, no! I have no problems with sleeping in the same bed", Rob assured him.

"Do you want to keep your jeans on or anything?, Paul asked.

"Oh, okay!" Rob answered sarcastically, "Maybe I should wear some tight swimming trunks with no fly… or maybe you have a cast-iron athletic cup that I could wear!"

Paul rolled his eyes in mock exasperation "Just light that small lamp by the door, will you? I'm going to turn off this lamp".

When Rob returned from his shower, the room was dark save for a glow from the small night-light and a moon which shone brightly into the room. He was wearing the bath towel sarong-fashion. His clothes in his hand. He took a clean pair of under-shorts from his bag and turned the night-light off. He then finished drying off, see-sawing the towel across his back, then his arms and legs, rubbing them very briskly. Despite the darkness, the moonlight placed something of a golden aura: a pale, blue "fuzz" of sorts. From the bed, Paul was aware of the movements and motions of the smooth, darkened form in the room, parts of it catching touches of light from time to time. Rob moved to a chair, the light from the window showing him to be carefully draping his towel over the chair back. He then moved softly and smoothly on the balls of his feet to the side of the bed. He lifted one leg and then the other, stepping into his undershorts, which he then pulled up and into place. Picking up a corner of the bed clothes, he slipped between the sheets. As Rob slid down into the bed, Paul rolled over on his side, his back to Rob.

"Good night, Rob", came his voice from beyond the back and shoulder.

Rob did not immediately respond. He lay on his back for a minute, maybe two, after which time he rolled onto his side towards his friend's back. He hesitated for a moment, then moved his arm under Paul's, around his torso, placing his hand on Paul's left rib cage.

"Good night, Paul", he answered.

Rob awoke to the sounds and smells of breakfast preparations coming to him from the kitchen downstairs. He sat up in bed after carefully removing Paul's arm, which had been across his chest. glancing at the still sleeping Paul, he carefully swung his feet over the edge of the bed, stretched and yawned then got up and stepped into his jeans which had lain on the chair, then pulling them up into place and grabbing the towel from his shower of the night before, he moved towards the door.

"Good morning!", Paul drawled before yawning and stretching.

"Good Morning", Rob returned hastily. "I'd love to stay and visit, but I have to piss like a race horse!" With that he bolted out the door towards the bathroom. When he returned, Paul was half dressed, also obviously in need of the facilities. Paul came back into the bedroom shortly thereafter and grabbed his undershirt and socks to finish getting dressed.

"Did you sleep all right, Robbie?", Paul asked while pulling a sock onto one foot. "You didn't lay awake worrying or anything, did you?"

"No," Rob said simply. I went right to sleep. Then, grinning maliciously he asked, "Why? Did I miss anything while I was sleeping?"

"Hey, buddy!", Paul wise-cracked, "You don't give me much credit! Believe me: if anything had happened, you would carry that cherished memory to your grave!"

Gramma King had once again outdone herself for the boys' breakfast (to her they would always be "the boys").

"Now Robbie, I've made some scones for you to take along with you and I have also done up some of that Johnny Cake, so you mustn't forget and leave them behind when you go!"

"Sure, Gramma! Go ahead and clean out the house and pantry for our sweet little Robbie!", Paul teased.

"Oh, you!" she gestured as if to cuff him on the back of his head.

"Yeah, Paul!, Rob countered, "What are you worrying about? I'm just helping you to not make a pig of yourself! You have this great cooking all the time! You have to learn to share with the less fortunate!"

"I think that one of you is as bad as the other!", Gramma remarked. "You should have been brothers!"

"Yeah!", Paul mused, "I could live with that!"

"No kidding!", Rob agreed, ""I could learn to live with that too, I guess" Knowing that Gramma was facing away from them both, Rob smiled wickedly at Paul, who once again, closed his eyes and shook his head in disbelief, then mouthed the words without sound: "You are BAD!"

When Rob was leaving, he hugged Gramma King at the back door and thanked her for everything. He promised that he would write to her when he finally got back to school. Paul walked out to the car with him. From the back door, Grandma King watched the two young men walking together, watched them stand by the car for a few minutes, talking, then she saw them awkwardly throw their arms around one another. Rob turned abruptly and got into the car behind the wheel, wiping his forearm across his eyes. Paul stood watching as the car backed onto the roadway, then raised his arm and waved. Rob waved back to him in return, then started for the town and the highway. The two of them had learned much in the summer of 1972. Both had grown considerably in their abilities to give to others, accept the differences of others. They had dealt with prejudices and matters of self-identity. Over the years Rob would look back and remember that summer as one of the most important learning experiences of his life. For Paul it was as much or more. He took on an attitude of helpfulness, kindness and an optimism which won him love and respect time and time again. He would come to win the admiration and the trust of many men for his sense of decency, his manly loyalty and fairness.

CHAPTER 17

PART II

Rob was happily welcomed at the MacKinnon home. Kathy was full of enthusiasm about Martin's engagement.

"He's always been such an old 'sober-sides'! I wondered if he'd ever find a young lady!", Kathy said.

"Well this girl is one well worth waiting for!", Robert MacKinnon announced. "Just as sweet and kind as she is pretty!"

"Praise from Caesar is praise indeed!", Rob said. "When do I get to meet this young Lady? What did you say her name is?"

"Diane." Kathy told him. "Diane Greer."

"A clanswoman of the MacGregors?" Rob asked.

"Well, by golly, I believe you're right, Rob!" MacKinnon said.

"She never said as much, but she may be." Kathy added.

"So, when do I meet the future Mrs. Craig?", Rob asked.

"Not for a couple of days yet, Rob," Kathy said. "She

is at her parents' home just now. Martin is going to pick her up on Wednesday, unless, of course there's been a change in plan".

"He'll be stopping by this afternoon. You can find out from him," Robert MacKinnon said. "There'd better not be any serious change of plans, by gum! There's a reception for them here on Wednesday night!"

Later that same day, Martin stopped by and Rob went with him up to the old home place. They took Martin's jeep this time, for Martin had been doing some work up there. Rob was surprised to see that the lawn was now defined, some pruning and trimming of the shrubbery was much in evidence, and that the house itself had been freshly painted.

"Wow! The place looks great!" Rob said.

"It's a hell of a place to get in and out of in the winter," Martin said, "But it's going to be our house come hell or high water!"

"You're going to be living here, then?" Rob asked with more enthusiasm than surprise.

"Yep! You think I'm out of my mind?"

"Out of your mind? No way! I think that it's a great idea!"

"Well, Diane loves the place. She has her master's in education and she has been teaching for three years. There was and opening in the High School, for which she applied and has been accepted. In fact, she starts her new job in about a week and a half."

"What does she teach?"

"English. She's qualified to teach French too, but English will be her assignment."

"That's great! What about yourself?", Rob asked.

"Renovation and restoration work is big right now. I may have to take on the construction work from time to time, but I guess that I have a pretty good name out there. I can't think of doing anything else."

"Nice going! I am impressed." Rob said, "Really!"

They walked up the steps and into the big old house. Martin went into the dining room area, took out a pencil and pad of paper and his measuring tape.

"I have to take some measurements. We're going to somehow save this big old window in here. Why don't you take another look around? Make yourself at home."

Rob was grateful for the invitation, the opportunity. He had gone through the place briefly before with Martin, but he welcomed the chance to simply poke around on his own. He wandered through the rooms looking at the few remaining pieces of furniture; things that had been left in the house. He stopped to admire a recently carved, but very well-executed Celtic cross, of what appeared to be cherry wood. The intricate inter-lacings and the way in which light and shadow worked on the over-all design gave it a mystique, a power all its own. It had been simply laid on a side table in the main room of the house. Rob traced over the inter-lacings with the tip of his index finger, staring out the window as he did so, such patterns have an almost hypnotic effect. One cannot but be pulled into them.

Wandering into the hallway and onto the staircase leading to the upper hall, he allowed his hand to glide over the smooth, railing, feeling the polished wood. Not long afterwards he found himself standing in the upper gallery, staring at the picture of Alan MacKinnon. Looking at that image captured in time: that of a young man who had lived long before his own generation: The soft, gentle, dark eyes, the full mouth and well-formed brows, nose and cheeks, The man in the portrait seemed to be looking back at him, even a trace of humor in the eyes. Something about the eyes reminded him of a similar quality in those of Paul, but there the similarity ended. It wasn't as if there was any resemblance between them, In fact, he was surprised to see much about the portrait that made for an image of himself.

"What a fine-looking man, you are Alan MacKinnon! I wish that I had your looks.", he murmured aloud.

"Ah, but you have Rob! That is you, or you are he. You're an absolute look-alike!"

Rob started. He hadn't heard Martin approach.

"Wow! You surprised me!" Rob blurted. "Caught me talking to a picture." He flushed in embarrassment.

"I think that we all do things like that once in a while. How else can we speak to the past? Whether people pray in front of icons or saints images, or talk to ancestors through pictures… it is more common than we might care to admit. It's even more than addressing the past; it's keeping the 'past' alive and with us", Martin suggested.

"This is a fabulous house!" Rob said, changing the

subject. Looking around the hallway, taking it in. The fine woodwork and paneling, he went on: "I told my grandfather that his grandfather had built this place, what a great place it is. He said that he had had no idea that Lachlan had done anything but fail in a business venture in Pennsylvania. I guess that ol' great great grannie Jeanie hadn't been thoroughly truthful in what she told her sons." Mart remained silent, half smiling.

"Oh!, by the way!" Rob said, remembering something. "That beautiful Celtic cross downstairs: who carved it?"

"Well, I did." Martin Said.I take it you like it."

"It's fantastic! Where are you going to hang it?"

"That's what I wanted to do! 'Glad you reminded me, Rob! I want to center it over the fireplace in the dining room. That's the east wall you know, 'sacred space,' hearth of the family. Let's go do it right now. Then it's done."

A Few minutes later, Rob was holding the cross while Mart was measuring to find the mid-point of the center-most panel over the fireplace. Rob watched as Martin took what appeared to be a brass nail and tapped it into the panel where he had made a small 'x.' Martin then made a cruciform gesture over the spot with his right hand, The thumb of his hand over the third finger, leaving the other fingers straight. He then took the cross to its place. How priestly the movements of Martin appeared to be! Martin then put both hands on the horizontal, touching his forehead to that same mantle. He was offering a silent prayer, for after a minute, he stood back and crossed himself in the Eastern fashion: from right shoulder to left. Rob asked, "… Am I right in assuming that you will be the next Co-Arb?"

Martin looked quickly at him with a look of surprise.

"Oh, no, Rob. I can't be the next Co-Arb. It doesn't work like that."

"Who is he, then?… The next Co-Arb?"

"We don't know. We'll have to wait and see, I guess. We will get some sign or 'signs.' It always happens." Martin had acted a bit flustered in his response.

Rob looked at the Celtic cross in its place. It belonged in that spot. "It's rather confusing, this business of Co-Arbs and such."

"Yes," Martin agreed," but yet it's always rather simple and even quite direct." He paused, then said, "Well, Rob! Take a blessing from the new cross. Touch your fingers to your lips then your fingers to the cross center."

Rob smiled and agreed. He touched the interwoven center with his fingers, conveying as it were, a kiss to the cross.His hands came to the mantelpiece and in admiration he ran his fingertips along the upper edge of the massive piece of very old oak. Moving to the right, his hand went along that side of the mantle.

"Hey, Martin. C'mere."

"What?"

"You must have knocked something loose. You'll have to fix this"… and at that a large piece of the mantel piece molding came away in his hand. He stood there awkwardly staring at the wood that he still held.

"What did you do, Rob? You have to be careful!"

"I didn't do anything! This piece of wood had started to come loose." He tried to put it back but it would not fit back into place. "Something has gotten in the way. Here Mart! Hold this," he murmured as he handed the mantle's wooden end piece to him. Rob then peered into a square void left by the piece of mantle.

"I can't see what is holding it back…" and having said that, he moved his right hand up and into the void and ran his finger inside the obstruction and soon was pulling out a long cylinder which he handed to Mart. "Wait! There's some other thing in here! 'like a block of wood or something" and with that pulled out a small, leather bound book, and after that a very dusty box of brass and very worn wine-colored velvet, both of which he laid gently on the floor beside him. He had had to extend his right forearm into the cavity for this last item.

"Give me the end-piece. It will probably go back into place now," Rob said. Martin, stunned, stared at the objects on the floor as he absently handed the wooden piece to him. The carved piece slid back into place with no trouble. Rob turned to see Martin's face still a mask of wonder and disbelief, staring at him.

"Oh my good God! Oh my great and Good God!", he stammered staring at Robbie. He picked up the cylinder, and handing it to Rob, said: "Put these things on the table! Sit down there! Don't move until I come back. Don't

Move! I'll be right back!"

Robbie sat down on the wide window ledge, staring at the three objects on the table. He wanted to open the book, open the box, look into the cylinder, but figured that he had better wait. He contented himself with wiping dust off of the objects as he heard Mart's jeep screech out of the driveway.

In a very short time, the elder MacKinnon and Kathy were entering the house with Mart. He was talking to them very excitedly:

"......then he went to the side of the mantle and just pulled a piece of wood away as if he knew exactly what would happen."

"What've we got here, young man?" MacKinnon asked Rob.

"I don't know, sir. I was waiting, like Mart told me."

"Sir? You're calling me 'sir'? Mart came busting into the house calling me Grandfather. He hasn't called me anything respectful in twenty years! Boy! This must be the second coming or something!" Picking up the cylinder, he pulled away a wrapping of very heavy paper.

"Why, this is just a roll of papers, Mart.", but he unrolled them and found there to be about ten sheets of paper all rolled together, the sheets were about 18" wide by 20 or 24 inches long. On the top most one were several writings on the page; Obviously bits of verse. "Well," he muttered. "Well, well, well! It's either pretty terrible spelling in English or Scots Gaelic. What do you know about that!" He continued to look at the page and said to Kathy, "...We better flatten these slowly by pressing them under glass. I don't want to ruin them! Why don't you see what's in that pretty sad-looking box, Kath?"

"Oh, for land's sake!" Kathy exclaimed upon opening what they had thought to be a box. It was in fact a Victorian double picture frame. All of them looked at the old pictures in their oval matts: a handsome, proud looking man on one side; a well-dressed pretty woman on the other. "Robbie! This could be you! My word, but it looks like you!", Kath exclaimed. Rob stared in disbelief. It was not his own likeness which rattled him, but the picture of the woman. "Gwynne!", He whispered to himself, staring with awe.

"What? What did you say?" Robert MacKinnon asked. "Yes. There they are: Your great, great grandparents, Rob: Lachlan and Síne MacKinnon! 'Quite a handsome pair. Beautiful woman!"

Rob continued to stare, feeling a chill come over him,

"Well, lets see what this book is! We have to be ver-ry ver-ry careful here!", Robert said while slowly opening the book.

He turned pages carefully, frowning in his intensity. He would occasionally make short sounds of surprise of recognition.

"I wish I were more familiar with the Gaelic," he finally said. "But what this is, is of tremendous importance to the family and to Celtic Christianity especially. This is a Co-Arb's book: hand written and never to be published. You see… it is opinions and information written by a Co-Arb during his period of guidance. Celtic Christianity is deep and mystical, pretty esoteric in its own way. Then too, it cannot be published for fear that it would 'sell' and make money. Celtic Christianity forbids 'selling' anything of a spiritual nature."

"But was Lachlann a Co-Arb?", Martin asked.

"No but his brother, my great grandfather, was. Lachlan may have been asked to act as 'Dewar' or guardian for some things." Robert looked back to the front page and drew the attention of the others:

"Look here. 'How different the handwriting is from Lachlann's. But look at the title: "Rach as Shealladh!"

"Which means…?" Kath asked.

"Which means 'to go from view', 'going from view' or 'going from sight':It is Celtic Christianity's last line of defense: to vanish or to 'appear to disappear.' Well", Robert said, "We have to keep this book for the next Co-Arb."

Martin and Kathy suddenly turned their faces toward Rob, then to Robert.

"I'm sure that we'll know before long," Robert said cryptically.

That evening they had little time to go over what had been found earlier in the day. Rob noticed however, that Robert MacKinnon, rather than squirrel the three items away, had left them on a desk in the study in case one of them had a wish to look at them, and in fact, had made a point of saying as much. Martin stayed at the house of Robert and Kathy that night, planning to drive up close to

Bradford to pick up Diane the following morning. Robert and Kathy made it fairly clear that they had planned to retire a bit earlier that evening leaving Martin and Rob to visit, look at the book and writings, or whatever else they wanted to do. Rob was not unhappy in the least at this turn of events, for he wanted to talk to Mart.

"You caused quite a stir today, Robbie," Mart said as they sat in the living room having some coffee and tea by themselves.

"I don't see why I should get any special notice. We just found some things, that's all. I'm sure that in the course of restoration you would have found them, Martin."

"I'm not so sure. You should have seen yourself! You went to that mantle as if you expected to find something… as if you knew there was something there. When I saw you start to pull things out of that long hollow in the mantle, I felt the hair rise up on my neck!"

"You're reading a bit more into this than is there, Martin", Robbie advised him.

"Perhaps," Martin shrugged but smiled as his blue eyes danced with amusement.

"Seriously, Mart. If I can change the subject, I would like to ask you a question,… well, really I'd like to ask you if you'd do something," Rob began. "Now if you'd rather not, or if you feel uncomfortable and decide that you'd rather not, please don't think that I wouldn't understand… okay?"

"Okay." Martin turned to face Rob squarely, his eyes now very serious.

"Well, when I was last here, Robert told me a great many things... about highland ways, about the old faith and all... and he spoke of the importance of the Anam Caraid, the soul friend: 'How you send a twelve year out to meet his soul friend, how the soul friend is bound by the seal of confession and all?"

"Yes," Martin agreed. "The soul friend is very important. It is one of the strengths of the old faith, for not even an abbot or a bishop can interfere with a soul friend's discharge of his holy office; mainly, I suppose, because there is no way of anyone ever knowing what has been said or not said. If one disagrees with a soul friend, he or she walks away. If one doesn't heed a soul friend, he or she, the soul friend, can walk away."

"Well, it sounds like a great system."

"It seems to work very well for us, Rob, if that's what you mean. So what do you want to know about it?"

Martin, would you act as my Anam Caraid?"

"I would do so gladly, Rob. However I must have your trust."

"I do trust you, Mart.

"Well, okay!" Martin leaned forward and put his hand on Rob's shoulder." I will always do my best for you."
"Would you... hear my confession,... now?"

"If that's what you want. Surely", Martin agreed

Rob unloaded the story of the summer and his relationship with Paul and his grandmother, of what his personal relationship with Paul had finally come to, how he had dealt with it and so on. As he unfolded the events of the last few weeks and particularly the past three days, Martin sat motionless, hunched forward with his forearms resting on his thighs, his hands clasped together. He seemed to be staring at the floor while listening, although every once in a while his steady blue eyes would turn up to read those of Rob, then return to the study of floor space before him. When Rob came to the end of the story, his leaving the farm and his goodbyes, Martin continued to gaze forward. Without looking up he said to Rob: "It's essential that you are totally honest with me. I must have your trust and you must be willing to accept what I say as the best answer which I can come up with."

"Okay, I can do that." Rob said.

"What you did was good as far as your willingness to accept who he is… although…" Martin looked toward the ceiling.

"Although? Although what?" Rob asked.

"Such a friendship will be very hard to maintain. It might be difficult for you to understand his need for something other than a strictly platonic relationship. You can't overlook the fact that a part of his feeling for you is based on a physical attraction… which you may resent from time to time. It is not an easy path, this one which you have chosen."

"I don't know what to do." Rob said. There was a note of sadness, but perhaps an even greater desperation in his voice. "I really do like the guy. I guess that I even love him."

Martin nodded his head, understanding. His kind, blue eyes looked into Robbie's again. There was a definite compassion registered on Martin's face along with a certain sadness. "So you're asking me what you should do…"

"Well, yes."

"I think that you need to listen to your heart and the 'inner voice,' … but after having asked the Almighty. You must learn to trust that inner voice… even if it means going against what you might think you want.", Martin explained.

"Rather like 'conscience' vs. rationalization.", Rob mused.

"You've got it!", Martin said.

Rob frowned as if in thought then said, "I guess that I have already done that, Mart, and yes, I have begun to understand the power play between the 'voice within', the Holy Spirit, as opposed to my own rationalizations. It's a tough battle sometimes, I might add. In this case something has come to me as almost what I would call a 'revelation.' Could you accept it, Mart?

"I would certainly try, Rob," Mart told him.

"Well, Rob Explained, "It occurs to me that both Paul and I are facing some need for, and an opportunity to gain, some discipline here. We both must accept one another for who he is. We both need to learn to give love with no expectation of reward.

"Rob, that is.. beautiful and it is good! It is what real love is all about!", Mart said softly.

Martin grew silent again, smiled slightly as he sat

thoughtfully with his hands in his lap, staring again at the design in the carpet.

"There's another strange thing; a coincidence, or something of that sort, Martin. It is almost beyond belief!", Rob stated.

"Oh?" Martin asked. "That much of a coincidence? What is it Rob?

"Well, today while you were looking up into the hollow of the fireplace mantle, all bent over and trying to see up in there where I had pulled those things out, I noticed something you were wearing. I noticed that a deer-antler cross fell out of your shirt and was hanging around your neck, just kind of swinging there!"

"Oh, yes! My 'Caberfeídh' (Kahber-fay), Mart said.

"Well, if this isn't the damndest thing!" Rob told him, "My friend Paul… the guy I was just telling you about?… He wears a deer-horn cross too. He says that it was an uncle who gave it to him. He wouldn't take it off for anything!"

"Your friend Paul, for whatever confusion or unhappiness he may have been experiencing, must be greatly respected by someone. The antler cross is something that you'll never find in antique stores. They are either passed to another, younger person when a man marries, or else cast into deep water somewhere where they'll never be found or seen again. Anyway, a young fellow who wears the Caberfeídh can be trusted to hear your innermost troubles!"

There was a pause in the conversation, then Martin went on: "Robbie, when Diane and I are Married, I would very much like it if you would allow me to pass my own Caberfeídh on to you."

"Martin, that would be a tremendous honor for me!" Rob replied with a rush of joy through his being.

"Well!   That's that then!", Martin said, rising and stretching. "Now we must trudge off to get some sleep!"

The two young fellows shook hands lightly hugged, and turned to go. Rob turned and asked,

"One more thing, Martin!"

Martin turned, waiting for the question.

"Who was Co-Arb before your grandfather?"

"Why, it was Robert Donald, son of Lachlann. Robert Donald was your Great Grandfather, Rob! I thought that you knew that!", Martin said simply.

"Martin, before coming here and spending time with you folks, I had never even heard the word 'Co-Arb'!"

Rob was to build a lasting friendship with Martin in the years which followed and Martin turned to Rob for advice from time to time. In fact, on the very evening of the engagement party Rob was asked to perform a service which, once he assumed the task, started him toward his true life.

CHAPTER 18

PART II

There were a great many people gathered at Robert and Kathy's home. Some of the men who attended wore kilts. In fact, Robert and Martin were wearing Highland dress. Rob couldn't help thinking how very 'natural' these MacKinnons, Robert and grandson, looked in kilt and sporran. When Martin had come through the door just behind his fianceé he seemed to Rob to be the epitome of what a clansman should be; what a fit Highland Gael should look like. Certainly there was no doubt that he was proud of Diane. She was as lovely, and attractive as Kathy and Robert had said. A ginger-haired girl of small delicate build, her eyes were soft green-brown and her complexion was fair but rosy. She seemed to take the time to listen to anyone who spoke to her; not in a hurry to move on. That she had a deep fondness for Martin's grandparents was quite evident. It was her demeanor around Martin which endeared her to Robbie. She seemed to adore him and yet she was not hanging on him, clutching him,… not physically nor in her aspect. When he spoke a light came into her eyes. When he spoke to her or of her, she took praise with humility and always returned a compliment to him. Martin was a different person around her. Rob had never been able to see any hint of boyishness in Martin, nor had he seen him glow with affection as was now the case when he was in Diane's company.

Robbie was introduced to so many people that he felt that he was being absolutely over-run with names and the many relationships of these people to the MacKinnons. Robert MacKinnon would say to someone, his hand on Robbie's shoulder: "I want you to meet my Kinsman and dear young friend Rob Currie.", "Alan MacKinnon was our ancestor in common," he told others. Something deep inside of him gave Rob a feeling that he was being introduced, in some cases at least, to people who had heard of him previously. A slip-up on Diane's part convinced him that his 'gut feeling' was not without foundation. She had been talking to him about the renovations on Ardachy, how much Martin had been doing and how she hoped that they would be able to keep up such a huge house.

"Marty says that you are very much taken with the house," she said.

"Oh, yes. It's a great place! You are definitely the couple for the house. Of course it is a lot of house for two people but, once some kids come along…" He then shook his head, slapped his open palm against his forehead.

"Shees! What a dumb thing to be saying!"

"Au Contraire! It's part of marriage; the most important part, I would imagine," laughing, she lowered her head and looked up at him, smiling. "Rob! You're blushing! Oh I am going to like you!" She touched his arm and went on: "Marty is very impressed with you… and Robert thinks the world of you, not to mention Kathy's feelings! But why not? The problem of the succession…. Of …. The…Co." She stopped, looking at the surprise on his face. "Oh, dear!" At that moment it was Diane who was red-faced, as if she wanted to run and hide somewhere.

"Did you… let some kind of cat out of some kind of bag?", Rob asked with a trace of a smile. He continued: "Well, I very much fear that such a position would prove itself to be far beyond my capabilities. In any case, I wouldn't worry about having almost having given away a top secret if I were you."

"Oh! I always pride myself on not talking too much. Oh, no!" Her hand came up to her forehead as if she had suddenly had a migraine, as if she felt ill. Rob grasped the situation and was surprised to hear himself say "This will just have to be our secret, Diane!" He smiled and put his hand on her forearm. "Okay?"

Martin appeared as if from nowhere and looked from one of them to the other. "Is everything alright?" His concern was very evident.

"Everything's fine, hon'! Your fiancée and a very handsome young man are sharing a secret, that's all," she said smiling.

"Something that you'll carry to your grave, no doubt," Mart said with a trace of humor now.

"Absolutely! Wild horses couldn't drag it out of me." Turning to Rob she said, "Don't worry. I'll never betray our secret."

"Wow, thanks Diane! I'm relieved to hear that!", then to both of them Rob said, "Gosh, I'm getting to really like you two."

Rob drifted away from them only a few feet and Kathy appeared ready to lead him off to meet someone else: another friend and guest.

"What on earth was that all about?" Mart asked Diane.

"I was trying to get that gorgeous kid to run away with me", she said playfully.

Mart shook his head, took her arm and led her off with him, he teased, "But that would make me feel terribly lost, no madness in my life."

"Oh, I am sure that you would be able to find some madness!", she replied with conviction.

Much later, the last guests left the MacKinnon home, Rob started picking up plates, glasses and trays with remaining cakes, hors d'oeuvres and such and started carrying them toward the kitchen.

"Oh, Robbie! Don't worry about those things!", Kathy said to him with just a hint of fatigue in her voice. "I will put the left-overs under cover, but the glasses and cups can wait 'til morning!"

"It's no problem! You sure don't want to wake up to all of this tomorrow," he advised.

"Why don't you and Diane put the food wherever you want," Martin put in, "and let Rob and me wash up these things? We won't destroy all of your china and glassware!"

There was so much food left over! Kathy and Diane sorted much of it, planning to set some of it aside for the newly engaged couple, some quantities were ear-marked for an elderly neighbor, and still other assorted dishes, rolls and sweets for a family down the road, the children of that family having been foreseen to enjoy the extra goodies. The two women worked smoothly and easily together, almost anticipating the moves of one another. Martin washed the dishes, starting with the glassware, which was rinsed in very hot water and required very little in the way of drying with a dish towel. Rob did the drying and set all of the glasses to one side. Martin then washed the cake plates and such which were also lined up in the rack by the sink. These too, Rob dried and stacked according to their patterns and size. Considering all of the cake knives, forks, spoons and all, there were a great many things to wash and dry. There were, in fact so many odds and ends that Martin actually drained the wash water and refilled the sink to continue on. Diane came by and started putting the dried glasses and dishes away. She seemed to know where things were usually stored. The three of them managed to make fairly light work of what had initially appeared to have been a tremendous challenge. After their putting the house back in order, Kathy admitted that she was really grateful that she didn't have the monumental task of picking up to do the next day.

Rob sat down at the kitchen table as Martin went into the Living room to see what his grandfather might be doing and Kathy went into the laundry room with a great bunch of napkins, some small tablecloths and such things which would need to be washed the next day. Diane moved to the stove and started to heat up some coffee. Rob watched her absently, but taking in her graceful movements.He saw her push back a wisp of her hair which had strayed across her forehead, using the bend of her wrist to do so, her fingers remaining relaxed. "Gwynne does that same thing!", he thought. It appeared to him as a totally feminine gesture, one which would never even occur to a man, if a man could even use his hand or wrist in that same way. It was some of these movements which he saw to be so fascinating when with his own girlfriend.

"I'll bet that you would like a cup of coffee." She said to Rob. "Am I right?"

"I am getting to where I will always take a cup of coffee", he replied. "Having been a student and especially an art student, I find myself burning a lot of 'midnight oil' and it is coffee that keeps me going. Yes! I would love a cup of coffee! Are you going to have one with me?"

"Yes, I might just do that!", she replied. "Marty doesn't care all that much for coffee, as you know, but I seem to thrive on it!"

She placed a mug of coffee in front of him, then placed

a mug on the table for herself and sat down. Both of them were quiet for a short time, each in thought. Rob broke the silence:

"Diane, could I ask you a question?", he asked.

"Certainly, Robbie. If it isn't too difficult for me to answer!"

"Thinking of you and Martin getting married, I was wondering about something ", he said.

"It is pretty plain to see that you are both really good together and that you love one another, but, I can't help wondering…". He paused, then continued, "I remember my mother talking with another woman at one time about the minister of her church and both of them were of the opinion that it would be very difficult for a woman to be married to a man who had committed to Almighty God and who had to share himself with so many people. Both this other lady and my Mom said that they would not be able to do that. Well, here you are, marrying a man who is already a Ceile De, a priest. That has to be something that you might think about, I should imagine. Am I being too personal in asking about this?"

"You are right, Robbie. I have thought about it and I have wondered whether I have what it takes. You are not being too personal, by the way. In fact I am really happy to know that you would care about something like that. I really love Marty and I love who he is, the kind of man that he is. There is so very much love in him, Robbie! I suppose that there may be times when I have a hard time sharing him, perhaps even with God! Still, I have learned so very much from him in the time that we have spent together. He has taught me how to share my love with others too, although next to him I am a rank amateur! At this point I do not think that I could ever love a man and want to share my life with a man who could only love one person in his life. There is so much, so very much love in Marty that it simply must not be bottled up or held back. It's who he is and, since I love him, what he is I want to be too!"

Rob stared at her with admiration. "Wow!", he said softly, "You are quite a woman!"

Martin came into the kitchen, looked at the two of them and said: "You two just can't be left alone! Here you are again: conspiring, sharing secrets! Am I right?

"Oh, No! Rob! We have been caught again, red-handed!", Diane feigned surprise and fear!. Then to Martin she said, "I take full responsibility! I lured him to this table with some warmed –up coffee and he, being innocent and unsuspecting, has been like putty in my hands!"

Rob smiled shyly, shook his head slowly from side to side and said: "You two deserve each other!" They all laughed. At that moment Kathy appeared at the doorway.

"Well everyone, I am just about worn out for one day. I'm going to turn in," she announced. "Goodnight. And sleep as late as you wish. There is nothing pressing for tomorrow!"

Diane expressed the same feeling on her part: the need to call it a day and turn in. After she and Martin exchanged some words quietly at the foot of the stairs, they kissed goodnight and she went up to bed. Martin and Rob went into the Living room where Robert had been looking for something in the bookshelves.

MacKinnon sat down in his chair and dug out his pipe and tobacco pouch, seeming to have something to do, something yet to be resolved. Mart sat on the couch, then as if he had remembered something, he went to the bookshelves and opened one of the lower doors.

"Could we take another look at these things that Robbie rooted out of the fireplace mantle up the hill?"

By all means! Robert said. "I'd like to look at them again too. How about you, Robbie?" He added almost as an afterthought. "Which of those things did you find to be of greatest interest?"

Martin didn't look up as he brought out the small book and the brass-bound box-like folding frame. Rob realized that the question had directed at himself.

"Oh! Me?", he asked somewhat caught off guard. "I'm not sure. I guess that I would have to say the book, being the Co-Arb's book, hand written and all. Still, I am half afraid to touch it, it being so old!"

"Well, I doubt that it is that old", Robert said." It's maybe got 75 or 80 years on it. It could conceivably be a hundred years old, but it is meant to be read! A book which is left unopened is like any other solid, rectangular object, but it really ceases to be a book." "Let's all move to the dining room table. We can all look at it together," Mart suggested.

Mart lay the book on the table so that the three of them sitting side by side could look at it together. "Here, grandad, you sit in the middle," he said.

Robbie had never heard Mart call his grandfather by that name before. It made it all so clear, this generational difference, also their connectedness.

Mackinnon carefully opened the leather clad cover. It looked pretty fragile and appeared to be simply waiting to split at the binding. There was a blank page, and after it a title-page which had been hand-decorated; title letters and border in a design of inter-lacing and spirals. The colors were subdued from age, but overall, very beautiful: olive green, grey-blue, red orange and nut brown. The title was cleverly designed with letters which inter-acted with one another:

"Leabhair Chomh-Airbe Ard Achaidh"

"Book of the Co-Arb of Ardachy," MacKinnon translated.

"Is the book all in the Gaelic, then?", asked Martin.

"No. it's in English," MacKinnon said in a low murmur without moving his eyes from the book, "although it does contain some passages and verses in the Ghaidhlig with no translations. I looked at it earlier, and was surprised (as a matter of fact) that it is mainly written in English."

As he slowly turned the pages, it seemed quite evident that the whole had been written by one hand, for although there were variations in size of the letters and the number of lines to a page, there was no mistaking the employment of the same script throughout. Each new subject began with an 'illuminated' capital letter: very intricately decorated, sometimes with interlacing or other such designs trailing away and down the side of the page. Rob found himself to be wondering about the man who had worked at this book; hand-decorating letters, carefully executing each line of script through the use of Celtic uncials. What had been set down was the carefully kept theology of the ancestors, the out-pourings of a hereditary 'abbot': a 'rememberer,' father-figure and for his time and people, a living representitive of some long ago Druidic Christian abbot.

The elder MacKinnon sat back after a time and rubbed his eyes under his glasses.

"I'm afraid that I've had enough for one day," he said. Then, putting his glasses back in place, he went on: "Robbie, there's something that I want to ask you to do. Now, if you'd rather not do it, just say so. I won't think the worse of you should you refuse."

Rob looked up at the elder MacKinnon, then glanced sideways toward Martin, who was simply looking downward waiting for both the question, and the answer which would be given. Rob sensed that Martin knew somehow of what was about to be asked.

"Robbie, I would like to know if you would be willing to begin studying for Holy Orders in the Celtic faith. It has been revealed to me from within that you have a calling to the priesthood of this Church… and also that this call is no surprise to you; that you have even expected it."

Rob was unable to speak. He glanced from one of

them to the other. The older man looked at him, a kindly expression of trust on his face. Martin had the trace of a smile as he looked down upon the document before them. Finally, Rob was able to make a reply.

"I have, well....I had hoped, to be accepted into your circle, and yes... to be honest, I am not surprised. Anyway, I had a feeling that you might ask me. But…, I am not sure that I'm good enough. The word 'worthy' comes to mind…"

Martin's hand came up and onto Rob's shoulder.

"…and I doubt that I am worthy," Rob said solemnly. "Also, as you know, I am new to Celtic Christianity and there is so very much to learn! I would be willing to start on a course of study, of course, but I'm afraid that I might require a great amount of help. The main thing is that I have to wonder if I am, as I said, worthy."

Rob saw a broad smile on Martin's face. He looked to his grandfather.

"Well, now Mart!" the older man said. "How's that for an answer?"

"It's the traditional, 'correct' answer, for sure!"

Robert MacKinnon went on: "The fact of the matter is that among ourselves it is often said that if someone asks for ordination into the priesthood, he should not be ordained. In other words he or she should have great humility and certainly question his or her worthiness".

"You said, 'or she', right?" Rob asked. "Are women ordained as priests as well?"

"The rule is", MacKinnon explained, "that a woman, if

she is a mother or plans to be a mother, should wait until the youngest son or daughter reaches the age of eighteen. A woman as a mother has a lot of work cut out for her and being a Céilede is a twenty-four hour responsibility. Anyway, young man, you certainly cannot begin to start at any younger time in your life! I know that you will already have quite a bit 'on your plate', as they say, what with your regular course work toward attaining your degree, building and polishing a relationship with the young lady in your life and all other considerations. Even so…!"

The older man sat forward and stretching himself to the left, took up a small pile of books from the end of the table. Holding them for a moment in his two hands, he went on:

"Robbie, Martin and I have put our heads together to come up with some introductory material which you might care to study. Upon reading what we are loaning to you, it may somehow dawn on you that you already carry a great deal of Celtic Christianity and simply never realized it. What we are having you look at, read, digest and consider are some representative works having to do without 'old way': our world-view and its outer manifestations."

He handed to Rob one book at a time, explaining just a bit about each one: "The Winged Destiny-Studies in the Spiritual History of the Gael" by Fionna MacLeod; "Liturgy and Ritual of the Celtic Church" by F. E. Warren; "Homily on the Prologue to the Gospel of St John" by John Scotus Eriugena; "Carmina Gadelica" (Vol. II) by Thomas

Carlyle… a book of Celtic prayers and blessings gathered from the people of Scotland's Highlands and the Hebrides. This book was opened to show Rob how the prayers were printed in Gaelic with English text on each facing page. Last of all, Rob was handed a small book from Martin's hand.

"This book is yours to keep, Robbie," Martin told him. It was a small paper-back book entitled 'Gaelic', by Roderick MacKinnon and designed as a 'teach yourself' book.

"Oh, hey! Thanks a lot, Mart! I will really treasure this," Rob exclaimed. "It looks like I have some work ahead of me!"

"Well, the book has a good pronunciation guide,… or I think so anyway. It just came out two or three years ago," Martin explained.

Rob held the books in front of him with both hands. "Wow! This is so great! It's a whole new world opening up for me! All at once too! A bit overwhelming, really!"

Robert and Martin laughed.

The three of them sat in silence for a short time, Robbie finally asking a question:

"What is, or was, the Pelagian Controversy' all about? I have run into that here and there."

"Research it!", The elder MacKinnon commanded. "Ask your grand-parents about it and read up on it."

"It might be a good idea for you to look at some of the old Celtic illuminations and calligraphy too, and to try your hand at it. Calligraphy is a good discipline," Martin put in.

"If I get into all of this as you two are piling it on, I

will end up being the most 'disciplined' guy around! Well, thanks! Thanks a lot for your show of trust and faith in me. I will do my best.", Rob told them.

"Well, Robbie ", MacKinnon said," It will take a few years to prepare you for ordination, so research things carefully and well. We are more interested in seeing you to be a truly good guide to others and a man who will bear good witness, rather than to rush this study along. We have time on our side yet, for a few years, anyway".

Rob had a very hard time in getting to sleep that night. The great honor and trust which had been given to him, his telling Gwynne all about it, his family… Oh! The Family!

"My mother would be no less happy if I were to join the Communist party!" He couldn't help laughing to himself. "I'll hold off for a while before I totally wreck her life. I'll wait… for a few weeks, at least." He laughed again to himself and then thought: "I wonder what Gwynne might think of this!", a much more sobering consideration. He lay in the darkened room, looking into the darkness, the specks of whatever it is that seem to come with darkness. He listened to the sounds of chirping insects and at some point or other, he surrendered to sleep.

CHAPTER 19

PART II

Rob was happy enough to be back at college. Being somewhat established into the swing of the curriculum, he could begin to see how the various courses could be used in harmony one with the other. He found himself to be fairly well accepted by his fellow students and had been 'tapped' by one of the fraternities in his Freshman year, but somehow he could not bring himself to join. In his spare time, what there was of it, he found himself in the Library, poring over such books as Logan's 'Scottish Gael' or Adamnan's 'life of Columba'. He came upon a reprint of Spottiswood's 'History of the Church of Scotland' and devoured anything that he could find on Scottish Highland Folk ways.

In late Mid-November he received a letter from Paul. It was cheery enough, but there seemed to be an undertone which Rob could feel without his being able to pinpoint just what it might be. In the letter, Paul asked if it would be possible for him to stop by for an hour or two on his way home for Thanksgiving break. Rob responded to the letter and told Paul that he should try to be at Gramma King's on the following Saturday. At which time he would call from Ohio. Rob hoped that Paul would get his letter in time.

On Saturday evening Rob telephoned the farm as he had promised. Paul answered an there was some happy banter. Paul then put Gramma King on the phone, having explained that she was all but pacing the floor.

"Can you stop by and see us, Robbie?"

"No, Gramma, I'm afraid not. They're not giving us any vacation time to speak of. The first long break won't be until Christmas."

"Oh! Oh, that's too bad. That is really a shame. I was hoping that you could get together with us before… well, I'll let Paul tell you! I've probably said too much already."

Rob listened to the muffled voices on the end of the line as the receiver was being transferred. Paul was back on the phone.

"Rob?"

"Yeah, hi again, Pau…"

"Rob?"

"Yes. I'm here, Paul! Go ahead."

Rob, my…, my number came up. I have to report for a physical."

Rob felt as if he were sinking.

"When…? When do you have to report?"

"First week of December.", Paul told him

"Oh, God! That's… terrible! Why now? This freakin'

war is just about over!", Rob said with anger.

"Well, tell that to those selective service guys!", Paul said.

"How's Gramma taking it?", Rob asked him.

"Like a soldier… on the outside, anyway!"

There was a long pause. Neither of them seemed to know what to say. Finally Rob broke the silence.

"Paul? I'll call you back in about an hour, okay?"

"Well, yeah, Rob… but…?"

"Don't go away!   Stick around 'til I call back", Rob assured him.

After about two and a half hours, Rob called the King farm again. It was just a bit after 10:30. Paul answered the phone and Rob could hear the hesitancy in Paul's voice as he answered.

"Paul? This is Rob again. I'm sorry that I didn't call earlier but I had some things to do. Listen! I won't be able to make it until Wednesday, the day before,…. Thanksgiving. I will leave here on Wednesday forenoon. I figure that I won't get to your place before Thursday. If I'm really too tired to drive straight through I will stop half way. It's about a 12 hour trip, but wait! There's a guy who lives near Hamburg, just south of Buffalo and he has a driver's license and wants to go home for Thanksgiving… So we can switch off and take turns driving. That way it won't be bad at all!"

"Well, look Rob that's an awful trip for you to make! You'll be really beat! Even if you started at noon on Wednesday, you wouldn't get here 'til midnight or even two A.M.!", Paul told him.

"Hey, c'mon Paul! I want to see you before you leave! Don't sweat it! Ask Gramma if I'm invited for Thanksgiving dinner."

After a muffled voice at the other end, he heard the phone being taken up and Grandma King's voice:

"You just get here! You can sleep 'til Dinner time if you need to. We've got enough to feed you! Oh, Robbie this is grand! Absolutely grand! The back door will be unlocked and the Kitchen light will be on if you get here and we've gone to bed."

When Rob drove into the driveway at the King farm, it was a little after One A.M. His fellow student really flew when he drove. Rob had expected to see lights flashing behind them on several occasions but the kid from Hamburg, Karl Dreher, really seemed to have had a sense about such things.

Rob saw that there were two cars in the driveway in addition to Mrs. King's car and that the lights were still on throughout the house. The back door opened and a solitary figure, barefooted and hunched against the cold came onto the steps. As Rob pulled his bag out of the back, the figure came down from the steps and enveloped him with two strong farmer arms in a great bear hug. Rob dropped his bag and hugged his friend with both arms, surprising even himself as he kissed Paul on the neck!

Standing back, Rob said, "God! It's good to see you!"

Paul wiped his eyes with his forearm and grinned.

"I'd forgotten what a pussy college kid looks like!"

"Yeah, well… you should know, now that you're one too!", Rob said.

"You look great, Rob!"

"Good enough to eat?" Rob smirked as he asked.

"To Hell with you! C'mon in. There's a family to meet." Paul ordered.

As the two young men entered the Kitchen, Grandma King went over to Rob and gave him a great hug.

"This is Robbie, Paul's friend that I've been telling you about," she said to the people seated around the kitchen table. Rob saw two men and a woman and looked up to see another woman just entering the Kitchen.

"Robbie, this is my son David, Paul's dad, and this is Paul's step-mother Linda".

Rob shook hands with David King and nodded to his wife who sat beside him, looking up as if she had been appraising him since he entered the room.

"And this is my son Arthur. 'Art' to everyone who knows him."

Robbie shook Art's hand and as their eyes met he could sense that Paul's uncle was looking very deeply into his own eyes, a slightly amused expression on his face. Arthur held the handshake a bit longer than Rob found to be comfortable.

"And this is my daughter Martha," Mts. King concluded.

Rob smiled and nodded, feeling an instant liking for this fine-looking and friendly appearing lady.

Paul's father presented himself in Rob's mind to be a warm and uncomplicated man, but as someone who had had his share of hard knocks. Rob could see that Paul resembled his dad and the similarity allowed for a flash into the future of his friend in later life. At the same time, there was no mistaking a look of quiet, sad resignation that hung over David King's features; the traces of lost hopes, inner compromises and his having come to terms with crushing defeats.

As Rob looked across at Martha, there was a graciousness and natural refinement about her, but not without a hint of defiance. Her eyes were a soft hazel, but shone like polished stones. She gave him the feeling that she was no stranger to adversity, but that she had a lot of fight in her. The world was not going to run over her or grind *her* down into a rubble of ruined dreams!

It occurred to Rob that he had never envisioned there being more to the King family than Paul and Gramma, as if all of the others whose names he had heard many times, had been somehow relegated to old photos and shadows. He felt himself to be somewhat out of his element when after having taken a chair at the table, he was in the midst of memories and stories of events of a past which belonged to others, far removed in time and distance from his own life. Paul sensed Rob's awkwardness, and smiled at him from time to time from his place just around the table corner. It was a smile that had a glimpse of near grimace, but with it a look of reassurance all the same. After a story was told of

Martha and a High School boy-friend who had given her half of a box of chocolates, followed by all of the laughter, Rob heard himself being addressed. It was Martha

"So, how about you, Rob? Do you have someone special in your life?"

"Someone special?"

"Yes, such as a young lady?"

"Oh! Yeah! I mean yes!", he corrected himself. "I have a girl who is going to College… a different college. Her name is Gwynne."

"She goes to a different College from the one you're attending?", Linda, asked. "She has to be crazy to let you out of her sight!"

"Well…, thanks!... I guess!" Rob stammered as he felt himself redden and tried to smile.

"C'mon, Linda! You've embarrassed the guy!" David said trying to inject humor into what he said.

"Why would that embarrass him? Excuse me all to hell!" Linda got up and went to the sink and started running water. Martha looked at David, who responded by raising his eyebrows and shrugging his shoulders as an unspoken answer to his sister's silent question.

By about 2:00 A.M. the family members began to go off towards their beds. Paul took Rob's bag up to the same room which they had shared in the past. Somehow, Mrs. King had managed to get the family members quartered comfortably in the various rooms of the house, although Rob learned later that Martha had shared her mother's room during her stay.

Rob woke to find that he was quite alone and that he had slept until about 10:30. There was no sign of Paul and the only sounds in the house were those of women's voices down in the Kitchen. Everything from the night before seemed to be a mental blur: the table conversation, the faces of the family members who had been around him, the very bone-weary walk up the stairs, the great rush of happiness which had come over him when he had hugged Paul just before climbing into bed, all was as if it had been a part of a dream. He quickly pulled on his jeans, bending forward to pull up the zipper, grabbed his shaving kit, and made a dash for the bathroom. Once in the shower, flashes of the night before came to his mind; flashes of sounds and sensations, movements in pitch darkness; even the taste of another man's mouth." I can't believe I did that! …but, I guess that I did sure enough! Wow! Well, it's nothing that will kill me or become habit forming!"

Downstairs he saw Gramma King and Martha grinding up bread and onions with a cast iron grinder. Martha was turning the handle as her mother was stuffing dried bread and quartered onions into the wide-mouthed grinder's top.

Linda was mixing cranberries and pieces of orange, nuts and sugar in a large bowl.

"Well! Good Morning, Robbie!" Gramma King said looking up with a broad smile. "Did you get your sleep out?"

"Morning everybody! I can't believe that I've slept this late!"

"Well, after a long drive like that, you're certainly entitled to a late sleep!", Martha put in.

"There's cereal there in the cupboard, milk in the fridge and you know where the bowls are! Can I fry you an egg or two and some bacon? We're almost finished here," Gramma said.

"Oh no! Cereal will be fine. Plenty in fact!", Rob assured her.

"Take one of these bananas and slice it up for your cereal, Robbie," Linda offered.

"Oh great! That would be really good! Thanks!"

Rob fixed his bowl of cereal and sat down at a corner of the table. Grandma absently poured him a glass of orange juice and set it down in front of him.

"Where are all of the guys?", he asked.

"Oh, they're out at the barn, trying to do something about that one roof timber that snapped a while back. Lucky for them, they can do the job from inside since the haymow is so full. I wouldn't want them on the roof at this time of year!", Grandma said.

"What time did Paul come down?"

"It must've been around 8:30, wasn't it Ma?" Martha volunteered.

"Just shy of nine o'clock," Linda corrected. "He looked as if he was just busting to go!"

"Robbie somehow has that effect on Paul!" Grandma exclaimed. "It is amazing how much he seems to love his buddy Robbie!" Turning to Rob she said "I'm so glad that you could be here before he goes off to the Army, Robbie! It means so much to him! And it means a lot to me too!" Looking to Linda she asked, "Will you be able to get all of that into that one bowl, Linda? Oh, I guess that you know what you're doing! I'll just mind my own business!"

Rob was happy enough to finish his cereal and head out of this world of 'women talk' and the dinner preparations. He took his empty bowl to the sink, rinsed it out under the water tap and gently left the bowl inverted on the drainboard before doing the same with his coffee mug.

"Boy!" Linda exclaimed. "Not too many men are apt to pick up their dishes and such and rinse them out! Now, here's a young man who has been well-trained!"

"Yes, well, ... my mom runs a pretty tight ship!", he answered, just a bit sheepishly with a smile.

He was beginning to see Linda to be a really good person after all, despite a seemingly purposeful attempt to leave anyone new in her life with a bad first impression.

"I'm heading down to the barn to see if I can mess up whatever those other guys are doing.", he said, reaching for his jacket.

"Ask them if they want to stop for some coffee," Gramma called after him,

"Sure thing!" Rob answered.

"Oh, Ma! They're probably already into the beer!", Linda stated with a bit of a laugh.

The ground crunched underfoot when Rob went outside and he was surprised that it had been a much colder night than he had thought. The air was clear, crispy even, to the nose. As he looked toward the sky he could see that the clouds were giving way to that very blue, almost turquoise color which seems to present itself so much more clearly during the cold months. He stopped by an old apple tree by the back of the yard and looked up again through the branches, seeing the shapes of blue between the branches of varying angles and thickness and thought of how very much this could be likened unto a stained-glass window with the lead came dividing the shapes of, in this case, blue glass.

A shrill scolding interrupted his reverie: a tiny but very bossy chipmunk chattering and chirping for him to move on. He smiled to himself, the chipmunk still hurling insults and epithets in some rodent dialect, he walked towards the sounds of hammering.

Inside the barn's mow door, Rob peered about and then upward above the bales of hay. David King looked over the side and called down to him:

"Well, you timed that just about right! Hell! We're all but done with this widow maker now!"

Paul's torso presented itself as his friend added:

"Yeah! We're bustin' our asses out here while you're luxuriating in your morning wet dream!", Paul teased.

"Well, that's what you guys get for keeping me up all night, feeding me beer and shocking me with wild stories. Okay! Enough! What can I do to help?", Rob asked.

"Throw up that piece of four by four and then pass up those two lengths of two by six," David said. "Then pick up that pail of 30 penny spikes and bring them along up here."

The four of them managed to get the broken timber jacked up and in place, 'scabbing' the 2x6's on each side securely with the huge spikes. The bantering, never-ending insults were as much a part of the necessary equipment as anything else. Requirements and suggestions had been communicated the age old way of men working together. Despite the cold of the weather outside, the top of the mow, cramped for space and lacking in air, was very warm indeed. All of them were without jackets and perspiring.

Art put his hand on the repaired beam and proclaimed: "Yessir! That'll stand 'till it falls!" looking towards the others he asked: "Who wants a beer?"

"A beer?", Rob asked. "Now? At this time of day?"

"Hell!" Art said. "Beer don't know what time it is!"

Later in the day Rob called his folks in Balston to wish them a Happy Thanksgiving. He did not mention his being with the Kings. He figured that if he let his mother know that he was in New York State, Shiela would make it the 'Thanksgiving from Hell' for other family members.

He called Gwynne and spoke with her for a while. He told her that he was spending the Holiday with Paul and his family before Paul's departure for the Army. She said that that was a nice thing for him to do but that he had better not mention it to his mom. Gwynne had come to understand Sheila pretty well.

The Thanksgiving dinner was picture-perfect; one which could well have served as a picture of the Norman

Rockwell version of America at her best. The assembled Kings were all in high spirits and at the end of the feast, after the Pumpkin Pie and while drinking coffee, Arthur had started telling old stories of the days when they all lived on the farm. David would add a bit, as would Martha and before too long everyone was laughing. Gramma King was laughing herself to tears; so many memories, so very much that had been happy, funny and wonderful. All of her children were home! The various scars of their adulthood wounds carefully tucked away, covered by the levity of the moment: a family tradition in itself; old as the human race.

Rob was enjoying the family fun, and he was happy to be so included, such a part of it all, yet, he looked over toward Gramma King at one point and saw in her eyes something apart from the general merriment. She was looking toward Paul, an expression akin to fear in her eyes.

Rob stayed at the farm until Saturday morning. He said his goodbyes just after breakfast. Paul's dad took him aside and somewhat self-consciously thanked him for having been such a good friend to his son.

"You've been good for Paul, Rob. I was afraid that he was going to drop through the cracks. I hope that you guys will keep in touch."

Paul walked down to Rob's car with him. They stood there, both of them somewhat self-conscious.

"Well… I guess that this is all she wrote for now." Paul said.

"Yeah," Rob agreed. "I guess it is. Next time I see you,

you'll be a mean-assed soldier and I'll still be a wimpy civilian!"

"You ever gonna write to me, old buddy?" Paul's voice cracked, breaking over the question as a stick underfoot.

"God, yes!" Rob threw his arms around Paul, They hugged, slapped each other on the back.Each rubbed his eyes, felt the tears and also the hurt of a separation never experienced before in their young lives.

"Write to me as soon as you can, Paul!"

"Right! I will do that!"

"Call me if you get a chance!", Rob added.

"Right! I'll do that too, good buddy!", Paul promised.

As Rob backed the car out of the driveway and onto the road, he looked back toward the house. Paul was still there, looking towards him. He paused to wave back towards him and saw the rest of the Kings moving up to surround Paul. All were waving their "goodbyes" to him. Gramma was with them, wiping her eyes with one hand and waving with the other. Rob waved back and honked the horn before heading down the road. "Wow!", he thought to himself, "what 'family' I have just seems to keep on growing!" . He reached for a Kleenex tissue, having found that he too needed to wipe his eyes.

He went up to route 20 and followed it to Auburn, where he went north to get onto the New York State Thruway, Interstate 90. It would be faster, he reckoned, despite having to pay a toll. The Interstate had been completed in the mid 50's and tolls were originally promised to be lifted as soon as the then "Thomas E. Dewey Thruway" was paid for, but now, about eighteen years later, tolls were still being charged. Rob intended to go west towards Buffalo and South to Hamburg, where he would pick up his fellow student, Karl Dreher, who had driven part of the way up with him. Karl would take up a part of the drive back to Athens and that would be a welcome bit of assistance. The fact that Karl was also helping with the cost of fuel was a great help as well. Karl was a good enough sort of guy, like a very great many people from the Hamburg, New York area, he was very "German" in many ways. Two world wars and anti-German feeling in America during both of those conflicts, had made little more than a dent in their identity. Some were Lutherans, others Catholic, but they held onto a very strong pride in their Teutonic heritage. They had served bravely and well during the American Civil War, a great many of them hardly landed on these shores before joining the Union Army, some of them still hardly acquainted with the English language. A lot of men from Hamburg had met their end in Petersburg and Hatcher's Run. Nor had German-Americans held back from fighting for America against their old-country cousins in two world wars. The Germans, like the Irish, the Scots, Poles and Italians, Russian Jews, Ukrainians and Heaven only knows how many others, these dispossessed of Europe, all felt that they had "earned their spurs". They took pride in knowing that they were good Americans now.

Rob thought about this as he drove along. How could

we transplants continue to love the customs, dances, music and foods of countries which had disowned us? What are we hanging onto, he wondered, and why are we so reluctant to let go? He remembered then, something that an old lady had said at a Scottish gathering when an English fellow in attendance asked why Americans could or should wear the kilt. She had nodded towards him and said: "If the cat has her kittens in the hen house, that doesn't mean that she gives birth to chicks!" "The Scots!", he thought, "We are the worst of the lot!"

CHAPTER 20

PART II

In early November of 1973 Robbie realized that it had been quite a while since the Thanksgiving at the King farm and his last time spent with Paul. As everyone had been saying, the war in Vietnam was said to be winding down. In January of the same year a Cease-Fire had been signed, to go into effect on January 28th. History books tell us that the last American Combat troops left the country by April 29th, save for about 8,500 personnel kept on to maintain security. Paul had indeed been sent to Vietnam not long before this.

For a long time Rob had received and sent out letters on a fairly regular basis, but there had been a few months now during which time there had been no word from Paul. Robbie began to think seriously about calling Mrs. King. They had remained in contact and Rob had made a point of visiting her during his summer recess whenever he could. Finally, he had decided on one day to make a phone call that evening after dinner. As it turned out he found that he had a message waiting for him after his last class of the day. His room-mate had taken the message for him and had left a note:

Currie- some man called and left a request that you call the Kings A.S.A.P. Sounded urgent.

-Eric-

Rob went to a telephone and dialed the number which he readily recognized, and soon found himself talking to David King, Paul's father. The family had been informed that Paul had been listed as missing in action. Mr. King's voice was thick with emotion and Rob heard his voice break once or twice. Rob felt old, tired, angry and terrified all at the same time. In his mind he saw his friend's eyes, his strong arms, his half-sarcastic grin all in one flash. Then, he stumbled within himself to remember Paul's face. "Oh God! Oh, my Good God!!", he heard himself exclaim.

"Robbie, I know you are probably busier than a cat on a hot tin roof, but… if you could spare us a day or two of your time, It would mean a lot to my mother,… to all of us, if you could come up to the farm. I'm really kinda scared, Rob! My mother 'Gramma King,' just isn't herself!"

"I'll be up there as soon as I can get there, Dave! Don't go off and away! Wait for me. Okay?"

"Rob, I'll be here! I can't tell you how much this means to us!"

When Rob pulled into the driveway at the farm he saw several cars in the driveway. As well as Gramma's grey

Chevy he counted three other vehicles: two cars and a pick-up truck. He recognized the pickup as Art's and figured that one of the other cars must have been Dave's.

Rob let himself in the back door as he had done so many times by now. The house was strangely quiet. Three people sat around the kitchen table. Grandma King was nowhere in sight. Usually she would be bustling about, knowing well ahead of time when someone would be stopping by. David, his wife Linda, and Art were talking in low tones at the table and it was Art who first saw Robbie's coming through the door, and who rose and went to him. He actually hugged Rob.

"We're really glad you've come, Rob! This is a pretty hard time for everybody." He turned, one hand on Rob's shoulder and steered him toward the others, and at that same time, Martha came into the kitchen from another room. Moving over to them she hugged Rob, kissing him on the cheek. She started to speak, and her voice caught in her throat:

"Oh, Robbie! What're we going to do? We can't go on without Paul! It can never be the same!"

She paused, wiped one eye then the other with the back of her hand before saying: "I'll get mom. She's been asking for you."

Art and Rob went over to join the others at the table. David stood up and moved toward Rob, holding him to himself as if he were Paul's proxy or representative, which indeed seems to have been his place, his position in the family, at this time.

From the other room could be heard Martha speaking softly: "Yes, mom. Robbie. Robbie Currie is here."

"Robbie? Oh, for heaven's sake! I knew he'd come! I'll be right out!" The words came out more slowly, more full of fatigue than was usually the case with Gramma King.

Martha entered the kitchen with her mother. The wonderful elderly lady looked to be years older, drained of energy. As she moved into the room, Rob went toward her and put his arms around her as she also held him closely to her. She cried softly.

"Oh Robbie! I am so afraid! I am so terrified that something bad has happened!"

David rose to help Rob escort his mother towards the table.

"C'mon Ma. Sit down over here with us. Rob's driven a long way."

"I've made fresh tea, and there's coffee", Linda announced, "Ma, can I get you a cup of tea? Rob, How about you. Tea or coffee?"

"Uh, yes please. Coffee would be great," Rob said.

There was a great deal of silence between remarks and observations. As in such situations, no one knew what to say.

Art finally spoke up in earnest. He toyed with the spoon in his coffee cup, looking down as he spoke.

"I can't claim to know more than anyone else, but I've been in 'Nam on a couple tours of duty. It's a different kind of war. The older guys who have been in Korea have said it often, and the few guys who were in the service during the big 'W.W.' swear that it is not so much of a war as it is one huge cluster f____! Er! 'Sorry Ma!" Mrs. King looked perplexed, not realizing that he had almost spat out an expletive. She stared at him, frowning, searching for meaning. Art went on:

"We're trying to get out of 'Nam. You've all seen it on the T.V. Trying to haul ass out of there! Nothing is functioning (not that it ever was in this war!) There were never any, what we could call, 'battle lines'; just patches of ground, bases 'er outposts here an' there, connected by helicopters. Communications are sometimes excellent, at other times non-existent! It's a case of one hand not knowing what the other hand is doing! What I'm trying to say is that… we should not give up hope. Paul's unit could have been isolated, cut off, forced to take evasive action, come a long way around Robin Hood's barn, as they say, to get back to their own base of operations. We don't know. There are countless possibilities, not the least of which could be a lazy C.O. or Company Clerk sending out letters to 'blanket' what is not known. We have to just keep hoping and praying that he's okay. We have to keep hoping! We can't give up!"

"The thought of him being lost, or hurt, or wounded, captured, maybe mistreated, is just too much to bear!", Mrs. King said. "Why did it have to be Paul? Hasn't that poor boy been through enough?"

Everyone fell very silent. No one knew what to say, what

to add. Finally Rob broke the silence. He cleared his throat and began to speak very slowly, carefully and quietly:

"I, uh… I am not a family member here, but I am close to Paul too…"

"As far as I'm concerned you are pretty much 'family', Rob!", David interrupted. "Go ahead!"

"Well, I don't quite know how to say this. To tell you the truth, my friendship with Paul has been the strangest thing in my life. We started out just about hating each other. We've had a lot of disagreements, we've hurt each other's feelings. I've never been able to understand it. I don't think Paul has ever figured it out either. Despite everything, when we would meet I'd feel all over-joyed, not be able to keep from smiling."

"Honey, that sounds like a love-affair!" Linda put in.

"Linda! For Christ's sake, shut up for once!" David said evenly, menacingly. Linda shrugged her shoulders.

"No!", Rob answered. "It's okay, Dave! Really! I guess I can live with that! Two years ago, probably not, but now, today? Yes. Men can love one another, and deeply. I have thought from time to time that I hope that he has a buddy in 'Nam who is looking after him: some guy who pisses him off, gets in his face, but who'd take a knock in the head for him. Love affair? Okay. Whatever! But that's not what I want to say. It's hard to put into words.

Somehow I began to realize about a year ago that I would always know when he was nearby or planning to get in touch; kind of like when Gramma knows that one of you folks will be dropping by, you know? About a year ago it dawned on me that I always would know and that he always knew in the same way about me. At the same time, if a time was at hand when he was supposed to come by and something came up to prevent him from doing that, I would somehow know not to expect him. Oddly enough, when we reached that point, that kind of 'communication' or whatever you might call it, we also stopped fighting one another. Okay! Call it what you will. A love affair? Maybe. Something homo-erotic? Definitely not! Psychologists can make of it whatever they want, but…"

Rob stopped for a moment and looked towards Art who had just lit a cigarette. Rob looked at the table, shook his head and said "Wow! I can't believe I'm saying all of this!" Looking again at Art he held out his hand towards Art's cigarette, which Art passed to him without a moment's hesitation, as if they had been buddies forever. Rob sucked in a deep breath of smoke and held it briefly before exhaling and handing the cigarette back to Art.

David started to say: "Rob, when did you start…", but Rob held up his hand briefly as if to say, "Wait. I have to finish." Rob went on, as every family member watched his face.

"What I really want to say and what I would really like you to believe is this: when David called me and told me the news, I was devastated. It was like a kick in the solar plexus, you know?… where you can't even catch your breath? But there was something missing. All the way up here, all that long drive, I thought and thought and… thought. I don't want to seem to be giving any false hopes or anything… I have to say this: I don't feel him 'gone', or lost or 'tortured'. I don't feel him 'missing'. Wherever he is, he's okay. I would know it, I'm sure, if anything was really wrong. And, although she's still feeling the 'kick in the solar plexus', I think that Gramma knows too, that he's wandering around out there."

Everyone was very silent, all looking down towards the table top now, only Linda staring at him, her eyes riveted to his face. Rob looked across at her, and without knowing why, feeling a slight smile come to his mouth he said simply:

"Linda?"

"My good God! You scare the hell out of me! But I believe you! I really believe every word you've said! Who *are* you?"

"Just a friend, Linda.", Rob said softly.

"No, you're not 'just a friend', Robbie!" Gramma King said. "You are a member of this family and right now, at this moment a young man doing the work of an Angel!", The matriarch had spoken. Gramma king looked over at him with gratitude and love.

A serious and intense silence followed Mrs. King's statement broken finally by Art.

"Na! A great guy, but no angel!", Did you see him suck up half my cigarette in one drag?" Everyone smiled.

"Well, can't angels smoke? Maybe that's where 'holy smoke comes from!", Martha put in with a chuckle. Everyone there were relieved to have even this tiny bit of levity.

"Maybe I'm just nervous!" Rob said with a sheepish smile.

Gramma King rose slowly from her chair, came over to him and put her hand on his back. "Don't you ever, ever feel the need to be nervous in this house, Rob!".

As it turned out, Paul did manage to return home from Vietnam, for after about three months after Rob's meeting with the King family he received a telephone call from his very dear friend who called from an army hospital in California.

"Paul!", Rob exclaimed. "Great God almighty! It's really you! I – I don't know what to say! Are… are you alright? I mean, how are you doing? Are you still in one piece?"

"Hey! Slow down!!" Paul laughed, "I'm okay! I took some shrapnel, lost a little chunk out of my upper left leg, but all in all I'll still be the best-built guy on the beach!"

"Wow!… Wow!", Rob stammered. "Have you called Gramma and your dad? I have been calling the farm at least once a week. Your grandmother is a real trooper: holding onto hope like you wouldn't believe!"

"Yeah, I know. She told me that you've kept in touch. "Says that she found you to be a real 'angel' to her! I'll never forget this, Rob. No, not ever. I mean it!", Paul assured him.

"So, do you know when you might be coming home?", Rob asked.

"The doctor says that they want to keep me here for a

few weeks. Tests, maybe a bit more prodding and probing; that kind of happy horse shit. After that they'll run me through all of the separation and discharge bull-crap. I figure that I will be seeing your sorry ass in about a month and a half. I'll send you a letter with an address so you can write to me if you find some time."

"Find some time? You silly shit! I will most definitely find some time! Just get that address to me!"

"Hey, Rob…?"

"Yes, buddy! What is it?"

"If I fly into Rochester or Syracuse when they send me home, could you meet my plane?"

"I'll be there with bells on!", Rob exclaimed. "I'm hoping to get you cleaned up and presentable enough in a few months for you to be my best man!"

"No freakin' way! You're finally gonna marry that beautiful woman? Wow! This is great!"

Well, I haven't asked her yet, but I think she'll accept me." Rob smiled.

After a pause, Paul continued:

"Gotta go! I'll be in touch! Thanks again!"

Rob hung up the phone, sat still for a time, closed his eyes and whispered, 'thank you, Lord!' Then he picked up the telephone again and dialed Gwynn's number. He had been calling her more and more frequently in the past several months. He shared details of his progress, what he had been working on, new things learned about their Celtic heritage. After all, Gwynne was of Celtic background too: Welsh, but just as much a Celt in pride and spirit as he had found himself to be. Mainly, he simply liked talking with her, kidding her, teasing her. He discovered that what he liked most about her was the way in which she was comfortable with his teasing, that she rejoiced in her own strength without using it as a weapon.

After a couple of rings he heard the voice of her roommate answer.

"Hi, Simone! This is Rob. Is Gwynne there?"

"Oh! Hi, Rob! Wait."… a muffled sound, then, as if far off, he heard, "Gwynne! Your dreamboat's on the phone!"

"Hello, Robbie!" Gwynne answered. "I swear that that girl has a 'thing' for you!"

"Are you jealous?' he teased.

"You'd better believe it! I wouldn't let you out of my sight with her around! You are too innocent and naïve for someone like her."

"Gwynne! I just got the greatest news!"

"Paul's alive!", Gwynne said.

"Yes!! You don't sound surprised", he observed.

"Well, Robbie, I have been believing in your own 'gut feelings' about him. I have come to accept that somehow you have a sense about things." She paused and went on: "But yes! It's great news and I am about to cry like a baby."

Rob went on to tell her of his conversation with Paul and that he had been wounded but would be coming home for good; also that Paul had asked him to pick him up when he arrived.

"He's probably seen some terrible things. He may have had to do some pretty awful things. I suppose he may be carrying some serious mental or emotional pain as well," Gwynne suggested.

"You know, Gwynne: when we had that long conversation at your mom and dad's during mid-winter break? You know, about the war and all? I have given all of those things a lot of thought. We seem so often to be reading from the same page about so many things. We really need to have more time together."

"Well, Robbie, we spent a lot of time together then, when you come to think of it. Your mother seemed to think that we were going to get tired of one another."

"Yeah, I know," Rob said half laughing. "That's my mom alright! Still, Gwynne, I really want to see more of you."

"Well," Gwynne teased, using his words against him, "You don't mean that we should play strip poker or some such thing? How much more of me do you want to see?"

"C'mon, Gwynne! That too, of course, but I want to spend more time with you,. We have Spring break, which seems to mesh pretty well. Why don't you consider making a trip down into P.A. with me? I'd like you to meet Robert, Kathy. Marty and his new wife, Diane. Think about it and maybe run it by your parents."

"Rob, my parents like you, trust you and would be fine with the idea, but I can hear the silence in your mom and dad's house already. Your mom would be livid. I would be a scarlet woman in her eyes for running off somewhere with her son!"

"Well, Gwynne, if Mom gets mad she'll just have to get glad somehow. Think about it, okay?"

"I already have thought about it, Rob! Let's plan on it. I can't see where there would be a problem at my end."

"Great, Gwynne! Love you!"

"I love you too, Robbie. 'Bye.'"

Spring break came soon after Rob's suggestion that he and Gwynne spend most of that time together. In one of their telephone conversations Gwynne had suggested that she could save him some extra driving if she were to meet him in Olean, where a fellow student lived, but Rob said that he preferred to drive up to Syracuse and pick her up at the University and the two of them go on 'home' to Balston from there. He told her that while he appreciated her concern and her suggestion, he really needed to go to Balston with her first. He mentioned also that he had some very good news to share with her.

It was pleasant and reassuring for them to see the familiar look of their home-town during this Easter season. Springtime had come forth on schedule: the return of clouds of Red-winged blackbirds, the greening and flowering of the land. It all seemed so 'right', so familiar to them. Even Gwynne's parents were doing yard work: her father using an edging spade along a stretch of a flower border, her mother on her knees using a small hand-rake to clear the ground under already blossoming yellow forsythia bushes.

As the young couple approached the gate, the older folks stood up, smiled and rushed toward them. They appeared to be as genuinely happy to see Rob as they were to see Gwynne. They hugged and exchanged small talk for a brief time before moving towards the house, Rob carrying two suitcases of Gwynne's things into the foyer behind them.

After a glass of Lemonade, Rob said that he had to go home and greet his own parents as well as to make some preparations for the following day, which would be Good Friday. He explained that he would follow the custom of 'going from view'… into the woods for the afternoon, and that he had planned to join his grandparents in the evening.

"I'll drop by later this evening, that is, if it's alright with you folks," Rob suggested.

"Of course it's alright, Rob!", Mrs Williams told him.

"Huh!" Mr. Williams grunted. "Nobody asked me what I thought about that idea!"

Rob turned, a bit surprised by the remark, only to see the man's stern remark replaced with a broad smile.

"Hell, yeah! Rob. If you come over, she might even let me break out a beer or two!"

"As if you need an excuse!", his wife muttered.

Things were great at Rob's house as well, for a while at least. Shiela Currie had come in, through the house, to find Jim and Rob on the back deck. Rob had given his mother a great hug which had been greeted with a delighted squeal from her. She sat down and began to speak of how beautiful the church looked after an afternoon of dusting, polishing and decking it with spring flowers.

"You will like our new minister, Robbie. He is younger, of course, and he has a wonderful approach to things. We are having a Good Friday service tomorrow, as a matter of fact. You will meet him then."

Rob and his father exchanged looks, which Sheila noticed immediately.

"What?", she asked, it being more of an accusation."

"Rob has something else planned for tomorrow afternoon, Sheila," his father stated quite simply.

"You mean that you can't give Our Lord an hour of your time on Good Friday?", this time an outright accusation from her.

"I'm prepared to give Our Lord more than an hour of my time, Mom. I just have to do it alone, that's all."

"Oh, no! My parents have got you into that old Celtic 'pagandom,' right? You are going to the woods for three hours?", Shiela's voice growing louder as she spoke.

"I haven't seen Gram and Grandad since I was home at Mid-Winter break, Mom. No. This I decided to do on my own."

"Well, decide again! I want you to go to the service tomorrow!"

"Sorry, Mom. This is important to me. I feel that I have to do this. I will go with you to Church for the Easter Sunday service."

"Great!", Sheila erupted, bolting to the back door. "One of my kids is now a Jew and the other is going back to Druidism! I must've done something wrong somewhere along the way!" Cupboard doors slammed within the house.

"Is Carole already a Jew, Dad?", Rob asked.

"Well, she is Carole Lewis now. Henry is Jewish and Carole is converting", Jim answered. "After all, why not?"

"Yes", Rob agreed, "Why not? She would want to keep her family in the one religion".

"Besides that", Jim went on, "Little Josh can't be counted as a Jew unless his mother is Jewish. She wants him to have the option to be of the faith of his father's people. He has been circumcised. If his mother converts, he's good to go! About twelve years down the line we may be putting on yarmulkes, attending his Bar Mitzvah!" They both smiled and after a pause, Rob decided to run something by his father:

"That's another thing I have been wanting to talk to you about, Dad", he said. "I have been keeping the old Sabbath for a while, like Mom's Mom and Dad".

"Do you think that I haven't suspected as much?", Jim asked softly.

"It doesn't bother you in any way?", Rob asked.

"Why should it bother me? You're a good young man, you're clean and honorable. What path you choose to God is your concern and something not to be interfered with. Hey! I have seen the Celtic cross on the east wall of your room, the candlesticks and the Bible", Jim said. He paused for a moment and added: "You know what else I think?"

"What's that, Dad?", Rob asked.

"I think that you should celebrate Shabbat with your grandparents tomorrow evening".

CHAPTER 21

PART 2

Rob and Gwynne went down to Pennsylvania for a few days close to the end of their Spring Break. It was a pleasant trip for them and during that time Robbie revealed several things to Gwynne. He was a bit wary of mentioning too much about his religious studies and even more reticent about the possibility of his entering into Holy Orders. Gwynne made it a bit easier for him when suddenly she said:

"I suppose that one of these trips we'll be going down to see you ordained."

Robbie swung his head suddenly to look at her.

"Why do you say that?" He asked.

"Come on, Robbie! I do know you, after all!" she said, smiling at him. She squeezed his knee.

"Would that bother you?", he asked.

"No, not if that is what you want, or what God wants",

she replied.

"You're amazing!", he said smiling at her.

Nothing was said for a while as they rode on. At length, Gwynne asked him a very direct question:

"When you were at my house on Thursday evening, what were you talking to my parents about?"

"Do you really want to know?", he teased.

"Yes, I do!", She replied.

"Well, now! Let's see if I can remember." He said slowly as if trying to recall the conversation. Suddenly then he said, "I told them that I was going to ask you to marry me! I told them that we would not have a wedding 'til after we graduate next year, but that I was going to ask you now."

Gwynne kept silent. He looked towards her, pulled the car to the side of the highway and stopped.

"So, will you Marry me?", he asked.

"Can we have a Highland wedding?" she asked him.

"Certainly! I would love that!" he replied.

"I will certainly think about it then," she teased.

He turned off the engine, exited the car, walked around to the passenger side and opened the door. Bowing stiffly, he offered her his hand. She too left the car and was led by Rob to the rear of the vehicle. He then dropped to one knee on the ground and effected his best 19th century manner:

"Miss Williams, I would be the most happy man in this world were you to become my wife."

Gwynne was laughing, half covering her face. Cars passed, honking their horns. A young guy yelled out. "Way to go, Man!"

"Robbie, you fool! Get up!", she laughed.

"Your answer?" he inquired.

"Yes! Yes! Now get up!", she laughed.

There, at the rear of the vehicle, two young, usually sensible people, went into a long, lasting kiss, for the whole world to see, to the waves, shouts and car horns of passing cars and trucks.

The MacKinnons, Mart and Diane took to Gwynne immediately. Kathy and Diane taking her to one side to do one thing or another, especially once the engagement had been announced. For two days and nights Gwynne was to enjoy the warmth and hospitality of these fine people. She saw the home-place and was especially interested in the fact that Mart was outfitting a room to be a nursery.

"So, you are expecting a baby?", Gwynne asked.

"Yes! We are both so excited about it!", Diane exclaimed. Their lives were taking on such new meanings, for all of them: Gwynne and Rob, Martin, Diane, Robert and Kathy. Somehow they felt themselves to be all coming together as well. On the way back to Balston Spa Gwynne had been speaking with Rob as to how she shared his feelings for the Pennsylvania folk.

"Robbie?", she asked, "Do you think that when we have our wedding we could ask Martin to do the Service?"

Two weeks later, Rob was driving North again from his college. He was to pick up his dear friend Paul at the Syracuse airport. It had meant his having to cut two days from school. He had spoken with his Faculty Advisor and it all seemed to be within the realm of possibility.

"Yes, Currie," he had said, "This is important. Let's just hope and pray that your friend recovers from the ravages of war and the physical as well as psychological wounds."

Rob waited for the incoming passengers and watched the throng of people coming from the baggage pick-up area. There were several of them in uniform. Finally he spotted Paul, walking with a crutch. Beside him was a sailor pushing a cart with two canvas bags: one a white sea bag, the other an olive drab duffle bag.

Paul fell on Rob's neck, hugging him and trying not to lose his balance. His crutch fell. The sailor picked it up and positioned it under his left arm.

"This is Petty Officer Second Class Mario Pellicone, Rob. He's been like a brother to me on this flight."

Rob and Mario shook hands.

"What's your rate, sailor?", Rob asked.

"Hospital Corpsman", he answered.

"Wow! I'm impressed," Rob said. "I've heard some pretty good things about you guys! You are the Medics for the Marines, right?"

"When we're not patching up other sailors or dispensing aspirins, some of us get sent to work in the front lines, yeah!", Mario said. "As for now, I am homeward bound! I won't join nothin', not even the church, after this! Well, bein' Italian I won't be able to give up the church! Anyway, I'm sure that you catch my drift!"

After a bit more small talk, Rob picked up the canvas bag and walked with Paul out to the car. A cop had told Rob he could leave it outside of the entrance when Rob had explained that he was there to pick up a wounded soldier. Just short of the doorway they heard:

"Think about what I said, King!" It was Mario.

"I will, Mario!" Paul called back, turning his head, waving with his right hand. "Thanks for Everything!"

From this point in their lives all would somehow come together in very unexpected ways, Each of them would embark upon paths which, while taking them in different directions, would also serve to reinforce the bonds of youth in ways which they would never have thought possible.

Paul was soon able to put his crutch in storage and began to work and study in the field of Physical therapy, thus fulfilling to a great extent the advice given to him by a sailor whom he had befriended on the way home: "The best way to get yourself 'squared away' is to help other guys who have been damaged", Pellicone had told him.

Maybe Mario had been one of those "Angels" who come into our lives at just the right time. Who knows?

Not long afterward, Rob received his Bachelor of Fine Arts degree and Gwynne also left Syracuse with her own Bachelor of Arts degree. She had majored in the Humanities, particularly in the area of Cultural Anthropology. With some extra summer course-work she could be pretty certain of receiving a temporary Teacher Certification.

Both Gwynne and Rob had a very busy summer, Rob at the feed mill to be close at hand for all of the preparations for their coming wedding, which would be in late August. He had also been accepted as a designer for the Olean Tile company in Olean, New York. This meant that he and Gwynne had to find a place to live in or close to that town. They looked at apartments in Olean and found nothing too appealing to them. One day they chanced upon something which had never occurred to them. They had stopped for a sandwich in a small diner near Allegany and the man behind the counter spoke to them.

"Are you two students at St. Bonaventure?", he asked.

"No, Sir. We both just received out degrees in May, but not from St. Bonaventure," Rob told him. "Actually, we are looking for a place to live in this area."

"That's sure something different!" the man said, "Most young folks can't wait to get out of here!"

"Well, I have been accepted for a position in a local business," Rob told him, "We are to be married in August, not long before I start work."

"There's not much around here in the way of places to live," the man said, looking past them towards the street. "Oh, I am sure that some folks have some rental properties, but not much to write home about!"

"We are beginning to see that," Gwynne said.

The man didn't respond right away. He seemed to be deep in thought. Finally, he turned to Rob and asked him: "Are you handy with tools and such?"

"My dad always said that if a guy grew up in rural New York State and couldn't frame up a building by the time he was eighteen that he hadn't been paying attention," Rob said, smiling.

"There you go!" the man answered. He turned and moved to the opening in the wall behind the counter and called: "Hey, Earl! Can you come out here for a minute?"

A young fellow with a brush-cut came through the door. He was thin, very light in complexion and gave the impression of a farm hand. The man asked him: "Is your aunt still trying to sell her Ma's farm house?"

"Well, yes. She is, Tom," Earl answered. "There's only ten acres left to go with the house 'though. Most of the farm's been sold off already."

"What shape is the house in?", Rob asked.

"It needs a lot of work. 'Foundation's good. Chimneys and roof line look good and straight," Earl explained.

He went on to tell them that when the grandmother died she had left the house to her two daughters. Those two had never been able to agree what to do with the place, so it sat empty for about ten years. Finally, one of them had died, leaving the surviving sister to do as she wished. She put the house and the farm acreage on the market.

"Could you tell us where it is located?", Rob asked.

"I get off work in a couple of hours. Hell! I'll take you right to it! It's not far from here," Earl offered.

"Take them out there right now!", Tom offered. "Hell! It's deader than four AM here today and Leo's back there to do what might be needed. Go on ahead!"

Not long after Earl had got in the car with them, directing Rob just a bit out of town, up a dusty dirt road for about a mile, he told him to pull into a driveway.

"This is it!", Earl stated.

They exited the car and looked across a lawn knee-deep in long unmown grass and weeds towards a grey, weathered house on a slight rise. It would have been white with dark green shutters gracing the windows at one time. The shutters too had lost most of their paint. One of them had been dislodged by an apple or crabapple tree, the long unpruned branches of which, scraped against the window. The corners of the house had wide, thick boards running from base to the bottoms of the side soffits. The front doorway was framed by wide molding, topped by a decorative lintel, and showing glass side lights on each side of the door.

"Greek Revival!", Gwynne murmured. "It's beautiful!"

"Just an old farmhouse!", Earl said. "If you didn't want to bother with all of the work it needs, you could just tear it down and put a trailer there!"

Rob was silent, continuing to look things over. Finally he asked: "Is there any chance we could look inside?"

"C'mon round back of the house," Earl said.

They walked through tall grass and weeds, some of which was almost waist high, to the back of the house. Gwynne pointed out an old stand-pump outside the back door. Earl told them that the last he knew, it still worked, but would need a new valve by this time.

"The house has got electric!", he proclaimed, "It's plumbed for running water and there's a' indoor bathroom and toilet too," he added, after which he produced a key from somewhere and used it to open a padlock which had been holding some heavy metal straps, inelegantly attached to (and nearly ruining) the heavy back door.

They entered into a kitchen area, marked by a side or working table, a rather simple sink arrangement, and an old cast iron stove, the pipe of which went to an opening in one of those chimneys which are set upon a simple, but sturdy shelf of sorts, about six feet above the floor. Rob was already thinking that that was one thing that had to be replaced by something more structurally sound.

A door from the kitchen opened into what had to have been a dining room. To the left was a door which opened onto a side porch. In summer months, men would wash hands and faces out there before entering the house to be fed, but that was a situation which would have been observed only into the mid-20th century. There was one piece of remaining furniture in the dining room: oddly enough, an old parlor organ.

From the dining room a doorway led to a hallway which extended to the front door of the house. On the right was a stairway to the second floor, and close to the front of the house two doorways: one to the right, one to the left, each of which opened into a bright, well-windowed room.

"Yes," Rob assured Gwynne," It's a perfect Greek Revival

house!" He pointed to the wainscoting in each of these rooms: panels of wood rising to about thirty inches; well-done, well fitted together.

By the front door the floor boards had buckled from cold and damp and the front door could only be opened to about six or eight inches because of the swollen floorboards. "That could be fixed," Rob thought to himself.

They went up the stairs and found that there were two large rooms, one on each side of the hallway, each over one of the downstairs front rooms. At the end of the hallway, at the front of the house was centered a window of regular size, having on each side of it two narrower windows as additional 'side-lights'.

"Oh!" Gwynne exclaimed. "Look at the beautiful molding around that window!"

"Yes", Rob agreed, "and when this house was built, I'd judge around 1840, all of that would have been done by hand, with block planes!"

At the far end of the hallway was another door. They opened it to find one very large room, somewhat unfinished. There was a large window at the far end but no other save for some low windows, about three, along each side, for the roof tapered to this point. The room obviously covered the area of the dining room and kitchen below.

"Some dormers would help", Rob said. "A person would have to proceed carefully however, so as to not detract from the architectural style of the house. This room was probably used mainly for storage."

"No," Earl put in, "They was kids who slept in there years ago!"

"I'd want a bit more light for our kids," Rob said, then looked towards Gwynne, a bit embarrassed for perhaps having 'jumped the gun'. She smiled back at him.

Outside once again, Gwynne took his arm in both of her hands and looked up at him with dancing eyes.

"What!" He said to her, smiling.

"Oh, Robbie! I love this house!"

He looked towards a small barn and another small building. "A work shop maybe?" he thought.

"Do those buildings come with the house, Earl?", he asked their guide.

"Well, that bigger one? It's not a barn it's a' old horse barn. The main barn had the roof tore right off in the hurricane of '54 they tell me. 'Had to be tore down," Earl explained, "But yeah! There's those buildings and the house, sittin' on ten acres!"

Rob stood silently looking at the house. "It would take a lot of work!", he remarked. "I ought to get Dad down here to look it over if I thought about us buying it." He turned to Earl. "How much does your aunt figure she has to have for it?", he asked.

"Prob'ly more than it's worth!", Earl smiled. "Hell! Make her an offer! Even she knows it aint gonna stand here forever without some work!"

"Let's talk to our Dads about it, Gwynne, and see what they think," Rob suggested.

"Your Dad maybe, Rob! As much as I love mine, he'd be turning over figures about annual depreciation and that sort of Insurance Agent thing!", Gwynne replied.

Having taken Earl back into town, they sat in the car for a few minutes.

"What do you think, Gwynne?", Rob asked.

"I love the place! Not just the house, but the whole thing," Gwynne said. "The horse barn would make a fine work-space for you, I love the lawns and the house very much!"

"Should we get our Dads down here to look at it?", Rob asked.

"I don't know, Robbie! My father is so very 'practical' that he may want to talk us out of it"

"Well, I think that we should include both of them, Gwynne, your dad and mine. Why not?", Rob asserted.

Two weeks later, Rob, Gwynne and both sets of parents went down to look at the place. Sheila was enraptured with it, which surprised Rob to no end. Jim, his father, concluded that it was a good, sound looking building but that a lot of work would be required. Gwynne's mother said that it would be a lot of work for two young people to take on. Owen Williams, to Gwynne's surprise, said, "It's an old place. It needs a lot of tender, loving, care, but, 'what the Hell'! I'd go for it!"

Later on, Jim and Sheila told Gwynne's parents that since they as parents of the bride, were paying out so much for the wedding, that the Curries would, as a wedding gift, put up $5,000.00 toward the purchase price. The house and land were finally sold for the sum of $9,000.00.

Rob kept in touch with Paul since his return from 'Nam, calling him often. He went out to the King farm where he was warmly received as usual. Gramma King was overjoyed at the news of Rob's coming marriage and wanted very much to meet Gwynne, this young lady of whom Paul spoke so highly. Rob promised to bring Gwynne with him on the next visit, wondering within himself as to how sleeping arrangements might be made. As it happened, the matter was resolved on his first stay-over at the farm.

"Rob," Paul said to him when it was time to turn in for the night, "You know where everything is. You'll stay in the same room." He seemed rather shy, embarrassed even as he paused before adding: "I'm going to sleep in Art's room."

But why, Paul?" Rob asked, a bit surprised. "I don't want to put you out of your own room! Just because I'm soon to be an old married man…"

"No Rob. That's not it," Paul cut him off. He pulled out his cigarettes, took one, tapped it, put it between his lips and lit it. Rob waited for him to continue speaking.

"Old Buddy, I have some bad nights sometimes," he explained. "I might wake up screaming, in a cold sweat. I guess that I've been known to cry in my sleep."

He passed his cigarette to Rob saying to him: You want to take a drag and make this thing hotter'n hell again for me, like you've always done?" It was his attempt to temper his words with some levity.

Rob took the cigarette from his friend, took a deep drag, blew out the smoke and with eyes squinted against that white cloud, he looked directly at Paul and while returning the butt to him he said, "Paul, I'd understand. I'd want to help." He placed his hand on his friend's shoulder.

"No, Rob. This is something I have to work through. I know you'd understand how I feel about that, okay?"

"Okay, Paul," Rob said softly. "I guess that we all have to face down our own demons and I suspect that you've managed to find a few where you've been." His smile was warm, compassionate and understanding. His arm went around Paul's shoulders as he added, "I will miss your warm form next to me," he joked.

"Yeah me too," Paul said.

Later in the summer, Paul went with Rob down to the Southern Tier to help in working on the house which would be Rob and Gwynne's home. Rob had been gifted with a two-week 'vacation' from his work at the feed mill, which had come to him as a complete surprise.

Buck had appeared at the Currie home on Sunday afternoon, August 3rd, his usual, somewhat shy self. Everyone wondered why he might have come around unexpectedly, but he was warmly welcomed and he happily accepted some coffee and a piece of pie. Sheila was exceptionally happy (her demeanor had changed considerably since the announcement of the wedding). After some small talk, Buck said"

"Well, to cut to the chase, as they say: Rob, I've got a job for you. It's going to take a while, a couple of weeks, in fact."

"Sure, Buck," Rob nodded. "What is it?"

"Well," Buck said, "I want you to take that truck and some stuff down to the Southern Tier. Pick it up tomorrow. It is loaded and tarped over. I want you to take that stuff down there and use it up on the job. You have two weeks. So, I expect to see you, my unloaded and undamaged truck back at the mill on Monday, the 18th. Okay?" Rob nodded, somewhat confused.

"Here's the address," Buck said, handing him a card with some writing.

Rob looked at the card, read the address, as his mouth and eyes opened wide in surprise.

"That's our new house!" Rob exclaimed.

"Yeah, well," Buck said, "Lets call this stuff a wedding present!"

Later that evening he told Gwynne the good news.

"Oh, Robbie! That's wonderful! We might even be able to move in and be there to start our new jobs!," she enthused. "Everything seems to be really working out for us!" After a pause, she asked: "Have you told Paul?"

"No, why?" he asked.

"Well, maybe he would like this opportunity to help us out!" she suggested.

"Do you really think so, Gwynne?" he asked.

"Robbie, I think he might even be hurt if you didn't ask him for some help," she suggested.

"You are something else!", he told her. "You are already

acting like a wife!", he wise-cracked.

"Well, Rob," she told him, "I signed my contract as Gwynne Williams, but when school starts I will be Mrs. Currie." I already feel myself growing old pretty fast! Anyway! So, are you going to call him?"

"Now?", he asked.

"Why not?", she countered, "No time like the present!"

He called the King Farm and Paul answered.

"Hi, farm guy!", Rob began. "Got your hay in yet?"

"Pretty much. How the hell are you, Rob?"

"Really great!", Rob answered. "Would you want to help a buddy out?"

"What's up? Nothing bad, I hope," Paul responded.

Rob explained the situation and Paul sounded to be truly enthusiastic.

"Yeah, well… It's just as well that I help you, just to make sure that you don't make a mess of everything!", Paul told him. "Besides, Art is here and I'm sure he could do the chores. Should we take some sleeping bags? I'd rather not sleep on the floor-boards!"

"Oh wow!" Rob exclaimed. "I didn't even think of that!"

"See?", Paul taunted. "Yep! 'Good thing that I'll be there to watch over you. When will you be by to pick me up?"

"Probably late morning or early afternoon tomorrow, okay?", Rob asked.

"Sounds like a plan, Rob!", Paul said.

By Tuesday afternoon, Paul and Rob were tearing out broken plaster and old laths and preparing a room for new wall board.

CHAPTER 22

PART 2

The Church of Gwynne's young life saw its first Highland Wedding on the 23rd of August that year. Martin acted as celebrant and the resident Methodist Minister, who was not at all adverse to there being a rite of the ancient Celtic faith in his church, offered up the final prayer. Gwynne's former room-mate and now a very dear friend was the Bridesmaid and Paul stood as Rob's Best Man. There was, of course a piper who performed his duties extremely well. There were several men present in Highland dress: Rob of course, wearing the tartan of Clan Ranald, as did his father who had purchased a kilt for the occasion. Paul was resplendent in his bright red MacGregor kilt and plaid, looking all the world as if this was his usual mode of dress. Many of the women present wore Tartan sashes over their right shoulders, often pinned with a clan crest. Sheila, her mother, Diane, even Grandma King all appeared with the tartans of their clans or those of the families into which they had been married. Sheila sat in the front row on the "Groom's family side, wearing the Clan Ranald tartan and holding a sash of that same clan neatly folded on her lap. She appeared to be especially radiant on this day and she did something quite wonderful and unexpected.

It is always the mother of the groom who holds the tartan sash which will be draped over the shoulder and wrapped around her son's bride. The last vestige of an ancient matriarchy? Perhaps, but who can tell? The bride's donning of her husband's tartan does not signal any loss of her own identity. Indeed, it is a means by which a family demonstrates their 'adoption' of the young bride of their son. With this, especially among Gaels, the young woman has all the rights of inheritance that a daughter of that family's bloodline might expect.

After the vows had been made, after the giving and receiving of rings, Paul as best man turned and walked to Rob's mother in order to take the sash of the Currie family's tartan back to Rob that he might wrap it around Gwynne and pin it to her shoulder with a clan crest. When Paul bent towards her, Sheila raised her left hand to the back of his neck, pulled him closer and kissed his cheek. With both hands she presented the tartan and the crest to him. He smiled, slightly flustered but also just a bit tearful, certainly grateful for her unexpected gesture of friendship. Jim Currie smiled at Paul, then looked at his wife with a renewed respect.

The wedding reception was spectacular, held at a country place which provided a fine hall and wonderful lawns and gardens. There were a couple of reels and the piper outdid himself in providing the music for them. There was, of course, the dances more familiar to most Americans: slow, romantic ones as well as some of the music of the younger set of those times.

Paul's wedding toast was eloquent, deeply moving and salted with humor which had everyone laughing almost to tears. His ending remark made a lasting impression on Gwynne's family:

"We all were told by Father Martin how Gwynne's wearing her new husband's tartan makes her as a daughter to the Curries." He turned toward Gwynne's parents and continued: "I am sure that the Curries hope that Rob will come also to the Williams family as a good son. You have one son, Evan. Let us all hope that he will have a wonderful new brother. Now, let's raise our glasses to the most wonderful couple I have ever known: Gwynne and Rob Currie!"

Simone had been quite taken with Paul from the first time that they met at the rehearsal. Paul had been at his most charming, showing her attention, smiling mischievously and acting quite gentlemanly. In fact, Rob upon noticing this, thought to himself: "Paul, for a guy who has expressed doubts about his sexuality, you sure know how to turn on the charm around women!" As they were often paired: she as bridesmaid and Paul as Groomsman, not only had Paul acted as her escort, but they danced together several times. When Rob was called aside on one occasion, Gwynne turned to her right and asked Simone: "Are you going to be able to hold together?"

"Gwynne! He's as gorgeous as Rob!"

"Does this mean that you'll stop drooling over my husband now?", Gwynne teased.

"Oh, yes! Well, most of the time, anyway!" Simone answered. "But, Gwynne, do you think that he thinks that I'm making a play for him?"

"Who? My husband?", Gwynne teased.

"No!, Paul! Do you think that he can read how I feel?"

"Simone, Paul is a male animal. He is naturally vain and would think you were crazy were you not to fall head over heels for him!", Gwynne said with authority and wisdom.

"Alright, Gwynne," Simone countered, "But your beyond belief handsome husband is a male animal too. Is he also vain?"

"You'd better believe it Simone!", Gwynne readily replied, "I accept it and wouldn't have him any other way! But now he's *my* male animal and I just hope that whatever vanity he may have will help him to remain the great man that I think and hope that I am accepting as my husband."

All in all, it had been a wonderful wedding. Robert and Kathy MacKinnon stayed with Hugh and Allison for three days. During that time the men talked long into each night, catching up on all of those things which had been taking place since they last saw one another so many years before. Kathy and Allison took a liking to one another from their first meeting. Paul and "Gramma" King were told by Gwynne's parents that they were to have no choice other than staying with them. Paul and Owen Williams had a lot in common and Gramma King found them to be 'wonderful people'. Martin, Diane and little Alasdair stayed at the Curries' along with Carole, Henry and little Josh and the Elder Curries, down from Vermont. Martin and Henry talked about Judaism and how similar certain aspects were to be found in Celtic Christianity. Everyone had laughed when, at the reception after the newlyweds had drunk their wedding pledge, Rob had said, "and that is the last pledge from this glass!" and threw it against the back of the fireplace, where it shattered into many pieces, Henry, without even thinking about it had yelled "Mozel Tov!" Sheila had loved it and hugged her son-in-law, all tears and smiles. Carole, for her part, had come to see her mother in a different light, for Josh and his Gram' Currie really brought out the best in one another.

Rob and Gwynne had opted to have no honey-moon, but to go directly to their Greek Revival home near Allegany. Two days after the wedding, the men were loading a rented 'U-Haul' trailer with odds and ends of furniture, lighting fixtures, beds, box springs and mattresses: the gleanings of three households. These were articles that sets of both parents and the MacKinnons had insisted upon their taking to their own new/ old home. Finer things such as handmade quilts, crocheted table cloths and embroideries were stored along with the wedding gifts in the back seat and trunk of the car. Gwynne had said so many times, upon different occasions, "Oh! I can't take that! It's a family heirloom!", only to be told that it was now hers to care for.

Paul had told them at the reception that he would come down on Labor Day weekend to help on getting anything done which still needed attention. Since Labor Day was Monday, September first, both Rob and Gwynne would be starting their new jobs on the 2nd, Rob as a young designer and Gwynne as 'Mrs. Currie', a Junior and Senior High school English teacher. As the two of them left Balston Spa, on the long drive to Cattaraugus County, they were convinced that they were the happiest and the most blessed couple on Planet Earth.

Rob and Gwynne had said that instead of their taking a Honeymoon when they married, that they would go to their new home and that they would take the 'Honeymoon' a year later. That was not to be. As it turned out, on 20 May of 1976, just a few days shy of nine months after their marriage, Gwynne brought forth their first child: a little boy. They named him 'Ian Robert'. They took him to 'Ardachy', the MacKinnon 'home place' near Emporium a month later, where he received his 'Child Blessing' with Martin acting as the officiating priest. Rob's parents and those of Gwynne travelled down to be on hand and quite to Rob's surprise, his mother not only accepted this sworn adoption of her grandson into the Celtic faith and the promises of the faithful to safeguard of young Ian, she actually appeared to rejoice in the rite.

Two years later, a second son presented himself to the family, whom Gwynne and Rob had named 'Owen James.' Once again, Martin Performed the Rite, but at Rob and Gwynne's own home, again with all of the grandparents on hand. By this time, Gwynne had decided that she would continue on, for a while at least, as a 'stay-at-home mom'. She wanted to raise her boys, be there at home and see them into their own schooling at least.

By this time, everyone was saying that Rob and Gwynne had done wonders with the old place. Lawns hedged by flowering shrubs, planted fruit trees soon to give of their abundance and the house itself, well kept, painted white with its olive green shutters, had become something of a show-place. As well as having converted the old horse-barn into a studio and workshop, Rob, with Paul's help, had built some stone retaining walls for the lawn and garden areas. Paul came down from time to time, although he was doing a great deal towards helping Vietnam War veterans towards finding their places in society again. Rob often wondered how Paul was managing with his own life. Paul always had insisted on sleeping in the loft, the former hay-mow, of the horse barn which had become a studio/ workshop. He and Rob had actually partitioned a part of it to provide a living space of sorts for Paul. By this time, Gwynne had stopped asking why Paul preferred to be off by himself. She, like her husband, had come to understand that Paul had his own demons to confront and in his own way.

After the birth of Owen, Ian now being two years old, Rob bought a spinet for Gwynne and it was placed in a corner of the living room. Gwynne began to practice her playing again and there were many times when the men would stop whatever they were doing to listen to the music of the piano wafting across the lawns. This music became a great part of their lives. Later on, the children would sing along with their mother and upon hearing them, Rob on more than one occasion, would find himself wiping his eyes.

In 1981, three years after the birth of Owen, a third son came into the world. Gwynne had insisted that this time it would be a daughter, but when she brought forth another son on the first of March, they named him after St. David of Wales, whose feast day it was. David Alan Currie was Gwynne's and Rob's third and last child. Gwynne said at the time: "Oh, well! I wouldn't know how to raise a daughter now if I'd had one! I guess that I'm happy to have my boys: all four of them!"

She had said that very thing to her father-in-law one day when they had come down for the Child Blessing.

He asked her, "Do you think of Rob as a boy?", a twinkle in his eye.

"Rob is definitely a boy in so many ways! He is gifted, intelligent and knowledgeable beyond belief, but Papa Jim, he is, in so many ways a boy!"

"Well then, Honey, you deserve a lot of credit," he said softly. "It takes a good and strong woman to bring out the best in a man and yet allow him to retain that boyishness!"

She said to him, "When Rob and I were saying goodbye to my mom and dad after we were married, my dad hugged me and kissed me on the forehead. Then he did the same thing to Rob. He told me that I was always welcome to come 'home', but that I should never come back without my husband."

"Your father is a fine and good man, Gwynne. It takes a lot of man to say such a thing to a precious daughter, believe me!", Jim told her.

"I love you, Papa Jim!" she said.

"I love you too, Honey. A man couldn't ask for a better daughter", Jim said softly. "You are a wonderful wife to my son and a truly fine mother."

CHAPTER 23

PART 2

Paul stopped by from time to time, but less frequently now. He found himself to be needed by so many of the Veterans: veterans of WW II, Korea, and the many often disoriented survivals of his own nightmare, Viet Nam. He had also taken up some work with an old Italian boot-maker who had helped him to learn enough in the way of working with leather that he was able to involve some of his veterans in simple leather-craft. On one of his visits, he had stood young Ian onto a piece of leather, traced around his foot with a black marking pen, then done the same with Owen. Three days later, the little boys were given, each of them, a pair of moccasins. The boys, for their part, dearly loved their 'uncle Paul'. He always did 'neat stuff'! Not that they did not think of their dad as anything less than a genius. They would go out with him to his workshop and put things together from the odd shapes of wood scraps left from his wall sculptures. One part of the shop was dedicated to work done with clay. Their dad always seemed to allow them to use as much clay as they wanted and he would help them to glaze their creations before firing them in the wood fired kiln out back of the studio. Gwynne was the recipient of countless little sculptures and pots made by her boys.

In 1986 some new possibilities presented themselves to Rob and Gwynne. David had reached his fifth birthday, which meant that he would be going to school in September. Owen would be seeing his eighth birthday in August and entering into the third grade in School come Fall, and Ian had turned ten in May. He would be entering into the Fifth grade in the new academic year. Since all of the boys would be going to school, Gwynne had decided to trade in her 'stay-at-home mom' apron and return to teaching. The school was the same 'K-12' Central School where the boys would be enrolled. The boys would be able to ride to and from school with her each day. When she first mentioned the matter to Rob, she was not all that certain that he would go along with the idea. She was wrong.

"Honey," Rob told her, "You have just taken a great load off my mind! To tell you the truth, I have been wondering about you being here all day in an empty house."

"Are you afraid that I might become an alcoholic house wife?", she teased.

"Good Lord, No!", he retorted. "But, you would be here locked away from the world. Besides that, those kids can certainly use a really good-looking, understanding and helpful teacher. I never had a really pretty teacher when I was a kid!"

"You really are a flatterer, Rob!", Gwynne said as she punched his arm. "You're incorrigible!"

"Hey!" he replied, "My flattery has got me three kids!" She answered him by pummeling him repeatedly with a cushion.

After that, they sat quietly for a while. Rob broke the silence.

"This has been a good year, Gwynne. My commission for the church sculptures has come as a great boost to our financial situation. We never did have a Honeymoon. Let's all of us go over to Britain this year."

"You mean Scotland, right?", Gwynne asked.

"No, I mean Britain", he replied. "We can fly into Prestwick, take a few days in the West Highlands and the Isle of Skye. After that, we could travel south, along the western side of Britain, England actually.I want to check out a place in Wales called Llyswen before going down and into Cornwall."

"Llyswen?", Gwynne asked, "In Wales?"

"Yeah! It's in the Brecon Mountain area, Brecon Hills or whatever," he replied.

"That's where my Gran and Granddad Williams came from!", she said.

"I know," Rob replied. "The boys need to see where their mom's folks came from as well as their Scottish ancestors' homeland."

"You never cease to amaze me, Robbie! You are a hopeless Romantic, and I love you for it!"

The folk who still reside in the old lands are quite accustomed to tourists coming among them. Yet, now and then, they find themselves to be somewhat surprised when an American, Canadian or Australian visits and seems to sense that he or she recognizes something about the place. It was like that for Rob when he was at Sleat on Skye and later, looking at the Five Sisters of Kintail, those five mountain peaks on the mainland, tears came to Rob's eyes. He had felt elation at first, then a sense of longing, followed by an inner anger which he could not possibly have explained. Gwynne saw it, felt it in him, but observed quietly. Later, when they left Dornie and headed south, Rob swung the car around and returned for another look. Finally, they headed down through GlenShiel, towards Spean Bridge, towards Fort William: South and through the Scottish lowlands and into England.

Wales they found to be an enchanting place. At the Bed and Breakfast place in Llyswen, the Lady of the house did not want to charge them for their stay. Her "cooker" had suffered some malfunction and breakfast had been late. She had cooked their breakfast at the house next-door. The poor woman was beside herself. After breakfast, young Ian gathered the plates from the table and took them to the sink in her wee kitchen.

"There's a lad who has been well brought up!", the woman said with delight.

"His mum runs a pretty tight ship!" Rob replied, after which he took the lady aside and insisted that she take the full amount to which they had agreed when they had first arrived at the house. The poor woman was almost in tears and was still wiping her eyes as she waved them goodbye from her cottage door when they left.

Gwynne loved Cornwall: 'a stone land' in the words of the English poet, David H.W. Grubb, a strange, Celtic land where villages seem to grow out of the landscape: stone, slate-walled buildings rising from more stone and slate, to the point where it was often difficult to determine where the landscape gave way to human habitations. It is a land still marked by stone crosses, stone circles and always a reminder: this is not England! This is Cornwall!

What surprised Gwynne most of all was the way in which her sons, these little boys, seemed to have felt so much at ease here, as they had in the Scottish Highlands. "They really are little Celts!", she thought. "They almost act as if they have come 'home'!" Well, the sons and daughters of a people may be born in a land far across the sea, but there is something of their forebears carried on. "Just because the cat may have her kittens in the corner of a hen house does not see her giving birth to chicks!", as the older folk would say.

Rob, Gwynne and the boys returned to the Highlands five years later, In 1991. Ian was now a teen-ager of fifteen years. Rob and the boys walked over the rocky, sometimes boggy ground, to the Fall of Glomach, highest waterfall in

Britain, in the mountains of Kintail. Gwynne happily left them to it. She had learned to love walking by the sea, or in this case, by the banks of Loch Duich. On that trip they went to StrathGlass and St. Mary's Church there, with its graveyard filled with standing stone Celtic Crosses, they stopped by the Holy Well near Munlochy, The magic of it all going on and on. They went to the Battlefield at Culloden and saw the long rows of common graves: the final resting place of the Jacobite clansmen. They looked upon all of this in silence. A man in Inverness had asked them why they would want to go to Culloden. Rob had answered, "Because I am a Currie and a MacKinnon."

"Aye, well, there's a lot of both, MacVurrich and MacKinnon buried at Culloden!", the man had answered solemnly. There was unmistakable respect in his tone.

Upon their return to the 'States, Rob, Gwynne and the boys drove up to Balston. They thought to end their trip by seeing parents and grandparents, having also brought some gifts for them as before. The family's older members were slowing down, probably not to be around much longer. Hugh had had several strokes and Allison was preparing herself for the inevitable.

"Your mother has been a God-send, Robbie!", she said to him when they were alone. "She is here to help me every day! I couldn't manage alone. Denny and Madeleine have come down from Canada twice now."

After a pause, she added: "Go to your Ordination, Robbie. We will need a priest before long and your

Grandfather has said that his final passing would be complete were you to see to his Soul Leading and final farewell."

"I had planned to do that, Gram'. I'll see to it right away," he said softly. "I know that I am not worthy, but I guess that I am as ready as I'll ever be."

He was ordained at Ardachy House a month later and by Robert MacKinnon, CoArb. In addition to Gwynne and the sons, a great many people were present. Rob saw for the first time how much older and how frail his elder kinsman had become. In fact, Martin left the gathering just after Robert and Kathy had some Coffee and Tea, in order to drive them home. Robert could not last very long at gatherings anymore. He needed his rest.

Only three weeks later on, Rob, Gwynne and the boys went up to Balston Spa. Hugh was in hospital, not expected to live more than a few days.

Rob was in the room as his grandfather was breathing the last minutes of his life. Rob moved to the bedside, where his grandmother, seated beside the bed, held the hand of her life-long partner. Rob invoked the 'Soul Leading' after which the old man opened his eyes and smiled ever so slightly. When he closed his eyes again, his breathing stopped within minutes. Rob heard a choking cry from his grandmother. She stood up, kissed her husband's forehead before falling into Denny's arms, her head against his shoulder, her own shoulders shaking as she wept.

Rob took out the small bottle of oil, donned his stole

and anointed the forehead of his grandfather. After a prayer, his priestly function accomplished, he turned to Gwynne. He was simply another one of the mourners now. After removing his stole, he sobbed once and his shoulders shook as she held him in her arms. All three sons encircled their mom and dad with their arms around them.

When Robert MacKinnon died a year and a half later, followed by Gramma King four months after that, Rob realized that now, even their own parents were growing old. Sheila had become the kind of 'Gram' to her grandchildren that her mother had been. Carole's and Henry's Josh was in second year of Law School at Columbia (a 'Jewish Prince' his father's people called such a station in life), his sister Miriam was a Junior in High School.

After 'Gramma' King's funeral the family gathered at the farm. Rob was overjoyed to see all of them again and they all expressed their joy as well. David and Linda spoke with him as if he too were a son, and Martha, warm and kind as always, expressed her happiness to have him present at such a time. Art came up to them on one occasion and having just 'lit up' a cigarette he addressed Rob:

"Hey, Robbie, do you still suck up half a cigarette in one drag?"

Rob held out his hand, took Art's cigarette and inhaled deeply and after a moment exhaled a cloud of smoke. His three sons,.. and their mother... stared, open mouthed at him.

"Christ on a crutch!, Oops!   Sorry, Father," Art

exclaimed. "You've done it again!"

Ian, still staring said, "Dad! I didn't know that you smoke!"

"I don't!" Rob smiled at him.

"Maybe Dad's a "Closet Smoker!", Owen joked.

Paul later took Rob to one side and thanked him for all that he had done for the family. He then reached in his pocket and pulled out a small leather pouch.

"Gramma' asked me before she died to take care of these," Paul said, pouring the two Crowned Lion Head buttons into his palm. "She also asked me if I would mind giving one to you. I told her that it would make me very happy to do so."

"Paul!", Rob protested, "I can't take…"

"Yes! You can and you will!", Paul insisted. "Besides," he smiled, "You're still my first love, Rob!"

"And you're still a dumb, stupid guy, but a hell of an 'uncle' to my kids!" Rob said. He accepted the silver button and they hugged.

Looking on from a distance, Owen said to his mother:

"Uncle Paul really loves Dad, doesn't he, mom?"

"He always has, Owie! Your Dad loves him too," she said softly. "Sometimes men form very strong bonds. I hope that you may someday bond with someone so strongly."

"Yeah. Me too," Owen replied. There was something in the way that he replied. A slight shiver came over her. She raised her eyebrows, glanced towards him, then smiled.

Their third and final trip to Scotland was in the early

summer of 1994. Ian had graduated from High School the year before and had worked in an animal shelter for a year. He had been accepted at Penn State where he hoped to work towards Veterinary Medicine. He agreed to go with the family only if he were to be allowed to pay for his own Air Fare and Lodging. He also wanted to bring along a girl whom he had been dating since High School. Her name was Angela Bjorno, of Danish and German parentage. In keeping with that heritage, the girl always insisted that her first name was to be pronounced "Ahn GAY la" Gwynne liked her very much and saw no harm in the idea. Rob fell silent and set his jaw, not entirely pleased with the proposition at all.

"They want to go back-packing through a part of the Highlands," Rob said. "Is that a good idea?"

"They're beautiful young people and they are in love," Gwynne said simply.

In the end, the very lovely Angela and her adored Ian were to be booked on the same flight. Actually, Rob had come to really like the beautiful, blonde Angela. Many of her mannerism reminded him of Gwynne at that same age. Rob's parting shot on the subject had been when he said to his wife:

"It's a good thing your Aunt Lucy isn't alive to see this, Gwynne!"

It was a good trip. The family stayed together for about a week. From time to time, Ian drove the car. They went through Glen Lyon, Mac Gregor country, one of Scotland's best kept secrets. It is the longest of all the glens, passing between rugged, craggy outcroppings and forested ledges. The Glen Lyon road comes to an end at the Bridge of Balgie. There is an old post office there where the proprietors have a small shop where various items are sold as well as some baked goods and food served on the premises, above which they rent out lodging. The old stone bridge arcs over a fast flowing River Lyon and the scene is of post-card subject matter. It is there that Ian and Angela took up their backpacks and struck out, saying that they would meet up again with the family at Killin two days later. All went well and similar side trips resulted in similar arrangements.

"Where did Ian learn to be such an outdoorsman?" Rob asked on one such parting.

Gwynn, Owen and David all laughed.

"I wonder!" Gwynne said. "You practically raised these boys in the woods!"

"Yeah…", Rob pondered. "We spend a lot of time in the woods, don't we?"

Owen lowered his voice and imitated his father:

"If you've grown up in the Alleghenies and can't find a way to stay dry and warm in the woods by the time you're twelve years old, you just haven't been paying attention!"

David started laughing hysterically and said, "You sound just like Dad, Owie!"

Gwynne laughed as well and turning her head to glance at her husband, she saw him shake his head from side to side, trying not to laugh, but he was smiling.

Prologue to
PART THREE

PROLOGUE TO PART 3

Seven years later, the America which they had known would evolve drastically. Changes had come about, surely: computers, the internet, an almost total dependence upon scanning prices of goods in supermarkets. All of this had been taken in stride. But the year 2001 would bring with it an age of surveillance, restrictions, increased security at airports and border crossings. Various types of regulation would lead to an almost paranoia throughout American society. Smokers would be stigmatized, possession of knives and even aspirin by school children would be grounds for suspension from school. Words or expressions would be disallowed as they could be construed to signify racism, sexism or evidence of 'hate crimes'. Children no longer played out of doors due to a wide-spread fear of child abductions. Those who would attend candle light vigils to save seals and whales would rally for the right of abortion of human fetuses on demand and those who were 'pro-life' would, as often as not, be in favor of capital punishment. There were those who believed that citizens should have a right to own guns and those who saw ownership of any firearm to be anachronistic at best and a threat to order and safety at worst.

The famed American 'love affair with the automobile' would soon see the love affair with the computer, internet messaging and 'texting' on various, ever-updated 'phones take on a place of equal standing. The Federal government 'pushed' computers and 'computer literacy' and at the same time took over Health Care, Education and a broad program of 'Welfare Reform." Many states discontinued the teaching of Cursive Writing altogether and by the end of the first decade of the 21st century better than 40% of Americans were living on government welfare and food stamps. With so much that served to divide Americans without too many people noticing any differences the government took to surveillance of the citizenry which it was meant to serve. 'Security cameras' in city streets, inside of public buildings and even schools, became not only accepted, but expected.

Foreign wars, US complicity in 'secretly' toppling governments and a 'war on drugs' poured almost unbelievable amounts of the nation's wealth into the 'off-shore' bank accounts of those who were hired as 'contractors'. Billions of dollars were wasted, left 'unaccounted for' and the government simply printed more money. Our security agencies had been monitoring e-mails, telephone conversations and filing away information of millions of our citizens. Few people seemed to sense that all of these things signaled the end of Empire, the collapse of a social order. Chaos merchants: those who made unbelievable profits by feeding a war machine and supplying arms, literally 'bought' the politicians who in turn, obligingly fanned the flames of war, sold more arms and 'services' to the government. It was an open secret that the government had been training troops for riot control, some of those troops being from other countries. With electronic devices, un-manned flying devices called 'drones, the vast surveillance in place, there was little doubt that the government had the upper hand. Two factors would serve to take away any such control. One of them was the fact that somewhere between eighty and one hundred million Americans were armed, knew how to use their weapons and had also been accumulating such 'archaic' but still silent and deadly back-ups as crossbows and very accurate bows and arrows. Laughable? Not really. After all, the sophisticated tools of the government depended upon electrical power. A Wide-spread power outage would leave countless screens and monitors blank. Radio and telephone towers could be easily disabled. They were often on hill tops, often in heavily forested areas. A good hunter with the aid of a good scope on his rifle could disable them. The government would be forced to put the well-trained troops on the ground. The men and women who lived in a given landscape would know that ground. Every creek-bed, every grove of trees and certainly any forest would serve as a site for possible ambush.

Finally, it happened:

First there had been a power outage. A third of the nation had no electricity. At the end of the second week without power, stores and supermarkets stood dark and empty with shattered windows looking out upon the street as if with sightless eyes. The debris of the looted items formed an ugly, scattered carpet underfoot, from inside each store out onto the pavements. The floor within often revealed broken, trampled bags containing flour, Corn Meal or Rice, overlooked initially by mobs who went first for the frozen foods or canned items, two-liter bottles of carbonated beverages, peanuts and potato chips. The collapse of any system is ugly at best. Most of the looted frozen foodstuffs were unfit for human consumption three days later, there being no way to keep them.

Police were no match for so very many people and when the various officers tried to employ the government supplied equipment which had been accepted by police precincts, the crowds became even more frenzied. National Guardsmen who had been called out often went over to the people, taking their weapons with them. In some areas soldiers wearing the blue UN helmets came onto the scene. They soon stopped wearing any identifying colors or insignia. The lesson could not have been made any more clear: Foreign soldiers on U.S. soil were fair game!

The America of too many laws and regulations had become lawless, and almost overnight at that.

Some historians have put forth the opinion that America lost her innocence with the Viet Nam War, but the murder of four students and the wounding of many others by National Guardsmen at Kent State in 1970 was not the first time that troops fired upon citizens. During the Anti-Draft Riots in New York in 1863, Naval ships bombarded lower Manhattan. After that terrible war the United States embarked upon upon an all-out war against the Plains Indians which went on until our War with Spain. In 1922 Veterans of the First World War marched to Washington, DC demanding the bonuses which they had been promised. They were charged by mounted troops with sabers. The army also used the machine gun against them.

Is it any wonder that this land, peopled at first by the dispossessed of Europe who were later joined by the outcasts of the Orient and finally the former Southern slaves which people once grew and harvested the most profitable crops to go forth to the North and to Europe, is there any wonder at all as to why these peoples have never completely trusted anyone in authority? Here and there, neighbors gathered into groups for the purpose of mutual protection. In rural areas a simple farm of a few hundred acres would often become a well protected 'island of security', providing food, housing and safety to neighboring folk who would lend support towards the production of food and protection of the holding. The 'clan system' had been brought back to life, not only among Americans of Celtic blood, for Italian Americans recalled Sicilian 'Familia' very well. It is amazing how so many people were forced to, able to, recall the past measures and strengths of their forebears.

For a while, America too would experience a taste, and a very bitter taste at that, of what we had at one time labeled another period which had followed the collapse of empire: 'The Dark Ages'.

CHAPTER 1

PART 3

Families are much older than nations and one family can outlive many empires. The deer has no concern for the deeds in the court house registry and the fox has nothing to render unto any Caesar. Man's laws move only as far and are only as valid as his armies can reach to enforce them. In ancient times all families had 'soldiers', if one chooses to call them that, but as mankind progressed into animal husbandry, into the pastoral state of his culture, he did not drop one thing to become another. Instead, he simply put his weaponry in the corner of his dwelling until he needed such things, then he went out to shear his sheep or mend his fences or nets. Yet, he was no less the warrior and no less the hunter.

When men and women left the tribe to dwell in cities they left everything behind, especially that sense of being needed and belonging to something. The visit to the city has been frightening, hilarious, mad and certainly enlightening, but all days must come to an end. It is time to return to the tribe; time to go home, if only we haven't lost the way. You say that you will not forfeit a world of change for one of tradition? Why, the oldest and most certain tradition of all is change and change is cyclical, is it not? Just be patient.

The herdsman left his splitting maul to stand by itself in a small drift of snow which clung to the shady side of a stump of a recently felled tree. It wasn't a really warm day, by any means, but the splitting of cord wood makes a man realize that a winter jacket isn't needed. He had never needed anyone to tell him that a good suit of long-johns with jeans, a flannel shirt and leather vest was all a person really needed on an average winter day for working in the woods provided, of course, that his feet were warm and dry. That's the most important thing. If the feet are cold and wet, there is no outer clothing that can be piled on a human frame that can keep that body warm. His flannel shirt sleeves were rolled back, revealing the white of the winter underwear and he passed his left arm across his forehead to wipe away the sweat, pushing his hat back as he did so. His right hand went around to his hip pocket at almost exactly the same time, fumbling for just a fraction of a minute before his fingers found the soft, crumpled package half-filled with 'chew'. He continued to watch the figures in front of him not more than ten or fifteen yards away while he transferred the package to his left hand, opened it with his right and took out a quantity of tobacco which he then mechanically transferred to his mouth and lower jaw just inside of his left cheek. The people moving about in front of him either sensed his disapproval or just plain didn't care, for they never stopped long enough to look in his direction. Even when the chain saw motor stopped, further up on the hillside behind the herdsman, not one of them looked up.

"I wonder that they don't feel a little embarrassed or something," he thought, "Always coming in where other folks are doing their work, just like a flock of crows or buzzards picking over the leavings of some dead thing. Damn!" He spat out a stream of fresh tobacco juice and half-consciously watched it discolor the snow, some of it clinging to an upright twig like a torn rain-drenched banner of some army of tiny forest men.

He noticed the quiet of the woods with the chainsaw no longer running. "You aren't quitting yet are you?", he called up to the shepherd with the chainsaw. The shepherd moved down the hill and closer to where he stood.

"Hell, no! But this saw might run if a man would put some gas into it! Besides it isn't even eleven o'clock yet! I figure we can knock down a few more of the dying beech before lunch time."

The shepherd moved down toward the herdsman and set the chainsaw on the stump.The herdsman watched him absently, watching the care with which the chainsaw was being balanced, the shepherd treating the machine with an obvious concern. A chainsaw is a noisy, foul-smelling, smoke-belching monster, but the hours of drudgery that a man is spared makes it worth putting up with. An inoperative chainsaw, one that has suffered neglect or has not been kept up serves as a nagging reminder of the sloth of its owner. A saw that could do so much in a short period of time, thereby liberating its owner from many extra hours or days of backbreaking work, deserves and does, in fact receive, a certain respect from one who knows what the alternative must be and who knows that from necessity he would have to accept that alternative. So important had this one tool become, that almost any gasoline which could be found in these days was, as a rule, saved for the chainsaw.

The herdsman pushed his hat further back on his head, revealing a line across his forehead where the leather had pressed into his flesh. Thick curly black hair just a bit clinging and damp from the work of splitting wood showed itself beneath the tipped back hat. He reached into his pocket and brought out the package again and without looking at the Shepherd directly but rather more in the direction of the forest floor he held out the crumpled pouch.

"Chew?", he asked.

"Well yes! Since you're buying I'll just have some of that!", the shepherd replied.

The shepherd took out a good sized pinch, leaned his head and jaw out slightly to make sure that none was dropped from his fingers before lodging it in his mouth. Carefully he folded the top of the package down on the original creases and handed it back to his friend.

"Thanks."

"Oh that's alright. I wouldn't want to see you do without a good chew after knocking over all them trees."

The two men stood silently looking ahead of them for awhile. Words aren't really necessary to men who have worked together since boyhood. It isn't really a matter of telepathy, although that might have a small part of it. It's more than that: two human beings sharing the same work because it's simply too much for one to do alone begin to function as a single organism. More than that, they held a common heritage of clanship and religion. They had become a part of their own North American land with its cruel winters and the poor soil which cheated them year after year. But even after several generations they were holding on to something from another place. They would often, in everyday speech, take on the funny, farmer-dialect of the Allegheny region. They were aware of it too and even jokingly referred to the speech pattern as 'Alléganish' or 'a-LEG-anish'. It wasn't something that they 'put on' as city people trying to imitate farmers or Yankees trying to imitate southerners. No it was genuinely theirs. They grew up with it and it was an extension of themselves. The English spoken to older people of culture and that which was used by them in polite conversation was as good as any to be found on the continent; better than most, although there was a slight Scots coloring to it; even a bit British. Lastly, and that tongue reserved for the intimate, inner circle… for toasts to the long exiled house of Stuart, for songs sung at ceílidhs… there was 'the Gaelic'. Each generation carried a tremendously heavy load. Each generation feared that theirs could be the last to carry it and be known for ever as 'the last to wear the tartan or sing in the Gaelic'.

It wasn't 'nationalism' as we know it, for Scotland was another country and years in North American had mixed German blood and English blood with Scottish. Still there was this Celtic something which could not be shaken and there was also 'the clan' and the Celtic Christianity, half pagan but very meaningful to them.

"Dad always said it would come to this." The shepherd was speaking as much to the ground, the soft but heavy air around them, as he was to the herdsman.

"Well, he wasn't ever known to be a dumb man, that's sure," the herdsman responded through the same channel of earth air and silence. Then a smile came across his face and two short bursts of air came through his teeth; a short laugh of sorts. The herdsman looked up sideways toward his friend without turning his head, his face still aimed toward the earth at his feet and went on:

"Your dad could really get me to laughing. He'd always act so serious about things but he could really cut up sometimes. I was just thinkin' about the time he put us up to stealin' that chair from that hotel. "I'd really like to have that chair!", he said, so we went to all that work to get it and bring it all the way back here and then he blistered us for takin' it! He even made us take it all the way back there! You remember that?"

"Yeah, I remember. But that kind of crap could wear a little thin sometimes. It's a little different when you live with it all the time."

"Maybe so, but he was the closest thing in this century to somebody like Cluny MacPherson or the MacNab. He was kind of what a highland chief would have been like or what they were supposed to be like, back in the days of the clan uprisings like the '15 or the '45. Anyway he was colorful. You gotta admit that!"

"Hell!" The shepherd laughed. "We're *all* colorful! Even those damned scavengers over there are colorful! Looking toward the people a few yards away with a nod of his head. He started to turn his face toward the herdsman and quickly swung back to the people picking up brush. One young man was holding up a tree limb about as big around as a man's arm while an older woman hacked at the small branches growing out of it with an old kitchen meat cleaver.

"Hey!", the shepherd yelled.

The young man and the older woman froze in their movements and looked up toward the two men by the chainsaw. The otherpeople who had been gathering brush stopped for a moment, then seeing that the problem was something belonging to someone else, they went on breaking small branches and twigs into small pieces about two feet in length. In fact they paid or pretended to pay even less attention to the two men, the young man and older woman, than they had previously shown. The young man who had been stopped, dropped the big limb to the ground and started walking slowly toward the shepherd who had just yelled at him. The older woman still stood in the same position, like a figure in a mechanical Old-World clock; cleaver still in hand, arm still bent, her face showing no signs of her thoughts, just a great blank.

The herdsman thought of how much the older woman looked like a figure from out of a painting by Breugel. She had a headscarf covering her hair and tucked down into an oversized cloth coat that was held together at the neck by a large horse blanket pin and around the waist by a leather belt with one of those large, bronze buckles that were all the rage in the '70's and the '80's,… probably the trademark of some beer company or motorcycle manufacturer. Perhaps the belt was drawn somewhat snuggly about the coat, causing the cloth to form large puckering folds both above and below the clean line of leather. 'Looks like a sack of oats tied in the middle', he thought. The belt had been passed through the handles of a beat-up old purse which had once been a faddy, bright orchid, but being made of some kind of cheap vinyl it was now peeling and cracked. The herdsman thought that it probably contained everything that the woman prized in life. "I wonder", he thought, "What they do carry in those old pocket books. Hell! They don't own anything or have anything, yet an awful lot of those women carry their purses hanging from a belt like that. The men don't seem to have anything, but the women are never without that purse and belt, even if the belt is made out of braided bailing twine and the purse is a cloth sack." He couldn't stop looking at the woman, her legs covered by a pair of sleeves cut off an old sweater and pulled up over her slacks, covering also the rubber over-shoes, the bottoms of the overshoes which showed themselves were covered with pieces of plastic tape. "No, he thought, 'Breughel's peasants had better clothing than that!"

The young man was now standing in front of them, looking at the shepherd; head slightly cocked to one side, waiting for the shepherd to speak. He wore a pair of faded blue Jeans with ripped out knees and a ripped pocket and these holes revealed another pair of jeans under the first and in not much better repair. An old Army coat (an Army dress blouse, really), but with faded rectangles and circles showing where once patches had been, made up the rest of his outfit. The shepherd began to speak.

"Now I don't like to have to remind you of this and I don't think that you're so damned dumb but what you've got to be told… ", The shepherd waved his hand toward the brush piles and in the general direction of the men and women a few yards away, one hand pressed into his waistline. Before going on he turned his head and shoulders and spit out the cud of tobacco that he had newly put into his mouth. It took about three spits, some sweeping action with his tongue and a fourth spit before he went on.

"Look! We ain't knockin' down these damn trees for the hell of it! We've got other work to do! Now you know that we let you people come in here to gather up brush but you have been told over and over that those limbs are to be left alone. You can have the small stuff. It's good for us and it's good for you to get it out of here. But I'm only going to say this one more time. Anything bigger around than your thumb gets left alone! If it's still got twigs or little branches growing out of it and its bigger than that then we haven't trimmed it yet! After… I said 'After' weve trimmed it you can have the trimmings. Nobody ordered you into this woodlot but I'll damn-straight order you out of here if you start puttin' yer hand in my pocket! Now I don't mean to talk to you about this ever again!"

The young man was still standing there with his head cocked to one side, his thumbs were hooked into his belt loops, his wrists pushing the army tunic back on each side, revealing a filthy green sweater: a texture of snags and pilled wool; sooty noils of a cheap, man-made fiber. On his head or surrounding it was a hood of common-cotton like material which was a dull faded orange disappeared into the neck of the tunic and sweater. The hood hung loosely, as did the two ends of a drawstring. The day wasn't all that cold really and gathering wood is warm work anyway. He looked, at first glance, as most of the scavenger people looked: ragged clothing, cast-off things either given by someone in a spirit of pity, perhaps charity, or else fished out of a refuse pile. In the towns and villages there were often covered receptacles where people could leave old things: clothing, worn bedding, shoes and boots; even old pans and dishes. Anything that might still have a month's use to another human being was left in the town's receptacle. These collection centers were usually back of a fire hall or Police station although any out-of-the way place was acceptable. No one ever saw any of the deposited items being taken, but the bins would be picked clean by sunrise each day. In fact there were usually no bins left. They too would have been carried away, leaving only the commonplace four uprights supporting a roof of sorts. The young man standing there would have been outfitted from such charity and refuse piles since the time of these troubles had begun. No, he didn't really look very different from the rest of the scavengers, and yet, there was something. The shepherd noticed it and tried to figure it out. Was it the face? No not the face. It was a young man's face; an unmarried young scavenger's face (well, unmated anyway. Scavengers didn't 'marry', they mated.) His lack of a beard showed that he was still trying to look his best for a young woman; still trying to look attractive and oddly enough, he was a fairly nice looking guy. His eyes were pretty lifeless, 'though. Dull. Scavengers had a way of making their eyes and expressions go dead when they spoke to the men who worked the land.

The young man took his right hand from his belt loop, ran a knuckle under his nose and spoke as if to the ground at his feet.

"We wasn't try'n to rob nothin', Mister." He glanced back at the shepherd, the herdsman, then back to the shepherd before looking toward the earth again.

"I ain't sayin' you was!" the shepherd scolded, "but it looked like you was and you know better. Like they say, a man doesn't tie his shoe in his neighbor's melon patch, nor straighten his hat in his neighbor's orchard! You look smart enough to know that!" The shepherd was feeling a bit embarrassed, but a man had to stand his ground with these people. The hills abounded with stories of what happened to people who appeared to be timid, like the story of an old farmer who was alone on his place and in poor health. It started with people moving into his shed, which burnt to the ground one night. Then his hen house. It wasn't any time at all before they started tearing the barn apart for firewood. They ended up by cleaning him out of food and everything he had. His older son had come up from the city and found his father alone in one room of the old house. Scavengers had sold things and bought wine and whiskey and were having a party in the kitchen. The son had dusted about three of them with his hunting gun, clubbed another one to death with the gun butt then turned himself in. Of course, the son was let off. The County Judge said that it was as sure a case of justifiable homicide as she'd ever heard. She wasn't known to be an easy judge by any means, but she accepted a plea of temporary insanity even 'though that plea hadn't washed in a court of law for over twenty years. It didn't help the farm 'though. The farm was ruined: all of those buildings gone and no money with which to replace them. No. A man had to be firm and stand his ground when he dealt with the scavengers.

The young man looked up again and this time there was expression in his eyes: kind of a half hurt, half pleading look. He ran his hand under his nose again before he spoke.

"Mister that woman back there's awful sick. I gotta get her back to where she can lay down and warm up some. We were trimmin' that limb for the brush so's we could get our bundles made up an' go. We weren't gonna take any of your limbs. Honest to God!

The shepherd felt foolish. 'Probably he'd have a good laugh if I showed any kindness,' he thought. 'Yeah they'd all be yukkin' it up among themselves but hell, how do I know whether he's telling the truth or not?'

"Well you listen to me, fella. If you trim brush on my place you're working here and you know that you aren't working for me! We've got our own men and women pulling together and that's all we've got space for, so you aren't working for me! You take what we leave for you. We make the leavings not you!" The shepherd studied his face for a moment, then: "By the way are you one of the people we agreed could take from here? Who the hell are you, anyway?"

"He's been here before," the herdsman said. The herdsman had slowly lowered himself into a hunter's crouch during the conversation. Now, he half-knelt on the earth with one knee, an arm laid loosely over his other, raised knee as he looked up to the shepherd. His hunting knife glinted in the pale sunlight which struggled through the overcast. With the knife he had been cutting away at a piece of punky wood, trying to remain away and out of the exchange between the two other men. Something had prompted him to come to the young man's defense, to support him in some way. The shepherd looked a bit startled that the herdsman had spoken and glanced first at his friend, then to the young man. He looked past the scavenger then to the older woman. She continued to stand there, staring up toward the three men. Her hands now hung loosely at her sides, the kitchen cleaver drooping like a wet rag, an extension of her right hand. She just stared in their direction as very young children will stare: no attempt to disguise the wondering; the questions brought on by the moment.

"Is that woman over there your mother?", the shepherd asked.

"No, Sir. She's my girl's mother. Well, the mother of a girl I used to be with a lot. The girl's gone. She run off somewhere or other. 'Left the old lady. I kinda look out for her now. The old lady, I mean, she's been pretty bad off since about November. Fact is she doesn't come out too much anymore. Her kid usually comes with me to gather. He's about sixteen. She figured it best to leave him to watch the place today... you know... what with claim jumpers an' all."

They knew about 'claim jumpers', all right. The two men had heard of the constant quarreling among these rootless people. They fought and even died trying to protect ...or take... whatever passed for a dwelling: an old bus or car, a deserted root cellar or even a lean-to. The herdsman spoke again:

"Where are you livin'?"

"Beyond the second creek, into those thorn apples ", the young man replied, nodding to the north east with a quick jerk of his head. "There's an old sugar shack. I fixed the roof on it. It was kind of caved in when I found it".

The shepherd's eyes shot sideways toward the herdsman whose eyes were already meeting his. It was just a flicker, a second's reaction to the words they'd just heard, they in the next instant they were back to the brush gatherer. The shepherd spoke:

"That's practically on my boundary line!"

There was a lightly veiled warning in his words; just in the way that he'd said then. It was also clear that the gatherer understood instantly that this man could be more than a trifle concerned. This shepherd was much more than a keeper of sheep and a few head of cattle. He was a landowner who lived in a large and very old house. He had been educated, had been in other countries and had a family tradition that extended back in history to times and places which were already old when the first Europeans began arriving in the New World. He lived in a world of people and ideas that always made a virtue of loyalty and where hard work was thought to be a blessing from on high. A man who could not work was pitied in his world and a person who had no skills was thought to be already dead. The land and the family… and the word itself: 'clan', means "children". These were the priorities of the shepherd's world and the brush gatherer knew of the shepherd's world. Running and leaping into the tall brush at the side of a road or path at the sound of voices or horses hooves, he had, many times in his life, watched a party of men ride by, sometimes in a solemn, quiet single file; other times joking and talking to one another. These were the 'stewards', people who lived on the land, managed it and guarded it. They thinned out the weaker trees to provide room for the stronger ones just as they culled the less desirable sheep and cattle from their flocks and herds. They had reasons for all that they did, cures for ills among animals and plants, and mental records and religious ceremonies to fill their generations. The shepherds, the herdsman, hunters and artisans clung to their way of life as they held to one another. The land was dotted with such holdings which were, themselves, islands of work, loyalty and purpose in a world that had lost its reason for being. Anything or anyone approaching such a holding, such an 'island' of security, was watched very, very carefully.

The young gatherer answered the shepherd; his eyes toward the base of the tree stump, while with the toe of his boot he made little patterns in a small patch of snow and mud.

"Yeah we knew we was close to this holding when we fixed up that sugar shack." After a pause and hearing no question he went on:

"Fact of the matter is we did it a-purpose." At this point he glanced up at the shepherd and to the herdsman with just a hint of fear that he might have sounded threatening. He let his explanation tumble from his mouth like apples being poured from a bushel. See we want to be near this place because it's safer than most. They ain't many who'd want to mess with you folks. People kinda figure that men who'd shoot a dog who got into their sheep or young stock without so much as blinkin' an eye wouldn't lose too much more sleep if they was to dust anything else, man or beast, who looked to threaten their family."

"Well, you've got that right!" the shepherd said, then:

"I didn't catch your name." He knew that no name had been given, but thought to be a bit polite about it.

"I'm Glen Olsen."

The herdsman stood up, turned from the waist and spat out some tobacco juice, rubbed his knife blade against his jeans; first one side of the blade, then the other, before putting it back into the sheath that hung over his right hip. This maneuver took both hands because the little leather strap had to be snapped back around the knife handle. He reached out and put his hand on the splitting maul, leaning on it like a cane. He straightened his hat then spoke to the young gatherer.

"Well, Glen Olsen, I sure have been admiring those leather lace-ups you're wearing. Where'd you come onto a pair of boots like that?"

The implication was very plain. The gatherer's boots were pretty much out of keeping with the rest of his outfit. They looked new, well-made and expensive. They weren't the kind of item normally found on the refuse piles, that was certain. The young man could feel the blood come up to his cheeks from around his collar. He felt hot and a little dry in the mouth. 'O, God', he thought 'they're gonna shoot me for a looter or even worse. They might think I robbed them from a man or knocked somebody over the head.' For the first time he noticed that both men were armed; that there was a six-gun hanging on the right flank of each of them. "Of course they're armed" he thought. "A man doesn't have to look to know that! They're always armed. I'd be armed if I was them and that's the truth!"

"I noticed the boots too." The shepherd was looking at him. Hard. Two steel blue eyes registered nothing save for their being aimed at the gatherer. A Question had been asked.

"You think I stole the boots don't you?" It was the accused turn to accuse. He managed a look of righteous indignation, looking each man right in the eye, first one and then the other. The eyes before him never so much as flickered. The herdsman took up the questioning now; his voice like a patient father's.

"Well, did you?" Two dark, almost black eyes, normally kind and accepting eyes, were smoldering just a little.

"No! I did not!"

"They're pretty nice boots!" The tone of the voice was almost singing, soothing but the implied accusation remained.

"Look I know that this looks bad, but…"

"It sure doesn't look very good!", the herdsman interrupted."

I come by these boots honest."

"You earned them? What kind of work did you do to earn them?" The herdsman's voice was beginning to rise.

The scavenger turned very red in the face and stared at his prized boots, the most beautiful possession of his life. He wished that he had never put them on. They had given him trouble enough in the last week. There had been the terrible experience with the man with the bad eye and his rat-like friend. Glen had made the mistake of taking a short cut through the college ruins. That's where they were, huddled around a fire emptying out a battered old purse. He remembered how he had come upon them suddenly in what was left of some walls. They had a roof made of poles and the beds of two old pick-up trucks slung over a low, narrow section of what might have once been a basement corridor. He remembered stopping dead in his tracks like a deer does when it catches sight or scent of man. He remembered how they had risen slowly without taking their eyes away from him: Three eyes looking right at him and one dull, lifeless eye looking past his shoulder. He had had to run and had become cornered by them. Had it not been for a metal sign attached to its metal post they would have done him in. He couldn't forget the three eyes seeming to be carrying their lifeless counterpart along with them, nor the club in one man's hand, the knife in the hand of the other. He had seized onto the metal post as if it were all he held dear in the world. He had swung arcs with the sign to keep the men away. Then when he had seen one man, the little one, try to race in and under his only defenses he had used that sign like a battle-axe, smashing the little rat collar bone, breaking his leg and the little rat had screamed. Bad eye had begun to to back away, waited for his chance, then he had turned and run. Ron had gone to the top of the knoll above the ruins on the hillside, dragging his sign and post with him. He remembered how he had slumped down on a rock or slab of concrete and how he shook all over and felt sick. He had even taken the boots off and flung them into the bushes, only to go back and retrieve them later. He had wished that he could have found a bed of mud… something to disguise their quality and newness, but that had been a very cold day; nothing but clean snow.

"Well, the way I see it," the herdsman was saying half to the shepherd, half to the scavenger on trial for his boots, "either this fella's thinking up an answer or is too ashamed to tell us what it is he done to get those boots."

"I didn't steal them!"

"Of course you didn't. You said you earned them." Then, suddenly, the herdsman turned away, spat on the ground and just as suddenly wheeled around to face him again. This time his eyes were blazing. He bent his arm to bring his hand up almost even with his shoulder, making a right angle with his forearm at the wrist. His finger shot straight out toward Glen, making jabbing motions at the air just inches from Glen's chest. His voice was much louder now.

"Listen, friend! A man I know must've given his jacket to one of you characters just about the same way somebody gave you those boots. Funny thing is he doesn't remember hiring anybody for anything or giving anything to anybody! All he knew was that he woke up in the hospital with a half busted skull!"

The woman with the cleaver put her chopping tool into an over-sized coat pocket and started moving up the slope toward the three men. She could see that this was more than an average laying down the law. The voices had become louder, the gestures more violent. 'I hope he ain't sassin' those men', she thought. 'Where would we go for wood? This isn't too bad here. We don't have to lug it too far nor leave our place for too long at a time. These young men always have to prove somethin' to somebody! Look at him up there!"

In the short few yards walk toward the men so much flashed through her mind: first her 'old man' running out on her, leaving her to make do for Steve and Rose. Then Rose brought Glen back one day and him all beat to a pulp. "I just want to get him back to where he can fend for himself, mama." That had been almost two years before. Rose worshipped that boy! He had been about nineteen then and Rose only about seventeen. He had earned his keep, well enough, and even a young fellow in his 'teens might pass for an older man around the place from a distance. Well then even the barn that had been home was taken from them then it was the old school bus. He wasn't such a big man when Rose left. He just moped around and he even cried! Finally, he got himself straightened out and revealed his 'surprise': the old sugar shack. Why, he'd even fixed the door and got the windows so that there was glass in every space that needed it; 'made a stove out of an old 55-gallon drum and found enough tin to fix the old stack to the sugarhouse. 'Stevie' likes Glen too, 'thinks the world of him. "That little sugar house is the only real home I've known in two years," she thought. "Oh Glen don't! Please God, don't let him make those men mad enough to run us off!" But if she was worried it never showed on her face as she stopped next to Glen, her breathing hard and heavy, gulping for as much air as she could take.

"We"… she tried to breathe "We… never meant to cause no trouble! Oh…" her hand went to her chest, "I've got to sit down!"

"Here!" The shepherd swung the chainsaw off the stump and onto the ground. "Sit here." He glanced at her. He and the herdsman glanced at each other. Glen the scavenger, the accused boot-thief, put his arm around her and crouched down next to her.

"You okay, Mama? Velma? Are you alright?"

She waved or half waved. "Just short of breath!"

Glen stood up slowly, his hand trailing from her shoulder as his arm came away. He continued to eye her a bit nervously.

"Glennie, what do these men want? What did we do or what do they think we've done?"

"It's the boots, Velma."

"Oh, Glen! I knew that those boots would get us into trouble! I told you not to wear them!"

"Why's that?" The shepherd was asking.

"Because they're too new, too good for folks like us! People are bound to think he stole them," she said.

"And you know that he didn't!", the herdsman snorted.

"He told me he didn't and I'll tell you something. This boy is wild, and cocky and bull-headed, but he hasn't got a mean bone in his body! He's never lied to me and if he says that he didn't steal them, then I believe him!"

A fourth man had come to the little group. The other brush gatherers had been quietly picking up their bundles and slipping away. Two women and a boy were all that were left and they were moving away too. The man was one of the clan, the holders. He carried a rifle, but other than that it looked as if his clothing had come from the same source as that worn by the other two: all three men had small, trim beards, Jeans, boots, plaid shirts and leather vests. All three wore broad-brimmed hats with a sprig of plant issuing forth from out of the hat band. This was the plant badge: a symbol of coming down from druid times of the clansman, clan law and a religion centered around nature. The fourth man had come to help the others. He too was an animal husbandman, a herder. He was, like his friends, a hunter as well. He spoke or called, just under his breath to the herdsman.

"Magnus!" Then the herdsman motioned to him with

his head to come over to them.

"What's going on? Were they stealing wood?"

"Oh it's a long story," Magnus the herdsman said. "The fact of the matter is… we're more concerned about the boots that fella's wearing than anything else."

"What?"

"His boots." The herdsman pointed to his own leather lace ups then jerked his thumb over his shoulder toward the young scavenger.

The hunter craned his neck and raised his head up to see past the herdsman to the figure of Glen Olsen.

"Holy Mother!", he exclaimed. "Where'd he get *them*?"

"I don't know but I'll tell you one thing, 'Laddie-buck'! If those boots are what the well- dressed young brush hog is wearing these days, I'm busting my tail bone for nothin'!"

"Well, Hell! All you have to do is go steal a pair a' boots and you've got the best of both worlds: his and yours. That's where he got them! Where else is somebody like that going to get that kind of gear?"

"Well, anyway," Magnus went on, "I don't know what the Captain over there is going to do, but he'll have to do *something*! They're living right over there, right on the boundary of Ardachy as it is!"

The woman, Velma was crying, the young man beside her with his hand on her shoulder, looking off into the woods. The 'Captain', the shepherd, was speaking in a low voice to the two of them:

"Someday the world will be different, but as it stands

now, things are just too risky, too shaky. You two are living at the fringe of my holding and what I hold is for many, many people. We can't have anyone crowding us and if it looks like a man who might have been stealing things can move in on us, other people might feel tempted to test us in other ways. There are people who follow me, trust me to do what's right for them". He paused for a short space of time, looked around and towards the tree tops, squinted once or twice, then went on: "You'll have to move on, find another place to live. I will be fair. I'll give you until the day after tomorrow….." He was interrupted by the woman, who slid off of the tree trunk onto all fours on the ground. The other men turned to look at the pitiful woman in an astonishment colored with a sense of sadness. The Captain's hand shot out to take hold of her arm, but stopped before making contact with her. Glen sank to his knees beside her with his arm around her, his head down and next to hers, whispering to her, trying to calm her. Her back shook and shook like some great comical, malfunctioning machine, but no one present could even think of smiling at such a sight.

Somewhere from beneath this ragged bundle on the ground a little, choking voice came forth to meet the cold air:

"Oh, Mister, Mister!...you just don't know! You just can't know! I know that you hate us, but you can't hate us as much as that!" She rocked back and forth, shaking with terrible, choking, sobbing sounds. The men stood there, filled with pity, but not knowing what to do.

"Velma?", Glen half crooned to her. "Mama? Com'on.

Let's go home, Mama…"

She stopped crying then, lifted her head and looked at him Her face was still wet, her eyes red, and her nose had begun to run. She wiped her nose with the end of her head scarf. She looked around as if she were taking it all in for the first time. "Yes", she said absently, "Home. For another twenty four hours we have a home".

The two of them, Glen supporting the weary and nearly broken Velma, turned without further word or plea, without the slightest sign of anger, and began to move away. Once again their eyes took into them the dull, almost unseeing look of so many of the gatherers. It has been said that the body can enter into something of a suspension once it has been subjected to too much pain. So too, the human spirit retreats into some similar escape. If it is true that our eyes are 'mirrors of our souls', then the eyes of the 'gatherers' may well be forgiven the dullness, the appearance of emptiness; perhaps the spirit behind them being not 'at home', but travelling somewhere else and in a happier time. Such an inner spirit may indeed have packed up and left the body. After all, ancient annals of the Gael tell of the Tuatha De Danaan, those half-otherworld beings who once inhabited Eireann. When finally they had been subdued by the Sons of Mil they betook themselves to the inner-world of the land itself, becoming the "Sithe", the nature spirits of that land. Since they had ceased to be the proprietors of the land, they became one with that land: always there, rarely seen, but often 'felt' by a sensitive man or woman. The folk who have peopled those Celtic lands, not Eire alone, but

Scotland, Wales, the Isle of Man, Cornwall and Brittany, have come to live with and understand such concepts. Even the language of the Celt places emphasis on 'being' and the condition, rather than the act. The idea of 'possession' is hard to verbalize. This is what finally comes upon a people when they have been forced to come to grips, repeatedly, with the reality of existence. "To be a Gael is to never be far from tears", and whether the tears be born of sorrow or from an almost impossible glimpse of something truly beautiful, it doesn't really matter, for at such times we know that we are truly alive!

The men of the land quietly gathered up their tools. "Time for lunch". Magnus the herdsman and the hunter Erc stole glances at one another and then, at almost the same time looked toward the Captain and the shepherd, who had picked up the chain saw, for he was staring at the ground. Without setting the saw down, he reached over and picked something up.

"What did you find?", Erc asked him

"Oh, nothing really", he replied. "That old woman must've dropped her cleaver". He wrapped the cleaver in a piece of rag, laid it on the top shelf of his small, metal tool box, then snapped the lid shut. The men began to retrieve and put onto themselves their jackets. They would need them now that they weren't to be hard at work.

"Damned scavengers!", the Captain muttered, "They've brought this on themselves!"

The men started walking slowly together, silently, up towards the main house.

CHAPTER 2

PART 3

An abandoned Sugar Shack can be made into a fairly decent shelter with a bit of work and some imagination. Of course, it is necessary to change the roof structure, for it would impossible to retain any heat with the long roof vent. The vent was, after all, made to let out steam when boiling maple sap to syrup. At such a time, no one worried about keeping the heat inside the building. It takes about forty gallons of sap to produce one gallon of syrup. The process requires a roaring fire and with that kind of requirement, a cord of wood does not last very long at all.

When the Sugar Shack had been left unused and left to fall back into the earth, the metal chimney stack had been taken down and put inside. There were also inside two large, square sap pans and a quantity of metal sap buckets, also a caved in 'arch' made of fire-bricks and some iron grates when Glen had first found the building. For over two weeks,

Glen had disappeared for a few hours of each day. He had been glad to have something extra to occupy his time. It was far better than entertaining all of the bitterness and hurt which had been brought on by Rose's departure. He had begun by trying tp prop up the badly sagging roof, but lacking the tools, such an endeavor proved to be quite difficult. He decided to begin by removing the vent-roof which covered an eight foot long hole in the peak of the building's roof and which rose to a heighth of about two feet above the ridge. He had managed to pry some of it away by use of some of the stronger ironwood poles which he had found here and there in the woods by the creek. He almost wept for joy when, much to his surprise, an old hatchet fell out of the beam-work. Someone years before had slid it up onto the plate which supported one side of the roof. It was one of those hatchets which had a head which, being sharpened to an axe-like shape on one side, had also a flat, hammer-like quality at the other. The sharp end was also in pretty good shape. His work went well after that. He had been able to cut some poles, replace some broken struts, and by using the vent boards and shingles from the roof, he had been able to seal the roof to the peak on both sides, thus making a covering which would shed completely rain water and snow. An old oil drum from an abandoned farm made into a fair stove, although he regretted having to use the sharp corners of his hatchet to cut a door and a pipe hole in the metal of the drum. He mounted some of the sap pans on one of the walls to make a mouse and rat-proof storage area. He built some shelves from some extra boards which he had found. It had been easy to build a fairly decent hearth area for the stove with the fire-brick and the metal stack needed less in the way of repair than he had originally estimated. When at last the work was done, he inspected the building over and over, thought of things which could be added. Before he knew it, the night had fallen, so he stayed there through the night.

It was not all that cold, but it was indeed cold. He lit a fire and sat by the burning wood, gazing into the flames and listening to the crackling wood as it was consumed. His mind went back to Hank and what he had told him of his own life as a kid on a farm:

"We used to milk the cows by hand", Hank had told him. "I guess that we raised most of what we ate, right there on that farm. I remember going out in the morning to the stable, before getting washed up for school. I would sometimes be still waking up, yawning and getting into the day. I would sometimes put my forehead to the side of a cow, still waking up as I washed her udder and sitting on the three-legged stool, start to pull on her teats, milking her. It was a different time, Glennie. I guess that it was a hard life, but if it was hard, we didn't really know it at the time. There was something really good about it: simple, plain, but good. We would skim off the cream of the milk we took up to the house and when we had enough, we'd put it into a churn and dash the cream until we felt the hard lumps of butter forming. Sometimes it came fairly quickly, that cream to butter. Sometimes it would take a while. It could sometimes tax our patience, but we'd keep on dashing that plunger into the churn with its sour cream. We sometimes used an old rhyme, or whatever you might want to call it:

"Come butter come. Come butter come, Peter waiting at the gate, Waiting for a butter cake, Come, butter, come"

"They were good times, Glennie. We worked hard, but oh!, what a wonderful life it was! That's all gone now".

Glen thought about that, about Hank and the scenes from Hank's own childhood which he would pour forth. He wasn't all that sure that he would want to return to such a way of life, but suddenly the thought came upon him: "We have so much less than even that now! Where did this older America go? When did it go? Didn't anyone even notice that it was slipping away?"

The very first thing in the morning, Glen headed back to the old school bus to rejoin Velma and Steve. He was very anxious to share the surprise of the new dwelling which he had brought into being with the two of them. He ran up the last slope to where the overgrown field met the small grove of trees, the place where the old bus, half sunk into mud, was listing slightly to one side, like a war-damaged ship, waiting to return to the earth. No one was there!

He sat beside the bus for a while, his mind racing from one horror to another. He blamed himself for having left them alone. He thought of the bad types of people who wandered about, taking from others; people less capable of defending themselves. He wondered if perhaps Velma and Steve had been run off, maybe even killed. Still, he thought, no one would have removed their dead bodies! Just to be sure, he looked around again. He went into the woodlot a short distance, circled around and came out. No bodies. They must have been run off. Maybe one of those "citizens' Committees" had come to throw a scare into them. Blaming himself again and again, he froze at the sound of a high-pitched screaming sound. No! It wasn't a scream, not a scream of terror anyway. It was old Millie Pike, running towards him across the clearing with her skinny old arms and legs flailing away like a paper in the wind. She hadn't been screaming, but just calling to him. Millie was a rural version of a city "bag lady", but instead of shopping bags, she used old gunny-sacks, old feed bags. She would cut a hole through both sides of a feed bag when it was laid flat and it was in that way that she could slip her head and one arm and shoulder through the opening, leaving the bottom half of the sack for storage. She normally wore two of them: one on each side of her body and it made quite a picture: a skinny old lady with two big loads, one on each side of her, with her skinny legs and flapping arms. She had something of the look of an old and scrawny White Leghorn hen. To complete her costume, she always wore a crocheted red-orange cap with a chin-strap, winter and summer and her long, white hair was left to fly in every possible direction. As she ran up to him, she kept making her loud-pitched, near screaming attention-getting sounds, which did not come forth so much as "Yoo-Hoo", but rather something like "Eeee'ooo".

The very sight of this flapping apparition running across the landscape in the daytime or the night would surely be enough to scare off even the meanest thief! Anyway, it wasn't night, and Glen knew her to be simply a stubborn but gentle old lady who simply did not want to be tied to any place at any time. She ran up to him, not really stopping, but as if she meant to pause just long enough to say a few words before resuming her race against time and fate.

"Velma ain't here!", the hen-voice said. She waved a boney hand towards the valley and its village. "She an' Stevie went to get their stores from the government truck! The government truck comes today! I'll bet that you forgot that!"

The Government Truck! The Government Truck was the last vestige of and old social services program. In fact, it was an attempt on the part of politicians to pretend that someone, somewhere, was still in control of things. About once a week, sometimes only twice a month, a large van would pull into some designated area: in one village a parking lot of a church,; in another town it could be near the local fire hall or school. Uniformed men, three of four of them, would accompany the main vehicle and a small check-point would be established: a table would be set up at which some official with a list of people who were not growing their own food. Next to the table, supported by portable posts, would be some sectioning off by use of some long ropes. People would form a line beside the rope, being careful not to pass the post nearest the checking table until a green light was flashed on. Anyone who neglected to wait for the green light and passed by the post would be sent back to the end of the line, if not totally refused any service at all. Once a person had submitted a card for food, the card was punched in one of the appropriate spaces around the card. He or she would be given a share of each item being distributed that day: cornmeal, flour, rice, pasta, a block of processed cheese, cooking oil, a carton or two of powdered milk and sometimes even a can or two of canned meat. Rarely there would be some cartons of a concentrated orange juice or cider, but these were always bitter, watery and no one looked forward to getting either of them. Often water-purifying tablets were dispensed, since so many people were taking water from creeks. People were very careful to not cause any problems. The personnel in charge did not "suffer fools gladly" and the least provocation would serve as an excuse to simply pack up and drive the van away. After receipt of the allotment, a recipient would have a stamp inked on the back of the right hand with a second stamp in the middle of the forehead.

There was little else that people could do. If anyone who was 'signed up' for the program tried to grow or raise anything on his own, the card would be taken away and he or she would be thenceforth "ineligible". It was almost as if someone in a high office had actually wanted to keep the citizenry dependent upon the government. Anyone who wished to 'break loose' from the system had to be very, very certain that he could provide for himself from then on, for the new found 'freedom' might end up becoming a ticket to starvation. Some people did manage to find some place to raise some food, or someone who needed help: someone who might provide a place to live and a small wage, perhaps even their own garden plot. For many, it remained an impossible dream and the majority of the people were reluctant to lose whatever advantages the government might offer. It had not gone unnoticed that the packages and boxes had been getting smaller, yet people seemed to reckon that it was better than nothing at all.

Glen had been thinking of all of this and his train of thought broke as he looked over to the empty sack left on the table for him. "My share! The Stores!" He thought of grabbing up the bag and heading down through the woodlot towards the town and the government van, but realized that by the time he got there it would be too late. Thinking that it would be worth a try, he snatched up the sack and headed out the door and into the old apple orchard. He didn't get very far at all when he met Velma and Steve walking towards him. Sure enough, they had been down to the government truck. Velma was puffing her way up a steep rise, Steve just behind her, carrying both of their bundles. He had taken the two shares, rolled them into a blanket and having secured both ends of the blanket roll with some twine, he had slung the load onto his back. When they came face to face with him, Velma did not try to disguise her anger.

"Must be nice!", she began,:Just sittin' up here! You're too late now! What are you planning to do for food this next week? You know that you have to pick up your own stores! They wouldn't dream of giving any of your allotment to anyone else!"

"Velma, I forgot about what day this is. I don't know what got into me! Even after Millie Pike told me where you'd gone, I just hung around here. I'm really sorry ", Glen said in the way of an apology.

"Yes, Glen, you should have. We haven't got enough to see us through without your share. Well, the truck will be long gone by now. No use crying over spilt milk, I guess!", She replied.

"I'll snare us something, Velma", Glen said to her, "I'll find a way to make up for it, for I don't want to live off of you and Steve".

Velma reached out and put her hand on his shoulder and looked into his eyes with a concerned, searching, yet loving expression.

"Glen", she said to him, "We're a family now and you know that you are more than welcome to a part of whatever we have. Besides, you always have managed to more than pay your way". Removing her hand and drawing Steve in to her. He had been standing by somewhat awkwardly. "Steve feels that way too, don't you, Honey?"

"Sure, Ma", he answered. "Glen's the only brother I got." Then, with a mischievous look towards Glen he went on:" Even if he is so stinkin' mean and nasty!"

Velma drew the two of them close to her and pulled their heads towards her own, one on each side of her. She then announced: "The three of us can take on the world, boys!"

"Jeez!", Steve said with feigned wonder," I thought that that is what we've been doin' all along!"

It had been difficult to get Velma to go to the sugar shack without telling her the reason and thus spoiling the surprise. The trip to the government truck had been all that she had felt to be up to that day. Glen and Steve went out alone that afternoon to gather some wood: some wind-fall not too far away. Glen had decided to take Steve to their new dwelling and share the surprise with him at least. He reckoned that they would somehow get Velma to go the next day without telling her the reason for a walk through the trees. He was able to keep Steve quiet about it, although Steve did raise the question of how far they would have to go from the Sugar shack to get wood, whereas there was quite a bit to be found in the woodlot near the old school bus. He had become pretty sullen, in fact, by the time that they reached the shack, but his delight upon seeing the place and what Glen had managed to do was worth the extra "hassle' to Glen, once Steve accepted the fact that they were not moving into a space which had been already claimed by someone else. Glen was not all that certain that he wanted to go through all of this again with Velma, but Steve was as eager to see his mother so surprised and delighted as he had been. The next morning they found themselves to be bringing a very dour, and grumbling "Mama" across the marshy ground, down through the tall weeds and briars, through the grove of Locust and Ash trees, to the thorn apples and untended fruit trees which had been growing wild for years. Once again, there had been the apprehension and doubt, followed by complete joy on Velma's part. Glen and Steve had left Velma to gather some dead apple limbs and start a fire, while the two young fellows went back to the old school bus to bring anything worth having and of course, the food. This had always been stashed in a hollow tree not far from the bus which they had named "the cupboard". It had taken them three trips back and forth, trying each time to slip away unseen by anyone.

That had been just over three months ago when Glen had missed the government hand-outs after just having completed his work on the cabin. It had been a wonderful three months for them. Tonight, this night, was to be the last night that they could stay there. The events of the day, the episode concerning his boots and those who held the land all seemed unreal somehow. They had even celebrated Christmas here and had even had a "Christmas tree": a pine sapling which they had decorated with bits and pieces of anything bright or shiny. That had been Velma's surprise to the "boys". Now, this night, too tired and heartsick to move, she simply sat off to one side, her pan of bean soup untouched. Steve had even found some wild leeks and cut them up, which had added some extra flavor to the soup, but Velma hadn't touched her food.

After the supper things had been washed up, Glen silently watched Steve as he was working on a small carving. He was going to stitch up a leather bag, but he somehow could not shake the heavy mood, the regret and the sense of loss which hung over him. Steve would run his thumb along the wood in his hand, then follow it with another cut from his knife, almost as if the thumb acted as an advance scout for each cut into the wood. Glen had showed him all that he had learned from Hank. Steve had taken to whittling and carving like the proverbial "Duck to water" It was clear that he had a natural aptitude for working with wood; something really rather special. In fact, Glen felt that where wood was concerned, Steve had already gone on ahead of him. "The kid has a real gift for carving!", Glen thought, "Who knows? When things return to normal, if they ever do, Steve might very well be able to sell some of his carvings". Sometimes Steve would take a piece of paper bag or some such thing and draw out a design with a piece of charred wood from the fire. The designs were good, full of imagination. As far as his drawings of trees, rocks, and other natural forms were quite fine, almost beyond belief. Glen would smile to himself when Steve was drawing, for the boy would really get into his work, his eyebrows and mouth often working as he worked with the charcoal.

Glen tried to avoid looking at Velma. He was embarrassed and heart-sick at the misfortune that he had brought upon these, his only friends, his 'family'. He wanted desperately to go back in time, to erase the whole day, or at least go back to the time before telling those men where it was that the three of them were living. "How could everything be so good, so bright and promising one minute, and so totally lost a few minutes later?", he asked himself. "I don't know much about God, but He must be something else: a real Rip-snorter! Well, God, I hope that this has all been funny to *you*, because it hasn't been all that bright and rosy for *us*!" He mentally snorted at himself:" Listen to me! Giving God a piece of my mind!"

Glen did look over at Velma, however. He watched her as she sat there, all alone with her thoughts....or was she thinking of anything at all? In a way, it almost appeared as if she were just 'suspended' somehow, somewhere else perhaps, numb to the here and now; beyond feeling or caring. Glen wondered at that moment how old Velma would be. He thought, "Rose is about 18 now and Velma was about eighteen or nineteen when she was married.... What!? She's only about thirty-eight years old! Can't be! She has to be older than that!" He could see that she must have been quite pretty when she was young. She still had a sweet, rather pretty face, nice eyes: soft, grey-green. Her hair had some gray, but it was still showing itself as mainly a light brown color. His eyes went to her hands: the limp, motionless hands in her lap. Her hands! They were an old lady's hands: heavy and thick. Older farm women, women who have worked hard all of their lives have hands like that...and there isn't anything wrong with that at all. In fact it seems to lend to them an aura of strength and integrity. Such are the hands perhaps, of Medieval women, perhaps pioneer women. Such people whose lives were filled with doing for others day in and day out: tasks that are done simply because they need doing. Hank said that a man would move Heaven and earth for a warm meal, some clean clothes and some praise. A man has to have some kind of recognition, some evidence too of his achievements. Women, on the other hand have worked for centuries at countless tasks which were often undone as soon as they were accomplished, often with not the slightest expectation of thanks or praise; no milestones to mark their achievements along the way. Hank had said that in this way women are stronger than men because of woman's ability to endure, to hide her disappointments and move on in the face of silence. "Still", Glen thought, looking at Velma's hands again, "those hands are too old for a thirty-eight year old woman!".

It was at that moment that Glen came to a decision. He made it and as soon as he had reached that resolve, he promised himself to see it through, no matter what might happen. He felt the fear, the numbing, the chill and the tingling, almost electric, shock enveloping his body. He felt it in his arms and in his legs, even up to his groin.

"I will go to that 'Captain', that landholder, shepherd-guy, whoever he is. I will tell him to blame me. To sue me before a court as a trespasser, even jail me or whatever he wants to do, but to leave Velma and Stevie alone. I'll even give him the damned boots if that's what he wants, but to leave Velma and Stevie alone!"

He felt good that he had come to a decision. At the bottom of it there was a glint of hope. Glen stood up and stretched as hard as he could, snapping back when he suddenly felt a stabbing pain in his neck, in the base of his skull. There was a knot, a thudding pain which almost caused him to pass out. With that, a fear, a reminder of his mortality, his comparative impotence returned to him. "They won't believe me. I won't get near the place before I am stopped, by somebody or other and get accused of stealing something". He rubbed the back of his neck and felt the pain subside, but the fear was still there: deep within him. That fear did not remove itself easily, by any means. "Well", he thought within himself, "I have to do this! I have to do it right away, before I get too scared to see it through. That way, at least Velma and Steve can stay. I'll go up there first thing in the morning!" He paused and thought again: a mental "double-take". "No! I have to go up there now! This very night!. Right now!"

Steve appeared to be very engrossed, absorbed, by his carving, yet Glen knew that there was not very much which was escaping Steve's notice.

"Take care of Ma, Steve", Glen said. "I'm going out for a while."

Steve didn't look up, his eyes intent upon the carving in his hand by his lap. He nodded with his head and said, "Yeah, okay Glen. But, don't do anything dumb, okay?"

Glen put his hand on Steve's shoulder, then tasseled his hair. The light from the fire and the oil lantern made a hazy glow, an outline of golden fuzz, a halo almost, around the boy's head. Quickly, Glen turned and with a glance towards

Velma, he opened the door.

"I'll be back directly, Velma", he said

Velma absently nodded her head. Glen walked out, into the darkness of the night-time forest; a still night, and moving through the trees with only the mouth-music of the creek, he walked towards the silence and the holding which they called "Ardachaidh": The High Field.

CHAPTER 3

PART 3

Glen was met by the Co-Arb of Cowall. Of course, he did not know that he was meeting a Co-Arb and had probably only heard the very term a few times in his life. Had it not been for a very unusual background, it is doubtful that he would have ever heard the word at all. At the moment, all he knew was that as he had been approaching the main house, taking a short-cut across the meadow just to the north of the out-buildings of the farmstead, he had practically run into a solitary figure standing almost in the middle of that pasture-land.At first, he had had a chilling feeling, coupled with a heaviness within himself; as if a great lump of dough was falling to the very bottom of his stomach, a sense of terror that he had come upon some kind of "look-out", a retainer or a family member of the proprietor of the land. For a second or two, he half expected to be shot at, or even to see a club winging through the air towards his head. The lonely figure simply and quite calmly turned to look at him as if someone had asked him a question, or was about to ask him a question. The dark figure spoke to him:

"It is going to be cold tonight".

"It's already getting that way", Glen replied. He felt a bit uneasy, but somewhat relieved that he had been addressed, spoken to, rather than shot at.

The dark figure made no move towards him, continuing to occupy the same spot as if he had been cemented to it in some way. The moon was rising behind him, making it very difficult for him to make out any facial features. In fact, the upper part of the man's body appeared silhouetted against the light of the unusually large, rose-colored moon, almost as if the human form before him figured as a part of a religious painting or perhaps a stage set. To Glen at the time there was something eerie about the scene; either eerie or terribly mystical and in the face of this lone figure in the field, he felt himself to be diminished, somehow having become a fourteen –year-old again, for it was the feelings of his early teens which he felt to be returning to him, washing over him in an instant in time and space. Nor was it a warm wave of the past either, but rather one of cold, carrying like flotsam on the tide of time: helpless feelings of youth which he had thought himself to have forgotten. Like the old Beatles' lyrics: "alone again, naturally….". In that instant, the feelings of the not too distant past returned to him: the knot in the stomach, fear, helplessness, and above all else the loneliness, anger and that returning sense of smallness, washing over him and drenching him to the very soul. Even so, he chose that moment to speak, if for no other reason than the need to say or do something, other than to simply and stupidly stand there.

"The moon is really big tonight. Huge!", Glen said

"Yes", the silhouette replied as if the statement had been made already, earlier, his response almost overlapping Ron's remark. "It is the Spring Moon! It usually looms up large and reddish, just as it is tonight, but not always." As an afterthought the Co-Arb added, "There are those years too, when because of rain or clouds we do not see it at all, but of course, it is still there. The fact that we cannot see it does not mean that it is not there, does it ?"

The figure had moved away from its moon aura or halo and now that the face of the Co-Arb was turned towards the light, Ron could easily see the face of a mortal man. It was a kind face and in it, a rather remarkable beauty or clarity to be seen there; an outward appearance of great dignity, but with it a sense of calm and patience. As the two men approached one another, Glen could see a darkly handsome, older man , the eyes of whom were remarkable in their gentleness; dark pools of dark memories and understandings. There was a sadness about the face and eyes, yet there was also present the warmth of an almost parental smile. Dark brown, full hair swept back along the sides of his head, the streaks of gray of which picked up the reflected moonlight, as did the silvery slivers of light in a closely cropped beard. Ron found himself thinking that it would be difficult to judge the age of this man, for although the features were not terribly wrinkled or old, the signs of patience, acceptance and peace which were inscribed upon that tablet of a man's life could only have come to one who had known many years of self discipline and concern for others, perhaps even personal sacrifice and suffering. What Glen found to be difficult to fathom was the hint of an almost child-like trust and a willingness to meet new people. Of course, all of this had been taken in very quickly by Glen, for he did not wish to be seen as one who was staring, despite a sense that this lone figure did not expect anything other than to be assessed, nor was he objecting to the scrutiny in the least. Indeed, Glen detected what he thought to be a very buried amusement in the Co-Arb. What also came as something of a surprise to him was the realization that he had been, so carefully, somewhat clinically, taking mental notes of another human being, or that he should even have cared to do so to such an extent. There was in fact, a degree of pride inside of himself to discover that he had been effecting a thorough inspection, perhaps even a bit surprised that he had even cared to do so! As far as his last statement had been concerned, the Co-Arb seemed neither to expect a response or to really care that much to have one forthcoming., as he went on:

"The Spring Moon is very important to the men who will begin the duties connected with lambing and calving. By custom, very few of them would think of such things before this time and its lunar sign".

"Do you assist with that?", Glen asked.

"No, not anymore, although I did at one time".

"You probably got tired of it or maybe you just have other, important things to do ". Glen felt a bit embarrassed, realizing how out-spoken he had been while addressing someone who belonged here, was rooted here, when, after all, he himself was not. Here he was, an "interloper" on his way even now to beg permission simply to remain and live in a shack, even at the edge of these lands.

The Co-Arb turned his face towards Glen, but there was no hint of any wounded pride or whatever, nor was there any indication that any trespass had been made or acknowledged In fact, the eyes of the monk-figure looked to be, appeared to be, thoughtful and focused on nothing in the immediate vicinity, nor the near-by forest, or even the hills beyond, yet he did appear to be deeply thinking of something. His response to Glen betrayed an attempt to draw himself away from another, deeper, thought and back to the courtesy of the 'small talk' at hand:

"Yes, ….yes, there are and there were other things which have somehow presented themselves to be of greater importance."

For a full minute or even more than a minute, only the silence of the night lay upon the two figures in the meadow: the Co-Arb whose mind had become a guest house of forest things, star music and the peaceful night surrounding them, and Glenn who was feeling no great anxiety in this man's presence, but rather the great quiet which lay on the land and this night of the Vernal, or Spring Moon. Even so, with a kind, slow and gentle manner, almost as one would wake someone from a deep sleep so as not to give alarm, the dark, older man spoke to Glenn as if to remind him of a detail which was not to be over-looked, but for which there was no over-riding concern:

"You'll be on your way to the Main House. It might be as well to go now and get this business of yours over and done with."

"Yes", Glen replied simply. "I can't imagine that they'll be too happy to see me anyway. I wish I knew what to expect from the owner, 'proprietor'. Or whoever he is!"

"The Owner". The Co-Arb repeated the words as if he too were making a statement. He looked down towards the earth and poked at a clod of some kind with what appeared to be a long walking stick, topped as it was with a piece of deer antler. He said, "Alisdair is not a bad man, nor even a hard man, but his is a great responsibility, and he takes that responsibility very, very seriously. After all, he holds this land in trust for the people whom he leads; the people who 'belong' to this bit of land. I am certain that he does not think so much of being the owner of this land, but rather as one who, we might even say, is owned by this land. If he were to manage things badly, the loss of cropland and animals would not only be his loss alone, but the loss of a great many people other than himself, and their many families, other than his own, would suffer. Many people who presently have homes and some status would be out on the road; landless and without hope."

"Like a Gleaner!", Glen said in a voice just above a whisper with a strong hint of sarcasm.

"Yes! Like a Gleaner, if such a person were even that fortunate! It could be much worse. Gleaners aren't as bad off as some others. In fact, we have had the odd Gleaner accepted into our group and such person has often taken on a position of responsibility, respect and trust."

"But what would this Alisdair know of such things?", Glen asked. "He is a 'Proprietor' of the land, a man with followers and a pedigree as long as his arm, going all the way back to the Lord God Almighty!"

At this point, the Culdee, Colm, raised his head, and it fell far back. A slow sound like a cry began to rise and come forth from deep within the man: a very deep laugh, so deep, in fact that it seemed to Glen that it was causing the man pain and depriving him of a chance to catch his breath! He then bowed forward so that his head faced the ground before him. He straightened slowly, holding his hand over his face, wiping his eyes with his thumb and forefinger simultaneously. His shoulders still shaking, he said:

"You had better go to the main house now. The chieftain will be wondering what happened to you if he is expecting you"

"Oh, he isn't expecting me, at all!", Glen stated quite simply.

"You're not expected?" The face before Ron was serious now. In fact, an expression came across the face and in the eyes of the Co-Arb which conveyed something in the way of a warning. Not even a trace of the man's earlier humor remained. He went on: "You plan to simply walk up, past that line of trees there, and on to the main house and knock on the door?"

Glen threw his head back, facing skyward, rolling his eyes upward as well, thinking "Here we go again! 'Time to get knocked back into my proper place! A minute ago a man was talking to me as if I might be a human being. Now the truth is out: I have been discovered to be some kind of germ or something! "Not expected", which translates to: I might get my ass shot off!"

"You're pretty naïve.", the Co-Arb was saying

"Which means....?"

"In this case, 'naïve' might mean something like your not knowing how the world really is." The Culdee turned himself and pointed to the line of trees ahead of them towards the south, at the edge of the meadow. "Now, of course you see that line of trees. What else do you see there?"

"I see a line of trees. Just some trees!", Glen answered. He tucked his thumbs into his belt loops and cocked his head to one side. His hood from his sweatshirt fell back and he could feel the faintest trace of cold wind lift up his hair and let it fall. Glen felt awkward, not at all good about himself. He knew that he looked tattered, picked over. He felt that even his ragged shirt beneath his sweatshirt, and even his torn, hidden away undershorts were all prominently on display. These settled people knew, they could weigh a guy, X-ray him; smell and taste his poverty, his lack of rootedness when he did not measure up. Still, he felt the need to stand his ground, to at least show some defiance.

"Some trees.", the CoArb repeated. "And in those trees, my dear young man, are eyes and behind those eyes, men with guns. They're watching us even now!"

Glen turned his head back towards the line of trees again, immediately regretting the too sudden movement. He looked back to the CoArb, still allowing his eyes to move to that edge of the pastureland.

"Hell!, he said. Why don't they just pick me off right now and get 'er done?" Glen's rising anger and frustration was becoming very obvious. His wounded pride left him pretty incapable of hiding his sense of helplessness.

"No, they wouldn't do that" Colm said. "Not while I am in this meadow and on this night. Still, I can almost guarantee that you would not get as far as the lawns of the main house before being turned back. You would at least be stopped, questioned, and perhaps even badly treated. When people are afraid of outsiders they do not always act well ".

"Wonderful!", Glen muttered.

"Is that so hard for you to understand?" The Co-Arb asked him. "Wouldn't you, given the dangers of the time in which we live, be careful, perhaps even a bit fearful, of allowing people who are unknown to you to approach your dwelling?"

The CoArb looked at Glen's face and did not shift his gaze until he had engaged his eyes and the two men looked into the eyes of one another. He waited for an answer, although he probably did not expect a reply to his question at all. Glen felt a certain surprise at his detecting in the face of the CoArb a look of concern, a very genuine concern for humanity in this man's eyes. The intensity he saw was a not only surprising but also unsettling and he felt uneasy., for he had not known people to be caring, as a rule, nor did they ever appear to assume any responsibility for the actions and opinions of others in this way.

"All I want is a chance to speak with the proprietor, this Mr. Mac Alisdair", Ron said.

"Alisdair". Colm corrected.

"Right!! MacAlisdair. Mr.Alisdair! Isn't that what I said?"

"His name is Alisdair, not Mr. Alisdair. Alisdair is who he is, but it is not his surname! He is 'The MacAllisdair' or even 'Ardachy', which is the name of the land, but never would he be called Mister MacAllisdair!"

"This is pretty confusing!"

"Yes, isn't it? Still, I wouldn't worry about it if I were you." Once again, a gentle, absent-minded smile crossed the CoArb's face, for he did appear to be thinking of something else or remembering something as he spoke. In a sudden movement, quite full of the presence of the moment, he drew his walking stick to his side with a strong left hand and motioning with his right hand, palm turned upward, in the general direction of the trees and that house which lay somewhere beyond them, he said, "I'll walk there with you", and with a sly note of humor he added as an afterthought, "Surely, one of the two of us has a chance of reaching the house without being gunned down!"

The Two men began to move across the pastureland toward the line of trees, their paces being measured, every other one, by the arcs traced forward and back by the stick which the CoArb carried. Glen noticed how smooth the older man's movements were and how steady and unhurried his gait was for an older fellow. From time to time, he glanced sideways at this man who now served as his escort, and saw there a fine profile of a face accustomed to hard work and severe weather. There was a gentle beauty about the face despite the marks of years and climate and Glen established in his mind that this man beside him must at one time have been a very handsome young fellow, Colm's mouth seemed to naturally approach smiling without actually doing so. Glen's furtive glances and observations also took in his companion's clothing and mode of dress: soft boots with no soles, laced up the front, moving quietly over earth that had become just a bit hard from the cold temperature of that night. Glen could not determine the length, which is to say the height of the boots, for they disappeared beneath a long black coat-like garment which reached to about mid-way down the calf of the man's legs. The coat-like garment was fastened about the middle with a leather belt, quite simple in design, having only a square brass buckle. Hanging on the Culdee's chest Glen saw a cross of dark metal or bone which bounced from side to side of the man as he walked along. Glen was somewhat hypnotized by the bouncing, swinging movement and could not resist stealing several glances. When he stumbled over a small clump of some kind on the ground, he shot a glance sideways to meet the eyes of the CoArb's smile, his eyes crinkled with amusement. At the time when they reached the tree line, he felt that they were indeed being watched, but could not see a single part of any form of a man anywhere.

"A Good Evening to you, and God's Blessings!", the CoArb said to the trees.

"And also to you!", A voice answered from out of one of them. Glen did his best to hide his surprise, but knew full well that he had failed in this endeavor.

Walking along some kind of driveway or road now, they soon came to a gate in a stone wall, which after having entered into an enclosure, turned into a stone path to what had to be the back of the Main House of Ardachy. Other buildings formed a sort of quadrangle of green lawn in their midst and there was some low shrubbery, somewhat bare, on this northern side of the house. Colm moved along with a familiarity which did seem to be a bit strange to Glen, for he did not stop to knock upon the door, but simply lifted the latch and walked on into an entryway. Turning to Glen, who expected to be left waiting outside, he said, "Come in! Come in! Let's not try to heat the entire out-of-doors!" Another door was opened and light streamed out, along with the wonderful aroma of baking and cooking, of wood-fires and candles. Once again, Glen was prepared to wait, and again his guide bade him to enter, this time actually stepping to one side and indicating that Glen was meant to precede him into the room, the kitchen of the main house.

As he entered the kitchen, the first thing that his eyes took in was a large corner fireplace, with a cheerful, mass of brightly flaming logs; a friendly fire, not the too active, leaping fire which can become hostile and spend its energies trying to escape up the flue and start a chimney fire. Glen remembered someone saying once that people do not know how to think to a fire anymore, or to deer or a tree or a plant, for that matter. This fire had occupied a place of honor for a very long time, its glint at each kindling being blown into a soft flame with a prayer each morning, and its being bedded down each night with a "smooring" blessing. Glen had heard of the old Celtic way of things, and figured that he had come face to face with its continuum, here in the 21st century. The room was filled with the warmth and contentment of a way of life, something which cannot be measured or weighed, only felt and appreciated. He was told to stand by the fire, which he did quite readily, extending his hands towards the flames in man's age-old, timeless homage to fire. He realized than he had not noticed that the evening had become quite chilly.

The Culdee moved across the room towards a wood stove, speaking in low tones to a young, dark-haired woman who was washing some plates and glasses nearby. At a sturdy wooden table a young man sat, enjoying a mug of some steaming beverage. The young man looked up at Glen in the half-challenging, half appraising manner which men seem to maintain throughout all ages, then he looked back to Colm. A low greeting was exchanged and nothing more. The young woman handed the CoArb two mugs which he took from her and placed on a sideboard. He then poured a bit of spirit into each mug, added a spoonful of something or other to each mug, before taking a tea kettle from the stove and filling each with hot water. He handed one of the steaming mugs to Glen, then pulled out a chair. Motioning to the chair, he half invited, half ordered Glen: "Sit!", and that is all he said. The young woman took a large tray of glassware and left the room, the door which she opened let in the sound of several voices and some music being played in the background. As the door closed behind her, the stillness returned to the kitchen: only the sounds of the crackling fire and the hissing of the logs and the tea kettle. Glen found himself to be transfixed by the sight of a plume of blue flame shooting out the side of one of the burning logs. It burned long and smooth and steady, as a propane torch might do. He watched it out of interest, but also because he did not know where else to turn his eyes. He wanted to look at more of his surroundings, but did not wish to appear to be too interested in the room for fear that someone might think that he was storing information in his mind for a robbery, what used to be called "casing" the place! He looked sidewise to see the CoArb talking to the man at the table, whose head was bent down as he was using the point of a knife on a sliver in his hand.

"Is 'himself' real busy just now?" Colm asked the young man.

"I don't think so. If he is, it won't be for long. Someone came by to buy some young stock or to talk about buying some, but they'll be leaving soon if they haven't done so already!" He kept working away at his sliver without looking up, adding: "There's nothing worse than old hemlock wood for slivers! This has to be the meanest one I've ever had!"

"Do you want me to have a go at it?". Colm asked.

"Not bloody likely! You almost killed me the last time you took out a sliver! I thought that I was going to lose the use of one hand forever!"

"Poor lad! You never did learn to suffer in silence, did you? Oh well! At least I offered!"

"Yes, Well….your offer has been noted. Thank you." Both men were smiling, obviously enjoying what must have been a typical exchange among the folk here. Glen hadn't expected to find much in the way of humor at all in this place. He thought to himself: "They can afford to have some humor and some friendship; to be funny or happy or whatever! They belong here, and to one another. Maybe they use their humor up among themselves and that is why they are so freakin' mean and nasty to outsiders!" The stories of such people and their dealings with outsiders were legion and sometimes pretty terrible. As for "settled" folk, they preferred not to alter the outsiders' perceptions of them, not even a little bit. It made it easier to keep their homes and property intact.

"Sit here by the fire and drink your toddie" Colm said to Glen. "I'll go and see if Alisdair is able to have a word with you."

Ron felt himself covered with needles, ice and a shiver from his toes to his privates all in one flash. "Oh, my God!", he half thought aloud before taking a big gulp of his toddie. He hardly was aware of the heat of the drink or the sting of the alcohol. It was warm and sweet and hit his stomach hard. He was more surprised that the liquid could so easily pass the lump in his throat. "I have been delivered into the hand of a man who hates me, I am sitting by his fire and drinking his spirits!"

As the CoArb disappeared into the sounds of the other room and the stillness returned to the kitchen as the door closed behind him, Glen ventured to look across the room, towards the man at the table. The sliver must either have been extracted or granted the victory, for the young man was now honing the knife which had been his surgical instrument, having managed to produce a sharpening stone from somewhere. The man's gaze was intent upon the slow, to and fro movements of the blade on the whetstone, his brows forming a frown of concentration or study. Aware of Glen's watching him, he glanced up only once, but looked him squarely in the eye as he did so, after a moment returning to his honing, preferring, no doubt, to give the task his attention. Still intent upon his sharpening, he asked Glen without looking up: "Where did you run onto Colm, or where did he meet up with you?

"Who?", Glen asked

"Colm! The guy you came in with!"

"Oh!", Glen replied. "I didn't know his name." I met him in the pasture back there."

Looking up now, the young man said, "I hope that you didn't interrupt anything that he was doing!"

"I don't think so", Glen answered." He was just standing there when I saw him. What was he supposed to be doing?"

"Making sure that we have a good birthing season"

"Oh!" Glen wanted to ask more about what was meant by such a remark, but thought better of the idea and changed the subject. "I figured him to be some kind of priest", he said.

"That's what he is! A damned good one too!"

"Seems to be a very nice guy!", Glen ventured.

"He is! Too good! He trusts everybody!"

"I guess that I would have to admit that that could be dangerous", Glen agreed.

"Not for Colm! He's got God on his side! It's the rest of us poor bastards who have to be careful!"

Glen smiled at the attempt at humor, the first act even resembling anything in the way of acceptance towards him by anyone other than the CoArb. He was silent for a moment before saying: "I guess that I should introduce myself".

"You don't have to! I know who you are. You're Glen Somebody or other: the guy with no home or clan or anything, but a damned good pair of boots! Well, you're under the roof and that gives you some protection because of the old Rule of Hospitality. Just respect our ways while you're here and you'll do alright!"

The young man, having spoken his mind, went back to his honing. He had not felt any obligation to introduce himself in return. The sound of the metal on the abrasive, the hissing of the fire and the kettle were the only sounds again, somehow making the silence even more intense, less peopled. Glen felt himself to be naked, an object displaced or cast adrift. The way that he had just been "put in his place" annoyed him. Ordinarily he would probably just stand up, tell the other guy to go screw himself and walk out. He couldn't walk out He had to see this through. At the same time a feeling came over him that he could not simply allow this to pass, this remark which, along with its implied promise of safety, offered nothing in the way of kindness or warmth. He had almost been told that he could not be expected to behave responsibly around good people. Within him was a strong urge to lash out in some equally nasty way, even if it might provoke a fight with the cocky knife-honer. He was so close to doing just that: to leap across the room and knock the guy off his chair and beat the crap out of him. That's the mental image that crossed his mind, that almost catapulted him into action. It also flashed immediately in his mind that were he to do anything other than to take this abuse, it would only prove some very negative ideas which others here might be harboring where he was concerned; that he would prove them right and appear to be the rootless, mindless, "low-life" that the other young man and his folk probably thought him to be. He decided to let the matter pass, but was determined to say something, anything, to show that he had no fear and could stand his ground. A question:

"What do you mean, "the Rule of Hospitality" ? Is it some kind of law?"

The other young man did not look up, save for a quick glance before responding:

"You are under the roof of this house. In case you didn't notice, you were given something to drink even before you were asked to sit down. That means that you are, for the time being, to be treated as a guest".

"That's a law?", Glen asked.

"Not a Federal law!", said the honer, looking at him as if he had asked the dumbest of all possible dumb questions. "But", he went on, "with us it is something of a law, and a very ancient one at that!"

Glen wanted to ask more about this law, what he had meant by "ancient", and why these people had laws of their own, apart from Federal and State laws. Several questions came into his mind, but at that moment the door to the dining room opened and Colm entered the room. Holding the door still half open, he nodded his head to a side in a fast movement toward the inner room.

"Come with me", he said, looking at Glen. "Alisdair wants to see you".

Glen looked toward the other young man and said sarcastically: "Aren't you going to wish me luck?"

"Good Luck!", the other guy smiled. Ron did a double-take. Yes, it was a smile. Not a smirk, but an honest smile!

The dining room at Ardachy is not huge, only big enough to accommodate a score of people at a high meal, yet large enough to serve as a gathering place should the need arise. Probably it is about twenty-five feet in length and sixteen or eighteen feet in width. High panels of wood, hand-made and hand-carved furniture, parquet floors, all make for an environment of polished wood, bearing also the aroma of very old polished wood as well. A large wrought iron candelabra stood on a side-board, casting a rosy glow over the room Two candle holders of cut glass on the great dining table twinkled with light reflected from the lone candle which each of them held, the table itself glowing in two streaks of candle light shining on its waxed and oiled very smooth wooden top. Even in good times the dining room at Ardachy had made visitors feel as if they had stumbled into another place, another time. In these bad times, the room served only as a reminder that security and even a simple grace in living could be had only in such tucked away, well-guarded isles of refuge. Brass gleamed from the wall: platters and trays reflecting the dancing light from the great fireplace at the end of the room.

Glen had walked into the room ahead of the CoArb, who had stood aside and motioned him forward. Upon hearing the door close behind him and retreated footsteps on the kitchen side of the door, he knew better than to look to see if Colm were still behind him. The CoArb had let him into the room, but left him to speak privately to the proprietor, the man whom he assumed was the shadowy figure sitting alone at the far end of the long dining table. That lone figure did indeed rise at that moment, moved to a corner of the table nearby and pulled out a chair, his hand indicating that Glen was being invited to sit there.

"Have a chair!" Glen stepped towards the table end and chair, looking at the same cold eyes which had stared mercilessly at him earlier in that same day. Alisder moved as quickly to his own place at the end of the table and the two of them sat at the same instant, Glen with a great apprehension. He felt clumsy, after all, suspecting that as he sat his manner and his gestures matched his ragged, tied and pinned-together appearance; betraying not only his nervousness, but what might be perceived to be a savage, ill-bred manner. Surrounded as he was by polished wood, gleaming brass and glass, the many signs of stability and tradition, he wondered if he did not look like something spat up from the raw earth itself: a clod of soft, muddy earth suddenly to land with a "splat" on the parquet floor, about to muddy even now a well-polished side chair. Glancing nervously towards Alisdair, he saw on the proprietor's face no sign of anything being out of the ordinary. The chieftain simply raised his eyebrows and began to speak, sounding more tired than angry or inconvenienced:

"Either you've balls as big as an elephant's or you're just

damned awfully stupid, coming up here this way! I told you to stay clear of my boundaries and here you are, sitting in my house! I hope that you have a pretty good reason for coming here like this!" Sitting at the end of his table with his elbows resting on the arms of the chair which held him, his body slumped down sufficiently to allow the thumbs of his clasped hands to touch the underside of his bottom lip as he spoke, he allowed his eyes to flash at Glen for no more than a second or two before focusing on a spot on the ceiling. Glen thought that Alisdair looked something like a priest hearing confession after hours, months, years of hearing confessions, as if this were a large part of his job, this listening, this hoping that something brought forth might make some sense somewhere.

Glen began by explaining to the landlord that he really hadn't meant to cause trouble, over-step or arouse suspicion in an way. He explained about the sugar shack on the boundary line and of the sickness in the old lady and that he couldn't take the chance that another move might be too much for her to take physically or mentally; that it was the only shelter that they had. He mentioned that he really could not leave her alone, that indeed he suspected that she might even have a serious heart condition. Admitting that they had over-stepped where the fire wood was concerned, he had meant no harm, but had simply become obsessed with the idea of getting what wood they could gather and get Velma back to shelter. As he spoke, he noticed that Alisdair's eyes never left from staring at the same spot in the ceiling, blinking now and then, maybe even closing his eyes for a few seconds at a time. Finally, his eyes even closed and stayed closed. Glen glanced, then stared and stopped talking.

"Go on!" Alisdair said, his tone even, not at all sleepily. His eyes did remain closed however. In another part of the house, a clock was chiming out the hour or a part of some hour. The piano music had stopped for a time and then someone had started playing again.

Glen went on, and on. He found himself telling about a great many things: his life in another time, in another place, a more secure place in a more careless America. He spoke of his teen years, his beatings, of kindnesses received, of people he'd been with and who had come into and out of his life almost as quickly an as evenly as a weaver's shuttle, gliding over and through the warp of the loom. Suddenly, he simply stopped speaking. Total silence, save for the hissing of a log in the fire, the distant chords and melody of a piano, but for some reason, these distant sounds seemed only to emphasize the quietude: total silence. Alisdair did neither stir nor even flicker an eye lash. Glen was almost afraid to look around. He felt something akin to panic begin to creep onto him. He contented himself to watch the patterns of reflected light from the fire on the polished wood able top. He caught a sudden glimpse of himself sitting there, as if through the eyes of someone about to enter the room, and the image of himself looked to be silly, looking as if just about to bolt for the door! He certainly thought that he had most definitely been shut out yet again. Christ! Was Alisdair asleep, or what!?

The landowner's left hand took leave of its mate which held its place by chin and lower lip and that moving hand went up to cover the still closed eyes in a tired, thoughtful gesture, the thumb and third finger of that left hand rubbing the eyes deep into their corners by the bridge of the nose. He moved the knuckle of that hand across the left eye and then quite suddenly opened his eyes and pulled himself up to sit upright in the chair. He grimaced and began to speak:

"Yeah, I know! It's not the same country anymore; not the one that I grew up in either. Oh, we always worked hard, I suppose, and we had our difficulties, but still, things were different.; a *lot* different! I remember this very room where we are sitting now, all lit up with candles all over the place. Lots and lots of people. My father used to go all out for the big gatherings: the "Ceilidhs". They'd dance to the wee hours of the morning. One year we had about two hundred guests for the St. Andrews Celidh. You won't find that nowadays. A man or a woman would be crazy to be out late at night in these times! You wouldn't have to be looking for trouble! Trouble would find you! But…, we can't turn the clock back, now can we?"

"Two Hundred people!" Glen was impressed

"Oh, yes!" Alisdair went on, "I can remember that my father would shore up under these old floors with extra timbers before a big gathering"

Alisdair went on, telling of the people and the music, the poems read aloud, the songs sung in both English and Scots Gaelic. As he spoke Glen stared in fascination into the fire, almost calling up the past, envisioning those evenings filled with fellowship and tradition. The lilting words and phrases of Alisdair, soft spoken and almost poetic, filled the room with warmth and energy, dispelling for a short time the very quiet gloom. Glen found himself thinking of this man, and of how different he appeared to be on closer inspection, on his own hearth, than the very brusque and cold man that had spoken to him earlier that day in the woodlot. Suddenly, almost as if the proprietor had read Glen's thoughts, a half smile that had been on his face disappeared as he came out of his descriptions and thoughts of another time, to confront the less hospitable, somewhat cruel world of the present.

"It's fun to remember all of that, those other times, but it doesn't help us to confront the problems of our own time, now does it? It doesn't do a damned thing towards helping us maintain harmony and peace in these less happy times, does it? Here we are: a fellow shows up looking all the world like he's overstepping his limits, and over-stepping those limits in a pair of fine damned good-looking boots which are obviously the work of an old-world boot maker, wooden pegs, 'last and all' boots such are hardly ever seen even among the super rich polo players down east, when by the look of the guy, he probably would see a pair of clean socks as the best Christmas present he might ever have given to him….., well, it kinda gets a man to thinking, if you know what I mean. He might be asking himself, "Who is this guy, anyway?" Now, I have to admit that you do not look like any hardened criminal that I might have seen a picture of on the post office wall, or walking around nearby either, but something here just isn't adding up You look alright. You sound alright. In fact, you're a good-looking kid who looks like you have had some upbringing somewhere along the line. I see that. I'd like to help you out, but I don't see how I can do that!"

"You've *got* to! "Glen blurted out, so fast that he hadn't had time to think of how this might sound. Too late! He felt the hair rise on the back of his neck: fear perhaps, regret maybe.

"I've GOT to!?" Alisdair was sitting bolt upright, staring in a none too friendly way at the young man beside him. "I've GOT to do WHAT ? I've got to hold this land together is what "I've GOT" to do! That's all I've got to do and I'm not sure that any one man could even begin to pull that rabbit out of a hat!....even with a whole tribe of people behind him!"

Alisdair rose from his chair and as he did so, Glen was on his feet in the same instant. It was obvious to Glen that he was being signaled that the talk was over; that he would have to go, to vacate the room, the land, the Sugar Shack. He felt the bitter taste of bile, of panic in the back of his throat., knowing that he had failed miserably, that if anything, he had probably turned the proprietor even more against him. His thoughts raced! It mustn't end like this! Glen grasped at straws, grasped at something, anything to say.

"Sir, please believe me! I didn't hurt anyone for these boots, nor did I steal them! Really, I didn't! They are mine fair and square! They look to be too good for me and they are, but they really are mine!

"Wonderful! I am truly happy to hear that!, Alisdair said coldly, very coldly in sarcasm. "So, then, Where did they come from?" The landowner turned and waited for an answer. Glen's arms dropped to his sides.

"A man made them for me. He was a soldier once and a medic, but someone taught him how to build boots in the old Italian way. He gave them to me. He actually almost built them to me."

"Where is this man now?"

"He is running a make-shift medical center up in New York State".

"Goodnight, young man!"

"But, Sir, honestly….."

"I said 'Good night, young man'!"

He was ushered out of the house by the young knife-honer, who escorted him out past the line of trees and into the center of the great field where he had met the CoArb and somewhere close to that same spot they stopped.

"Okay!," the honer said. By the time I'm halfway back to those trees, those guys are going to start putting some shots into the air. I suggest that you haul your ass out of here!"

Glen walked for the cover of the forest, then half ran, half dove into it, falling head-long down over the bank of a creek bed. His knee ached from hitting something and he lay there half laughing and swearing with the pain, but was surprised to find himself crying.

"Rotten sons o' bitches! Bastards! Nobody cares about anybody any more! Nobody gives a fiddler's fuck whether you live or die! Oh God! God! I'm so tired of this! I want out of here! I want to go home!" Then it came to him: "Home" wasn't a place. It was a time somewhere in the past. "Home" no longer existed, save for some idea in one's memory.

CHAPTER 4

PART 3

In the dining room of Ardachy House the flames in the fireplace cast long shadows across the room; flickering shadows playing an age-old game, a dance of sorts, with the skipping lights. In this dimly lit room (even candles were a luxury in these times, often home-made from the wax of the bees on the place and sometimes of tallow taken from butchered deer or cattle), shadow and light played their age-old game, not unlike silent music, in fact. They acted out their parts on the furniture, the brass trays on the high shelf above the paneling, upon the panels themselves, even upon the usually unnoticed parts of moldings and pieces of furniture. Certainly the glassware accepted their attention, shining out as it was from the leaded glass wall cabinets. Only the carved family Coat of Arms, high on the wall, dusty and aloof, seemed to repel their magic. It resisted such foolish dancing, as if it recognized its high station and function as a symbol of the great ancestors. It held to its lofty status and long pedigree, the only object in the room to remain apart from such games.

Alisdair too, sat apart from it all, slumped as he was in his chair at the end of the long table. It was his place to sit there, farthest from the fireplace and at that other end. It had been his place, this chair farthest from the fire, since he was seated there when he had turned eighteen. He had never moved to the other end of the table where his father had once sat, even after his father had been gathered to his ancestors. Somehow he had never felt that he wanted to do so. At this time, on this night so long afterwards, he was deep in thought. The glowing table top, so carefully polished year in and year out with beeswax and turpentine, did not take his notice this night as he stared along its length and into the fire beyond. He could not shake the ugly, sad feeling so deep inside of himself since he had spoken with the young man in the woodlot. He had wanted to hear something that he might have fastened onto; some little thing, anything which might have provided him an opportunity to relax his position, his decision on the matter. He simply could not get the image of that young man out of his mind: this no-name nobody from nowhere, a fellow with no roots, no tradition and no family, who had been sitting at this same table just a short time before. Well, with all that the kid did *not* have, he certainly did not seem to lack for a certain pride! Imagine! Oh, he hadn't seemed to have been a bad young fellow really, nor had he appeared to be lazy or totally helpless. In fact, Alisdair had to concede to himself a certain liking for the young man. Well now! Enough of that kind of nonsense! Alisdair realized and was determined to draw his mind away from *that* kind of thinking straightaway! Yes, the lad had seemed different right enough: perhaps shrewd, a bit more clever perhaps than others of his kind, and *that* made him more dangerous! Damn these people! Why can't they stay where they belong? Why does one of them simply barge into another man's life, expecting to get things to which he is in no way entitled?

The door opened from behind Alisdair, from the further parts of the house. Colm came quietly into the room as if someone might be sleeping there. He had sensed that the proprietor would be deep in thought. Although aware of the Co-arb's presence, Alisdair did not turn his head, although he did speak:

"Why don't you pour us a dram, Monk?"

"Do you feel a need for one at this time, Alisdair?", Colm asked.

"No, but I would like to have one!"

"Good!, then you are remembering that it is not good for one to drink alone", Colm teased. "In your present state of mind perhaps that would not be beyond the realm of possibility"

"Hah!", Alisdair retorted, "A man would have to be a chief of all sneaks to drink alone here, in this house!"

Colm smiled as he moved to the cupboard with the leaded glass doors which was set into the paneling where the glassware was kept, took out three dram glasses which he carried over and set down on the table to the left and front of Alisdair. He then moved to the side board and brought forth a bottle of whisky, one of the few bottles which were left,which he also set down onto the table. His movements and the ease and familiarity of the house, its contents and cupboards were more akin to those of an old family servant, such as a butler, rather than those which one might expect from a cleric. Yet Colm had known this house from his youth, long before he had entered into Holy Orders. Throughout all of this, followed by the uncorking of the bottle and the pouring out of the liquor, the brooding proprietor had neither moved or spoken. As if thinking aloud, the words came forth from his lips:

"What does he want from us?"

"He wants a home, I suppose", Colm answered, knowing of whom his friend was speaking

"Well, there's no anchor tied to his ass! Let him go and find one....but somewhere else!", Alisdair spat out.

"Ah, but there is indeed an anchor tied to his ass, as you say. In fact, there are *many* anchors: poverty, lack of education, having been cast out of whatever life he once had with a great empire now on the rocks, with too many people and no way to keep them fed, housed or gainfully employed....Do you want me to go on?" Colm asked gently.

"No! Don't hand me that shit!", Alisdair huffed, "I'm not in the mood for any bleeding-heart crap tonight!"

"Or perhaps any night", Colm gently admonished

"That's right!...or *any* night! I have had enough work

cut out for me just to keep things together as it is!" Alisdair heaved himself forward and stood up after having said that and taking ahold of his glass, he held it aloft, towards the Co-arb.

"Slainte!", pronounced the land-holder. The Co-arb picked up his own glass and held it in like manner towards his old friend:

"Slainte Mhath!"

After each of them had taken a swallow from his glass, they sat down, the Co-arb in the chair at Alisdair's left where not long before the young "gleaner" had been sitting and Alisdair resumed his chair at the table's end. It was all as if it had been carefully drilled, practiced and acted out many times before over the years, which in a way, had been the case. Neither of them spoke for a time, although each man was aware that the other wanted to say something. Alisdair broke the silence, nodding towards the table:

"Why did you put three glasses on the table? Why the extra glass?"

"Oh! I did put three glasses on the table, didn't I ?" Colm asked absently "Well, I thought that since Erc is in the house…."

"How long has he been here? I didn't know that he had stopped by!"

"Well, he was here when I brought the young man up to see you. He was in the kitchen, honing a knife as I recall. I don't know how long he had been here before that…", Colm answered simply.

"He has probably left by now!", Alisdair said. "He usually goes to bed at a pretty early hour".

Hell! We are all getting old, but Erc has acted old all of his life!"

"I really do not think that he has left. I am pretty certain that he is here somewhere. I got the impression that he was waiting to see you", Colm said as he toyed with his glass, turning the glass in a clock-wise motion with his thumb and forefinger. He was focused on the glint of reflected light at the edge of the glass. It was something for which he had come to be noted. Those who had known him over the years often wondered if he did not use such a study of reflected light as something akin to his deep spirituality; as if he were looking into another dimension at such times. Neither man spoke, relaxed and confident in their place in the scheme of things. Alisdair broke the silence, as Colm knew he would and almost had heard his words in advance: "Waitng to see me ? Why didn't he come on in and sit down? He doesn't have to stand on formality!"

"Well, now, Alisdair, I think that all of us could see that there has been something a bit different about tonight", Colm explained. "I knew, I think that we all knew, that you needed to talk privately with the young man. Erc felt the same way, I'm sure".

"Why did that young guy have to come here, anyway?", Alisdair asked.

"Perhaps he came to redeem us", was Colm's simple answer.

"Oh, hell! Don't start preaching at me! I'm not talking about Jesus Christ! I'm talking about that free-loader in the hand-made boots!", Alisdair said impatiently, pointing in the direction of the North boundary.

"So am I, Alisdair", Colm replied calmly as he turned his glass.

"And don't start playing mind games with me, either! Whatever you say, I see the guy to be a miserable grabber, just trying to weasel in here, where he doesn't belong!", Alisdair stated flatly before taking up his glass and swallowing a quantity of his Single Malt. With the glass still in his hand, his little finger just beneath the glass and pointing towards Colm, he went on:" I have a job to do here and I aim to do it. I still have to pay taxes, guard what we have and there are people to feed! I never asked for this job, but I have damned straight ended up with it.....so don't try to make me look like some unfeeling son of a bitch just because I don't invite every down and out freeloader to sit his ass down at my supper table!"

"Is that what I'm doing?", Colm asked, smiling.

"And don't pull that crap, either! ...answering questions with questions and all that bull!"

"Did you ask a question?" Colm's eyes twinkled with amusement and for that matter, Alisdair, at this point, could hardly keep from laughing as well. Not that he wasn't a bit angry, for he was indeed upset and angry and perhaps even feeling a twinge of compassion and guilt at the same time. He did feel the humor of this very old game, played out many times before throughout the years. The co-arb was once again holding up a mirror before him. He knew that Colm did indeed care about his feelings, understood his situation, but also this was his way of asking his old friend to be sure of both: what he was doing and of his innermost feelings.

There was a knocking on the door which led into the room from the kitchen, after which it was opened. Erc silently entered the room and stopped, stood and then stared at Alisdair. It was a mock stare, really. Anyone who did not know these men might have thought that one or the other was about to reach for a weapon, or at least hurl an insult towards the other fellow. The eyes of Erc could be made by him to look lifeless, cold yet penetrating; not even penetrating, but able to appear to look through another person, seemingly without seeing him. Alisdair continued in his own version of the cold stare. This was a drama which the two of them had been acting out for many years. Erc nodded his head and Alisdair did the same before finally speaking to him:

"Are you just going to stand there, staring at decent people, or will you join us in a dram?"

"Well, I don't see too many decent people here, but I would gladly have a dram with you", Erc replied

"You won't be putting yourself out on our account?", Alisdair asked

"Oh, no! I haven't anything better to do".

"Well, thank you!", Alisdair said sarcastically as he

began to pour from the bottle into the empty glass.

"You are more than welcome!", Erc returned, taking off his hat and moving toward the table to the chair to the right of the proprietor. He waited until Alisdair and Colm rose to their feet and they all made the customary toast, until they all swallowed a bit of the liquid, before pulling out the chair to seat himself. After a very short time, Erc said to Alisdair:

"You must have scared that kid half to death!"

"What kid?", Alisdair asked. He knew of whom Erc spoke but he somehow felt the need to ask the question anyhow.

"That kid with the expensive-looking boots!", Erc replied.

"Oh, yeah….Well, I do not think that he could have been too scared ", Alisdair snorted. "Somehow I got the feeling that he felt himself to be more inconvenienced than anything else!"

"I don't know", Erc persisted, "He went across that pasture and did not look back, not even once!"

"That doesn't mean that he was frightened", Colm put in. Alisdair and Erc both swung their heads toward him. It wasn't that he had said what he had, but rather something in the way in which he had said it. There was an implied sorrow combined with warning in his tone

"What do you mean, Colm?", Erc asked. Alisdair leaned forward to replenish the glasses He poured for Erc, but when he had barely begun to give more to Colm, the cleric shook two fingers back and forth by the glass.

"That's more than enough for me", Colm stated. I have to go home to my wife and read my nightly office. It also seems that I have been asked to offer up many prayers for others: for those who are ill or dying".

"You must be getting old...like Erc!", Alisdair said jokingly. The Co-arb smiled but said nothing. Erc persisted in his question of a few moments before:

"What did you mean, when you said that did not mean that the kid was scared, Colm?"

"No, *you* said that you thought that he was frightened because of the way he did not look back. I simply said that his not looking back did not necessarily mean that it was because he was full of fear", Colm explained.

"Well, then, What do you think that it meant? He never said a word!", Erc explained. "I walked with him myself to the far side of the north pasture. I told him that by the time that I walked back up to the tree line the guys on watch would open fire on anything or anyone left in the field that didn't belong there. I told him, "you'd better haul ass out of here", and he took off like a turpentined cat for the woods." Erc could see that Alisdair's heart wasn't totally into the humor of the incident.

Colm had a very serious expression on his face, directing his gaze to a candle flame. The wick had gone to one side and the candle was burning unevenly, sending small rivulets of melted wax down and onto the base of the candle holder. He wet his thumb and forefinger with his tongue, then reached over and pinched out the flame. The three of them sat in the light of three remaining candles and the dying light of the fireplace. They stared absently at the curls of smoke from the newly extinguished flame. No one said anything for a minute or two. Finally Colm spoke:

"No, gentlemen. I don't think that it was fear. Embarrassment perhaps, anger, frustration, maybe even despair, but I don't think that it was fear."

"A guy like that doesn't need or have the right to feel any of those things. What does a guy like that do to deserve anything at all?" Erc sounded peevish, almost petulant as he spoke.

Colm stood up, shrugged his shoulders and raised his palms on each side of him. "What do any of us do to deserve all that comes to us?"

"C'mon, Colm. I know that it's your job to bleed for all mankind, but Erc's got a point," Alisdair said. "Christ!"

"That's a start!", Colm smiled as he turned.

"Don't start that!", Alisdair said.

"Alright, listen then." Colm walked to the far end of the table by the fireplace, took a poker and pushed the glowing chunks of wood together at the back of the firewall. Almost immediately the flames leapt out of the smoldering embers. He hung the poker back in its place and turned toward Alisdair and Erc. Putting his hands behind him, between the fireplace and his back, he began to explain his feeling:

A long time ago, in this very room although it doesn't seem all that long ago, we saw what was happening. We more than saw it; we could feel it in the air. People all around us spoke of the shrinking middle class and of how many people were accepting handouts from the government. People like ourselves seemed to be anachronisms: hanging onto a clan-type lifestyle, working a sixteen hour day. We saw young people go into jobs with computers and electronic equipment making five times what we could make. We saw farming and animal husbandry become nearly extinct. The big money was in technology, war-material and the service and entertainment industries: 'fast food joints', motels, video games, televisions, computers, sports… anything but farming or shepherding!" Colm was gesturing with his arms as if to visually encompass and contain late 20th century thought. "They spoke of the Arms Race, of Space exploration, undersea exploration; of saving seals and whales and aborting human infants. Those whose hearts bled for seals thought nothing of destroying a human fetus and those who screamed for the life of the human fetus thought nothing of poisoning the air, the rain and the earth itself with chemical or radioactive waste."

"So?", nodded Erc, "what are you getting at? We all know this stuff."

"We do and we don't", Colm went on. "Alisdair, I can remember your father saying, back around 1980, that the reason the middle class had to let the government hand out all that help was because it was so much cheaper than hiring, feeding, clothing and transporting soldiers for the purpose of food-riot control. He was convinced that it was an attempt on the part of the employed, educated and wealthier classes to buy off the people who either couldn't or wouldn't find work."

"Yes," Alisdair conceded, "I remember him saying that. So?"

"What he didn't know and what none of us realized at the time was that more and more people would find themselves unequipped to find work. Technology became so complex and continued to become more and more so at such an alarming rate, that soon a very large group of people, many of them once considered to be skilled in one way or another, would find themselves homeless, jobless and with nowhere to go; with no way of supporting themselves."

"We all know that, Colm.", Erc said.

"Yes," Colm went on, "But it isn't what we know as much as it is what we have forgotten! Some of these 'gleaners', 'freeloaders', whatever we may choose to call them, were once educated, respected members of society. In other words out there somewhere wearing an old coat with a rope around it. Might be a great, really great, writer or poet; maybe a 'could have been' dancer or singer or artist. How would we know the difference? And if Jesus Christ were to return tonight or tomorrow, would we recognize him?"

"And you think that I've just turned Jesus Christ out of my house and Erc even told him to 'haul ass' out of the North pasture!", Alisdair teased.

"No, but I'm convinced that that young man is a very unusual 'gleaner'. I think that we could have given him a bit more of our time."

"Good Sweet Screaming Jesus!" Alisdair exclaimed in feined exasperation (as the CoArb squinted shut his eyes and grimaced), "What more could I have done? I let that young guy into my house, set him down in this room and listened to him. He didn't even try to meet me halfway! He stood his ground on what were already his conditions. He wouldn't even answer one question for me. Now, how 'fair' is fair?"

"I presume you refer to his boots," Colm said, "or why do a nice pair of boots like those end up on a dirt-bag like you", that kind of question?"

"Yes! Damn it, I want to know! And while we're on the subject I'd like to know why this matters so much to you!" Alisdair's eyes were wide open and fixed on the CoArb in much the same way that an angry father's might be fixed on a careless or thoughtless son who had somehow broken the household rules and needed to explain himself. Colm half smiled and his eyes turned slowly, thoughtfully toward the fire. He seemed to be deep into self-questioning or perhaps, as the other men thought, a means of putting his thoughts into words.

"The answer to that can only be complex because it is so simple," he said at last, turning to face them.

"And what is that?", asked Alisdair.

"Because," Colm said plainly, "I really believe that we are supposed to help this young man… and before you say anything else to me, listen for a minute!"

"I'm listening!", Alisdair assured him.

"No-I mean *really* listen!" This time it was Colm who was the father speaking to the son. There was a command in his voice and with it the hint of a plea. He walked from the fire to a chair next to Erc, sat down on it and leaned on the table almost in front of Erc and facing Alisdair just beyond and at the table's end. He faced Alisdair first, but looked at Erc as well as he began to speak. He spoke slowly and with certainty and as he spoke the other men listened.

"Never have I interfered in your running of things. I was loyal to your father and I have given what loyalty I can give to you. I wasn't, of course, always a cleric when your father was a Chieftain. He knew that when I took Holy Orders that I must first serve God. This I have tried to do, although I confess that I sometimes question my rate of success. Alisdair, I feel that you are a good man and an honest man. You have done well for all who look to you for guidance. Yet, I would not be, myself, an honest man if I did not tell you what I am about to say."

"Say it!", Alisdair nodded.

"I shall." Colm said, "Something very wonderful was brought to these shores long, long ago as we all know. When our ancestors left the highlands they carried with them this ancient faith. It has sustained us and has seen us through some very hard times. But we have locked ourselves up in it or what is worse we have locked the faith within a wall of militant clansmen. The beauty of our faith is that it allows for individual differences as well as binding us to the earth.

We never tried to make others into copies of ourselves. Joining us has never been a prerequisite to receiving our friendship. We have had to guard ourselves carefully and you have done well in helping us to maintain ourselves. Without such leadership we might be homeless, landless 'gleaners.'" He looked at first one of them, then the other.

"Alisdair, Erc, listen to me, for I may wince at your cussing and wink at your jokes, but I am really being called upon now to do *my* job and I'm trying terribly hard not to make a mess of it." His voice was steady and low as he went on, looking each of them in the face. He lightly stabbed at the table top with his finger as he spoke.

"Tonight… in the North Pasture, just after reciting the Rann for the good lambing and calving… I turned to see the moon rising and yet I was aware of a light over my left shoulder. I turned and saw, as it were, rays of light coming out of the corner of the woods. I blinked my eyes because I thought perhaps tears from the Rann had caused it. The light was there yet, but fading, and ahead of, or just in front of a light area I saw a figure approach and I saw an aura around that figure and the next thing I know he was addressing me."

Erc and Alisdair both looked at the table top as he finished.

"Salt of the earth, listen. I believe that he was sent here for a reason."

Alisdair was a bit vexed, probably not so much with the holy man, Colm, as he was with fate or maybe even God

Himself. He shifted in his chair, picked up the bottle and poured a small amount for Erc, held the bottle toward Colm as a question which Colm answered with a negative shake of his head, then poured only a tiny amount for himself. He sighed, rested his elbow on the table and his head in his hand, half rubbing his temples with his thumb and fingers, rubbing his hair with the palm of his hand at the same time.

"Well," he said without looking up, "what do you propose to do? I can't go back on my word and look 'wishy-washy.'"

"Let me go to this young man and talk with him. Perhaps if I can convince him to tell me whether or not he is a thief or rather if he came by his boots or any such thing in a dishonest way, I can set your mind at ease", Colm suggested.

"How the hell can you do that? You can't break the seal of confession!"

"Of course I can't. Yet you would accept my word if I found no fault in him. I would simply give you my endorsement of his character."

"And if he is guilty?", Alisdair asked.

"Why, we would leave things where they stand."

Erc was nodding his head slowly looking upward and steadily into the Co-Arb's face, his eyes almost squinting shut.

"That seems fair, Alisdair," Erc said.

"Fair for whom? If I'm right nobody knows. If I'm wrong, everybody knows! He looked up and saw both Erc and Colm smiling to themselves. He was giving in, they both knew. "And what's so damned funny about that? Win, draw or lose, the Chieftain is a shit!"

"Why change now, at this late date?", asked Colm.

"To hell with you, monk!"

"Probably. All in good time," Colm answered.

"When would you find out?", Alisdair asked.

"Soon. Very soon. Before they go."

"Okay, Okay, Okay! Do it! But if you're wrong…", Alisdair pronounced this with his head tilted as if in warning.

"I doubt that I am in this case," Colm said rising. Alisdair stood up with him. "I must go to read my office."

"Well, offer up a prayer for me. I wonder what I'll be doing in a year's time with my clan over-run with gleaners and holy freeloaders!" Alisdair rose from his place and walked to the side door with Colm.

"Goodnight, Erc," Colm turned to say.

"Goodnight, Father Abbot," Erc answered.

By the door, Colm put his hand on Alisdair's shoulder and said in a low voice. "Thank you. I know that this is not easy for you. I appreciate your confidence in me."

"Hell! After all these years what choice do I have? I can't help wishing that you are wrong, yet I'm about prepared to find out that you're right. Have a good night. Give my love to your lovely wife".

"And a goodnight to you, Alisdair", Colm replied. "Give my best to your wife and your mother, as well"

Returning to the table, Alisdair slumped down in his chair, picked up the glass with the tiny amount in and tossed it back, neither he nor Erc spoke for quite a while. Erc simply looked into space with just a touch of a frown on his face, finally Alisdair spoke.

"You know what pisses me off about Colm, Erc?"

"Erc raised his eyes toward his friend and raised his eyebrows also in the form of a question.

"The thing that pisses me off about Colm is that he really *is* a holy man!"

Erc smiled and nodded his head, "I know. Ain't that a bitch?"

CHAPTER 5

PART 3

Glen was angry, soaked, totally fatigued and brimming with a sorrow which he could hardly contain. He leaned against a young tree, not yet ready or capable of re-entering a shack which had become a home, a source of hope and even a lifeline connecting three disowned and dispossessed people to some sense of dignity. The 'sugar-shack' even that 'sugar shack'; a falling down ruin restored for the purpose of sheltering human beings had been declared "too good", beyond the reach of Glen and his two companions. Overcome with frustration, anger and powerlessness, Glen put his forehead against the smooth bark of the young Beech tree and felt hot, butter tears stream down his face.

He had stood there, forehead to tree bark for some time before he became aware of the cold sweeping over him; over his wet clothing from evening damp and the creek bed, hair wet from perspiration. The cold of the air, coupled with the cold of fear. It all swept over him as a wave from a northern sea. He shivered violently, stood back, and moved toward the gray building turned silver in the light of a very bright moon.

Half lifting the door as he pushed it open, avoiding the frozen mud of the earth, he entered into the warmth of the small building. A good fire had been set in the improvised stove: the steel drum with the makeshift door: a piece of metal held in place by two piled fire bricks. Glen looked into the fire bed and nodded with satisfaction at the great bed of orange, glowing coals. He took the door aside, threw another bunch of short wood pieces inside, carefully closed the door again, and began to take off his jacket. From the other side of the stove area, he could hear the deep breathing and occasional cough of Velma. She coughed even in her sleep these days, he noticed.

Glen took off his boots, stripped down to somewhat tattered long-johns, hanging his outer garments to dry by the fire. The boots he took with him, up a make-shift ladder to a loft, sleeping area which he shared with Steve. He moved quietly as possible, neither wishing to wake anyone or talk with anyone of the night's fruitless, cruel outcome. He lifted the edge of the battered moving-blanket which served as a quilt in the space shared with Steve and attempted to slide onto the pad and beneath the cover without waking his bed-fellow. Steve was already awake. He had not slept since Glen had left. Steve was awake! Steve wanted to talk! "Oh, Hell!", Glen thought, "not tonight."

"Are you alright, Glen?", Steve asked.

"Yeah I'm fine!"

"Nothing bad happened to you?"

"Nothing bad happened", Glen sighed. "They wouldn't listen, treated me like I'm a piece of shit, told me that we had to get out of here, but, other than that, everything's peachy-keen!"

There was a long, a very long, silence. In fact, Glen thought that perhaps Steve had simply dozed off. No such luck! He turned on his side, towards Glen who was on his back, arms beneath his head.

"You always find a way, Glen!", Steve told him.

"You think so?" Glen asked, "Right now, the 'ways' are getting fewer and farther between, Steve! I feel like we're running out of 'options' or possibilities!"

"Not you Glen! You always find a way!" insisted Steve.

"Well you just keep saying that, Buddy Boy. You might even come to believe it!" (Wow! Sophie in the "Razor's Edge!" Glen thought. "Not very original of me, was it? Funny that I'd remember that from High School!")

"My sister has to be stupid to have left something, er, someone like you, Glen," Steve suddenly replied.

Freudian Slip?, "something", Glen thought. "What am I a "something"? Is that what guys are? As a matter of fact, yes! Women's great problem with men, despite their always complaining about being treated as 'sex objects', is that they project the same classifications and definitions to men. We are "some things" before we're 'some ones'. Wow!

Am I getting cynical? Not bitter, I hope! Still, why do I get the feeling that Steve's sister was more taken with my equipment, than with me? Why do I still love that bitch? Stupid, I guess! Yep. Men are stupid! We deserve what we get!" Glen said aloud to Josh:

"We'd be smart never to get involved. It's a trap, but if we don't get involved, we are giving up on life. Face it, Steve! God designed men to be dumb!"

"But is that all there is to it? I mean if you love somebody it's okay to get real involved, right?", Steve asked.

"Well, yeah, but you really make it sound pretty simple. It's a little more than that. I guess that you have to want to be with somebody a long time. You make a promise to yourself to always be there… when that person needs you, when she hasn't got anybody else, you know?"

"Well my sister didn't keep any promises, did she?", Steve persisted.

"No Steve, but maybe she didn't feel that she had made me any promise,"

"Glen, if I had been her and had somebody like you I never could run off like she did. I just want you to know that."

"Go to sleep, Steve."

You aren't mad at me, Glen?"

"Steve! For crying out loud! Go to sleep! I like you fine, but just go to sleep!"

He lay there with the sounds of the place all around him: Velma's coughing down below them, the wood crackling in the stove, the too quiet breathing of Steve beside him. He knew that Steve was still awake, thinking. He too had thinking to do. Where would they go? They were safe here simply because they were so close to the lands of Ardachy. Somebody would think twice before raiding a cabin so close to the border of a well-armed, well patrolled holding like that. Now they'd be back on the road; probably find an abandoned vehicle or have to build a lean-to. No sense going to the government forest. That was a regular no-man's land.

He thought of many things. He thought of a fine house a very long time ago. He thought of his mother, but could well remember the man who had raised him and taught him things. He reached his hand to his chest, to the carved antler that he wore on a thong about his neck. He felt around for it and finally found it nestled in the crack between his chest and his other arm. He felt the form of it: a crude cross with a circle. "Don't ever take this off 'til you're married. When you marry, give it to another young fellow who can be trusted to keep a lad's secrets. This is a holy thing and someday, somewhere, a person will recognize it, although if no one ever does it doesn't matter… not as long as you know what you're wearing." He almost laughed aloud when he thought of the Creek, and yes, we were naked and we were clowning around. That's when my deer horn, my 'Cahberfay' landed on her chest. Must be Steve didn't stick around or he would have seen that nothing, absolutely *No Thing* happened. She was scared of this thing. 'Wouldn't have anything to do with me because of it. What the hell are we going to do? How did I get saddled with a family?

Finally, much later he did manage get to sleep.

When Colm returned to his home, he felt heavily burdened in body and soul. After having walked over the fields and down the hill from Ardachy, he came to the back yard area of the house. Stopping to look upon the yard, past the carriage house which had long since become a work shop, he reflected upon the first time that he had been here as a young College student so many years before, helping Robert MacKinnon. He waved to a solitary figure whom he had spotted moving amidst the shrubbery: one of the men taking his turn at night-time surveillance. He liked the walk from Ardachy House and on a night such as this, when bright moonlight danced upon the lightly frosted branches of trees, plants, stalks of weed, and pasture stubble, the sense of the magic of it all came back to him. Soon, with a light layer of snow, certain to come upon the land before long, the trees would cast long, blue shadows across the landscape on such a moon-lit night. As many times as he had experienced this throughout his lifetime, the pure beauty and magic of it all never seemed to wane. If anything, his senses had become ever more sharpened and he had continued with each year to find something in it all which would make itself known; something never really noticed before on prior walks. Walks. People did a lot of walking these days. What power people might be able to generate could not be wasted on motor vehicles. Even most chain-saws had become powered by means of solar electricity.

Gwynne had left a light in the kitchen window for him. Rob unlocked the back door and entered into the house. Home! This had been home for a number of years at this time, ever since Martin and Diane had taken a quite elderly Kathy to live with them at Ardachy. Her mind had remained quite sharp, but her body could no longer perform the tasks of house-keeping and preparing meals. Ian, Rob and Gwynne's eldest son, now lived at their old Greek Revival home outside of Allegany where all of the boys had grown up. Now Ian also had a wife, a son and a daughter.

Rob took the solar light from the window and carried it with him through the dining room towards the dimly lit living room where Gwynne was seated, reading. She looked up at her husband with a warm smile, took off her glasses and marking her place in the book with a card, she closed the volume and laid it on the coffee table.

"I was beginning to worry about you!", she announced.

"You weren't really worried, were you?", he asked.

"Robbie, you aren't a boy anymore, nor are you a young man! Of course I am sometimes concerned. You could easily have had a fall and no one around to see you or help you.", she stated with frankness and even some scolding in her tone.

He smiled, bent down and kissed her forehead.

"And don't think that a kiss on the forehead is going to make everything just fine and dandy!", she warned.

Still smiling he moved towards the closet, preparing to remove his coat and tam. Opening the front closet door, he broke into an outright grin and shook his head.

"And you can quit smiling too!" came her voice from behind him. At this, he went into a slight laugh.

He liked being with her. After so many years together they could read one another; at times even think to one another. Colm the Co-arb, the "Holy Man", the Abbot was, in his own home, a husband who loved his wife deeply. She knew how others looked to him for leadership and Gwynne had no doubt whatsoever that he truly was a deeply spiritual, compassionate man Still, she knew that he entertained doubts as to his own capabilities from time to time. It may well have been that that particular side of her husband which was dearest to her. She was aware of his humility, his humanity, and that her husband whom she had loved since her High School years, looked to her for support along the path of his calling; that he loved her and trusted her sufficiently to turn to her for advice when great problems might arise.

He closed the closet door and re-entered the living room where he sat down in the chair opposite his wife. She had not returned to her reading.

"You're still concerned about that young man, aren't you?", she asked

"Yes, I am", he replied. "I can not really explain just

why, but I can' t get him, his situation and how I first saw him, out of my mind. I did speak to Alisdair about the matter a while ago. Erc was present at the time. Alisdair is in a tight spot: between the proverbial "rock and a hard place". He had ordered the young fellow and his family, or friends, whomever they were, to leave the area. It would be difficult for him if he were to reverse his decision. Certainly, I can understand that he does not wish to be seen as weak in any way".

"Is there anything else that you might do?", she asked.

"As things now stand, Alisdair has agreed that if I speak with this stranger and can find a valid reason to give him my recommendation, that he will accept my endorsement. I will have to move quickly, Gwynne. Those people may be packing up to leave even as we speak".

"Can you see the young man first thing in the morning?", Gwynne asked.

"That's what I will have to do", he said, looking deeply troubled. "Still, what if I am wrong?"

"Well", she answered, "For my own part, I have come to believe that when something causes this much concern to you, there is a very good reason for it. In any case, I'm pretty sure that you have been thinking on the matter during your walk from Ardachy. Do what you have always done: pray on the matter after your nightly office before you come to bed, then do whatever first comes to you in the morning when you first wake up. It has always worked for you before, Rob"

Rob looked across at his wife, nodded his head, then he

said, "You are amazing, do you know that?"

"You don't need to start sweet-talking me. I'm still angry with you!", she told him, a slight frown on her face.

Rob looked at her and started to smile'

"What!?", she returned trying to maintain her stern look. Rob continued to smile at her.

"It's not funny, Robbie!", she insisted, trying to avoid being pulled into a smile herself. He pointed at her and began to laugh.

"Oh! You think that that's funny, do you?" She flew from her chair, snatching a side cushion from the couch and began to pummel him with it, which made him laugh all the more as his arms came up to defend himself.

"Robbie, you….are…. such…a …creep!", her every word being followed by another buffeting.

Suddenly his arms shot forth and pulled her onto himself, into his lap, still laughing, bursts of air coming forth from his mouth. Two people, already well past middle age, having more than begun their old age, held one another. His head rested against her breast as she reached up and pushed back his hair from his forehead. It was really more of a caress, almost a petting gesture.

"You're a silly old fool, Robbie!", Gwynne informed him.

"I know.", he answered.

"But I really like you, Rob", she said.

A shiver went through him, tears came to his eyes. Finally he answered her: "I have come to kinda like you too, Gwynne".

CHAPTER 6

PART 3

Just about daybreak, when the lighted clouds, but not yet the sun, were looming up over the forested hills of the East, with just the tiniest frost-hairs reflecting golden light while clinging to every branch, twig and stalk of grass or tall weed, Steve went running and hopping over the frosty ground in his bare feet, an old quilt gathered about him over his ragged underwear. He looked like a ragged deposed King who had refused to discard his Robe no matter how tattered it had become. He hopped over to a clump of trees and brush a stone's throw from the sugar shack and fumbled with his undershorts, almost dropping his covering. Then grabbing up his quilt and already beginning to make water, cursed when he discovered that a strong stream of urine had hit the edge of that once noble covering, the blanket clutched around him. He danced from one foot to the other, wishing that, at that moment at least, men could piss as fast as women. At least women don't wake up with an erection which makes urinating next to impossible. It was at that most private of moments that he was aware of someone close by, for there, not more than ten or twenty yards away, a lone figure stood looking toward the source of light in the distant hills to the East. How could he sneak back to the sugar shack without being seen? He decided that he couldn't no matter what he did. Anyway, when he finished that for which he had come out of doors to accomplish, was when the figure turned around and faced him squarely.

"A good morning to you," the man said. It was, after all, a man. Steve could not be sure at first: the long garment, belted in the middle could have covered one of the women. Yet, the voice was a man's voice and as the figure moved toward him, gliding as a hunter, noiseless in the woods, yet striding in away, Steve knew it was a man.

"Good morning," Steve replied, aware that his voice was high, that it sounded weak, or even maybe what the stranger would think of as betraying some fear.

"You could use something on your feet," the man said.

"I just ran out to take a leak," Steve said in return, thinking how dumb, how really stupid, that sounded.

"Yes, well, you'd best get back inside, but I wonder if the young fellow,… is he your brother? I can't recall his surname,… Glen, is he up and about?"

"No, he's asleep," Steve replied. "He was pretty tired. What d' you want him for? Is he in some kind of trouble or something?"

"Oh, no. No! I just would like to have a word with him. I can wait", the stranger said.

Steve looked at the man who was now quite close to him. The man didn't look dangerous or 'bad' in any way. In fact, he had a kind, gentle face, what you could see of it. His long brown and grey hair and beard didn't leave much of the face to be seen; but the eyes! The eyes had a beautiful, humorous something that was also sad. Dark pools of brown, greenish secrets in hiding.

"Well, okay, but I don't know when he'll be up.", Steve smiled.

"Have you had your breakfast?", the man asked.

"No. Sometimes we don't eat until later", Steve replied

"Well why don't I supply the breakfast then?" the man had a kind of satchel of cloth slung over his shoulder which he slung off and in front of him. "I have a feeling breakfast might cheer him up a bit."

"Well, I don't know. You see, we don't make up too fast to people we don't know.", Steve said warily.

"Of course you don't." The stranger agreed. "These are hard times, but they won't last forever. Here." He handed the satchel to Steve. "This won't bite. I'll just give this to you. Put the oats in water and boil it up... a cup of oats and three cups of water. There's butter there and a bit of maple syrup, and even some brown sugar. You can pretend that it is Christmas."

Steve didn't know how to respond. He took the satchel, said, "Thanks. Thanks a lot!" and ran for the cabin. Colm stood away off flapping his arms against the frosty air.

A few minutes later, Glen came out of the sugar shack cabin, tucking a heavy shirt into his jeans while trying to keep the tails of his jacket away from being tucked in with the shirt. He looked toward Colm, squinted and grunted something like, "Just a minute" and went a short ways into the woods. He came back a few minutes later, wiping water from his hands on his jeans. It was obvious that he had stopped at the creek nearby to wash his face, for his hair was wet in front as well as the hands he was now trying to dry. He walked up to Colm.

"Hi", he said cautiously.

"Good morning," Colm responded.

"Thanks for the food."

"You're very welcome."

"Did you already eat?", Glen asked him.

"No. As a matter of fact, I was hoping to have breakfast with you, that is, if you'll have me.", Colm smiled.

"Why?" Glen guardedly asked.

"Pardon?"

"Why would you want to eat with us?"

"That would take some explaining.", Colm said.

"You're the guy they call Colm, aren't you? I mean, I remember meeting you last night. I never did say thanks for taking me to the house.", Glen said.

"Don't bother. Just give me some breakfast!", Colm smiled.

"Yeah, C'mon in but don't expect anything fancy. We're

pretty poor in here", Glen explained.

Glen had been looking at the ground, feeling out of his element and caught off guard, but when he finally asked Colm to the cabin he had looked up and into his face. He turned his head toward the cabin and then swung his head back to stare at Colm's chest. There, on a thong was suspended a cross with a circle around it, very much like his own deer antler cross. It was the same shape, even having some of those woven designs and raised ball-like shapes. Colm's was made of metal with some light-green stones, but the center was deer antler.

If Colm noticed the surprise on Glen's face he did not show it in any way. He may have looked a bit puzzled or amused, but Glen couldn't tell for sure.

Velma was rushing about, clearing the makeshift table. She had been peering through the building's only window at the two men and watching them as they talked. When they turned toward the cabin she realized that Glen was bringing this man under the roof. What on earth is he thinking of? We don't know that man! Just because he brought a sack of oats... but enough oats for several meals! Who is he anyway?, She wondered.

As the two men entered, Colm took a black tam from his head. He stood by the door thinking of a house blessing while trying to look neither: judgmental or condescending. Actually, what he saw delighted him, for although everything in the place was cast-off or makeshift, the cabin had an air of surprising warmth about it. Everywhere could be seen examples of a remarkable resourcefulness, ingenuity. There were hooks made of tree crotches, the latch of wood, cupboards of slab wood which were well swept and uncluttered. A chair made from a barrel, cut and fitted with a seat, sat by the table, and two well-fashioned stools of tree limb and slab wood were on the other side. Even more impressive were some small bowls and drinking cups made of low-fire clay. Colm made a mental note to ask about these things before leaving.

Velma was clearing things away, breathing heavily as she moved about. For her everything was going wrong. As she would try to push one thing onto a shelf, some other object would fall. She hung a heavy coat on a wooden hook but it fell to the floor, another garment already having been hung there. The CoArb bent over and picked up the coat and handed it to her, just the trace of a smile on his face.

"Oh, dear! Thank you," Velma murmured. "I wouldn't have so much rushing around to do if I'd just had things picked up."

"On the other hand," Colm replied, "why should things be picked up at such an early hour? I'm afraid that I am being very rude stopping by at this time, catching people just as they're getting up. I apologize."

"I just wish that I could offer you something," Velma said. "Years ago, oh not years ago, but in better times, I would at least offer somebody a cup of coffee at such an early hour."

"Yes that would be nice. It was a good custom, but we've

all had to lay aside a lot of the old things. In the end we will probably be a better people for it.", he answered.

"Here," Velma motioned to the barrel chair, the only chair with a semblance of a cushion, for it had a seat padded with a few remnants of unused carpeting laid one atop the other. "You sit down over here and warm up a bit."

"Oh, thank you, but if you don't mind, I'll just stand by this stove for another minute or two.", he replied.

On the top of the makeshift stove a pot of water was already just beginning to simmer. Colm could see the oats rising and falling in the heating water. He stretched his hands toward the heat and could not help but watch the swirling, the rising and falling of the oats. How like nations and individuals, he was thinking: a brief rise to the top only to struggle there for the very shortest time before falling again. The microcosm of the macrocosm or is it the other way around? Oh well, no matter. What difference does it make? He thought to a greater spirit and yet inside of himself. Something special 'though, about boiling water. The patterns themselves like Celtic or Chinese or Maori pattern work. How many imaginations have been spurred on by the sight of boiling water, by the sheer magic of it all! Ceremonies, rituals… like the tea ceremony of Japan. Tea!

"Oh! I just remembered!", Colm said aloud, surprising everyone and shattering the somewhat uncomfortable silence, "I just remembered that I brought tea with me as well as oats and butter. You probably missed it in that satchel, for it is in another bag just below the bag of oats. I remember that I put the two bags inside of one larger bag."

Glen came forward at that moment from where he had been standing or rather, from where he had been hanging back. He hadn't had a word to say since his invitation to Colm to enter the cabin. His initial surprise had slowly turned to a very sullen silence. Now he wanted to speak.

"Listen, I don't want to appear unfriendly and I don't want to seem ungrateful either. I mean… you helped me out last night and I appreciate it, but you must know that I've been told to get out of here. They must have told you that. Now, here you are down here passing out food to us and even tea! Tea! My God, man! We don't want anything from you people! Nothing! The one thing we wanted wouldn't have cost anybody one bit of anything and your land boss up there couldn't even hear me out! We're poor and we're lost and we don't have a place to live and a lot of the time we're hungry, but we aren't trash! We don't steal and we work for everything that we can work for. Why don't all of you just leave us be?"

Velma sat down in the barrel chair and started crying into a piece of her scarf. They hadn't talked yet this morning and this was the first that she had learned that they definitely had to leave. She shook her head from side to side as her shoulders heaved up and down. Colm felt that he had really made a terrible mess of things. This was supposed to have been a good day, a morning of hope, for somewhere deep inside of himself he knew that this young man was good. More than that, he knew that Glen had somehow been brought here to fulfill something very special. His problem at this point was to convince Glen, Velma and Steve that all was not as bad as it seemed. He felt lost for words.

"I am truly sorry! Really I am!" he told them, "I had hoped to be bringing you better news, perhaps a bit of hope. I guess that I've really botched things badly." Preparing to put his tam back on his head before going out he said to Glen, "Please use the Tea. See that the lady has some and she should have some porridge. Try to get her to eat. Then, later when you folks have settled a bit, don't immediately start gathering up your things. I may be able to help you, but we must talk about it, you and I."

"What's the use?" Glen asked, "Hell, we always knew that it's only a question of time before we'd get run out," he said bitterly.

"Oh? I don't know about that." Colm said, "Sooner or later people get tired of running. Sooner or later they have to turn around and face whatever it is that's chasing them."

"You think so, huh? Well, that's how much *you* know about it. You've never had to run!"

"Oh, haven't I! And that's how much *you* know!" Coln clapped his tam on his head, opened the door and started out, then turning he said, "You and I have a lot to discuss. I mean to finish this conversation about an hour from now. I will be back!"

"Don't bother!", Steve said coldly.

"I said I'll be back!", Colm stated with a certain

finality and with that he stalked off under the Apple and Maple trees.

Glen stood leaning against the door frame of the cabin having come in and shut the door. He had his mouth twisted up on one side, daydreaming in the general direction of the edge of the loft where the boots were just visible. Well, he thought, I could never in my wildest dreams have thought that a pair of boots could have caused so much trouble! I ought to burn the damned things and get it over with… but what the hell! It's done now and they won't look so new forever, not even for very long. He ran his hand over his face and felt the stubble. He liked the feel of it. Shaving was a senseless thing to do, but a guy's face isn't young forever. Grow a beard and cover your face not to mention what little bit of youth you were given in a lifetime. He moved over to the stove and took down a small saucepan which always hung from a nail in a timber close to the stove. Dipping it into the large can of hot water that always simmered on the stove, he began to ladle some of the water into a stainless steel basin. When the basin was half full, he carried it over to a wide shelf which was attached to a horizontal beam which ran the length of the sugar house. Above this there was an old hand-mirror, hung upside down and suspended by a piece of twine from a nail in the wall. Glen knew that the others were feeling uncomfortable and that they were more than a little curious as to the identity of the man who had just supplied their breakfast. Something angry and mean and stubborn in him just wouldn't let him speak. He took off his shirt and laid it on the ledge a small distance from the basin of water, then taking a hunting knife and stropping it on a piece of leather, he took more time than usual inspecting it, looking at its edge and moving it back and forth for one small, light-reflecting surface on that edge which would declare the knife to be dull.

"Oh, my!" Velma was saying in a brighter than usual tone. "As sure as he said it, there is tea in this bag! We can have a nice cup of tea with our oatmeal porridge!" She spoke as if to Glen, over beyond the stove, but displayed the luxury to Steve, who felt the need to reinforce her happiness and also to break the heavy silence.

"Great! We can at least have a darn good breakfast! That's real butter in there, too!" Steve exclaimed.

Glen turned and looked absently in their direction: Velma putting the tea back in the satchel and Steve sitting down on a potato crate with a knife and stick. Glen knew that he had to say something.

"Don't put that tea back in there, mama. We might as well have some of it. Besides, we don't need any more stuff to carry than we have to." His words sounded bitter to him even though he meant to lighten the moment. He thought that he'd try again.

"How's that oatmeal coming, Steve? Why don't you get off your buns and give it a stir? I won't be but a minute!"

"Sure, Glen! I'll bet it's almost done." Steve got up and went over to the pot. 'Good thing I took a look at this! It's ready to boil over the top!"

"Push it off to a side, Steve the fire's too hot," Velma told him. "Take that wooden spoon and keep stirring it down. It won't boil over if you keep stirring it, but keep it more to the edge and not right over the hottest part!"

Glen took some soap and having wet his face with a cloth dipped into the warm water in the basin, he wet his hands, rubbing the soap between his palms. He rubbed soap from his palms into the stubble on his face and began to scrape the facial hair and the soap away in smooth swaths. From the stove, Steve watched him while his hand stirred the oatmeal. He followed every movement of the knife with his eyes. His mouth, partially opened, worked as Glen's face twisted one way and another under the knife.

Velma moved over to the make-shift stove beside Steve. "Here, I'll take over now. You pour a little of that hot water over there into this bowl." She took the heavy pot from the stove and carried it to the table, where se set it on a piece of smooth shale, for she had covered the table with a cloth and set three bowls around.

"Did you put that hot water in that bowl I gave you?", she asked Steve and when he told her that he had, she told him to pout the water back into the hot water can.

"That doesn't make any sense!", Steve complained.

"Oh, yes it does!," she answered. "You can't make a good pot of tea unless you warm the pot first. We haven't got a teapot, so that bowl will have to do."

Moving over to the stove she put a quantity of dry tea into the now-warmed bowl which Steve was holding.

"Put that on the table," she ordered, then picking up a saucepan with bubbling hot, boiling water with a cloth around its handle, she followed him to the table. When he had set the bowl down she poured the boiling water over the dry tea and almost filled the bowl. This she then covered with a small chipped plate. She glanced up at Glen and then at Steve. Both of them were staring at her at the table and had been following the tea making with fascination. Glen stood there with his knife in his hand, bits of soap still on his face, looking dumfounded.

"Well, for pity sake!", Velma chuckled, "What's the matter with you two? Didn't you ever see anybody make tea before?" She felt a bit self-conscious, yet sure of herself. There are still a few things she could do that they didn't know about!, she was proudly and brightly thinking. "Come over here and sit down!", she went on. "You'd better hurry up and finish and get that soap washed off your face, Glennie. If it dries and you leave it, you'll have a sore face for a few days!"

Glen finished and washed quickly, rubbing his face dry with a cloth, then wiped the knife blade carefully He put on his shirt and took the basin of water to the door. Holding the basin in one hand, he opened the door with the other, went out a few steps and threw the water to one side, away from the path. By the time that he had re-entered the cabin, poured a small amount of hot water into the basin, swished it around and thrown out the rinse water before returning the metal basin to its place behind the stove, Velma had dished up the porridge. She and Steve were waiting for him.

He sat down with them and felt a bit awkward, like something of a guest in his own dwelling. The table had been covered with a green cloth, upon which the three bowls of porridge steamed with a lump of butter atop each one and a small bowl containing brown sugar with a spoon had been set close by.

"What are we supposed to do with this butter on here?", Steve asked.

"Why, you spread it around over the hot porridge until it's all melted", Velma instructed.

Steve looked at Glen who returned his look, raised his eyebrows and shrugged his shoulders. They both took up their spoons and followed her directions.

"Then, "Velma went on, "you take brown sugar and try to sprinkle it over the butter. Of course, brown sugar doesn't sprinkle very well. You have to kind of help it along with your finger tips".

Steve and Glen watched her let clumps of the sugar distribute itself over the buttered porridge, then followed her lead. Steve tried his hand at it first and as Glen watched he could feel his mouth filling with saliva. By the time that Glen took his sugar, Velma was stirring the butter and sugar into the oat meal.

"Oh!" Velma said, looking up toward Steve, "Don't try to spoon it from the middle, Steve! It'll burn your mouth! You always eat hot porridge from the edge of the bowl where it's had a chance to cool a bit". He followed her instruction, took about half a spoonful to his mouth, tasted it and a smile came to his face. "Hey! This is really good!", he exclaimed.

As Velma removed the plate from the top of the bowl in which she had been brewing their tea, she thought of Steve's delight at the taste of plain old oatmeal porridge She was thinking to herself how, four years earlier a kid couldn't be driven to eat such fare, for everyone wanted the sugary, boxed cereals. She found herself thinking of the obscenely obese people in super markets, filling their shopping carts with every kind of "junk food", carbonated beverages, frozen pizzas: that sort of thing. She had thought back then that it was strange to see the really poor people who were so over-weight, walking starvation cases, for although they ate constantly, there was little in the way of nutritional value in their diets. Their bodies called for food and were filled instead with junk." Well", she thought," you don't see many over-weight people anymore. Maybe this collapse of our society hasn't been all bad!" The bowl was filled with a dark amber liquid, all of the leaves having settled to the bottom of the bowl. She ladled out a cup of the tea for each of them. They were eating silently now, for despite Velma's efforts the atmosphere was heavy, charged with uncertainty and sadness.

After a while, Velma sat back and looked very thoughtful for a few minutes, then she spoke:

"Boys, I have to say something and I want you to listen real careful". She paused as she seemed to hunt for the words and then went on: "This is a really different morning. It's pretty sad for us, but I think that we may be looking at a glass that is half full and only seeing that it's half empty" She looked at Glen in a way that he had never seen before. She didn't look beaten down and sick this morning. She had had another hard night, but her head was high and she looked almost proud.

"Glennie, I want you to know that it took a lot of man to do what you did last night", she told him.

"You mean, like getting us kicked out, run off?", he bitterly asked her.

"Now, I said that I have something to say and I want you to be quiet and listen until I've said what I have to say" she insisted. Glen looked down at the table top as she went on:

"Maybe things didn't work out like you had hoped and maybe we have still a long row to hoe ahead of us. There's no way of knowing. But look at what we do have! I couldn't be prouder of you two if you'd have gone out last night and brought a bag of gold nuggets back here to this place! Just look at all that we've been through together! We have every right to be ugly, bitter, mean people, but we're not and we have that to our credit. Both of you are good, decent young men and there's many a woman in a palace that can't say that about her sons. Boys, we are going to get through this. I just know that we will!"

CHAPTER 7

PART 3

True to his word, Colm was waiting for Glen. It was already getting a little warmer now that the sun had come up. He was sitting on the large trunk of a fallen tree when Glen first saw him: one of his legs drawn up, the knee of which supported his hands, while the other leg hung loosely, or appeared to do so, for really the foot of that leg was planted firmly on the ground. The raised, bent leg, the one onr the tree trunk itself, revealed a high-laced boot which had neither a sole nor a heel. Glen was put in mind of something that a Native American might have worn. Glen could also see more of the Co-Arb's mode of dress as well, for the black outer garment which fitted from neck to somewhere between the knee and ankle was really some kind of coat. Beneath that there was a heavy woolen and long tunic, perhaps even an extra long off-white shirt, very plain and gathered about the waist. As Glen approached, the Co-arb slowly moved his head to face him and then stood up. From somewhere on the other side of him, Colm produced the long walking stick which Glen had seen the night before in the moonlit field. He could not remember whether Colm had had the staff with him earlier that morning or not. Glen walked up to the Co-arb, feeling very awkward, even a bit ashamed of his own actions earlier and when in the face of the older man's generosity.

"I....I guess that I owe you some kind of apology", Glen said. "I'm sorry for the way I acted a while ago", he said.

"Why?", Colm asked. "I thought you had yourself under pretty fair control, considering the circumstances".

"Maybe", Glen countered, "But I could have at least thanked you for supplying our breakfast. We really liked it! I've never had anything like that, although Velma seemed to know how to cook it up".

Really?" Colm asked, "You have never had porridge before? Oh, it's really good for you. Oats have something special which our bodies require. I can't remember just what it is, but it is important. It's cheap fare too! Oatmeal does not cost a lot at all! Sometime you should try mixing some cheese with oatmeal porridge, or honey perhaps, although it is a bit sweet for my liking"

"Anyway", Glen persisted," I want you to know that we really are grateful. Thanks a lot!"

Colm started to walk and as he did so he gently nudged Glen's arm with his hand, indicating that he wanted him to walk with him. They moved along an old trail through the maple and ash trees, not quite side by side, for Colm was leading, although Glen was just a bit short of being at the cleric's side. Colm said nothing for a minute or more, then he spoke:

"When I was young, like yourself, and a novice at the time, I was told a parable. It seems that a very rich man sent a servant with some money, maybe a bag of gold dust, to a nun who was taking care of a large number of orphans. The servant went out as his master had directed him to do and when he returned, the master asked him if the nun had said anything. The servant told him that the nun had simply said:" Thanks be to God!", after which she had given him her blessing. The wealthy man thought long and hard on this matter and decided that perhaps, considering the number of children being fed and cared for by the good woman, it had been after all, too small a donation. The next day he sent a second gift: this time twice the amount of his first donation. When the servant returned, the master questioned him again and the servant revealed that the nun had said exactly the same words, after which she gave him her blessing, A day or two went by and the rich man sent his third and most generous donation. Again, when the servant returned, he gave to his master the same report. "Isn't it strange", the rich man thought, "that she never once expressed her thanks!" A few days later the wealthy man met the nun in the town's market. He asked her if she had received his donation, and the second, and before he asked her if she had received his third gift, she answered:" Yes, we have received three donations from you for the homeless little ones, Thanks be to God!" His mouth must have hung open a bit, for the nun then said:" You wonder why I am not giving thanks to you". The man, being polite assured her that her thanking him was not necessary. The nun then said, "Just so, for it is you who should be thanking me!"

The Co-arb then stopped and turned to Glen.

"I don't get it!", Glen said. "She sounds to have been pretty hard, pretty ungrateful!"

"Ah, but you see. Glen", Colm explained, "The rich man already had money, and he was able to derive a very good feeling as a result of his charity. The nun had only mouths to feed and now, more money with which to buy more food until someone else decided to do something in order for him also to feel good about himself!"

Ducking under a branch and holding it aside for Colm to pass by, Glen allowed it to spring back into place once they were past it. In answer to what Colm had explained, Glen asked him:

"So, I should not thank you? You should thank *me* because I need help. Is that it?"

Colm laughed, but in a friendly, kind way, as he found himself to be truly enjoying the exchange.

"Something like that, yes!", he answered, "Why not?"

"Well", Glen countered, "I could say that a refusal or a reluctance to accept words of thanks might be something far removed from Christian virtue, perhaps even a bit selfish! What if that needy recipient, or whatever he may be called, really feels a need to express his gratitude? Sure, maybe the donor, the generous guy, may not feel that he needs to be thanked. Maybe he prefers that he is given nothing in the way of thanks. So, what? If the recipient wants to thank him, feels a need to thank him, then the generous guy who is feeling so good about himself had better shut the fuck up and accept it!"

From somewhere deep down in Colm's mid-section a laugh which almost cut off his breathing began to rise upward, almost doubling him over. He looked at Glen, continuing to laugh.

"What!?", Glen asked, half smiling, surprised.

At that one word, Colm stared at Glen, the smile fading from his face as memory and recognition set in. It wasn't just the one word. Others had pronounced it in much the same way many times. Yet, some memory was triggered in his mind: a young man at the far end of a kitchen, a bucket in his hand, staring and immobile, asking: "What!?"

"What is it?", Glen asked.

"Nothing. Nothing, really. For a moment you put me in mind of someone whom I knew many years ago".

They walked on through what had once been an apple orchard. The trees had long since begun to show hard, brittle and dead branches; branches which would never again blossom or leaf out or bring forth fruit. Too many years had passed since they were cared for, pruned. There were too many shoots which had come forth and had thus deprived the tree of strength. The trees were, in effect, killing themselves.

Glen and Colm stopped beneath a large old tree which looked hard, brittle and silver-gray. Colm glanced towards Glen's chest and saw there a whitish antler cross-shaped form which rested there, suspended on a piece of thong which circled his neck. Colm reached over, took the cruciform and simply tucked it inside of Glen's shirt top, dropping it onto the young man's chest and out of sight. It was something of a fatherly gesture and Glen could remember Hank having done the same thing from time to time. Colm reminded him of Hank in some ways: older perhaps, but about the same age as Hank probably.

"That is a very fine Caberfeidh, Glen", Colm ventured. "Someone must have seen you to be quite special!"

"You know about the Cobberfay?, Glen asked.

"I have seen a few of them in my lifetime", Colm answered smiling.

"No kidding! Here was me thinking that it was some old Scottish Highland thing that has lost its meaning!"

"And so it is and almost has done!", Colm responded.

Glen stopped, turned to look at Colm and asked: "Am I supposed to *know* you? Who *ARE* you anyway?"

"More to the point", Colm answered, "for all of our sakes,….Who are *YOU*?"

"My name is Glen! My Birth Certificate has me as Glen Olsen!", the younger man was feigning exasperation, lifting his eyes skyward and then tilting his head to one side as if he were facing up to somebody who was challenging him to a street fight. He stared into Colm's eyes.

"Yes! Yes! Glen is your name, a label to distinguish you from other labeled beings! But, Glen, who are YOU?, who ARE you?, WHO are you?"

"Oh, right! Now we are going to play word games or mind games!", Glen said sarcastically.

"Come on, Glen! You know better than that!", Colm returned."You have a pretty fair idea as to what I am asking. You have already demonstrated that somewhere you have had some education and that you have a pretty sharp mind as well! Someone taught you to discuss ideas philosophically. It's time to drop the "dumb" act! I am dead serious about those three questions which refer to your identity and your self-identity! Once you' have established who you really are, you're on the home stretch!"

"You used to be a teacher, right?", Glen asked

"Don't change the subject!"

"I don't like to talk about myself, who I am or whatever", Glen protested.

"Well, I think that I may remind you that, things being as they are, you had better start telling *someone* more about yourself", Colm said gently.

"How do I know that I can trust…..you ?" Glen asked stubbornly.

"You know that you can! You have already figured that out, Glen".

The younger man stared at the ground at his feet saying nothing, Slowly he began to nod his head, as if to himself or to a voice within himself. He nodded his head once or twice more, then lifted his eyes to meet those of Colm.

"Okay", he said with resignation, almost inaudibly, then, he repeated, "Okay! But you have to promise me on your word as a holy man, priest or whatever, that you will not repeat any of what I tell you to any other person.! Not ever! Agreed?"

"I would be derelict in my Holy Office were I to reveal anything which I hear in confidence!", Colm assured him.

"Yeah!" Glen responded, nodding his head, "I kinda had that figured out! Let's go over here and sit down….err, No! Let's go back to the sugar shack and some heat so we don't have to listen to our teeth chattering!"

The two men almost glided through the intricate intertwining branches of the dying orchard; ducking, weaving, moving sideways until they came to the small clearing which had the sugar house at its center. Glen held the door open and waited for Colm to enter, at which point the younger fellow broke the silence:

"One thing about this palatial residence, Glen remarked," We don't have to worry about tracking up a floor that is already made up of earth!" Calling over to Velma, he asked, "Is there any of that tea left?" She answered that she had just recently poured some more hot water into the bowl as it looked to have become pretty strong. He saw that there was indeed some tea in the ceramic bowl when he removed the plate which served as a lid. He poured out some tea into two mugs, then handed one of them to Colm.

"Sorry that there's no milk to offer you,", he apologized.

"It will be wonderful, just as it is", Colm assured him. "To tell you the truth, I hadn't realized how cold that I'd become until we came in by this fire! This is marvelous!"

CHAPTER 8

PART 3

Glen had not known this man called Colm for much more than fourteen hours. The man seemed to be someone to be trusted and now he had been called upon by this "Co arb" to tell him of his background, to identify himself. Glen knew that a Co arb was a high-ranking priest-figure and that he appeared to be a man of great integrity, but the years since his childhood had also given him cause to be somewhat wary of strangers. At the same time, he realized that this might well be his only opportunity to convince, evenly marginally, these people in whose midst he found himself to be, that he posed no danger to them or to their way of life. He struggled within himself, but seeing this patient, seemingly kind, man before him, he decided that he would reveal himself, if perhaps, for the last time.

"You asked me who I am,", Glen began "Well, I will state

my name again. I am Glen Ronald Gilcannon. I am twenty-one years old and I was born near Syracuse, New York. I was raised mainly in the Finger Lakes region. My name at birth was Olsen, not Gilcannon, but I am a Gilcannon by blood. You see, my mom and dad split up, divorced, when I was quite young".

Glen paused for a moment and seeing that Colm simply sat quietly, staring towards the fire, waiting, he continued:

"It must have been a pretty nasty affair, that divorce, for my mother just would never seem to get over it. She didn't want my Dad to ever see me again and swore up and down that he was no good, just plain 'rotten'! Of course, I don't remember him that way at all! I was pretty young yet when the split came, but my memories of him are good ones. I remember him taking me out with him fishing and I remember how he would listen to me and how kind his eyes were when he looked at me when I was talking. He would take the time to explain things to me and reason with me whenever I was upset about something or other. I remember that he had tears in his eyes when he told me that I'd be with my Mom and that he wouldn't be living home anymore. I guess that I cried myself to sleep that night.

One day, not too long after that, I remember that my mother was rushing around, throwing things into suitcases and she was saying over and over, to her friend Marge, Boy! What a really hard case and man-hating bitch Marge was!…, that my father would never see me again, that we were going to go away where he would never be able to find us. I remember that my grandmother told her to stop and think and to not be silly, but then my mother started yelling at her too! We went on a long bus-ride and ended up in some little town. I remember that we lived upstairs over a restaurant for a while until we moved to an apartment house. That place was awful! My mother worked in a store for a while and then she worked in a tavern. We were in and out of one dump after another. It was kinda bad once I started school, because we would be pulling out of one place to go to another. Finally, we ended up in Bath, New York. Things were more stable after that."

"You must have liked living in Bath, I take it", Colm ventured. "It is a small, quiet town as I recall".

"Well", Glen replied, "It wasn't the place, the town, itself. This guy came to stay with us back then who really changed things for me. My mother had found a small house to rent on the outskirts of the village and she decided that if she could rent out, or sub-let, a room to someone, it would help towards paying the rent.

Anyway, there was a man, I guess in his fifties at that time. He worked with helping wounded and damaged veterans. He set up some workshops for them. There was a V.A. Center there, at Bath. I was only about seven years old and I remember thinking: "Who is this old guy, anyway?" As it turned out, he really made our lives more full somehow. He knew how to do just about anything and everything! I had never known anyone quite like him, and to tell the truth, I have not met anyone like him even since then! He played the guitar, he was a leather worker, a carpenter. He had a lot of heart. Well, like I said, he was always caring for disabled vets. He was like a grandfather to me: helping me with my homework, teaching me things. I think that there were times when my Mom might have even been a bit jealous of his friendship with me".

Glen stopped for a moment and he smiled, as if remembering, re-living different things.

"His name was "Hank", but that wasn't his name really. "Hank" was his nick-name from his army days", Glen went on. "His real name was Paul Henry King. When my Mom died, when I was ten years old, he kept the place and took care of me: packed my lunches, signed my report cards, helped me to learn things, did the laundry: everything! It was as if I was his own kid!"

"What did you say his name was?", Colm interrupted.

"Paul Henry King", Glen answered. "Like I said, he was an older guy. He wasn't a boyfriend to my Mom or anything like that, but he took care of us. In Mom's last year he looked after her all the time".

"And where is this fellow, "Hank" now?" Colm asked.

"He's been near Syracuse for almost a year now. When I took leave of him it was like to kill me!...." Glen's voice stopped as he glanced towards Colm. He could have sworn that he saw the older man's shoulders shake and that he caught the sound of a catch in his breathing.

"Well can I imagine your.... deep sense of loss", Colm put in." He sounds to have become...or, rather he must have been… a wonderful man".

"Oh, you got *that* right!", Glen agreed. "I have been able to keep my sanity and my hope in the midst of so much downright cruelty and suffering all around, just by thinking of him, by asking myself, What would Hank do ?" He paused for a moment, then continued:

"When I was seventeen, I told Hank that I wanted to, or felt that I should, see my father. I didn't know how Hank would take to the idea, but he told me that it would be good for both of us: my father and myself. I didn't have a clue as to where he might be or how to even go about looking for him. I went to see my Gramma Graham, my mother's mom. I thought that I'd ask her. Well, my grandmother was as mad as a wet hen! She asked who had put me up to a crazy idea like that, and why I'd want to go looking for a man who'd practically deserted me and my Mom. She had nothing good to say about him at all! She asked me if my Aunt Em had put this idea into my head. I heard her mumbling something about Emilie being an old busybody and how she wished that she would mind her own business. Even when I told Gramma that I had not seen Aunt Em since I was about twelve years old, Gramma acted as if she didn't believe that all of this wasn't Emilie's fault. Well, I got no help from my grandmother, so I figured that Aunt Em must know something. I looked through some of Mom's old Christmas card list and found her…Aunt Em's…address. She was living up near Lewiston in Niagara County, up by the Canadian border.

I had some money of my own, but Hank gave me some extra and I took a bus up to see her. What a trip that was! Buffalo was full of homeless people and it was pretty scary. Niagara Falls was even worse! Well, everyone knows what happened to the world soon after that.

Aunt Em wasn't as old as I had thought she'd be. She was Gramma's youngest cousin. She seemed really glad to see me again and she made me stay over at her place. She told me that my father was working at a place near Niagara Falls....if that plant hadn't also shut down by then. Well, I went to the plant and he was there. He had been an executive, but he was one of a few people still there, getting ready to close the place for keeps. He was in his shirt sleeves and sweaty when I saw him again after such a long time. He seemed really glad to see me and he kept looking me up and down and he kept saying over and over, "God! This is great!" and "I can't believe this!" : things like that.

"I met him after work for supper. He told me that he had remarried and that his wife was extremely jealous of anyone who claimed any part of his time or life. He told me that it almost destroyed him when my mother packed up and just took me off to someplace or other. When he would try to call the house of my grandmother by 'phone, she would just hang up on him and that when he had gone by to talk to my grandmother at her house she threw a bucketful of scrub water on him. Then, he said something that really rocked me to my foundation. He said, "You know, Glennie, I always loved you from day one. I know that I could not have loved you more if you were my own son". He looked like he was kicked when he saw how surprised I was when he said that! Then he said in a quiet way that some things are hard to understand, that I must always think well of my mother, that she had been young and unsure of herself.... and that now that she was no longer living we should try to forget the past. He told me:"Glennie, I would have given anything to be your father, but your Mom was almost two months pregnant when I married her, and we hadn't known each other in 'that way' for more than a couple of weeks. I'm sorry, son. I'm not your father. I wish that I could have been". Glen continued:

"I didn't want to say anything to anyone about it. All at once, I was completely without background, my mother was dead and I didn't even know who my father was! I was a bastard! All of those years my mother had been calling the man she had married, a guy who married her to give her kid a name, the man she divorced and hurt, a 'bastard'! She should have been referring to me! A bastard! When I got back from seeing Olsen, I told Hank about it, what had been said....but not right away! It took me a couple of days before I could let it all out. I was so ashamed!"

"What was Paul's,...I mean Hank's reaction ?", Colm asked.

"Well, that part of it was really weird! Hank didn't seem to want to say much at all. He just looked at me with those kind, somewhat sad but beautiful eyes of his. He has unbelievable eyes!"

"Like polished dark-grey-green granite….", Colm said softly.

"Yeah! Really!" Glen stared in wonder at Colm. "You really can read minds, can't you? I was just thinking about his eyes!"

Colm gave no answer.

Glen continued his story of his family and his growing up with Hank as his guardian:

"Hank looked really sad after he heard of my meeting with the man I had been believing was my father. He looked at me like he wanted to tell me something. All of a sudden he just came out and said to me "I know your real father, Glen." I couldn't believe it! I was kind of pissed off, y'know? I asked him why he had never said anything to me about it before."

"Hank knew who your biological father is?", Colm asked.

"Not 'is', but 'was'!", Glen replied. "My real father died when I was a kid according to Hank. My real dad was killed in Afghanistan, Iraq or something. There was a war going on over there."

"Yes," Colm said in a low voice. "We were a long time in that quagmire. We would never be the same after that."

"What did you call it? What was that word again?" Glen asked.

"Quagmire?" Colm asked.

"Yes!" Glen said in almost a whisper. "That is what Hank called it too! Quagmire! What a strange word!"

"How did Hank come to know your father?", Colm asked.

"Well," Glen responded, "That's a funny thing too! I was getting to that." He closed his eyes, frowning slightly as if recalling details and then continued:

"Hank met my dad's father in 'Nam. His name, my grandfather's, was Donald Gilcannon. According to Hank my grandfather saved his life once, when they got caught in an ambush. Hank said that he was hit with all sorts of flying metal and my grandfather scooped him up' over his shoulder and got him outta there. That's how Hank put it: "He scooped me up over his shoulder." They got to be pretty close friends and they both managed to come back home. Hank told me that my grandfather got married and that he remembered when my real dad was born, 1981 it was."

"Your grandfather and Hank had stayed in touch then, I take it," Colm suggested.

"Oh yeah! Hank did his work with returning soldiers for a long time! Well, he's still looking after people," Glen stated. "My grandfather worked near or in Corning, until he had to quit his job. Something about some chemical that they'd used in 'Nam. 'Agent Orange', they called it. It finally got to him. Hank was with him up until the time he died. My grandfather lived until I was about three years old. I kinda remember him."

"That must have been how your friend Hank came to know your father," Colm suggested.

"Oh, No!" Glen corrected. "Hank knew my birth father

from the time he was born! He spent a lot of time at my grandparents' place. They named the boy Douglas."

I can't help wondering," Colm said, "why Douglas Gilcannon and your mother never married."

"Hank told me that my birth father and my mom had loved each other since they were kids" Glen went on: "It was, according to Hank, the greatest 'open secret' among the Gilcannons. They never stopped loving one another. Yeah, my mom often spoke of her and her cousin Dougie going skinny-dipping after dark, of long walks in the woods; that kind of thing."

"I wonder why they didn't marry," Colm persisted.

"They were cousins!", Glen stated. "Hank said that my grandmother (my birth father's mother) would have had a shit fit! He said that my mom had flat out decided that she'd marry this other guy who had already asked her. That was Leonard Olsen."

Glen stopped, looked off as if daydreaming and wondered aloud: "why did she never tell me who my real father was? That is just not right! Not right at all!

"Anyway," Glen continued, "Hank and my grandfather discovered while they were soldiering over there that there was an ancient connectedness. Hank said that the caberfeidh he was wearing gave him away.

Hank always said that there was only one person, other than his grandmother who had practically raised him, who would ever mean more to him: some guy he knew as a young man. He talked about him often. He told me once that my grandfather had saved his physical life, but that this other guy, this "Rob" or "Robbie" had saved his sanity and his spirit when he was a young guy, really screwed up and mad at the world."

"Well, it sounds as if he really did more than simply pull himself together. Do you know where he is at this time?" Colm was very interested in all that Glen had been telling him.

"I may have mentioned that Hank had been working with medics. After he came back he got into that line of work. Now that some of the Veteran's Hospitals have closed down, he had set up a facility where he and a couple of other people were looking after some ex-servicemen who need help."

"Wonderful!   Such help is sorely needed," Colm observed.

Glen went on: "Hank is one of those people who just has to be helping others. Possessions mean nothing to him."

"Tell me, if you feel that you may do so," Colm said, "Those boots which seem to be causing so much trouble: did your friend Hank give them to you?"

"He practically *built* them "to me!... or "on me" from scratch! He had learned leatherworking somewhere and got in with some boot and moccasin maker who used to make such things and sell them or trade them at the 'rendezvous,"… kind of re-enactment events based on the Early American Fur trade. Anyway, no one would believe that some guy built a pair of boots like this for me. They would be sure that I stole them."

"Your friend Hank seems to have taken over as something of an 'uncle' or grandfather where you are concerned. He was obviously discharging what he felt to be his duty to your father and grandfather." Colm put in.

"He gave me a silver button to carry with me for a reminder of my heritage. He said that it was one of two buttons which had once belonged to Rob Roy. He said that the other he had given to his friend 'Rob.'"

Really! Colm appeared to be impressed. "May I see it?... the button?", he asked.

"You aren't going to think I stole it, I hope!", Glen said.

Glen reached inside his clothing and brought forth a small leather pouch with a drawstring. He loosed the strings, turned the pouch upside down and a small silver piece marked with a crowned lion head dropped into the palm of his hand. Colm looked at it closely, inspecting it, turning it over. At length, he reached into an inner pocket and brought out a small folded cloth which he opened. There, on the cloth, before Glen's startled, staring gaze was the mate of the button in his own hand: the crowned lion Head facing of a silver button.

"How the Hell..., where... did you get that!?" Glen stammered, clearly stunned.

"It was given to me by a very dear friend a long time ago. My name is Rob Currie, "Robbie"..., or it was at one time before I became CoArb of Ardachy."

"You are Robbie!?" YOU are Robbie? Oh...my... GOD!"

"My word! You sound to be terribly shocked or disappointed… or both!", Colm stated, smiling.

"No! I am in no way disappointed. I had heard so much about this young guy, Hank's friend. I naturally formed an image of someone much younger in my mind. Still, you appear to be the kind of man Robbie would become as he got older." Glen thought for a moment or two and went on: "I can't believe this! It is really kind of scary!" He shook his head as if to clear it then continued:

"But, I have heard of *you*, at least. You have never heard of *me*! You might still think of me as a young guy who stole these boots and this silver button, for that matter!"

"No, Glen you have told me too much about Paul,…. 'Hank', as you call him, too much which identifies his interests, his background and his character, for you to be anyone other than someone who spent a great deal of time with him; someone with whom he had chosen to share much of his background."

"Then, does this mean that I am no longer suspected of being a thieving and perhaps even a murderous piece of common crap?", Glen asked sarcastically.

Colm chose to ignore Glen's barb. He turned his face toward the young man and without warning or lead-in of any kind whatsoever, he asked a very direct question:

"Where is the staff, the ancient reliquary staff? Who is acting as 'Dewar', or 'keeper' of that relic?"

"I know what a 'Dewar' is," Glen replied. "what makes you think that I would know where the staff is, or anything about the staff, or who is acting as guardian just now?"

"Because your father was the last male of the Gilcannon line,... except for you!"

"There was another line of Gilcannons!" Glen volunteered, almost defensively.

"Yes, Glen, it would have been Paul ("Hank") or his father, David. They were descended from Duncan Gilcannon, but Paul would have seen to it that you carried your father's sacred charge."

"You asked who I am, but you already knew." At least, so it seems you hinted that I might be Dewar, the Keeper of some Holy things," Glen said.

"Well, are you?", Colm asked softly.

"Wait! Let's not get ahead of ourselves! Glen said "There is a lot to understand here. You know, I carry the 'Old Way' myself, after my fashion, and for a half-heathen Celtic Christian from the backwoods, like me, to meet up with someone like you... well! It's kinda like meeting the Dalai Lama! Part of you really leaves me about to bow; the other part of me wants to take off running for the hills!"

"Well, Glen," Colm ventured, laughing warmly, "my wife tells me that I had that kind of effect on many people many years before I became a 'Dalai Lama'!"

After a moment, Glen frowned and asked: "Did Hank (Paul) ever tell you that they thought that he might be asked to care for the relics? I'm sure that he had never met my grandfather before they were in Viet Nam together. It's a wonder, too, for they are distant cousins. It's funny how things work out."

Colm started to say something, then shook his head and motioned for Glen to continue.

"What I know of it, I learned from Hank. He was supposed to be Dewar if my father had no one to pass things on to. Hank filled me in on all of this about a year ago, maybe two and a half… just after I'd gone to see Leonard Olsen, the man who I thought was my father. I was pretty broken up. I called Hank and he wanted me to stop by his Uncle Art's farm near Cazenovia."

"Oh! Did Art take over the King farm?", Colm asked.

"Yes," Glen assured him. "He had been messed up for a while, but I guess that after Hank's Grandmother died, his Uncle Art pulled himself together. That's where they have that center for Veterans just now!"

"Wonderful!", Colm said, "Absolutely Wonderful!"

"Anyway," Glen continued, "Hank told me that he had been wanting to break some news to me and that he had had a heck of a time trying to find the right opportunity. See I still had no idea that Hank knew my father or he'd been in the army with him. At that time or up to that time Leonard Olsen was my father, as far as I knew.

Hank took me up to a room in the house where he had always stayed when he was there. He told me about his Grandmother, his dad, his friend Robbie who had meant so much to him, and…" Remembering a detail he said, "Hey!! Yes! He showed me a colored drawing that was hanging there of him done by his friend, Robbie… You!! Wow!

You're the one who did that!"

"It was one of the best portraits that I had ever done," Colm said. "I had no oils with me, but I used oil crayons. It had to be in color to capture his eyes! What fantastic eyes! My wife Gwynne always said that it isn't fair that a boy, a man, should have such pretty eyes!"

"Anyway," Glen went on, "Hank pulled two boxes out. One of them was a long, wooden box and it had been under that high bed. The other one was a footlocker such as soldiers use and he hauled that out of the closet. There was mostly pictures, mementos and such; some clothing and so forth in the foot locker. The other long box was what was to be so surprising. Hank kept glancing at me, kind of anxious-like when we got to that long wooden box or trunk.

When we opened the trunk it seemed mostly to be full of Doug's personal effects, keepsakes I guess you'd call them. There was an old kilt not in very good shape, a Scottish tam or 'bonnet', and an old dirk. There were some framed awards, a few old books, but mainly, a bundle of cloth. The bundle was long, going from a back left corner to a right front corner of the trunk and the trunk itself was about four feet long. The cloth was a fairly bright plaid or 'tartan' of a heavy weave and it was tied around with a thick twine. The twine had also an envelope tied in tightly but not so tight that it couldn't be pulled out. We pulled it out and I couldn't believe my eyes! It was addressed to me! I have kept the letter in an old leather tobacco pouch. I'll let you read it. Let me get it."

Glen went over by the improvised stove and pried up a flat stone just in front of it. Under the stone could be seen only more soil but this he quickly scraped aside and pulled up a tin box of rectangular shape which appeared to have been an old biscuit tin. It turned out to be a tin with a hinged top which read "Glenlivet Scotch Whisky" one of those old sales gimmicks for Christmas Season sales. He brought the tin over to the plank table and set it down. He then opened it, took out a leather pouch and out of that a letter, folded in half (envelope and all) which in turn was wrapped in clear plastic. He handed the plastic-covered letter to Colm. For a moment Colm hesitated, then took the letter and began to open the plastic sheet. He reached for a pair of reading glasses which he put on, laid the plastic on the table, took the letter out of the envelope which he also laid on the table, unfolded the paper and began to read.

"Dear Glen, Since you are reading this, it means that I never made it home from Iraq or else that I am in such bad shape that I cannot communicate with you. I was afraid that this might end up being the case, but there's really no such thing as death. Everything goes around. It also means that my very good friend Paul has once again lived up to my expectations.

I wish that I could have been more for you. The few times I picked you up when you were a kid, I never wanted to let go of you. I can't make any excuses. Your mother and I have thought the world of each other since we were children. We never intended for things to get out of hand, but instinct, biology or something, snuck up on us. You know that your mom and I are cousins. This may sound like some excuse now, but at the time, too many people stood to get hurt. Your mom took matters into her hands and got married. Olsen is a great guy. He really is. Yet, he is not your father. I have that honor and I mean to say that it is an honor. As far as most people know, I am the last of the Gilcannons of our line. The truth is, you are a Gilcannon and the line does not die with me.

This is no time for me to ask a favor of you, but I must do more than that. I must lay on your shoulders a tremendous responsibility. At first you may wish to walk away in angry refusal. That is understandable, but you cannot do it. You have a responsibility to carry something which has been carried for a very long time (for about 1300 years, I suppose) by other Gilcannons and you cannot dismiss this sacred trust.

Inside this tartan cloth are three things. I will name them, describe them, and tell you their function:

A long 'cane' or walking stick with unusual carvings around the top or 'crook'. At the very top of the crook you will notice a small hole or indentation the size of a nickel as if something has been pried out of it… which something has been pried out. This staff was carried by an ancient Celtic saint and has been in the keeping of the Gilcannons for centuries. It is very, very ancient and considered by many to be very holy.

A small silver bell minus a clapper, also ancient and very holy, having belonged once to the same saint.

A piece of vellum wrapped around the staff with a prophesy given in the 1600's by a West Highland seer or 'prophet'. You will not be able to read it, for it is written in Scottish Gaelic but if the prophesy is fulfilled the man whom you someday meet who has the clapper for the bell and the piece missing from the staff will translate it for you easily.

No matter what may come to pass, guard these things well, for they must be carried by one of us until all is joined again. Know that I love you that I have always loved you and that I'll love you outside of this body. Give my love to your mother. There has never been any other woman who has meant so much to me.

Your Father,
Douglas Gilcannon

Colm turned the letter over, then folded it and put it back into the envelope. This he laid on the table.

"Do you have the tartan bundle described in the letter?"

"Yes." Glen answered simply.

"Do you have it here?"

"Yes."

"May I see it?"

Glen hesitated for a moment, then looking toward this minister, priest, holy man, whatever he was, and sensing no guile, he rose and went over to an overturned syrup evaporator tin, beneath which was the arch once used for the fire for making syrup out of the sap. Out of this he pulled a long package wrapped in canvas. He brought the long package to the table and laid it before Colm. Colm made no move to open the package, although there was a noticeable anxiety about him.

"Please unwrap the package," he said simply,

It took Glen some time to pull off the duct tape which he had used to hold the canvas wrapping in place, but before long the table had the wrapping to one side and the bright tartan bundle beside it in front of Colm. Colm carefully unwound the cloth and sat staring at the stick, the tarnished bell and the vellum wrapped around the staff.

"Please, may I see the little scroll?", he asked.

Glen unwound the vellum and as he did so, Colm again donned a pair of glasses. Glen handed Colm the scroll which he carefully unrolled. The priest frowned, squinted, and looked closely at the paper.

Glen thought that he saw Colm's lips twitch or move as he studied this unintelligible message. Then he heard Colm speak slowly, a bit of hesitation now and then:

"Ah, My heart relates a sad thing.

The children of fortune shall see sorrow.

They shall cross the sea to the West

With them shall go the staff and bell,

Although not whole the two, of Cowall

Til shall meet the son of the Lion's :and of the cannon's servant who go there,

With the son of the folk
Who under the crownless Eagle dwell.
Then shall Gaeldom Rejoice
And Cowall's store be whole.
Out of a time of skulking Thieves
New order shall raise a proud banner."

Colm looked up at Glen, whose mouth was agape, his eyes staring.

"You… you read that!"

"Well nearly so. It's difficult to translate Gaelic into any other language." He then reached into his clothing and pulled out a silver chased cross which hung by a thong about his neck. He pulled the thong over his head and lay the cross on the table.

"May I have a knife?" he asked.

"A,- a knife?" Glen asked. "Yeah here!", he handed him a hunting knife, which Colm took and began to twist back each of four metal tongs in the center of the cross. Once all were pried back, he turned the cross over and, from its back, he pushed the whole center of the cross out onto the plank of the table. He then picked up the round center, studied it as he turned it between his thumb and index finger. He turned it several times before asking Glen to pick up the staff.

"Hold the staff flat on the table," he ordered, "with its crook with the hole facing up." Glen did as he was told to do. The Co Arb then took his round cross center and pushed it into the round space on the staff crook's head. Glen continued to stare in disbelief.

"What, I mean what is this supposed to mean?", he asked in wonder. "It fits perfectly!"

"The Clapper for the bell is in the shaft of the reliquary cross at Ardachy," Colm said calmly. Then "To answer your question, Gilcannon, it means that the Celtic Church has blossomed in the New World and that we have found our Dewar, the keeper of relics.

"I have been chosen to be the living representor of an ancient tribal Saint, Colm said, "and you? You are the living keeper of the relics of that saint!"

Glen asked, a bit of confusion written on his face, "But aren't you claiming these things now? Aren't you expecting to take them with you?"

"Oh," Colm said happily,"I will take them alright! But you have to go with them! You are the custodian! This afternoon or tomorrow morning, you and I will walk together proudly to Ardachy. The staff will be shown, you will be introduced. From time to time I will ask to borrow the staff and bell for a purpose, but they are always to be given back into your keeping."

"But," Glen asked, "Won't I have to leave? Alaisdair said that…"

"Alaisdair will be awestruck!", Colm interrupted. "Two Hundred years ago a Co- Arb and the relics left Scotland on the same ship. It has been a long wait, but the two have come together again! Leave? We won't ever want you to leave! You'll be given a proper home on the premises. You and your friends will be well looked-after!"

"According to the prophesy," Glen began…

"According to the prophesy, we shall see better times!" Colm reminded him, ""Now that we have met."

"Now that we have met," Glen repeated. "Now I can work alongside the others and have respect?"

"You can be sure of both, young man! Colm exclaimed, clapping his hand on his shoulder and pulling the young man's head beside his own, "What a Ceilidh will be had! I can't wait 'til I see Alisdair's face when he sees this staff! The house bell will be rung out of its crutch and the pipers will be taking turns throughout the night! We are complete again! Oh, thank you, thank you!... for coming to us, for putting up with us! You are finally home! My wonderful wife will cry like a baby in pure joy!"

THE FINAL IN-GATHERING

PART 3

On the morning after Glen's joyful meeting with Colm, just about mid, morning in fact, Colm re-appeared at the Sugar-shack. Erc was with him, as was the herdsman, Daraic. All of them were carrying bundles of clean clothing and having brought a horse and small wagon back to the other side of the creek, as close as they could come by way of wagon, they made ready to load whatever Glen, Velma and Steve might wish to take with them. Soon thereafter they heard the sound of a large animal coming through the trees. It was Alisdair, riding a horse. Riding in close to the sugar shack, he stopped and swung down from his saddle. Steve took the reins and tied them to a sapling, feeling himself to be in the presence of some knight or king, for Alisdair's arrival upon the scene was nothing if not somewhat lordly.

How different he was today! Alisdair had replaced his broad-brimmed hat for a highland Balmoral bonnet, complete with two feathers. He smiled broadly as he approached Glen. Taking the young man by both shoulders, he said loudly:

"You really are a royal pain in the ass, aren't you? Well then, you've come to the right place! You'll certainly be at home here, among us!"

He then turned and walked to the sugar shack, ducked as he went into the building. Everyone could hear him chuckling his delight. As he came out of the shack, he asked Glen:

" Did you do all of that fixing and fitting out by yourself? Now, here is a very innovative young man!", he announced to all present." Well then, young man", he said to Glen, "You should have no difficulty in turning our Co-Arb's carriage house into a suitable living space and work-shop, right?"

Glen looked to right and left, confused. Were they mocking him? No! They all seemed to be quite serious. He turned to Colm, rushed to him and fell to his knees, hugging the cleric's legs.

"Get up, Glen! I'm not really the Dalai Lama, you know!", Colm said, somewhat embarrassed, but smiling. He reached down and pulled Glen up and to himself. "Let's get things loaded up!"

Poor Velma was still in a state of near shock, looking from one of these strangers to the other. "Where are we going?", she asked.

"These people are asking us to come and live with them, Ma", Steve explained.

"And", Alisdair pronounced, "We are going to have you looked after by someone with some medical knowledge, Ma'am", Alisdair pronounced. "That's as nasty a case of asthma or whatever, that I have heard in quite a while! I have an idea that it can be taken care of, however! My own wife is a nurse practitioner, and a very good one. She and my mother are going to be looking after you while Glen and your son..."Steve", is it?...work on a new dwelling for you".

"Oh, I don't want anybody putting themselves out for me", Velma said to him. I can manage...."

Alisdair took her two hands, bent and looked into her eyes. "No, you can't!, he said softly but firmly," You need some help now. Let us do this!",

Glen was amazed at the gentleness of this man whom he had come to see as hard, unfeeling; a man he had almost come to hate. He felt an almost sick feeling of shame. How could everything have turned so completely around, and in such a short period of time?

Alisdair then turned about and said to the others:

"Now, Then! Let's let these folks wash up, put on some clean clothes before we make our great "entrance" to this new world order of ours! We must all look our best!" Turning to Glen he said, "Especially you! Good Lord! Our Co-Arb has me convinced that we are making way for a near miracle!" Bending close, he said, "If you think that your head is spinning, believe me: you have nothing on me!" Clapping his hand across Glen's back, he said, "Go ahead now! Get ready. You have a great many people to meet! Make sure that you shave, by the way! There are a few pretty good-looking young women up there!"

Things will have taken a while to return to what might have been called" normal", but in time, the nation will have struggled back towards a semblance of order. America will have come to have learned a great lesson. There would be no more talk of being "biggest and best", or of "empire". People will have come to be grateful for every blessing, however great or small. Once again, Americans would come to value contentment over "happiness" and for a while, they would be seen again to be a kindly, friendly, even a hospitable, people. Perhaps they will know or realize within themselves, that they had been given a tremendous test, which somehow they managed to pass. Perhaps there will be that inner fear that such a test, such an opportunity to address who they really were and had become, might never come again....and that if it ever did come upon them, it might be their final stroke of death. They will have come to know what it was to almost lose the soul as well as the body.

If we are to truly survive as a people, as a nation, we must learn to feel that we belong to the land rather than to stake out ownership of this or that part of the land. We must learn the ancient wisdom again which lurks in the corners of our minds: that "magic" and "miracles" are not illusions, but a reality which make themselves known in the sounds of crickets, the light of fire-flies, every birth of a child or a farm animal or a forest animal; the sound of the running creeks, blue shadows cast upon winter snow. We must learn to laugh again and we must learn to weep for the beautiful things which we encounter, for whether tears be of sorrow of joy, it does not really matter. It is then that we have proof of our being truly alive. If one of us should chance to meet with a boy wearing a stag-horn cross or a girl with the same cross carved of deer's rib-bone, we must know that this same young person has given someone, somewhere, cause to believe that tomorrow need not be feared. Sperandum est!... There is hope.

CPSIA information can be obtained at www.ICGtesting.com
Printed in the USA
BVOW05s0512210316

441114BV00005B/7/P

9 781634 132343